The Minister's Annual Manual
for Preaching and Worship Planning
2005–2006

Edited by
Rebecca H. Grothe

Compiled by
Sharilyn A. Figueroa

Logos Productions Inc.
6160 Carmen Avenue East
Inver Grove Heights, MN 55076-4422
1-800-328-0200
www.logosproductions.com

First Edition
Nineteenth Annual Volume

Published in the US by Logos Productions Inc.
6160 Carmen Avenue East
Inver Grove Heights, Minnesota 55076-4422
Phone: 800-328-0200
Fax: 651-457-4617
www.logosproductions.com

ISBN: 1-885361-78-5
ISSN: 0894-3966

Contents

Children's Time

Appendices

FREE Children's Sermon Index

Your paid subscription now includes FREE access to the *Children's Sermon Index* – **a database of children's sermons based on the Revised Common Lectionary for each Sunday of the year.** You can search by theme, season of the church year, or keyword.

- **Your activation code is MA908.**
- **In the US** visit **www.logosproductions.com** and click on "Online subscriptions."
- **In Canada visit** **www.woodlakebooks.com** and click on "Church resources."
- Follow the instructions to receive FREE access to the *Children's Sermon Index* for as long as you subscribe to *The Minister's Annual Manual.*

How to Use This Book

This book is intended for use from August 2005 through July 2006.

Because many ministers prefer to plan an entire year of preaching and worship during the summer, this manual is designed to assist in summer-to-summer planning. Included in this book are helpful suggestions to guide your worship planning for each Sunday, as well as for several special worship occasions.

Every minister develops his or her own style of preaching and worship planning. Methods, planning, study, writing, and delivery are all unique. Preaching practice comes from experiences over the years; therefore, use this book in whatever ways will benefit your worship and sermon preparation most fully. Its useful-ness is determined by your own style and manner of preparation.

Many ministers prefer to spend time several weeks in advance of a specific Sunday reviewing the texts for that day. The materials in this book will be most helpful for that task. Please read David H. Schmidt's "Resources for Preparing to Preach" on page 435. A variety of resource materials, commentaries, and translations are listed to help you in your exegeses.

For each worship experience, the writer has prepared brief explanatory notes for the lessons, notes that you can use to get a feel for the texts.

You can also use these notes in your Sunday bulletins to help your congregation grasp the central idea in the lessons for the day.

As your worship plans develop for a particular Sunday, please note the variety of prayers and calls to worship suggested by our writers to fit in with the theme for the day. You may use these in any way appropriate to your planning.

The children's time can be especially useful for those pastors who have difficulty developing ideas and presentations for this important ministry to children.

The sermon materials may be used as thought-starters for your own sermon preparation. In past years we included a "text" for each sermon heading.

Many pastors have informed us that they preach on the whole lectionary passage, not just one specific verse. The text references have, therefore, been omitted from the sermon materials.

Not all preachers use the lectionary lessons on a regular basis. If you don't use these texts for your preaching, the materials in this book can still be useful in providing sermon ideas and illustrations on specific texts appropriate for the time of year. On the other hand, if you are accustomed to using the lectionary lessons, you will find these materials especially suited to your preaching needs.

A large majority of denominations now follow the Revised Common Lectionary. Therefore, we are using the Revised Common Lectionary so that *Minister's Annual Manual* will be helpful to more people. You should have no difficulty adapting these materials to your own church calendar. The Consultation on Common Texts asks that we indicate the following:

For the Sundays following Pentecost, the Revised Common Lectionary provides two distinct patterns for readings from the Old Testament. One pattern offers a series of semi-continuous Old Testament readings over the course of these Sundays. The other pattern offers paired readings in which the Old Testament and gospel reading for each Sunday are closely related. In adopting the Revised Common Lectionary, the Presbyterian Church U.S.A., United

Church of Christ, and United Methodist Church elected to use the pattern of semi-continuous Old Testament readings. The other pattern of paired readings is found in *The Revised Common Lectionary* (Nashville: Abingdon Press, 1992).

—*The Revised Common Lectionary*, 1992
Consultation on Common Texts (CCT)

The following materials are included for each worship experience:

Lessons, assigned for liturgical preaching.
Introduction to the Lessons, a brief explanation of all texts.
Theme of the day's materials.
Thought for the Day to help set the tone for preaching.
Call to Worship for the beginning of the service.
Pastoral Prayer for the beginning of worship.
Prayer of Confession, asking for forgiveness and pardon.
Prayer of Dedication of Gifts and Self at the offering.
Sermon Summary for the day.
Hymn of the Day suggestions.
Children's Time for conversation with children.
The Sermon, including **hymns** and **scripture**.

Hymn of the Day selections were chosen from the following hymnals:

The United Methodist Hymnal, Nashville, TN: United Methodist Publishing House, 1989.

With One Voice: A Lutheran Resource for Worship, Minneapolis, MN: Augsburg Fortress, 1995.

Presbyterian Hymnal, Louisville, KY: Westminster John Knox Press, 1990.

Voices United: The Hymn and Worship Book of the United Church of Canada, Toronto: United Church Publishing House, 1996.

Common Ground: A Song Book for all the Churches, Edinburgh, UK: Saint Andrew Press, 1998.

The Faith We Sing, Nashville, TN: Abingdon Press, 2000.

New Century Hymnal, Cleveland, OH: Pilgrim Press, 1995.

This Far by Faith: An African American Resource for Worship, Minneapolis: Augsburg Fortress, 1999.

Many of the hymns suggested are available for congregational use through *LicenSing: Copyright Cleared Music for Churches.*™ For information on *LicenSing* in the United States, contact Logos Productions (1-800-328-0200, or www.logosproduction.com).

To assist in your planning, a four-year church year calendar is included in the appendices, as well as calendars for the years 2005 and 2006.

For even more worship planning helps, you may wish to use the 2005 May/June planning issue or the regular monthly issues of *The Clergy Journal.* These resources include additional sermons and hymn selections. The planning issue also includes more children's time ideas. Preachers who use this *Minister's Annual Manual 2005–2006* and also subscribe to *The Clergy Journal* will have valuable resources for worship planning that include:

- Three complete sets of sermons for every Sunday of the year: this book, the annual planning issue, plus "Preaching on the Lessons" in each issue of *The Clergy Journal.* (The sermon materials in all three publications have been cross–referenced so you will know at a glance which publication to use for a particular passage.)
- Two sets of children's time ideas.
- Almost three dozen additional sermons.
- Hymn selections to match the lectionary texts.
- Prayers and calls to worship.

Both *Minister's Annual Manual 2005-2006* and the 2005 May/June planning issue of *The Clergy Journal* will make excellent additions to your library.

– Rebecca H. Grothe
Spring 2005

August 7, 2005

12th Sunday after Pentecost (Proper 14)
RC/Pres: 19th Sunday in Ordinary Time

Lessons

RCL	Gen 37:1–4, 12–28	Rom 10:5–15	Mt 14:22–33
Roman Catholic	1 Kgs 19:9a, 11–13a	Rom 9:1–5	Mt 14:22–33
Episcopal (BCP)	Jonah 2:1–9	Rom 9:1–5	Mt 14:22–33
Lutheran	1 Kgs 19:9–18	Rom 10:5–15	Mt 14:22–33

Introduction to the Lessons
Lesson 1
(1) *Genesis 37:1–4, 12–28 (RCL)*
Joseph is his father's favorite, and his jealous brothers hate him. Their plot to kill him is thwarted by brothers Reuben and Judah, so the brothers decide to sell Joseph to the Ishmaelites as a slave – foreshadowing the Israelites' bondage in Egypt.

(2) *1 Kings 19:9a, 11–13a (RC); 1 Kings 19:9–18 (Luth)*
After his momentous victory over the prophets of Baal on Mt. Carmel, Elijah feels all alone and afraid for his life. He waits in a cave on a holy mountain for some encouragement from God.

(3) Jonah 2:1–9 (Epis)
Like an experience of death, Jonah is trapped in the belly of a fish. His first instinct is to pray, and he sings a thanksgiving psalm. Through metaphoric language, he reflects on his situation and the promise of deliverance.

Lesson 2
(1) *Romans 10:5–15 (RCL/Luth)*
How is one to be saved? Paul believes that accepting salvation from Jesus Christ is more inclusive than keeping the Law. It also has more to do with what God does than with what we do.

(2) Romans 9:1–5 (RC/Epis)

Paul is in anguish over the unresponsiveness of the Jews, his own people. His inability to understand their actions is aggravated by the knowledge that Jesus was one of them.

Gospel
Matthew 14:22–33 (RCL/RC/Epis/Luth)

Following the feeding of the five thousand, Jesus dismisses the crowds who had been amazed by this miracle. He sends the disciples to the other side of the lake, while he stays back to pray. A storm comes up and Jesus walks on water to go to them.

Theme

There are times when we feel like we are so far down that we can never get back up.

Thought for the Day

Wherever and whoever you are, you can find God. Wherever and whoever you are, God can find you.

Call to Worship

One:	The voice of the Lord is over the waters;
	the God of glory thunders over mighty waters.
All:	The voice of the Lord is powerful;
	the voice of the Lord is full of majesty.
One:	The Lord sits enthroned over the flood;
	the Lord sits enthroned as king forever.
All:	May the Lord give strength to God's people!
	May the Lord bless the people with peace!

– Based on Psalm 29:3–4, 10–11

Pastoral Prayer

Great and gracious God, how awesome it is to realize you know us well, and yet you continue to love us. How amazing it is to acknowledge that nothing can separate us from your love and that you are present in all places. Whether we are riding high on a mountaintop experience or struggling to find our way out of a valley of darkness, you are not far from us. You come to us regardless of the depth of our fears or the weakness of our faith. When we find life to be a voyage on rough waters, you draw near to bring us peace and calm. When it is hard for us to keep our heads above the water, you offer the life–preserving presence of your Son, Jesus Christ. We thank you for being the kind of God who is an everywhere, ever–present source of help. Amen.

Prayer of Confession

Forever-loving and forgiving God, when we feel overwhelmed by what life does to us, we confess that we find it hard to see beyond our own difficulties to how you are sending us hope and help. Though we know we are to keep our eyes upon Jesus, we often just see our problems. We confess to you that often when we feel overwhelmed and burdened, we forget that you are God-with-us. Forgive us when we only complain about what's wrong, rather than thank you for what you have already made right. When we are guilty of failing to look beyond our own troubles to the needs of others, remind us that we are to bear one another's burdens and so fulfill your will for us. Help us to do better. Amen.

Prayer of Dedication of Gifts and Self

Loving God, may these gifts be useful in your work of lifting the sprits of those who are feeling low – those who feel like no one cares. Use them to ease the burden of those who are being held down and held back, and who do not trust the rich and abundant life of your realm. As we offer our gifts, we offer ourselves to you. Amen.

Sermon Summary

Jesus reaches out to us, and often down to us, to pull us up and pull us along.

Hymn of the Day
"O God, Our Help in Ages Past"

Few biblical stories are more vivid than the account of Jesus walking on the water. We see the boat tossed by the waves. We hear the sounds of the disciples' terrified cries. We feel Peter's fear as he begins sinking into the swirling sea, overcome by doubt.

This hymn, set to the sturdy ST. ANNE, is a solid selection for this Sunday. Isaac Watts' text reminds us that God's pledge of protection and security has been and remains ours, no matter what "stormy blasts" may come. A contemporary alternative is Daniel Shutte's "Be Not Afraid."

Children's Time

Sink or Float?

Preparation: Bring a large clear plastic container filled halfway with water and an assortment of small objects – some that sink and some that float (for example: coin, rock, crayon, paper clip, feather, candy wrapper).

What is in this tub? Yes, water. What floats on water? (Boats, balls, and so on.) What sinks? (Stones, coins, and so on.) Do you think this coin will sink or float? (Have a child drop the coin in the water and call out the result. Repeat for all objects.)

In our Bible story, Jesus' disciples were floating in a boat, sailing across the lake. Jesus stayed behind to pray. There was a terrible storm that night. Early in the morning, Jesus set out across the water toward the boat. Do you think Jesus sank or floated? (Accept responses.) The Bible tells us that Jesus walked right on top of the water, all the way to the boat. No ordinary person can walk on water. But this was Jesus. Jesus walked on the water to help the disciples believe that he was God's Son and to trust that he would help them, no matter what.

Prayer: Help us, Lord Jesus, to grow in our faith and love for you. Amen.

The Sermon

In Over Our Heads

Hymns
Beginning of Worship: "Stand By Me"
Sermon Hymn: "Give to the Winds Thy Fears"
Closing Hymn: "Precious Lord, Take My Hand"

Scripture
Matthew 14:22–33 (For additional sermon materials on this passage, see the 2005 May/June Planning issue and the April 2005 issue of *The Clergy Journal*.)

A commercial shows a couple "drowning in a sea of debt." This could be one of the reasons we might have a "sinking feeling." Any number of things can be at work in our lives to pull us down and hold us down. We may feel buried, like the football player who is tackled and falls to the ground, only to have the opposing team pile on. Our troubles have a way of piling up.

During one of the worst hurricane seasons Florida had ever experienced, a good friend who was having a hard time of it emailed me and began his litany of troubles by saying, "I feel like Florida." He also could have said, "I feel like Job." In fact, he could have said, "I feel like the psalmist."

For my life is full of troubles,
and my life draws near to Sheol.
I am counted among those who go down to the Pit;
I am like those who have no help (Ps 88:3–4)

The psalmist spoke of his situation as being "in the depths of the Pit, in the regions dark and deep" (Ps 88:6). Haven't we all felt that way?

One thing we learn from reading the Psalms is that we are not the first to exaggerate a bit or to employ figurative language when it comes to describing our situation in life. When the psalmist said he felt like one who had gone down to "the Pit," he was echoing the actual experience of Joseph, who was put in a pit by his brothers, and Jeremiah, whose enemies put him into a pit. The pit referred to an experience of being rendered powerless. The word Sheol was similar. It was a place of nonexistence where one was removed from life and from God.

We may put different labels to the experience of being "in the pits." There was a time we described depression as being "down in the dumps." John Bunyan called it the "slough of despond." St. John of the Cross called it "the dark night of the soul." Whatever we call it, it is a description of those times when we call to God and anyone else who will listen from "out of the depths." There is nothing worse than feeling like we have been cut off from God and from others.

Isn't that how Peter must have felt out there on the lake, as he sank deeper and deeper? Sometime earlier, Jesus had put his friends into a boat so they could meet him on the other side of the lake. "I will be there when you get there," he may have assured them, and he went back to dismiss the crowds that had gotten caught up in his latest miracle (feeding the five thousand). Jesus felt the need to go off and pray, and while he was tending to the needs of his soul, the disciples were some distance from the shore. Not only that, but they were being beaten by the waves and wind. A sudden storm had caught them off guard. They were terrified.

Then Matthew tells us that Jesus came to them "early in the morning." The disciples see Jesus walking on water, and they believe him to be a ghost. (Don't lots of things look like ghosts when it's dark?) Jesus tries to calm them by telling them who he is. Peter gets out of the boat to walk to him on the water. He does fairly well as long as he keeps his eyes on Jesus, but when he sees nothing but the wind and the storm, he is overcome by fear and cries out, "Lord, save me!" And he begins to sink.

Many are the times you and I lose sight of God, and we can see nothing but the storms and stresses of life. Our fears and our problems overwhelm us, and we feel as if we "are sunk." That is the worst thing about those times of hitting bottom – we feel as if there is no help, no hope, no God to care about us and do anything for us. We frantically search for solid footing.

I believe that when we are at our absolute lowest point, God stretches out a hand to help us up and help us out. One woman related how her life had hit bottom. She became depressed. She withdrew from everyone and everything. She contemplated suicide. Through the church, she met Jesus Christ. Later, she said, she knew she had a long way to go but at least she felt she was going in the right direction: "When I trip, Jesus is there to reach down and give me a hand and set me back on my feet again. I have felt his touch many times."

That same thought is repeated throughout the psalms: God "drew me up from the desolate pit" (Ps 40:2) and "delivered my soul from the depths of Sheol" (Ps 86:13). Wherever we are, God can find us and put us back on our feet again. One of the ways God does that is through other people.

The story is told of a man in a prison for civilians in Singapore whose friend was sentenced to solitary confinement. He wondered what he could do to help him. He learned that the prisoners were allowed to have their hair cut once a month, so he applied for the job of barber. Though he was able to see his friend regularly, he could not give him anything or talk to him. So he would keep saying to him, "Please keep your chin up, keep your chin up!" while he snipped away at his hair. The guards thought it had something to do with barbering, but it was really an attempt to offer encouragement to a friend in a hopeless situation.

A final thought: The pit is sometimes another way of saying "pity." We need to think about things other than our own misery. One minister told a chronically gloomy woman that she was needed at church every Monday morning to pick up a list of people who were sick, homebound, and hospitalized. He told her to visit at least five of them every week for six months. Week by week a miracle took place in her life. She became one of the most radiant people in the congregation!

When you feel like you are about as low as you can go, keep your eyes upon Jesus. And look around to see if there might be someone to whom you might reach out.

– William M. Schwein

August 14, 2005

13th Sunday after Pentecost (Proper 15)
RC/Pres: 20th Sunday in Ordinary Time

Lessons

RCL	Gen 45:1–15	Rom 11:1–2a, 29–32	Mt 15:(10–20) 21–28
Roman Catholic	Isa 56:1, 6–7	Rom 11:13–15, 29–32	Mt 15:21–28
Episcopal (BCP)	Isa 56:1 (2–5), 6–7	Rom 11:13–15, 29–32	Mt 15:21–28
Lutheran	Isa 56:1, 6–8	Rom 11:1–2a, 29–32	Mt 15:(10–20) 21–28

Introduction to the Lessons

Lesson 1

(1) *Genesis 45:1–15 (RCL)*

Joseph sees God's hand at work in his life as he is reunited with his brothers. He sees his suffering as redemptive; God was at work through the events of this family's dysfunction.

(2) *Isaiah 56:1, 6–7 (RC); Isaiah 56:1 (2–5), 6–7 (Epis); Isaiah 56:1, 6–8 (Luth)*

God determines how persons qualify to be among God's people. The temple is to be available as a house of prayer for all people, including outcasts, eunuchs, and foreigners.

Lesson 2
Romans 11:1–2a, 29–32 (RCL/Luth);
Romans 11:13–15, 29–32 (RC/Epis)

Paul is an advocate for the inclusion of Gentiles in the church and for the church's mission to them. For Paul, this does not mean God has rejected the Jews.

Gospel
Matthew 15:(10–20) 21–28 (RCL/Luth);
Matthew 15:21–28 (RC/Epis)

Jesus seeks to convince the Pharisees that inner purity (clean hearts) is more important than outward ritual (clean hands). When a Canaanite woman – an outsider – whose daughter is ill confronts him, Jesus acts with a compassionate heart.

Theme
Good things can happen through people and events we may label as "bad."

Thought for the Day
The bud may have a bitter taste, but sweet will be the flower.

– William Cowper

Call to Worship

One: Call to mind the deeds of the Lord; remember God's wonders of old.

All: What god is so great as our God?

One: It is our God who works wonders; who has displayed might among the peoples.

All: With a strong arm God has redeemed the descendants of Jacob and Joseph.

– Based on Psalm 77

Pastoral Prayer
God, in these moments of worship, help us understand what is going on in our lives. Help us perceive your design and plan behind the events that seem to be chance and coincidence. May we be able to see where you have been at work – and a bit more sure of what you want to do for us and through us. We are grateful for what you have done in the past, and we anticipate what wonders you will yet perform. Give us grace to be patient and to wait for your kingdom. Strengthen our gratitude for all the ways you have already made our lives better. Amen.

Prayer of Confession

Gracious and merciful God, forgive us when we give up on you or give in to the difficulties we are experiencing. Forgive us when we forget that you can use any means to fulfill your purpose and that quite often your will is done in unexpected ways. We have taken for granted your creating power that made all things good, your redeeming power that shows how all things can be made new, and your sustaining power that leads us to believe all things will work out well in the end. Give us courage and confidence to work against all things that oppose your rule. Help us remember that because of you, all good things become possible. May you always have the last word. Amen.

Prayer of Dedication of Gifts and Self

Loving God, we are astounded at your greatness and goodness, yet we sometimes worship the things of this world rather than you. You have called on us to live in hope; help us to give with hope. May these gifts make a difference to those who have not yet known your healing and your help. May those who benefit from our giving see beyond the material blessings to know you as the source of all good. Amen.

Sermon Summary

Just as we believe that God's purpose ultimately will be fulfilled, the purpose of our lives should be the fulfillment of what God wants us to be and to do. As John Claypool once said in a sermon, "The worst things are never the last things."

Hymn of the Day
"I Need Thee Every Hour"

We may not know the name of the Canaanite woman in today's gospel lesson, yet her story is such that we feel we know her. She has a daughter in dire need, and so determined is she that Jesus can and should meet that need that he grants her what she asks. "Woman," he said, with words that surely humbled his disciples, "great is your faith!"

In Annie Hawks' hymn "I Need Thee Every Hour," set to the music of Robert Lowry, we can hear the voice of this Canaanite woman. Her simple, direct plea to Jesus was so filled with faith: "I need thee, O I need thee; every hour I need thee; O bless me now, my Savior, I come to thee."

Children's Time

Jesus' Steadfast Love

Preparation: Bring little star stickers.

Join me in singing "Twinkle, Twinkle Little Star."

Thanks for helping me sing today. All around the world the sun rises and sets every day. The stars twinkle in the sky, even when we can't see them because of clouds. Will the sun rise tomorrow? (Yes.) How do you know? (Accept responses.)

In today's Bible story we meet a woman who had a sick daughter. Like you, she watched the stars twinkling in the night sky. Like all mothers, she worried about her sick daughter. She wanted her daughter to get well. Then this woman heard that Jesus healed people who were sick. She heard that Jesus was God's Son. And she knew, as sure as she knew the stars would always twinkle in the night sky, that Jesus could heal her daughter. And she was right. Jesus healed her sick daughter.

(Place a star sticker on the back of each child's hand as you speak.) Wear this star sticker to remind you to have faith in Jesus' love and care for you.

Prayer: When we see stars twinkling in the nighttime sky, remind us, Jesus, that you always love us. And we love you, too. Amen.

The Sermon

When the Story Ended, What Had God Intended?

Hymns

Beginning of Worship: "Praise to the Lord, the Almighty"
Sermon Hymn: "God Will Take Care of You"
Closing Hymn: "If Thou But Suffer God to Guide Thee"

Scripture

Genesis 45:1–15 (For sermon materials on Matthew 15:(10–20) 21–28, see the 2005 May/June planning issue and the April 2005 issue of *The Clergy Journal*.)

Have you ever thought about what you might want on your tombstone? What epitaph would best summarize your life? There have been some interesting epitaphs throughout history. I understand Thomas Jefferson designed his own tombstone and wrote the inscription for it. He had served as governor of Virginia, a U.S. Minister to France, Secretary of State, Vice-President, and President. He had also achieved distinction as an architect, naturalist, and linguist. But he instructed that his epitaph say only, "Author of the Declaration of American Independence and of the Statute of Virginia for religious freedom, and Father of the University of Virginia," and "not a word more." Which of your accomplishments would best summarize how you want to be remembered?

Things do not always deliver as promised! There is no guarantee that life is going to work out as we hope and plan. It will be sad if we end up standing before our Maker and Judge and have to confess that we just never got around to doing what we knew God wanted us to do. How wonderful to be able to echo the words Jesus prayed in the final hours of his life, "I glorified you on earth by finishing the work that you gave me to do" (Jn 17:4).

The artist Rembrandt said that a picture was finished only when it truly and fully expressed the artist's intention. In the same way, we are to fully express the intentional design of our Creator. We are to live so that at the end we can say, as Jesus did, "I finished the work that you gave me to do."

Singer John Denver was once asked by an interviewer, "What would you like people to say about you when you are gone?" Denver answered, "I think I would like for them to say 'He became himself.'" Who is it you are to become? Are you coming to be that person more and more?

Few of us probably think of our lives in terms of its purpose or how God gives us work to do – what Frederich Buechner calls the "plot" of our lives. Churches spend time asking, "Are we doing what God is calling us to be and to do?" But how often do we ask ourselves, "Am I completing the work God gave me to do?" We don't always do a good job of seeing God's plan, design, purpose, or plot behind the everyday events of our lives or how they fit together.

In a similar way, we sometimes fail to see the "big picture" when we read the stories within the Bible. The passage from Genesis we read today brings us to the end of the ancestral story of Genesis, a story that began with a blessing and a promise. Every generation of God's people from the time of Abraham depended upon that promise. Abraham's descendents felt God was preparing them for their particular destiny and role in history. Memory made hope possible. They remained confident that they would be brought to a time of well-being and a place of abundance and peace. Even though some would conspire against God's plans, they believed God would ultimately defeat those evil plans, countering them always with good.

God's purposes are never defeated. Sometimes even the evil plans of sinful people can become tools by which God's plan is furthered. So when Joseph addressed his brothers in Egypt, he could see beyond the evil intent of his brothers to all the ways the purposes of God were being worked out. He could say, finally, "Even though you intended to do harm to me, God intended it for good, in order to preserve a numerous people, as he is doing today" (Gen 50:20). Though the brothers had plotted to eliminate Joseph, in the midst of their scheme was another plan being fulfilled that they did not see nor understand.

Leslie Weatherhead's little book, *The Will of God*, has helped many understand that in every situation, God's will is for good. Weatherhead wrote that while there is an intentional purpose of God for every person's life, our free will can create circumstances to thwart God's plans. Our free will can disturb God's intention for us. There is a will "within the will of God," what he calls the circumstantial will of God. Joseph did so well "under the circumstances" that the end of his story has provided me with a line that I have probably quoted and mentally noted more than almost any other verse of scripture: "Even though you intended to do harm to me, God intended it for good" (Gen 50:20).

Perhaps Paul committed that verse to memory, too, and that is why he could say later that "all things work together for good for those who love God" (Rom 8:28). In other words, God works for good in all things. Life's detours often reveal to us that God is a God of fresh alternatives. God works after the fact of tragedy and trouble to reveal new avenues of growth, hope, and opportunity.

Joseph's life was a testimony to how God can revise the game plan and defeat the most fervent efforts to thwart those plans. After Joseph was sold into slavery and was taken to Egypt, he made the most of the situation and ascended to a position of power. From foreign prisoner, he became Secretary of Agriculture for the entire kingdom of Egypt. During that time he had two sons. He named one of them Ephraim, which means "fruitful," because he believed "God has made me fruitful in the land of my misfortunes" (Gen 41:52). What a marvelous testimony!

Later, when his brothers came asking for food in order to survive a famine, Joseph said to them, "I am your brother, Joseph, whom you sold into Egypt. And now do not be distressed, or angry with yourselves, because you sold me here; for God sent me before you to preserve life" (Gen 45:4–5).

Joseph was aware of God's hand – leading, guiding, guarding, sending, and making all things work for good. Through all the twists and turns of his life, God was at work to bring something good and fruitful out of misfortune. Joseph paid attention to God and could affirm how God was involved in his life. In the end, the only thing that really mattered to him was what God had intended.

In the Royal Palace of Teheran, Iran, the grand entrance is resplendent in glittering, sparkling glass. It appears as if the domed ceiling, the side-walls, and the columns are all covered with diamonds. But they are not diamonds, nor cut crystal, but small pieces of mirrors. The edges of the little mirrors reflect the light, throwing out the colors of the rainbow. When the Royal Palace was planned, the architects sent an order to Paris for mirrors to cover the entrance walls. When the crates arrived and were opened, nothing but crushed pieces spilled out. They had all been smashed in transit. They were about to be junked when one creative man said, "No, maybe it will be more beautiful because they are broken." Then he took all the little pieces and fitted them together like an abstract mosaic. The result is striking.

In the same way, God can refit the broken pieces of our hope and dreams and make them into something even more beautiful than we had imagined.

– William M. Schwein

August 21, 2005

14th Sunday after Pentecost (Proper 16)
RC/Pres: 21st Sunday in Ordinary Time

Lessons

RCL	Ex 1:8–2:10	Rom 12:1–8	Mt 16:13–20
Roman Catholic	Isa 22:19–23	Rom 11:33–36	Mt 16:13–20
Episcopal (BCP)	Isa 51:1–6	Rom 11:33–36	Mt 16:13–20
Lutheran	Isa 51:1–6	Rom 12:1–8	Mt 16:13–20

Introduction to the Lessons
Lesson 1
(1) *Exodus 1:8–2:10 (RCL)*
Just as the ruler of Egypt had changed, so did the influence of the
Israelites. Their numbers increased and they became a threat to the king,
and suffered under their bondage.

(2) *Isaiah 22:19–23 (RC)*
God is concerned with the political problems of Isaiah's day. God
announces judgment against one of King Hezekiah's officials because of his
ambition, and promises to replace him.

(3) Isaiah 51:1–6 (Epis/Luth)
The prophet confidently announces God is near. The people are encouraged to remember God's promise to Abraham and to trust in God's
continuing care and comfort.

Lesson 2
(1) *Romans 12:1–8 (RCL/Luth)*
Paul calls on the Roman Christians to offer themselves to God in holiness
and humility. The call to God's service is the means by which the people
of God are united.

(2) *Romans 11:33–36 (RC/Epis)*
Paul has been arguing that God treats all persons (both Jew and Gentile) with amazing grace. Paul concludes with a familiar doxology used in Christian worship.

Gospel
Matthew 16:13–20 (RCL/RC/Epis/Luth)
Jesus asks his followers what others were saying about him. Then Jesus asks the disciples the same question. Peter declares Jesus to be the Messiah and the Son of God, and is given a new identity: the Rock.

Theme
We seek to know who Jesus was, who Jesus is, and who Jesus can be for us.

Thought for the Day
When Jesus asks me, "Who am I?" I know that it is not enough for me simply to say, "You are the Christ of God." The answer must become contemporary.

– D. T. Niles

Call to Worship
One: We see Jesus as Mary's son, as God's holy Son.
All: We see Jesus as the Christ of God, the life, the truth, the way.
One: We open our ears to hear his call, "Follow me!"
All: Christ, we are yours; we give ourselves to you.

Pastoral Prayer
Lord, in so many ways you reveal yourself to us, though we do not always recognize you. We yearn to learn more about you through the life, death, and resurrection of your Son, Jesus Christ. Thank you for the witness and testimony of others. Open our hearts and minds to know more about your action in our lives each day. Enable us to see you more clearly in order that we might follow your Son more nearly. Amen.

Prayer of Confession

Gracious and forgiving God, you sent your Son into the world to be an example for us, so that we might follow him fully and faithfully. We confess that we have failed to follow Jesus' guidance and to do your will. We have not done as Jesus did. Forgive us for listening to the words of Jesus without really taking them to heart. By the power of your Spirit, set us free to be more nearly what we claim to be. May the mind and spirit of Christ be in us, and may Christ direct our minds and govern our actions, so that we will become the persons you intend us to be. Amen.

Prayer of Dedication of Gifts and Self

Loving God, may these gifts be used to enable others to come to know Jesus Christ as your Son, as their friend, and as their Lord and Savior. May our offerings reflect the compassionate spirit of Jesus, so that others may see in us your love. Amen.

Sermon Summary

It is good to know what others believe about Jesus, but it is more important for us to know what we believe about Jesus, and how he is the Christ for us.

Hymn of the Day
"Built on a Rock"

More often than not, finding the hymn that is just right for a particular occasion requires a fair amount of pondering, leafing through hymnals, and imagination. Such is the case with today's texts, which offer several directions for the musician.

One intriguing possibility is Nikolai Grundvig's "Built on a Rock," set to the tune KIRKEN DEN ER ET GAMMELT HUS by Ludvig Lindeman. Grundvig's opening line echoes precisely Jesus' words to Peter in the gospel lesson, while the remainder of the hymn reflects ideas presented in the Romans text.

Children's Time

Peter, the Rock Man

Preparation: Bring small washed stones.

(Give each child a rock to hold.) What is in your hand? (A rock.) Did you know that Jesus named one of his disciples "the rock"?

In our Bible story today, Jesus was walking with his disciples. Along the way he asked them, "Who do you say that I am?" Peter gave the right answer, "You are the Messiah, the Son of the Living God." Jesus was pleased and said, "You are Peter and on this rock I will build my church." Peter helped to start the first Christian church by telling many people about Jesus.

Each one of you is Jesus' rock, too. Jesus continues to build up the church with you and me, just like he built his church with Peter, the rock man. How can we help to build up the church? (Tell others about Jesus, invite people to come to Sunday school, worship, pray, be kind to others.) Let's be rock people this week by inviting a friend to worship with us next Sunday.

Prayer: Dear Jesus, help us to be strong rock people for you. Be with us as we build your church on the good news of your love. Amen.

The Sermon

And Who Do You Say That He Is?

Hymns

> **Beginning of Worship:** "All Hail the Power of Jesus' Name"
> **Sermon Hymn:** "What a Friend We Have in Jesus"
> **Closing Hymn:** "O Young and Fearless Prophet"

Scripture

Matthew 16:13–20 (For additional sermon materials on this passage, see the 2005 May/June planning issue and the April 2005 issue of *The Clergy Journal.*)

In a sense, it was like a final exam. The course work of Discipleship 101 had been completed. All that remained was for Jesus to test what the disciples had learned over the past three years. There were only a couple questions. One sounded a bit like multiple-choice; the other was an essay question. The first question required research. The second was based on the disciples' own understanding and experience.

Jesus asked, "Who do people say that the Son of Man is?" Then Jesus asked, "Who do you say that I am?"

Jesus and his disciples had traveled to Caesarea Philippi in northern-most Israel, away from the distractions and confusion of Jerusalem. Jesus confronted his "students" with the question about the identity of "the Son of Man," Jesus' favorite term for himself as reported in Matthew. The disciples offered a series of possibilities pulled from tradition and from the past. These disciples, who had heard Jesus preach and teach, heal and feed, sought to explain Jesus by pigeonholing him into past identities brought back to life. They reported that some thought he was John the Baptist, or Elijah, or Jeremiah, or one of the other prophets.

When Jesus asked the disciples for their own assessment of who he was, Simon Peter ventured a reply: "You are the Christ." Someone jokingly suggested that "The disciples replied, 'You are the eschatological manifestation of the ground of our being.'" And Jesus said, "What?"

You can imagine how the other disciples might have reacted to exuberant Peter. He had popped up with the right answer before anyone else. That "good answer" was rewarded with a blessing. Jesus proclaimed that Peter would hold a special place in the life of the church. (James probably kicked the dust with his sandal, and muttered, "I was going to say that." Thomas might have angrily insisted, "I had my hand up first. You never call on me, Lord." And John may have whispered, "Peter, the teacher's pet, always gets called on. It's not fair!")

Jesus asks us, too, "Who do you say that I am?" Everything we might have learned or will ever learn hangs on how we answer this. In a way, one's whole life comes down to this question.

When he entered Jerusalem on Palm Sunday, Matthew tells us that when the parade had caught the attention of the religious pilgrims who were there for the Feast of the Passover, the crowds began to ask one another, "Who is this?" Some of the crowds offered an answer: "This is the prophet Jesus from Nazareth in Galilee" (Mt 21:10–11). It was their inability to correctly answer the question, "Who is this?" that led some to brand him as a common criminal while others lauded him as the Christ.

This is not the kind of question we expect to hear being asked in our world today, but several years ago, *Time* magazine had a cover story that asked, "Who was Jesus?" The article was prompted by the release of a controversial film, Martin Scorsese's *Last Temptation of Christ*. The article went on to offer what it called "a diversity of Jesuses," and encouraged the reader to "take one's pick." Is the question multiple-choice, one that can be answered with an "all of the above"? Perhaps no person in history has had more labels, titles, and names associated with her or him than Jesus: Itinerant sage, Hellenistic cynic, apocalyptic prophet, inspired rabbi, and so on. Even his enemies had a variety of descriptive terms: blasphemer, false prophet, madman. There are as many ideas and images about Jesus as there are people, it would seem. Maybe the question is really, "Which Christ?"

In spite of the centrality of Jesus Christ as Lord and Savior, what it says in the prologue to the Gospel of John is still true: "He was in the world, and the world came into being through him; yet the world did not know him" (Jn 1:10). Similarly, Jesus Christ is in his church, and the church came into being through him; yet the church does not know him well either. We talk about Jesus, sing about him, watch movies about him, teach our children about him, tell our children how much he loves them, and offer prayers in his name – even praying the prayer he taught us – and yet too few really know who Jesus is.

Too few know what happened between "born of the Virgin Mary" and "suffered under Pontius Pilate." M. Scott Peck has called Jesus "the best-kept secret of Christianity." There are some popular books that suggest that all of us need to have a new encounter with Jesus: Philip Yancey's *The Jesus I Never Knew* and Marcus Borg's *Meeting Jesus Again for the First Time*. Those two titles pretty well say it for us. Some of us really never knew Jesus. We may need to meet him again as if we are meeting him for the first time.

Some of us have what has been called a "term-paper attitude" toward Jesus. We rely on what we've heard others say about him. We have nothing but footnotes in our faith, and few original ideas. We may know all about Jesus, but still not know him. That's why the way we answer Jesus' question, "Who do you say that I am?" defines our relationship with him.

A couple things are worth noting about this question that Jesus asked the disciples. The timing was crucial. He did not give a quiz the first day they came together. He did not ask them what they thought of him when he recruited them, when they registered for Discipleship 101. He simply said, "Follow me." I doubt if any two of the original twelve had the same reasons for following Jesus. They may have followed out of boredom with their lives, or fascination with Jesus' new teachings, or simply out of curiosity. It was only after they had spent time with Jesus that they were called upon to make up their minds about him.

As in any personal relationship, our perceptions may change. Our understanding of who Jesus is should reflect a progressive, dynamic relationship. It requires time for us to come to know Jesus.

In *The Quest for the Historical Jesus*, Albert Schweitzer wrote that Jesus "comes to us as One unknown, without a name, as of old, by the lake-side, he came to those men who knew Him not. He speaks to us the same word: 'Follow thou me!'" Further, Schweitzer said, Jesus reveals himself "in the toils, the conflicts, the sufferings that they shall pass through in his fellowship" until finally "they shall learn in their own experience Who He is."

May that be true for each one of us.

– William M. Schwein

August 28, 2005

15th Sunday after Pentecost (Proper 17)
RC/Pres: 22nd Sunday in Ordinary Time

Lessons

RCL	Ex 3:1–15	Rom 12:9–21	Mt 16:21–28
Roman Catholic	Jer 20:7–9	Rom 12:1–2	Mt 16:21–27
Episcopal (BCP)	Jer 15:15–21	Rom 12:1–8	Mt 16:21–27
Lutheran	Jer 15:15–21	Rom 12:9–21	Mt 16:21–28

Introduction to the Lessons
Lesson 1
(1) *Exodus 3:1–15 (RCL)*

In this familiar story of the call of Moses, God speaks out of a burning bush that is not consumed. We are told who God is and how Moses understands God's call.

(2) *Jeremiah 20:7–9 (RC)*

The prophet is in turmoil because of the people's response to the message that God called him to deliver. Jeremiah wrestles with how such a powerful message could be dismissed so easily.

(3) *Jeremiah 15:15–21 (Epis/Luth)*

In torment, the prophet prays about the response he is getting to his message. God responds with a promise to strengthen Jeremiah if he remains faithful to the task.

Lesson 2
Romans 12:9–21 (RCL/Luth)

Paul exhorts the Romans to live out their faith by adhering to certain actions. All of his counsel is to enable good to overcome evil.

Gospel
Matthew 16:21–28 (RCL/Luth); Matthew 16:21–27 (RC/Epis)
Jesus seeks to explain to the disciples what it means for him to be God's Chosen One. Peter has other ideas about what this means. Jesus has the last word and points out that those who would follow him need to be selfless and obedient.

Theme
Though there is a cost attached to our discipleship, few of us are willing to pay full price.

Thought for the Day
Every one that I know whose discipleship has resulted in real power and service has somewhere had to pass through what for that person corresponded to the cross – some crisis of self-denial and self-giving.
– Sam Shoemaker

Call to Worship
One: I can hear my Savior calling, "Take thy cross and follow me."
All: He will give me grace and glory, and go with me all the way.
One: Where he leads me I will follow,
All: I'll go with him all the way.
–E. W. Blandy

Prayer of Confession
Gracious God, we come before you with the cares and concerns of life, and trust that you will meet us with grace and goodness. We thank you for renewing and redeeming what we have made of the lives you have given us. We thank you for the hard lessons we have learned from the difficult times of our lives. We thank you for the ways we have grown through adversity, won out over hardship, and developed character through suffering. We thank you that you have placed within us not only a capacity to cope with the worst that life offers, but also to hope for the best that your Son has to offer us. Give us the strength, the wisdom, and the courage to follow your will and your way through life. Amen.

Prayer of Dedication of Gifts and Self

Loving God, this is a time for us to give up our own selfish needs and to offer ourselves in selfless deeds. Help us to do the work that you want us to do in our time. Help us to be more sacrificial in our giving, just as your Son sacrificed his life as a gift to the world you love so much. Amen.

Sermon Summary

It is human nature to seek the easy way. Jesus tells us God's way is different. Peter represents each person who wants her or his religious experience to be more convenience than commitment.

Hymn of the Day
"Take Up Your Cross, the Savior Said"

Christianity's chief symbol is the cross – an assertion supported by its frequent appearance in Christian hymnody. Merely count the number of hymns whose titles contain the word *cross* to see how deeply it has inspired hymnwriters through the centuries.

"Take Up Your Cross, the Savior Said," by Charles Everest, has been set to a variety of tunes. BOURBON, a strong melody in the minor mode attributed to Freeman Lewis, is particularly effective in underscoring the gravity of Jesus' words to those who would follow him.

Children's Time

Follow Jesus

Preparation: Fill the baptismal font with water.

Follow my actions as we walk around the sanctuary. (Move on tiptoe, giant steps, baby steps, and marching. Include these actions: shaking hands with people in the congregation, raising hands high and saying, "Praise God!" and making the sign of the cross. End up at the font.)

In today's Bible story Jesus said to his disciples, "If any want to become my followers let them take up their cross and follow me." When we are baptized, we are marked with the sign of the cross. We become God's children. You are already Jesus' followers because you have been marked with the sign of the cross through your baptism. Jesus' love will always be with you.

Invite the children to dip their hands into the font and trace a wet cross on their foreheads.

Prayer: Teach the children to make the sign of the cross using this action prayer:

> God be in my head. (Touch forehead.)
> God be in my heart. (Touch center of chest.)
> God be on my left. (Touch left shoulder.)
> God be on my right. (Touch right shoulder.)
> Amen.

The Sermon

If It Had Been Up to Peter

Hymns

> **Beginning of Worship:** "God of Love and God of Power"
> **Sermon Hymn:** "O Jesus, I Have Promised"
> **Closing Hymn:** "Take Up Thy Cross"

Scripture

Matthew 16:21–28 (For additional sermon materials on this passage, see the 2005 May/June planning issue and the April 2005 issue of *The Clergy Journal.*)

Apparently the struggle Jesus had with Satan did not end when he came out of those forty days in the wilderness. We should have expected that. Luke tells us that, "When the devil had finished every test, he departed from him until an opportune time" (Lk 4:13). But who would have thought one of these "opportune" times would come in a conversation Jesus had with his disciples? Or that the devil would come back to speak through his friend, Peter?

This "temptation of Christ" had to do with whether or not Jesus would endure the betrayal, physical abuse, and painful death of the crucifixion – or enjoy life and die at a ripe old age back home in Nazareth. How interesting it is that this temptation was offered by his best friend, Peter!

Scholars say that in this text, Jesus is beginning to show his disciples what he had been talking about earlier. He had talked about the cost of following him, taking up a cross, denying themselves, losing their lives for his sake. But now he calls their attention to something they had apparently failed to perceive. There are times when someone needs to call our attention to some truth we may have missed, misunderstood, or omitted in our grasp of the Christian faith. In this case, it was sacrifice and suffering. For Jesus, it was show, and not just tell.

When Jesus tells his friends he is going to Jerusalem to die, to give his life for them and for others, Peter pulls him aside and says, "God forbid it, Lord! This can't happen to you. There must be an easier way. We won't let you do this to yourself. God won't either." Jesus responds with almost the very same words he had spoken to the devil during the temptation in the wilderness: "Get behind me, Satan!" (Mt 16:23). Matthew told us earlier that Jesus said to the devil, "Away with you, Satan!" (Mt 4:10). Back in the wilderness, as in this instance, it was the temptation to choose the easy way. Usually we think of the temptation to do evil as something completely different – to do wrong, something immoral, to break the law, to overeat, or to cheat. But as this story tells us, for the Christian, sometimes the temptation is to choose the easy, comfortable way.

Jesus reminds the disciples that it takes a painful effort to understand that God's thoughts are different from ours. There is a difference between "divine things" and "human things." What God has in mind for us may be totally different from what we have figured out for ourselves.

Peter may well have spoken for us all. Had it been up to Peter, Jesus would have avoided the cross and certainly not challenged us to take up our crosses. Peter, after all, would be more into "denial" than "self-denial," wouldn't he? Three times he would take the easy way out by denying that he had any sort of relationship with Jesus.

Most of us buy products that promise they are easy to use, easy to make, easy to put together. We wouldn't give things a second look if the packages said they were difficult to use, difficult to make, or difficult to put together. We want things in life to be easy. That may say something about the kind of Christianity many churches are promoting and offering these days.

One church I heard of sings songs like "Sunshiny Day" rather than challenging hymns of the faith. They took out the phrase "forgive us our sins" from the Lord's Prayer because people don't like to feel guilty. They don't use the word worship because worship has to do with awe and fear; they use the word celebration instead. They changed the "Prayer of Confession" to "Naming our Pain." I wouldn't be surprised if they removed the cross from the back of the chancel. It seems like a lot has been watered down in this church to make faith easy.

Are we overly hesitant to challenge people or confront them with a faith that might, at times, be inconvenient and uncomfortable? I once saw a cartoon that pictured a church billboard announcing "The Lite Church," with "24% fewer commitments, 10-minute sermons, 45-minute worship services, and only 8 commandments everything you've wanted in a church and less!"

Perhaps Sren Kierkegaard was right: when it's too easy to become a Christian, it is a lot harder to become a Christian. Little in life has value unless it costs us something. Few victories are won when there is no struggle or battle. Character is realized when we meet and overcome temptations – not when there is no hard decision to be made.

I've got to give Jesus credit for being honest. He told us what was involved in following him. He didn't water down the demands or soft sell the challenges. He came right out and spoke about denying ourselves, taking up crosses, and losing our lives for his sake.

Thankfully, many of Jesus' followers have been willing to pay the price. It has been pointed out that probably only one of the original disciples died a natural death and that 40 percent of the New Testament was written in prison.

What about us? Dean Inge once said, "We're losing our Christianity because Christianity is a religion for heroes, and we are just good-natured people who want to be left alone and have a good time."

I once read of a woman who reacted to an invitation to worship on World Communion Sunday that said her church would "partake of the cup and loaf with Christians around the world" by asking, "Is *loaf* a noun or a verb?" She suggested that if it were a verb, she would end up loafing with Christians around the world! Isn't that what most of us do through the week when it comes to living out the Christian life? We settle for mediocrity. We don't put much effort into it and consequently we don't get much out of it.

A little girl coming home from Sunday school told of her disappointment after the first day: "Jesus told us to go into all the world and make disciples of all nations, but we just sat at the table." Isn't that true of most all of us? If it had been up to Peter, that's probably all we would do.

– William M. Schwein

September 4, 2005

16th Sunday after Pentecost (Proper 18)
RC/Pres: 23rd Sunday in Ordinary Time

Lessons

RCL	Ex 12:1–14	Rom 13:8–14	Mt 18:15–20
Roman Catholic	Ezek 33:7–9	Rom 13:8–10	Mt 18:15–20
Episcopal (BCP)	Ezek 33:(1–6) 7–11	Rom 12:9–21	Mt 18:15–20
Lutheran	Ezek 33:7–11	Rom 13:8–14	Mt 18:15–20

Introduction to the Lessons

Lesson 1

(1) *Exodus 12:1–14 (RCL)*

The Lord tells Moses and Aaron to instruct the people how to prepare and eat the Passover lamb, smearing its blood on the doorposts so that the Lord will pass over the houses of the Israelites. This is the origin of the Jewish Passover and the last of the judgments against Pharaoh.

(2) *Ezekiel 33:7–9 (RC); Ezekiel 33:(1–6) 7–11 (Epis); Ezekiel 33:7–11 (Luth)*

The Lord instructs Ezekiel to prophesy against the shepherds of Israel who have neglected the people. The Lord will demand an accounting from the shepherds and rescue the sheep personally, so that the shepherds can no longer take advantage of them.

Lesson 2

(1) Romans 13:8–14 (RCL/Luth); Romans 13:8–10 (RC)

In this section of Paul's instruction on Christian conduct, he extols love as the fulfillment of all law, Mosaic as well as civil law, which, in the preceding verses, Paul had urged Christians to obey. This advice is all the more urgent and reasonable since the day of the Lord's return is at hand.

(2) Romans 12:9–21 (Epis)

In describing the conduct of Christians, Paul urges each one to respect the role of the others as members of one body. He then spells out what the unifying love of Christians looks like in practice.

Gospel
Matthew 18:15–20 (RCL/RC/Epis/Luth)
After the disciples are urged to seek out anyone who strays from the community, Jesus instructs them about what to do with someone who sins against them but remains in the community. The three steps are intended to show whether the sinner has the proper disposition to belong to the community or not.

Theme
The sin of a single member calls for the response of the whole community.

Thought for the Day
The sinful acts of a member of the church should be confronted directly and personally with the intention of regaining that person for the good of the church and the glory of God.

Call to Worship
One:	We come to worship as the Lord's community.
All:	We are responsible for one another.
One:	What we bind on earth is bound in heaven.
All:	What we loose on earth is loosed in heaven.
One:	Where two or three are gathered in prayer,
All:	The Lord is in their midst.

Pastoral Prayer
O patient and loving God, we gather as your community to praise you for the gifts you have bestowed upon us and to ask for courage, honesty, and love to face each other when we have been hurt or offended. We acknowledge that you have placed us in each other's care. Help us realize that we honor your trust when we are willing to confront the wrong we do, as Ezekiel confronted the wayward shepherds of Israel. Keep us mindful that love should govern all our actions and judgments, as Paul reminded the Christians in Rome.

We feel the awesome responsibility you have given us to pass binding judgments here on earth. Help us remember that we are to arrive at these judgments through prayerful consensus, for where two or three of us are gathered together, you are in our midst. Amen.

Prayer of Confession

Gracious and forgiving God, we come before you as a community of saints and sinners. Despite the outpouring of your love and your Son's sacrificial death on our behalf, we continue to sin against one another.

Sometimes we misuse our positions of power and authority to take advantage of others as the shepherds of Israel did at the time of Ezekiel. Forgive us.

Sometimes we forget to love, and try to fulfill your will by demanding conformity and imposing our own preferences on others. Remind us.

Sometimes we refuse to listen to the honest, caring intervention from members of our faith community who perceive us doing wrong. Open us.

Sometimes we pass judgment casually and rely on our personal feelings, rather than on prayerful discernment to determine right from wrong. Teach us.

Renew us during this time of worship and keep us responsible for one another in Christ Jesus our Lord. Amen.

Prayer of Dedication of Gifts and Self

O God of compassion and love, you have entrusted the whole of your creation to our care, but most especially you have made us responsible for one another. We humbly acknowledge this responsibility. As we offer material gifts to symbolize our gratitude for the physical world and to continue our good works in it, so too we offer ourselves, gathered in prayer, as a spiritual gift. We pledge that we will be for each other honest and supportive companions, correcting our faults, forgiving our sins, and healing our world so we may make a more perfect offering to you, our bountiful God, through Christ our Lord. Amen.

Sermon Summary

When one member of the faith community sins against another, every effort is made to regain the sinful member. The three steps that Matthew describes culminate in a binding decision, which is honored in heaven if it has been arrived at through prayer on earth.

Hymn of the Day
"God! When Human Bonds Are Broken"

In selecting a hymn for today I found myself responding to the two ideas Matthew joins together here – Jesus' prescription for dealing with conflict within the Christian community and Jesus' promise that where two or three are gathered, he is there. Fred Kaan's hymn, "God! When Human Bonds Are Broken," joined to a tune by William Monk respects the complexity of conflict while underscoring the hope of God's reconciling power in such times. "When we lack the love or skill to restore the hope of healing, give us grace and make us still."

Children's Time

What Is the Church?

Teach this action rhyme to the children. Invite the congregation to join you.

This is the church. (Place outside of hands together, lace fingers, fold hands with palms together with interlaced fingers hiding inside and thumbs side–by–side.)

This is the steeple. (Keep hands in same position, except raise index fingers to form a point.)

Open the door. (Open hands with fingers interlaced.)

And see all the people. (Wiggle interlaced fingers.)

What is a church? (Accept responses.) In today's Bible story Jesus taught the disciples about what it means to belong to a church. Jesus said, "For where two or three are gathered in my name, I am there among them." Did Jesus talk about a church building? (No.) How did Jesus describe his church? (Two or three people meeting together to worship Jesus.) Whenever and wherever people come together to worship Jesus, that is where the church is.

Prayer: Thank you, Jesus, for church buildings where we can gather to worship you and share your love. Amen.

The Sermon

Regaining a Sinful Member

Hymns

Beginning of Worship: "Save Us, O Lord"
Sermon Hymn: "Where Two or Three Have Gathered"
Closing Hymn: "There's a Wideness in God's Mercy"

Scripture

Matthew 18:15–20 (For additional sermon materials on this passage, see the 2005 May/June planning issue and the April 2005 issue of *The Clergy Journal.*)

Spouse abuse, alcoholism, child neglect, gambling addiction, spreading distorted reports that hurt another person's reputation – these and other personal wrongs are all too common in our society. And yet, it is just as common that family members and friends do not intervene to confront or prevent the harmful actions of others. In some cases a codependency has developed, making it as hard for the victim as for the victimizer to initiate a change in behavior. Sometimes a person is unwilling to get involved, fearing reprisals and even legal action. Sometimes a false sense of privacy prevails – summarized in the catch phrase, "it's none of my business." Whatever the reason, many of us are reluctant to confront others about their damaging behavior.

Today's gospel presents an alternative view. Echoing a biblical theme that goes back to the story of Cain and Abel, it presumes that we are responsible for one another, because we are already involved with each other by virtue of sharing a common faith life. The question for Matthew is not whether we should intervene but how.

The context for this instruction is the disciples' question, "Who is the greatest in the kingdom of heaven?" (Mt 18:1). Perhaps they had been debating about this among themselves – is it the wise scholar; is it the financial benefactor; is it the effective ruler? Typically, Jesus reversed their assumptions and drew their attention to the least member of their society, a child, who is the greatest in God's society. To drive the point home, Jesus warned about the consequences of harming or misleading a child – better to be drowned in the sea than do such a thing. He went on to emphasize the necessity of avoiding the cause of any personal sin, using the graphic image of cutting off one's hand or plucking out one's eye if need be.

To balance these harsh warnings, Jesus looks at the sinner from another point of view – God's. Jesus begins with an example familiar to his hearers, a shepherd watching over his flock and discovering that one of the sheep has gone astray. Leaving the ninety-nine, he goes in search of the wayward one and when he finds it, rejoices more than over the ninety-nine who stayed put. That's how God feels about anyone who goes astray.

This appealing image is translated into more practical terms in our gospel reading for today. Here the situation is not about a member who wanders away from the community, but one who sins against another and remains in the community. The spirit behind Matthew's recommendations is the same as the motivation of the good shepherd: to correct sinful behavior among the followers of Christ and bring the sinner back into harmony with the community. The process moves through three steps.

First, the one who is offended brings the situation to the attention of the offender privately. For example, perhaps a member of the congregation is spreading a false rumor that the youth minister is misusing church funds. The hope behind a personal confrontation is that the sinner will acknowledge the wrongdoing and correct the behavior. If that doesn't happen, then the one who is offended returns with two or three witnesses who can corroborate the offense. The youth minister may enlist parents and staff members who have heard the offending parishioner make innuendos and suggestions about the youth minister. This step is a reflection of Deuteronomy 19:15 and is an attempt to let the facts speak for themselves. This action is also taken in relative privacy to avoid undue public pressure or attention. If the sinner still refuses to listen to the truth and change, the matter is brought to the whole community. In the case of large congregations today, this may be a representative body such as a board of elders or pastoral council.

At this point the question is no longer primarily about the individual's behavior; it is about the individual's willingness and worthiness to be a member of Christ's followers. A person who stands against the whole community is already standing outside the community and should be recognized as doing so. In the derisive terms of Jewish life at the time, this one is to be considered as a Gentile and a tax collector.

The three steps that Matthew outlines are intended to pursue all reasonable efforts to help a person correct her or his sinful actions. They are meant for the good of the sinner and do not require that the person offended, the two or three witnesses, or the community as a whole be perfectly sinless. The issue is how to get one who sins back in harmony with the rest of the community.

This process is not just a pragmatic way of dealing with human conflict. It is an exercise of the judgment of God, made explicit by the assurance that whatever the community binds on earth is bound in heaven, and whatever the community looses on earth is loosed in heaven. This echoes the mandate which God gave to Ezekiel (33:7–11) to confront the house of Israel with their wrongdoing. Ezekiel's word is God's word and if he does not deliver it as God instructs, he is as guilty as those he is to warn.

The intimate association of God's people with God's will and judgment is carried one step further in the concluding verses. Should only two or three members of the community agree on what to ask God for, it will be granted to them because where only two or three are gathered together, God is there – fully, caringly, and powerfully.

The message of this gospel reminds us that we all are responsible for one another and are expected to speak up and intervene when we realize that a sister or brother is doing wrong. Whatever inhibitions we may have because of our personalities, our upbringing, or our cultural mores – we need to put them aside. We are called to seek out those who go astray by offending us personally or the faith community collectively. Obviously this is not a license to moralize or pass judgment on others based on our personal preferences. It is a responsibility rooted in love of one another and fidelity to the life of the community. We are responsible for one another and when one wrong has been corrected and one disciple is regained, the whole community is stronger, safer, and more pleasing to God.

– Robert L. Kinast

September 11, 2005

17th Sunday after Pentecost (Proper 19)
RC/Pres: 24th Sunday in Ordinary Time

Lessons

RCL	Ex 14:19–31	Rom 14:1–12	Mt 18:21–35
Roman Catholic	Sir 27:30–28:7	Rom 14:7–9	Mt 18:21–35
Episcopal (BCP)	Sir 27:30–28:7	Rom 14:5–12	Mt 18:21–35
Lutheran	Gen 50:15–21	Rom 14:1–12	Mt 18:21–35

Introduction to the Lessons
Lesson 1
(1) Exodus 14:19–31 (RCL)

The climactic moment in Israel's escape from Egypt occurs when Moses, at the Lord's command, parts the waters of the Red Sea, allowing the Israelites to cross safely while the Egyptian army is destroyed when the water closes in on them.

(2) Sirach 27:30—28:7 (RC/Epis)

After describing the harmful behavior of the wicked, Sirach urges readers/ listeners to forgiveness, reminding them that they are all sinners who will one day face their own deaths and the judgment of God.

(3) Genesis 50:15–21 (Luth)

After burying his father Jacob, Joseph returns to Egypt where his brothers beg forgiveness for their earlier plot against him. Joseph not only forgives them, but promises to take care of them as well.

Lesson 2
Romans 14:1–12 (RCL/Luth);
Romans 14:7–9 (RC);
Romans 14:5–12 (Epis)

Paul provides further instruction on Christian conduct, urging his readers to accept their differences, to avoid making judgments that belong only to God, and to be sure that their decisions are carried out for God's glory.

Gospel
Matthew 18:21–35 (RCL/RC/Epis/Luth)
In response to Peter's question about how often he must forgive someone who offends him, Jesus tells a parable that highlights the true meaning of forgiveness and the consequences of not forgiving one another.

Theme
The Limits of Forgiveness

Thought for the Day
As followers of Jesus, we are expected to forgive others as often as we are forgiven by our heavenly Father – that is, without limit.

Call to Worship
One:	We come to the Lord burdened by the debt of our sins,
All:	And desire the liberation of forgiveness.
One:	We hear God's freeing word,
All:	And feel release from our moral debt.
One:	We remember that we are to forgive others,
All:	As often as we have been forgiven by the Lord.

Pastoral Prayer
O gracious God, we give thanks that you hear our pleas for forgiveness when we sin against you. We do not deserve your understanding and pity, and yet you offer us reconciliation each time we ask for it. Your mercy is truly without limit.

Help us to imitate your example when others offend us. When we are pressured unfairly and forced to act against our will, as the Israelites who were enslaved by the Egyptians, help us to forgive.

When we are betrayed and exploited out of selfish motives, as Joseph who was mistreated by his brothers, help us to forgive.

When others deliberately seek to offend us by their attitudes, comments, and practices, help us to forgive.

Remind us, as Paul reminded the Roman Christians, to be tolerant of our differences and to do all things for the glory of you, our God, whose children we have become through Christ Jesus, our Lord. Amen.

Prayer of Confession

O good and forgiving God, we present ourselves to you as the servant in today's parable, asking for patience and pity as we try to make right the wrongs we have committed. At the same time we too often imitate that same servant in demanding restitution from our brothers and sisters, and withholding the forgiveness they sincerely seek from us. Forgive us when we act self-righteously, when we take advantage of another's weakness and vulnerability, when we demand more than we should, and when we make it virtually impossible for others to correct their mistakes. Purge our desire for vindication and dominance, and fill us with your spirit of forgiveness, which knows no limit. We ask all this through Christ, our Lord and Savior. Amen.

Prayer of Dedication of Gifts and Self

O God of infinite love and forgiveness, you have given us your spirit of compassion and understanding. Help us to use these spiritual gifts wisely and well as we shape our world according to your desire. In offering our material gifts today, we also offer ourselves as your servants, overlooking minor differences with others, preserving the goodness of our material world, supporting those who work for justice and peace, and forgiving those who act selfishly and harmfully. We thank you for the confidence you place in us as we recommit and dedicate ourselves to your service through the same Spirit who guided Jesus to fulfill your will. Amen.

Sermon Summary

In answer to Peter's question about how often to forgive, Jesus tells a parable that shifts the focus from how often to how well, emphasizing that our forgiveness of others is the measure of God's forgiveness of us.

Hymn of the Day
"O God of Every Nation"

Today marks the anniversary of the horrific felling of the World Trade Center in 2001. The gospel lesson from Matthew finds Jesus teaching about one of Christianity's most central topics: forgiveness. The coinciding of this anniversary and this text could hardly be more spiritually charged.

An excellent selection for this occasion is William Watkins Reid's "O God of Every Nation," a hymn found in many sources and set to a variety of tunes. "Keep bright in us the vision of days when war shall cease, When hatred and division give way to love and peace." Amen. Let it be so.

Children's Time

Forgive One Another

Preparation: Bring a cap and a teenage or adult guest to help act out the skit.

(Place the cap on your head.) This is my favorite cap. It was a birthday present from my best friend. (Have your guest remove the cap from your head and play "keep away" with it, tossing it to the other children.) Would you please return my cap to me? (Have your guest continue the game of "keep away.") Now, I'm getting angry! Please return my cap. You know it's my favorite! (Have your guest catch the cap and hand it to you while saying, "I'm sorry." Respond by saying, "I forgive you.")

We all make mistakes and do wrong things. And people we know sometimes hurt our feelings and make us feel sad too, like when you played "keep away" with my cap. What can we say when we do something wrong? Yes, we can say, "I'm sorry." And when someone tells us "I'm sorry," what can we say in return? Yes, we can say, "I forgive you." In today's Bible story, Jesus told a story about how God forgives us and wants us to forgive each other.

Prayer: Dear God, please help us to be kind and forgiving to others. Amen.

The Sermon

Not How Often, but How Well We Forgive

Hymns
Beginning of Worship: "Where Charity and Love Prevail"
Sermon Hymn: "We Live Not for Ourselves"
Closing Hymn: "Seek Ye First"

Scripture

Matthew 18:21–35 (For additional sermon materials on this passage, see the 2005 May/June planning issue and the April 2005 issue of *The Clergy Journal.*)

As creatures, we live with limits. We spend a limited time on earth; we deal with physical and intellectual limitations; we have limited financial resources and personal opportunities; and we face emotional limits as well. Most parents have a limit to their patience with children; volunteers have a limit to their availability; grieving persons have a limit to their pain; the oppressed have a limit to their tolerance of injustice.

So it is perfectly understandable that Peter would ask Jesus what the limit was on forgiveness, especially as his question came immediately after Jesus' instruction on how to handle a member of the community who sins against you. Whether Peter's question was hypothetical, simply for the sake of discussion, or real, because someone had sinned against him, Peter wanted to show Jesus how big-hearted he was. So Peter volunteered the answer to his own question: forgive up to seven times. The reference here may be a reversal of Genesis 4:24 where Lamech says that his ancestor, Cain, is avenged seven times. If so, then Jesus' response continues the allusion by reversing Lamech's own claim to avenge himself seventy-seven times.

In other words, Jesus tells Peter and all the disciples to forgive as often as they are offended. There is no limit on forgiveness if the person is truly sorry. (Of course, we may ask: if a person truly is sorry, will he or she continue to sin against you?) As he often does, Jesus drives home his point with a story – except that this one doesn't quite fit the question that prompted it. Instead of telling a story about how often to forgive, Jesus tells a story about the true meaning of forgiveness.

The situation is common. A servant was in debt to his lord, or master, in a big way. The modern equivalent might be tens of thousands of dollars owed on a credit card or perhaps a loan that a person cannot possibly pay back. The master in question had a simple solution: sell the man, his family, and whatever property he had to another slave master and use the money to pay off the debt, not unlike creditors today foreclosing on a person's home or other assets in lieu of repayment.

This desperate situation called for a desperate response. The slave pleaded with his master and asked for more time to settle accounts. The petition must have been persuasive because the master not only released him but forgave his debt as well. It's as if a credit card company or loan institution suddenly felt pity for a person and just wrote off the whole debt.

The story should have had a happy ending at that point, emphasizing again how God is merciful and forgiving when a person acknowledges their wrongs and the just obligations they incur as a result. But the story goes on because it is not about God's response to our moral debts, but about our response to one another (Peter's original question).

As the slave left his master's presence (note the symbolic distancing of himself from the forgiveness of the Lord), free of debt and punishment, he came upon a fellow slave who owed him a small amount, single digits rather than multiple digits. Instead of following his master's example and celebrating his good fortune by forgiving this minor debt, he abused his fellow slave and demanded payment. The debtor struck the same self-effacing pose as the first slave, begging for more time.

The response, however, is exactly the opposite of what the first slave had received. The first slave had the second one thrown in jail, where he could not possibly earn any money to repay the debt. It appears from this action that the first slave didn't want the money so much as the twisted satisfaction of making the second slave suffer. But his wicked indulgence didn't last very long. Other slaves heard what had happened and reported it to the master who immediately revoked his forgiveness and handed the wicked servant over to the torturers.

This long answer to Peter's short question can be summed up as follows. We are to forgive others as often as we have been forgiven by God, which is as often as we sincerely ask for forgiveness. We welcome this limitless spirit of forgiveness from God to ourselves, but sometimes we find it difficult to imitate that same spirit in our relationships with others. Perhaps the advice of Paul in the second reading today can help us head off the need for such forgiveness.

In writing to the Christians at Rome (Rom 14:1–12), Paul plays down the differences among us that often lead to harsh words, divisive judgments, and hurtful actions. So what, he asks, if some eat meat and others are vegetarians? What difference does it make if some think

Christmas is more important than Easter, or singing hymns is a better way to praise God than meditating silently on scripture? There is no difference in these matters, he insists, if everyone is doing them for the Lord's glory.

In other words, Paul reintroduces the priorities that should govern the Christian life. It is not insisting on incidental practices and personal preferences. It is "walking in love" (14:15) with one another, avoiding doing the things that offend or injure others, and overlooking the choices and attitudes that offend us. Obviously Paul is not referring here to core beliefs and practices that define the Christian life. These are not usually the things that cause us to judge and offend one another. It is usually the differences in the way we carry out our commitment to Jesus.

Needless to say, there are times when one member truly sins against another, violating a trust, speaking a falsehood, disrupting a family, and damaging a reputation. At such times, assuming the offending person expresses sorrow and asks for forgiveness, Jesus expects that we will have the same pity and compassion as God has with us rather than the vindictive spirit of the slave in the gospel. We are all servants of the Lord and beholden to God's mercy.

– Robert L. Kinast

September 18, 2005

18th Sunday after Pentecost (Proper 20)

RC/Pres: 25th Sunday in Ordinary Time

Lessons

RCL	Ex 16:2–15	Phil 1:21–30	Mt 20:1–16
Roman Catholic	Isa 55:6–9	Phil 1:20c–24, 27a	Mt 20:1–16a
Episcopal (BCP)	Jon 3:10–4:1	Phil 1:21–27	Mt 20:1–16
Lutheran	Jon 3:10–4:11	Phil 1:21–30	Mt 20:1–16

Introduction to the Lessons

Lesson 1

(1) Exodus 16:2–15 (RCL)

In response to the Israelites' complaints about being led into the desert, the Lord tells Moses to inform the people they will have flesh (quail) to eat in the evening and a fine, flaky substance in the morning, which Moses tells them is the bread (manna) the Lord has given them.

(2) Isaiah 55:6–9 (RC)

In this concluding part of the Book of Consolation, Isaiah urges the people to turn to the Lord, who, though infinitely superior to all creatures, is nonetheless forgiving and generous.

(3) Jonah 3:10—4:1 (Epis); Jonah 3:10—4:11 (Luth)

Jonah, who had previously tried to avoid the Lord's call, preaches repentance to the people of Nineveh. When they repent, Jonah is disappointed and asks the Lord to take his life. Instead the Lord teaches him a lesson about God's desire to save all people.

Lesson 2

Philippians 1:21–30 (RCL/Luth);
Philippians 1:20c–24, 27a (RC);
Philippians 1:21–27 (Epis)

Writing from prison, Paul is ready to die and be united with the Lord, yet he is also confident that he will visit the Philippians again. In the meantime he urges them to be strong in their faith and to count suffering for Christ as a privilege.

Gospel
Matthew 20:1–16 (RCL/Epis/Luth); Matthew 20:1–16a (RC)
Reinforcing his assurance to Peter that everyone who follows him will receive their reward, Jesus tells the parable of the vineyard owner who hires workers at different hours but pays them all the same wage, illustrating God's desire to bring all people into the Kingdom.

Theme
The privilege of suffering for Christ is part of discipleship.

Thought for the Day
Though no one wants to suffer, persecution for Christ's sake can be a stimulus for spreading the gospel and deepening the faith and courage of disciples.

Call to Worship
One: We gather as a free people exercising our right to worship.
All: Elsewhere in our world, brothers and sisters in the faith are persecuted and prevented from doing what we take for granted.
One: We offer our praise and thanks to God,
All: Mindful of those who are joined with us through their silent devotion.
One: We lift our voices and express our joy,
All: With them and for them as the Body of Christ.

Pastoral Prayer
O free and faithful God, you have called us to a way of life that sometimes leads to persecution and suffering. When we are intimidated by this prospect, remind us of the long line of faithful witnesses who have braved every threat and considered suffering for Christ as a privilege. Be with those in our community and throughout the world who pay the price for putting the gospel into practice when they defend the rights of others, advocate equality between men and women, and protect the lives of those who are vulnerable, dependent, and in need. Strengthen us to stand with

them and to do our part not only to support their advocacy, but also to make our own contributions as authentic, committed followers of our Lord, Jesus Christ, in whose name we pray. Amen.

Prayer of Confession

Lord of life and blessing, we profess to follow you no matter what the cost, but too often we shy away when we sense that others may disagree with our faith convictions and may criticize, ridicule, or embarrass us. We are sorry.

Too often we maintain silence rather than speak the word of correction when we hear others being stereotyped and their differences caricatured. We are sorry.

Too often we avoid the very people and situations you need us to confront so that the power of the gospel may spread more widely and rapidly. We are sorry.

Too often we imprison one another with our disagreements, our stubbornness, our control, and our egos. We are sorry.

Replace our sorrow with your healing grace so that we may live our lives in a manner worthy of the gospel of Christ, who was willing to suffer for us so that we may share life with you, now and forever. Amen.

Prayer of Dedication of Gifts and Self

O good and benevolent God, you have showered us with gifts of beauty, knowledge, freedom, and opportunity. We know that, at times, we take these blessings for granted. So now we consciously offer back to you signs of what you have given us. As we use these material and spiritual resources in our worship, we also pledge to use them as fully as we can in our daily lives to promote the spread of the gospel and to alleviate the suffering of others, especially those who are imprisoned in any way for their belief in you. We offer this prayer through Jesus Christ, the liberator of us all. Amen.

Sermon Summary

Writing from prison, Paul uses his situation to assert the priority of doing the Lord's will no matter what the circumstances and to bolster the unity of the Philippians, who should see that suffering for Christ is a privilege.

Hymn of the Day
"My Hope Is Built on Nothing Less"

The gospel reading for this Sunday shatters the illusion that God's grace works in any way akin to our earthly sense of justice. The idea of earning this or deserving that is washed away by Jesus' proclamation, "The last will be first, and the first will be last." It all depends on grace.

A wonderful hymn for today is Edward Mote's "My Hope Is Built on Nothing Less." Many know it to the melody by William Bradbury, but I prefer John Dykes' MELITA for its chromaticism. A sublime alternative is Frederick Faber's "There's a Wideness in God's Mercy," set to Calvin Hampton's ST. HELENA.

Children's Time

Be Happy

Preparation: Write "JOY" on a sheet of unlined paper. Roll up the paper and tie with a string to make a scroll.

Paul was one of Jesus' followers. He lived a long time ago. Paul traveled to many places to help people start Christian churches. Paul often sent letters like this one (hold up scroll) to the churches. This rolled paper is called a scroll. How is this letter different from the ones we send today? (No envelope, stamp, and it's rolled up.) Paul often wrote about this topic. (Unroll scroll.) What does my scroll say? (Joy.) Paul wrote that whenever we worship together and spread the good news of Jesus Christ, our lives will be filled with joy.

This may be a song Paul might have sung if he visited our churches today. (Sing "I've Got the Joy, Joy, Joy, Joy down in My Heart.")

Prayer: Thank you, Jesus, for sending people like Paul to encourage us to grow in our love for you. Amen.

The Sermon

The Paradox of Imprisonment

Hymns
Beginning of Worship: "Christ, Be Our Light"
Sermon Hymn: "I Have Loved You"
Closing Hymn: "Joyful, Joyful We Adore Thee"

Scripture
Philippians 1:21–30 (For additional sermon materials on this passage, see the 2005 May/June planning issue of *The Clergy Journal*; for sermon materials on Matthew 20:1–16, see the April 2005 issue of *The Clergy Journal.*)

Despite occasional jokes about country club jails and criminals earning their way to three meals a day, imprisonment is one of the harshest punishments human beings can impose on one another. It severely restricts a person's freedom and self-determination, two of the most important ingredients in human life. Inmates are expected to fit into the regimen of the prison and relinquish virtually all control over their own behavior and lifestyle. And, of course, prisoners are subject to physical, verbal, and emotional abuse from other prisoners and occasionally prison guards.

These conditions are even more intolerable when a person is imprisoned, not for a real crime, but for opposing the policies or practices of the ruling power. These political imprisonments are unjust and violate the human and social order that prisons are intended to protect.

And yet, despite the negative aspects of imprisonment, there is something uniquely powerful in the experience, especially for those imprisoned for opposing injustice. The life work and contributions of people like Nelson Mandela and Martin Luther King Jr. might not have been the same if they had never spent time behind bars. And the literature such prisoners have produced, often in the form of letters from jail, constitutes a testimony to the resilient human spirit.

Paul's letter to the Philippians is not only an example of this paradox of imprisonment; it is practically the origin of it in Christian tradition. Scholars cannot be sure during which of Paul's imprisonments this letter was written. It seems he is in the custody of the Romans (from his reference to the imperial guard in 1:13) and has been perceived as a serious enough threat that he might even be executed (v. 20), but you wouldn't know it from reading the letter. The dominant theme is Paul's joy at the faith of the Philippians and the spreading of the gospel.

In the first part of this letter, Paul declares that "what has happened to me has actually helped to spread the gospel" (v. 12). This is not wishful thinking; Paul can point to the way the gospel has become known throughout the imperial guard and elsewhere as people learn he is imprisoned for Christ. In addition, Paul knows that Christians in the city where he is being held are proclaiming the gospel more boldly and fearlessly because of his example. This is not an uncommon occurrence. When the leader of a movement is imprisoned, the movement often gains more public attention and the followers rally more strongly to the cause. It's one of the paradoxes of imprisonment.

A second paradox is that prison is supposed to break a person's will and make her or him conform to the laws and expectations of the ruling power, but it often has the opposite effect. Paul certainly sounds more self-determined than ever as he speculates on his future. He may be put to death, which for him is a gain because it will unite him with the Lord forever. If, on the other hand, he is released, it will enable him to continue preaching, which he also desires. Although Paul says he does not know which he prefers (v. 22), he basically faces a win-win situation. This is not what his opponents had in mind when they imprisoned him.

The third paradox Paul addresses is the privilege of suffering for Christ. Ordinarily human beings try to avoid suffering. Most people, unless they have a psychological disorder, view suffering as an unwanted and negative aspect of life, which they try to eliminate as quickly as possible. Suffering conflicts with our basic desire to be happy, secure, and content. Paul is certainly not promoting suffering nor is he yearning to make himself miserable, but he realizes that the message of Jesus makes some people uncomfortable because of the changes it requires in their lives. They in turn avoid the challenge by disposing of the messenger. When this happens, it is a sign that one is doing what the Lord expects – and what the Lord experienced in his own life.

Paul presents this point to the Philippians as an exhortation (the beginning of his first exhortation in this letter) not to be intimidated by their opponents. If these people think they are exonerating themselves by inflicting suffering on Christians, they are actually showing that their way of life is leading to destruction, whereas the suffering which Christians bear because of their union with the Lord is evidence of their salvation. (v. 28)

Once again, this is not hollow encouragement. Paul knows the Philippians are facing the same struggles and the same threats that he continues to face. He is confident they will remain steadfast, not primarily because of his example, but because such suffering for the Lord "is God's doing." It is the price one pays for living a godly life in a sinful world, but it is also the assurance one has that this very suffering deepens one's union with the Lord.

Few of us are likely to face the paradox of imprisonment because of our belief in Jesus, but most of us will face some degree of opposition, rejection, adversity, and even persecution when our embodiment of the Lord's life disturbs others. When we refuse to join in on racial comments or sexual jokes, when we are willing to articulate social and political positions that benefit minority and disadvantaged groups, when we make decisions about the economy and investment opportunities that are consistent with the priority of the common good, when we represent a true concern for the environment and refuse to give polluters a free hand, and when we voice opposition to the flaunting of moral standards in entertainment and advertising, we can expect to feel the repercussions.

The challenge for us in today's reading is whether we are able to do what Paul did when we encounter opposition and hostility. First of all, are we able to see such situations as a way to further the gospel and proclaim Jesus' values? Second, are we able to maintain the self-determination of our convictions and not compromise or cave in to make our lives more comfortable and conflict-free? Third, are we willing to accept the suffering that may result and affirm it as a privilege and sign that the Lord is working through us? God's strength and grace make it possible for us to respond, "Yes!"

– Robert L. Kinast

September 25, 2005

19th Sunday after Pentecost (Proper 21)

RC/Pres: 26th Sunday in Ordinary Time

Lessons

RCL	Ex 17:1–7	Phil 2:1–13	Mt 21:23–32
Roman Catholic	Ezek 18:25–28	Phil 2:1–11 or 1–5	Mt 21:28–32
Episcopal (BCP)	Ezek 18:1–4, 25–32	Phil 2:1–13	Mt 21:28–32
Lutheran	Ezek 18:1–4, 25–32	Phil 2:1–13	Mt 21:23–32

Introduction to the Lessons

Lesson 1

(1) Exodus 17:1–7 (RCL)

After being fed with quail and manna, the Israelites still complain, this time because they have no water. The Lord instructs Moses to strike a rock with the same staff he used to part the Red Sea. Moses renames this site as a reminder of their complaining and testing.

(2) Ezekiel 18:25–28 (RC); Ezekiel 18:1–4, 25–32 (Epis/Luth)

The Lord corrects a longstanding misconception in Israel's thinking that the sins of parents are inherited (along with their punishment) by their children. The Lord clarifies that each person is responsible for her or his own behavior and its consequences.

Lesson 2

Philippians 2:1–13 (RCL/Epis/Luth); Philippians 2:1–11 (RC)

In urging the Philippians to think first of others, Paul invokes the example of Jesus who did not exploit his equality with God, but became a humble servant whom God exalted above all creation.

Gospel

Matthew 21:23–32 (RCL/Luth); Matthew 21:28–32 (RC/Epis)

The day after Jesus drove the moneychangers from the Temple, the chief priests and elders ask by what authority he did so. Jesus responds with the parable of the two sons, implying that when good deeds are performed, they need no other authorization.

Theme

Looking to others' interests leads to exaltation by God.

Thought for the Day

To put on the mind of Christ is to do nothing from selfish ambition or conceit, but to look to the interests of others and humbly serve them.

Call to Worship

One: We come before the God of all creation,
All: Humbly acknowledging what God has done for us.
One: We too frequently complain,
All: When our needs and wishes are not met.
One: Through this worship may we cleanse our hearts,
All: And give fitting praise and thanks to our God.

Pastoral Prayer

O God of power and might, you call us to be of one mind and heart as we serve. Help us to look not to our own interests, but to the interests of others and to express the same concern for them that Jesus expressed for us when he emptied himself to become human.

We are especially mindful of those who do not have enough to eat or drink, of those parents who sacrifice their own interests to care for their children and model for them responsibility and love, and of those who contribute their time and talent to make worship a fitting gift to you. Bless and exalt all who humbly live their lives in Christ Jesus our Lord. Amen.

Prayer of Confession

O God, you have exalted Jesus above all creation because of his humble self-sacrifice on our behalf. We acknowledge that we have not always followed his example. We have at times acted from selfish ambition in our careers, our neighborhoods, and our church. We have at times acted from conceit to put others down, to artificially extol ourselves, to gain attention, or to win favor. We have at times regarded ourselves as better than those less educated, less wealthy, less influential, less attractive, or less athletic. Teach us humility and help us to look to the interests of others first so we may have the same mind that was in Christ Jesus, our Lord. Amen.

Prayer of Dedication of Gifts and Self

O God of love, you have given us the irreplaceable gifts of encouragement in Christ and sharing in the Spirit. As we have received, so do we wish to give, offering humble service to others, symbolized by the simple gifts we present to you this day. May this offering be a reminder to us that Christ our Savior did not cling to his equality with you but emptied himself to serve us. Through the letting go of these gifts, we pledge to let go of our presumed privileges so we may serve others with Christ, in whose name we pray. Amen.

Sermon Summary

Paul exhorts the Philippian Christians to imitate the example of Christ, who did not exploit his equality with God but emptied himself to become a humble servant, obedient even to death on the cross. This is the basis for his exaltation, and for ours.

Hymn of the Day
"The Great Creator of the Worlds"

The question posed to Jesus in today's gospel lesson is crucial. Who gave Jesus the authority to say what he said and do what he did? Were his words and deeds really sanctioned by God? The Christian answer, of course, is yes, and today's hymn, from the Epistle to Diognetus (ca. 150) and translated by F. Bland Tucker, points straight to the source of Jesus' authority. God sent Jesus, the text says, not in wrath and power, but in grace and peace; not to oppress, but to save.

Children's Time

What Would Jesus Do?

Preparation: Write "WWJD" on a large sheet of posterboard. On the back, write "What Would Jesus Do?" Bring a big box of fish crackers.

Let's say the names of these letters together: W-W-J-D. Does anyone know what these letters stand for? (What Would Jesus Do?)

Our Bible story today is part of a letter written by one of Jesus' followers named Paul. Paul wrote this letter to his favorite church, the church in Philippi. In his letter Paul reminded the people in the church to follow Jesus' teachings. It's a good reminder for us, too.

Look at my big box of crackers. And you all look like you might want a snack. (Hold up the WWJD poster.) What would Jesus do? (Give everyone one cracker.) Paul wrote that we should share what we have with others.

Paul wrote that Jesus wants us to worship God. One way to worship is by praying. Let us pray. Dear Jesus, every day help us to remember to follow you in the words we speak and the things we do. Help us to remember to ask ourselves: What would Jesus do? Amen.

The Sermon

Exaltation through Humble Service

Hymns

Beginning of Worship: "Speak, Lord"
Sermon Hymn: "At the Name of Jesus"
Closing Hymn: "From This Assembly"

Scripture

Philippians 2:1–13 (For additional sermon materials on this passage, see the 2005 May/June planning issue of *The Clergy Journal*; for sermon materials on Matthew 21:23–32, see the July/August 2005 issue of *The Clergy Journal*.)

At this time of the year, one of the great American traditions is in full swing – football. From pee-wee leagues through Pop Warner, high school, college, and the NFL, football is being played everywhere. Many consider football to be the ultimate team sport because every play involves every member of the team, and the success of the team usually depends on how well each player carries out his role (and now that women are playing football in their own leagues, how well each carries out her role).

The team concept is etched in football lore with famous half-time speeches by coaches, with timeless phrases like "win one for the Gipper," "there's no 'I' in team," and most recently in the description of a team's collective defense as a "we-fense."

The image of this melding of talent into one effective unit is often belied by the showboating antics of some individuals, but for the most part football remains a team effort. And the organizing force behind that effort is the coach, who blends the individual players into a coordinated whole. The coach has to convince each player that they get the greatest benefit by thinking of the team first and themselves second.

In many ways this is what Paul is doing in his letter to the Philippians. He had already given a positive spin to his own hardship and the struggles of the Philippian Christians against their opponents. Now he wants to reinforce their unity with one another and the reason for putting forth the effort required.

Paul begins by reminding them who they are – one might say what sort of team they belong to. The language is implicitly Trinitarian, referring to encouragement in Christ, consolation from love (of the Father), and sharing in the Spirit. In short, the Philippians are not Paul's team; they are God's. And they will make Paul proud if they perform as God desires – with the same mind, the same love, in full accord.

How are they to achieve this unanimity? By doing nothing from selfish ambition or conceit. No grandstanding, no comparing statistics, no hogging the ball or changing the play to showcase one's own abilities. It gets even more demanding: "in humility regard others as better than yourselves" (2:3). Paul clarifies his point in the next verse. "Let each of you look not to your own interests, but to the interests of others." Prior to self-awareness and self-concern is the awareness of others and their concerns. With this awareness a person can then channel her or his own skills, resources, and opportunities toward satisfying the interests of others and in the process, Paul implies, serve her or his own interests as well.

This is not pie-in-the-sky sentiment from Paul. The Philippian Christians had witnessed him doing this very thing – deferring to others, putting aside his own preferences, willingly taking on sacrifice and hardship for their sake. But Paul does not point to himself as the model they should imitate. Rather, Paul draws their attention to Christ Jesus, the supreme example of humble self-sacrifice they are all to imitate.

hymn of early church

When he turns to the image of his Savior, Paul abandons his own style of rhetorical exhortation and invokes what appears to be a hymn from the early church. The first stanza clearly asserts the equality of Jesus with God. And yet, although this equality was Jesus' by right, Jesus did not exploit it. Jesus did not insist upon his superior state to avoid or refuse the work God gave him to do, in the way the second son did in today's gospel.

Not only did Jesus not look to his own interests or consider himself better than others (which he actually was, of course), he emptied himself of all such entitlements and took the form not of God but of a slave. This second stanza is the basis for an entire theology of the self–emptying love and service of God's Son. Human comparisons can't begin to express the extent of this radical move. Kings may abdicate their thrones and presidents resign from office; millionaires may give away their wealth, and celebrities may jeopardize their careers by supporting controversial causes, but no one else has exchanged being in the form of God for being in the form of a human.

The third stanza drives the point home. In emptying himself, Jesus humbled himself, literally lowered himself to the dirt of the earth (the word humility comes from the same Latin word as ground, humus) and the fate of all humankind, death. But Jesus' death was not simply the termination of his life; it was the obedient acceptance of death on a cross. Jesus paid attention (the literal meaning of the word obedience from the Latin ob-audire, to listen to) to the purpose of his coming: to make a complete gift of his self-emptying and to absorb the worst effects of humanity's sinful condition.

At this point in the hymn, the focus shifts from Jesus to his Father, and from the example of humble self-giving to its outcome. From the lowest point imaginable at that time and in that culture – death on a cross – God steps in and exalts Jesus, giving him a name (an identity) and a status that is once again above all others. Clearly Paul is drawing the connection between this exaltation and the willing self–emptying that preceded it. God is not bestowing an arbitrary title from a motive of benevolence as an earthly ruler or a team's owner might.

You can almost hear the reverent silence that must have followed this rapturous outpouring of Paul's belief and hope. In a more subdued tone Paul draws the obvious conclusion. Just as the Philippians have always obeyed (listened to, learned from) Paul, whether he was with them or away

wow!

from them, so they should continue to obey God, who is at work in them. And in this way they will gain their salvation.

The implication of this brief passage from Paul's letter is clear. Each of us is gifted by the Lord to contribute our part to the saving work of Christ. But sometimes our own ambition or interests get in the way of the humble service we are to offer. So before the next football game you watch or play, take a moment to consider where you may be getting in the way of the ultimate team effort and let the same mind be in you that was in Christ Jesus – looking to the interests of others first.

– Robert L. Kinast

October 2, 2005

20th Sunday after Pentecost (Proper 22)

RC/Pres: 27th Sunday in Ordinary Time

Lessons

RCL	Ex 20:1–4, 7–9, 12–20	Phil 3:4b–14	Mt 21:33–46
Roman Catholic	Isa 5:1–7	Phil 4:6–9	Mt 21:33–43
Episcopal (BCP)	Isa 5:1–7	Phil 3:14–21	Mt 21:33–43
Lutheran	Isa 5:1–7	Phil 3:4b–14	Mt 21:33–46

Introduction to the Lessons

Lesson 1
(1) Exodus 20:1–4, 7–9, 12–20 (RCL)

The pyrotechnics displayed in preparation for Moses receiving the Ten Commandments and following their receipt puts to shame any modern rock band's theatrics. In fear and trembling, the people wait at the foot of Mt. Sinai to receive what is the heart of Torah.

(2) Isaiah 5:1–7 (Epis/Luth)

This love song blurs the line between heaven and earth. A metaphor for the stages in human/divine encounter, the life cycle of the vineyard illuminates the attraction, passion, hope, disappointment, and destruction inherent in a dream shattered by unfaithfulness.

Lesson 2
Philippians 3:4b–14 (RCL/Luth); Philippians 3:14–21 (Epis)
Philippians 4:6–9 (RC)

Paul cannot be outdone in his Jewishness or his allegiance to Christ. Yet, none of it matters, he insists, except union with Christ through faith, shared suffering, death, and ultimately, resurrection.

Gospel
Matthew 21:33–46 (RCL/Luth); Matthew 21:33–43 (RC/Epis)

Jesus makes his audience answer the question of what the vineyard owner will do upon discovering that his slaves and his son have been beaten and killed. The listeners are trapped. Their response is self-incriminating. Their choice is clear. Kill Jesus or accept responsibility. For the moment they chose neither.

Theme
The foundation of all that we do as Christians is our allegiance to Jesus Christ and his message.

Thought for the Day
What we think or what we believe is, in the end, of little consequence. The only thing of consequence is what we do.

– John Ruskin

Call to Worship

One: Friends, before we even gather in this place, Christ is with us – calling us, leading us, strengthening us into his body, the church.

All: May the words of our mouths and the meditations of our hearts be acceptable to you, O God, our rock, our redeemer.

Pastoral Prayer
God, your community in Christ is divided just as it was for Paul: conservative, liberal, Catholic, Protestant. Are we all part of one body? We point our fingers at one another, claim our truth, and fling our doctrines and positions into our courtrooms, classrooms, the media, and governments. Is this what you had in mind when you sent Jesus? Is this the community of love for which he died? We ask you, once again, in all our misguided assumptions, "transform our body of humiliation that it may be conformed to the body of Christ's glory." You alone have the power to do that. We alone have the power to accept. Increase our willingness to accept and to understand one another as one church, that with mutual respect and love we might, together, minister with compassion and justice to your world. For this is the vision of Jesus Christ. Amen.

Prayer of Confession

God, you set before us the ways of life and death. You gift us with rules to live by; people to show us the way. Yet, in the freedom you wove into our beings, we resist you. We play with your rules, we follow your people when it is convenient. We leave so much undone, so many unloved and ignored. Too often we walk away as if what we do or leave undone does not matter. You know what it would take to make us understand, to open our hearts to a true desire to do the right thing for nothing else but love of you, our neighbor, and ourselves. With fear and trembling, God, we ask you to do it. Confront us, transform us, encourage and sustain us that we might, with joy and thanksgiving, be more faithful in our witness to you in Christ's name. Amen.

Prayer of Dedication of Gifts and Self

We return to your work portions of what we have been blessed to earn. May our giving and our gifts be touched by your Spirit as they serve your people here and within the wider community. May the love and compassion of Jesus Christ infuse our offering with your grace. Amen.

Sermon Summary

In life, the going will be rough at times. When it is, remember who you are and why you do the things you do. Don't get sidetracked by the details.

Hymn of the Day
"Christ Is Made the Sure Foundation"

Hymnwriters have often used the image of a stone or cornerstone to write positively of Jesus' central place in Christianity. "Christ Is Made the Sure Foundation," a hymn found in the earliest sources of Christian hymnody from the eleventh century, is one such piece. This is one of 100 or so texts that John Mason Neale, an Anglican priest and founder of the Society of St. Margaret, translated from early Greek and Latin sources. Set to a variety of tunes, Dale Wood's EDEN CHURCH is especially good at conveying the cornerstone's weight through long, arching phrases in a minor mode.

Children's Time

Jesus Is Number One

Preparation: Write each of these numbers and letters – J E S U S I S # 1 – on a sheet of brightly colored copier paper. Place real money, a photo of a family, a little cross, a soccer ball, and a cell phone in a gift bag.

What do you think I have inside my bag? Let's see. (Pull out the items, one at a time, and have the children name them.) Which one of these do you think is the most important in our lives – money, our families, Jesus, sports, or cell phones? Why?

Today's Bible story is taken from a letter written by Paul. Paul was one of Jesus' followers. Paul traveled to many places, helping to start Christian churches. In his letter, Paul wrote about what should be most important in our lives. I have his answer right here, but I'll need your help to figure it out. (Distribute the nine sheets of paper you have prepared. Help the children with papers arrange themselves so their sheets spell out, "Jesus is #1.") Let's read these words together: Jesus is #1. What does this mean? (Accept responses.)

Prayer: Dear Jesus, help us to pray, worship, be kind and loving to others, and teach others about your love. Open our hearts to keep you number one in our lives. Amen.

The Sermon

The Devil in the Details

Hymns

> **Beginning of Worship:** "All Hail the Power of Jesus' Name"
> **Sermon Hymn:** "We Are Your People"
> **Closing Hymn:** "The Church of Christ, in Every Age"

Scripture

Philippians 3:4b–14 (For additional sermon material on this passage, see the 2005 May/June planning issue of *The Clergy Journal*; for sermon material on Matthew 21:33–46, see the July/August 2005 issue of *The Clergy Journal*.)

In the movie, "The Best Two Years," Elder Rogers, a Mormon on a two-year missionary tour in Holland, has lost his faith and his evangelistic zeal. This happens after his former missionary partner returns to Utah and marries Elder Rogers' fiancé. Since then, Rogers seems to have worn out every new partner assigned to him until Elder Calhoun arrives, looking and sounding as nerdy as Rogers' worst nightmare. Eventually the two bond. When Elder Calhoun asks Rogers why he is in Holland, he can't remember. As this funny story evolves, Elder Rogers rediscovers the answer to the question as he and Elder Calhoun convert a young optometrist to their faith.

Knowing who you are and why you're doing what you're doing is a pretty important bottom line for just about everyone. It's easy to lose a sense of this in the daily-ness of life's details, which is what Paul is writing about to his faithful flock in Philippi. As Elder Rogers learned, in the midst of life's challenges and sorrows it helps to keep one's rudder steady on the course. In the face of whatever criticisms are being directed at Paul or at his beloved church community, Paul cuts through the details of faith practices and traditions. He reminds the faithful just what keeps them true to course: "I regard everything as loss because of the surpassing value of knowing Christ Jesus my Lord" (v. 8).

It's hard to grow up in the United States and not have a taste for competition and winning. If we like to debate, even with ourselves, we become seasoned at making our case, listing our proofs for our theories and ideas, and finding holes and fault lines in the theories and ideas of others. We seem to think that if we stack up enough facts or reasonable arguments on our side, we will win. Sometimes it works that way. Sometimes it doesn't. It's possible that the person with the tallest stack of facts, arguments, and details is wrong. You've heard the sayings, "You can win the battle, but lose the war" and, "You can't see the forest for the trees." We can be so close to something that we miss the point entirely, because we are focused on extraneous details.

I like to weave. I once wove a transparency, a type of tapestry in which you are "drawing" with fiber on a warp (the vertical threads on the loom). Weaving any kind of tapestry is time and labor intensive. After weaving my first 6 inches, I hated it, decided it wasn't working, ripped it off my loom, and started over. I liked it better the second time, at least in the beginning. As the piece developed, I began to have doubts. When weaving on a traditional floor loom, all you can see of your work is the area right in front of you. For me, it was about 6 to 12 inches high by 36 inches wide. As you weave, you move forward – the completed work is wound around a beam on the back of the loom. What you've completed becomes hidden. The more I worked, the less confident I grew. Again, I thought about tearing it off. My daughters stopped me. To get some perspective, I stood on my weaving bench and looked down. I resisted the urge to tear it out. My daughters continued to encourage me to keep going.

Finally, it was finished. Truly, with fear and trembling I cut the piece off my loom, walked down a long hallway in my home and hung it on a wall without looking at it. I turned and walked far away from it as possible but still able to see it. Then I faced it. I loved it.

In the weeks it took to weave that piece, I lost track of where I was going. Not because I wasn't "going," but because, in the moment-to-moment intensity of such close and tedious work, I got lost. Details became everything and such close, critical scrutiny threatened to sink the project before it had a chance. I think that this is what Paul is cautioning his flock against in our reading today.

To those who claimed that one had to become a Jew before becoming a Christian, Paul said, not so. And he, more than anyone, knew why. He was a Jew among Jews: circumcised, descended from the tribe of Benjamin, learned student of Torah. While each one of those details was important to his development as a person of faith, they were, he declared, just details. Not one achievement or piece of knowledge held within it the power to redeem his life from the mess he had made of it. His rigid adherence to the details of Judaism had been his downfall. How could he ever forgive himself for standing by and doing nothing while Stephen was stoned to death (Acts 7:58)? How could God forgive him? Yes, Paul knew that the devil is in the detail. He learned the hard way that details did not and could not hold the key to his salvation – his lasting and eternal relationship with God.

"I regard everything as loss because of the surpassing value of knowing Christ Jesus my Lord" (v. 8).

For Paul, knowing Jesus Christ as his Lord was a moment of exquisite clarity. The scales that fell from his eyes in Damascus were like the details of his past life falling away (Acts 9:18). Amazingly, he could see clearly that the way of Jesus Christ – his message of love, forgiveness, and life purpose – was all that mattered. The rest was mere detail.

"Beloved, I do not consider that I have made it my own; but this one thing I do: forgetting what lies behind and straining forward to what lies ahead, I press on toward the goal for the prize of the heavenly call of God in Christ Jesus" (vv. 13–14).

Today, two thousand years after Paul wrestled to understand the bottom line of his life, we are invited to reconsider our own. Where is our energy, our treasure, our time, our money, and our peace? In the details of living, or in our deep connection with God, our neighbor, and ourselves? In the end, as Paul knew, there is one bottom line, and that is love. The rest, my friends, are details.

– Rosemary A. Rocha

October 9, 2005

21st Sunday after Pentecost (Proper 23)

RC/Pres: 28th Sunday in Ordinary Time

Lessons

RCL	Ex 32:1–14	Phil 4:1–9	Mt 22:1–14
Roman Catholic	Isa 25:6–10a	Phil 4:12–14, 19–20	Mt 22:1–14 or 22:1–10
Episcopal (BCP)	Isa 25:1–9	Phil 4:4–13	Mt 22:1–14
Lutheran	Isa 25:1–9	Phil 4:1–9	Mt 22:1–14

Introduction to the Lessons

Lesson 1

(1) Exodus 32:1–14 (RCL)

Like adolescents with their first taste of independence, the faithful flock turns faithless once Moses is out of sight. Focused on their immediate needs and wants, the faithful flock will never know to what ends Moses worked to secure their safety and their future.

(2) Isaiah 25:6–10a (RC); Isaiah 25:1–9 (Epis/Luth)

Verses 1–5 are a psalm of praise for the One who destroys enemies and provides shelter and refuge for the threatened. Verses 6–10 describe the celebration in Jerusalem, a place from which grief and even death will be forever banished by God's own hand.

Lesson 2

Philippians 4:1–9 (RCL/Luth);
Philippians 4:12–14, 19–20 (RC);
Philippians 4:1–13 (Epis)

"The Lord is near," from the Aramaic *marana tha*, is Paul's encouragement to the faithful to practice their faith in gentleness and with justice, even in the face of disagreement. Be positive, Paul reminds them, and continue to follow my lead.

Gospel
Matthew 22:1–14 (RCL/RC/Epis/Luth)

The two-stage Palestinian wedding invitation becomes the framework for the allegory of God's end time as wedding feast: an announcement that the feast was being prepared was followed by a second, that it was ready. Invited guests disregarded both. The wedding was held with new plans and new guests.

Theme

God calls us into community and through prophets, like Moses, Isaiah, and Paul, shows us the way to live into it.

Thought for the Day

I trust all joy.

– Theodore Roethke

Call to Worship

One: O Lord, you are my God; I will exalt you, I will praise your name.

All: You have been a refuge to the poor, a refuge to the needy in their distress,

One: This is our God for whom we have waited so that we might be saved.

All: This is God for whom we have waited; let us be glad and rejoice in God's salvation.

– adapted from Isaiah 25:1–9

Pastoral Prayer

God, you call us into community, but community is not easy. We try to love each other. Lead us not into the temptation of being judgmental.

We seek to do your will. When our fear of disagreement leaves us on shallow ground with one another and with you, give us courage to speak our minds with love; open our ears with understanding; change our thinking, if it would be your leading.

We reach beyond our lives into the world. Give us vision to see the thread that binds you to us, us to you, and all of us to one another.

Give us also, gracious God, the passion that was Paul's, that however long our time together might be, we might follow his lead, sharing your love in the message of Christ in all that we are and in all that we do. Amen.

Prayer of Confession

One: Remember me, O God, when you show favor to your people;

All: We have sinned.

One: Our ancestors made a calf at Horeb;

All: We worship money, good looks, and possessions.

One: Our ancestors exchanged your glory for the image of an ox that eats grass.

All: We exchange your glory for cars, perfect children, and younger skin.

One: Our ancestors forgot the great things you had done in Egypt, and awesome deeds by the Red Sea.

All: We forget you, too, O God, even though you continue to move in and through our lives.

One: Moses stood his ground with you and asked for a second chance.

All: Jesus Christ is our ground and our second chance.

One: Let us accept your love, O God, and live as if it matters.

All: May it be so. Amen.

Prayer of Dedication of Gifts and Self

Bless now, loving God, these things we offer – our money, earned though the labor of our minds and hands and hearts; our lives, busy with families and work, fun, and friends; and our church, a community of faith. Bless now, loving God, all these things, for we offer them to be your vehicles of compassion, justice, grace, and joy. In Christ's name, make it so. Amen.

Sermon Summary

Everyone needs affirmation and confirmation, especially from one we admire. Paul is generous with his words of affection and commendation to his beloved community at Philippi.

Hymn of the Day
"Christ for the World We Sing!"

Martin Luther believed the critical task of a theologian was to distinguish rightly between law and gospel, and it is an equally important one for church musicians. Here, the nugget of gospel is the king's command that his servants go out into the streets and invite everyone to the banquet. Samuel Wolcott's "Christ for the World We Sing!" reflects the zeal with which the king and his servants welcomed all to the banquet. A contemporary choice for a worship band is Tom Conry's "Anthem."

Children's Time

Peace Be with You

Preparation: Bring large cozy quilts or fleece blankets. Arrange for an organist or other musician to play soft, soothing music.

(On your cue, have the musician play peaceful music. Spread out the blankets. Invite the children to lie down in a comfortable position and listen to the music.) Close your eyes. Relax. Listen to the music. How do you feel? (Accept responses.) I feel peaceful. When we feel peaceful, we feel calm and safe and surrounded by God's love. While you are resting, listen to these words in the Bible from Paul's letter to his friends in the church: "Let your gentleness be known to everyone. The Lord is near. Do not worry about anything. And the peace of God will guard your hearts and your minds in Christ Jesus. The God of peace will be with you."

Have the children slowly sit up and hand you the blankets.

Prayer: Dear Jesus, thank you for noisy times and quiet times. Help us to talk to you during all kinds of times. Amen.

The Sermon

Advice from the Cheerleader

Hymns
Beginning of Worship: "Praise to the Lord, the Almighty"
Sermon Hymn: "For All the Saints"
Closing Hymn: "O God of All Your People Past"

Paul: cheerothem keep on keep on!

Scripture

Philippians 4:1–13 (For additional sermon materials on this passage, see the 2005 May/June planning issue of *The Clergy Journal*. For sermon materials on Matthew 22:1–14, see the July/August 2005 issue of *The Clergy Journal*.)

Every now and then, you need a cheerleader – someone to remind you of who you are and urge you on. Sometimes, you need someone else to hold the carrot out in front of your nose, shine the light on the dark path up ahead, and give your frightened soul a bit of a shove into an often fearsome world. Paul, the supreme cheerleader of Christ and his followers, does just that for the Christians at Philippi. Had he been living today, he may have found gainful employment, if not as an evangelist or local church pastor, then as a job consultant, professional coach, or personal trainer.

In the notes on this passage from the Interpreter's Bible, the commentator reminds us that, for Paul, "The Philippians were the convincing proof that he had 'not run in vain.' They were also his chief cause for rejoicing. The thought of them filled him with gladness, as if he were sitting at a feast instead of lying in prison."

Remembering from where Paul writes this letter makes us better understand his motivation in cheering on the Philippians, in reminding them of the best they could be. Divisions or disagreements, such as whatever was happening between Euodia and Syntyche, would have, understandably, gnawed at Paul. How can these people who are so good be so – human? Come on, people, get with it. Forgive, talk, reconcile.

end time

Paul had a sense that time was short. Christ would come soon. It was imperative that this community that had been such a joy for him in their adherence to the faith continue to be focused on the purpose and goal of their lives – commitment to Jesus Christ. And so Paul, ever the zealot, cheers them on with a few reminders of how they are to keep on keeping on.

First, "Rejoice in the Lord always." The Greek for "rejoice" was also used to say "good-bye." These Christians, facing what Paul believed was the end time, were to find joy in their life in Christ, even as they were saying good-bye to life as they knew it. Rejoice.

Second, "Do not worry about anything." I actually prefer the King James reading of this charge: "Be careful for nothing." In other words, act boldly, don't micromanage your life because, in just a little while, it will all be changed, permanently. "Be careful for nothing." Give all that you have to give, now. It reminds me of Jesus' admonition to not store things in our barns. The time is now, so live now, love now, be happy now – but always in faithfulness and service to Christ. Be careful for nothing.

(3) Third, pray honestly. I suspect that many Christians are afraid to pray. We don't want to treat God like some sugar daddy or mommy, so we hesitate to ask for "things" because it seems so greedy. Some Christians aren't convinced about this thing called prayer. We aren't sure that it works, that it's meaningful, or that it's real. And, some of us just don't believe in it, period. But, Paul believes differently. His life and his ministry have been deeply and profoundly infused with a power beyond his capability. He trusts, with his whole being, that there is purpose and meaning in prayer. If he charges his flock to be careful in nothing, that nothing includes their prayer life. " Let your requests be made known to God. And the peace of God, which surpasses all understanding, will guard your hearts and your minds in Christ Jesus." Pray honestly.

(4) Fourth, thank you. Like most pastors, teachers, and other caregivers, burnout is real. Paul, prevented from his passion of spreading the gospel by his confinement in prison, has time on his hands to think about his life – where he messed up, where he succeeded, and the great cloud of witnesses to whom he is and will be eternally grateful. The Philippians are his "joy and crown." And the word he uses for crown doesn't mean one made of gold, but one like those pictured on ancient Olympians, made of leaves and branches and given to those who win a race or lounge at a banquet table. Paul is grateful to the Philippians because they have shown concern for him, and because their behavior has made him feel victorious. In their faithfulness he has seen his life's work bear fruit. Everyone should be so blessed. Thank you.

(5) Fifth, carry on. This faithful group knows what is expected of them and how to do it. "Carry on," Paul tells them. "Keep on doing the things that you have learned and received and heard and seen in me." Most of us like to think that, after we die, someone will carry on the values and commitments to which we gave our lives. That's why grandparents like to have grandchildren. It's physical proof that some part of them will keep flowing on into the future. Paul is no different, though he sees that what is being carried on is not his to claim, but God's. Carry on.

Everyone needs a cheerleader sometimes, a life coach, a spiritual director. So, here it is from Paul to us, with love and passion: rejoice in God always, be careful for nothing, pray honestly, thank you, carry on.
Oh, and one more thing, "The God of peace be with you all." Now get out there!

– Rosemary A. Rocha

October 16, 2005

22nd Sunday after Pentecost (Proper 24)
RC/Pres: 29th Sunday in Ordinary Time

Lessons

RCL	Ex 33:12–23	1 Thess 1:1–10	Mt 22:15–22
Roman Catholic	Isa 45:1,4–6	1 Thess 1:1–5b	Mt 22:15–21
Episcopal (BCP)	Isa 45:1–7	1 Thess 1:1–10	Mt 22:15–22
Lutheran	Isa 45:1–7	1 Thess 1:1–10	Mt 22:15–22

Introduction to the Lessons
Lesson 1
(1) Exodus 33:12–23 (RCL)

Moses is a great leader. He loves God; he loves God's people. Having smashed the tablets with God's laws upon seeing his people worshiping golden statues, Moses now negotiates with God for his people's future and a reassuring sign that God is still with him.

(2) Isaiah 45:1, 4–6 (RC); Isaiah 45:1–7 (Epis/Luth)

The God, whom the Persian King Cyrus "does not know," calls Cyrus, in spite of that fact, to liberate the Israelites from their Babylonian captivity. Isaiah is clear. The God of Israel is the power behind the power with which Cyrus acts.

Lesson 2
1 Thessalonians 1:1–10 (RCL/Epis/Luth);
1 Thessalonians 1:1–5b (RC)

Writing from Athens, after being forced to leave Thessalonica because of hostilities towards them, Paul encourages and praises these new Christians. They are chosen by God and have, in turn, responded faithfully, "in spite of persecution." Their reputation for hospitality and steadfastness in the face of great challenges has spread.

Gospel
Matthew 22:15–22 (RCL/Epis/Luth); Matthew 22:15–21 (RC)
The Pharisees have just been stung by Jesus' parable of the wedding feast. They are out for revenge. A question of allegiance is intended to trick Jesus into saying something that will get him in trouble with Roman authorities. Jesus, however, will not be caught in this net.

Theme
The key to making wise choices is knowing to whom your heart belongs.

Thought for the Day
It's not that we have so little power, it's that we don't use the power we have.
– Danusha Veronica Goska, Sojourners magazine, August 2004

Call to Worship
One: Mighty God, lover of justice, you establish equality among your people.
All: We praise your awesome name.
One: Holy God, you spoke to your people in the pillar of cloud.
All: Speak to us now; shape our lives by your Spirit.
One: You alone are Holy.
All: You alone are God.
– based on Psalm 99

Pastoral Prayer
We pray, God, for leaders – the decisions they face, the powers they hold. Shower them with your Spirit, that they might see with understanding, hear with compassion, decide with wisdom, and love with your passion and justice.

We pray, God, for followers – the decisions they face, the power they hold. Give to them comprehension, wisdom, courage to question, and conviction to hold onto their power to choose.

We pray, God, for those too apathetic to care. Awaken their hearts to the world around them, redirect their inward focus to life beyond their personal concerns, empower them to accept the decisions they face, and give them the power to act.

Bind us together, God of leaders, followers, the unwilling, and the too willing. Implant in our hearts a commitment to community – that each one's choice may be for the greater good, that each power play be made from the honest desire to do your work and follow your way, in the spirit of Jesus our Christ. Amen.

Prayer of Confession

God, almost every day we wrestle with overwhelming choices – Caesar or God, life or death, love or hate, possessions or freedom. Often we choose wisely, but then there are those other times. Our wants get confused with our needs. Our "must haves" overshadow our satisfaction with ourselves, our loved ones, and even life itself. Give to us the vision and wisdom to see your way clearly. Then empower us with your grace and courage, that we might take the higher path. In all things keep us faithful to your gift of love – for you, for our neighbors, and for ourselves. In Christ's name we pray. Amen.

Prayer of Dedication of Gifts and Self

With these gifts we recognize the power of Caesar that, when used for good, helps bring about the work of your Spirit. Bless the gifts and our giving, that your way might be served, as Christ would have us do. Amen.

Sermon Summary

The question of allegiance is never an easy one to answer, particularly when the choices are between political and social realities that are the stuff of daily life and the values and directions of the Spirit's call.

Hymn of the Day
"God, Whose Giving Knows No Ending"

Biblical scholars have come to see the conflict stories in the synoptic tradition as products of careful shaping by the gospel writers, conveying multiple levels of meaning. That's what makes them so tantalizing for preachers but challenging to church musicians. I ponder what those in the pew hear in a reading, and in this case it may well be the question, "What does belong to God?" Robert Edwards' "God, Whose Giving Knows No Ending," set to the music of Parry, is my choice for today. "Gifted by you, we turn to you; Off'ring up ourselves in praise; Thankful song shall rise forever; Gracious donor of our days."

Children's Time

In God We Trust

Preparation: Soak pennies in 1/2 cup vinegar and 1 teaspoon of salt, then rinse and dry. Locate a few magnifying glasses.

(Give each child a penny.) Whose picture is on the front of the penny? (President Abraham Lincoln.) Why? (He was an important president and we want to honor him.) What words run across the top of the penny? (In God we trust.) Use one of these magnifying glasses to see the words more clearly. Why do you think we have "In God we trust" written on all of our coins? (Accept responses.)

In today's Bible story some people showed Jesus a coin. The leaders tried to trick Jesus, but instead Jesus taught them about God.

God created everything and all things belong to God. One way we can give thanks to God is by giving offering money to the church. All of our coins work together to help other people in our neighborhood, in our country, and throughout the world.

Please take your penny back to your seats and put it in the offering later to thank God for making a beautiful world and loving people to care for you.

Prayer: It's good to know, God, that all things belong to you, including us. Thank you for all of your good gifts. Amen.

The Sermon

God vs. Caesar – How Do We Decide?

Hymns

Beginning of Worship: "O How Glorious, Full of Wonder"
Sermon Hymn: "Breathe on Me Breath of God"
Closing Hymn: "God of Grace and God of Glory"

Scripture

Matthew 22:15–22 (For additional sermon materials on this passage, see the 2005 May/June planning issue of *The Clergy Journal*; for sermon materials on 1 Thessalonians 1:1–10, see the July/August 2005 issue of *The Clergy Journal*.).

For some of us the world is an either-or kind of place. Either you're with me or you're against me. During the Vietnam era the phrase, "America, love it or leave it" was a popular either-or response to anti-war activists.

For some, faith is an either-or experience. God is either for us or against us. If God exists, there would not be suffering, disease, terrorism. But, these things exist, therefore God must not exist. In seminary I discovered that doubt is not the opposite of faith but an element of faith. That helped me break free of some of my either-or thinking.

For some, life is a gray experience, sometimes good, sometimes not so good. Some have that grayness about faith or God. We think, "God loves me, but maybe God doesn't get involved in every little thing that happens in my life, or in the world. God is all-powerful, but maybe God lets people figure things out for themselves, even when they mess things up.
In today's gospel reading, Jesus is confronted by either-or thinking, but, it's the gray area in which he leaves his challengers standing. "Teacher...tell us, then, what you think. Is it lawful to pay taxes to the emperor, or not?" (v. 17).

We don't have to be biblical scholars to know a trick question. Those testing Jesus were from two groups, a lot like our political parties. The Pharisees were known for a strict legalism in interpreting Jewish laws and a respect for tradition. The other political party was the Herodians, Jews who were loyal to Herod and supportive of Rome's presence in Israel.

The Herodians probably supported paying taxes. The Pharisees probably would not have. In Torah law, which they held sacred, selling land to outsiders is forbidden because it belongs only to God (Lev 25:23). From their strict viewpoint, Caesar did not have a right to God's land and was, therefore, not entitled to collect taxes from God's people. Second, the coin held a graven image, a picture of Caesar, considered a god by the Romans. To touch it and use it was to acknowledge a god besides Yahweh. It's easy to imagine the insult this coin represented to the Pharisees who were forced to handle it day after day.

So consider Jesus in the midst of this group. If Jesus had said "pay the taxes," the Pharisees would have had one more issue to hold against him. If he had said, "don't pay the taxes," Roman loyalists might have had him arrested. This either-or situation is exactly where his audience wanted him to be, and Jesus knew it.

"Tell us, then, what you think. Is it lawful to pay taxes to the emperor, or not?" (v. 17).

Jesus refused to participate. "You hypocrites," he told his challengers. What is important, Jesus told them, is not paying taxes to Caesar, or the coin with which it is paid. What is important is remembering who you are and whose you are. "Give therefore to the emperor the things that are the emperor's, and to God the things that are God's" (v. 21).

In other words, Jesus tells them to give to the civic authority what belongs to them, and to give to God what belongs to God. And, Jesus could have added, "make sure you know the difference." Jesus did know the difference. Jesus was not concerned with politics; Jesus was concerned with love and justice. "Give to God what is God's" is a mandate to re-evaluate life. Knowing the difference between Caesar and God isn't an either-or kind of thing. Rather, it's a matter of love and justice, a matter of living in the way Jesus lived.

When I think of people who actively and creatively balance this giving to the society and giving to God, I think of former President Jimmy Carter. When Carter, a devout Christian, received the Nobel Peace Prize for his work to find peaceful solutions to international conflicts, the Nobel committee wrote in their press release from Oslo, Norway: "In a situation currently marked by threats of the use of power, Carter has stood by the principles that conflicts must as far as possible be resolved through media-tion and international cooperation based on international law, respect for human rights, and economic development." Jimmy Carter's deep commit-ment to this work has its basis in his deep faithfulness to Jesus Christ.

For some of us the world is an either–or kind of place. For some of us, God is an either-or kind of God. But for Jesus, the tension between Caesar and God did not exist. God was everything. To Caesar he gave respect, but never the authority over how he was to live or die. We see this most profoundly at the end of his life, when Jesus stood before Pilate, the highest Roman official in Israel, the one who had the power of Jesus' life and death in his hands.

"Pilate therefore said to him, 'Do you refuse to speak to me? Do you not know that I have power to release you, and power to crucify you?' Jesus answered him, 'You would have no power over me unless it had been given you from above.' From then on Pilate tried to release him, but the Jews cried out, 'If you release this man, you are no friend of the emperor.

Everyone who claims to be a king sets himself against the emperor'" (Jn 19:10–12).

While it's easy to focus on ourselves and to become overwhelmed by the stresses and demands of our daily lives, we need to look up and look out. We need to remember that we are part of something bigger: a larger community, a nation, a world. For Christians, the basis for our allegiance to our community, our nation, and our world is our faithfulness to God and our commitment to following the way of Jesus Christ in love, in justice, in forgiveness, and in peace.

"Give therefore to the emperor the things that are the emperor's, and to God the things that are God's."

With God's help – we will.

– Rosemary A. Rocha

October 23, 2005

23rd Sunday after Pentecost (Proper 25)
RC/Pres: 30th Sunday in Ordinary Time

Lessons

RCL	Deut 34:1–2	1 Thess 2:1–8	Mt 22:34–46
Roman Catholic	Ex 22:20–26	1 Thess 1:5c–10	Mt 22:34–40
Episcopal (BCP)	Ex 22:21–27	1 Thess 2:1–8	Mt 22:34–46
Lutheran	Lev 19:1–2, 15–18	1 Thess 2:1–8	Mt 22:34–46

Introduction to the Lessons
Lesson 1
(1) Deuteronomy 34:1–12 (RCL)
The wandering is over. Israel looks to its future in the land promised to Abraham. But Moses, their leader, sage, prophet, and liberator will not go with them. His journey ends at the boundary of his people's future.

(2) Exodus 22:20–26 (RC); Exodus 22:21–27 (Epis)
God cares passionately for the vulnerable. God's people are charged to remember their times as aliens and to use that memory to serve those in need. The warnings for going against this direction are dire: death by the sword, more widows and orphans.

(3) Leviticus 19:1–2, 15–18 (Luth)
This list of behaviors unacceptable to God's people provides guidelines on being holy. The question of not being partial to the poor seems to contradict laws in other parts of scripture.

Lesson 2
(1) 1 Thessalonians 2:1–8 (RCL/Epis/Luth)
Writing from Athens, Paul tries to encourage the faithful, reminding them to let their memories of his past words and deeds determine their present attitude toward him and his workers.

(2) 1 Thessalonians 1:5c–10 (RC)

Paul is grateful for the courage with which the Thessalonians received God's word in the face of persecution, and live the word as positive and powerful examples of faithfulness to Christ.

Gospel
Matthew 22:34–46 (RCL/Epis/Luth); Matthew 22:34–40 (RC)

Back in Jerusalem, Jesus' days are numbered. Following an unsuccessful attempt to trap him with questions of resurrection and paying taxes to Caesar, a lawyer challenges Jesus by inquiring about his understanding of the bottom line of Jewish law.

Theme

The great commandment is simple to understand, yet difficult to live. With God, all things are possible.

Thought for the Day

Love is not blind – it sees more, not less. But because it sees more, it is willing to see less.

– Rabbi Julius Gordon

Call to Worship

One: God, you have been our dwelling place in all generations.

All: Before the mountains were brought forth, before you had formed the earth and the world, from everlasting to everlasting you are God.

One: A thousand years in your sight are like yesterday.

All: Satisfy us in the morning with your steadfast love, so that we may rejoice and be glad all our days.

One: God, you have been our dwelling place in all generations,

All: From everlasting to everlasting you are God.

– adapted from Psalm 90

Pastoral Prayer

God of love, teach us love. When we are strong, remind us that you spur us on. When we are indifferent, give our eyes your vision of justice and mercy, so that we might see the paths you place us on. When we are callous, make us stumble over our unkind words and selfish acts, so that we may think loving thoughts and do loving deeds. When we are stubborn, make our love malleable, so that we may love you and your creation today and through the certain changes of tomorrow. When we are weary from caring, make us see you in the faces and places of all your creatures and creation. God of love, it is no simple thing to ask to know how to love. But still we ask, for in love only do we find you. Amen.

Prayer of Confession

To know you, to love you, to serve you. This, O God of time and eternity, is our call. This, O God of love and compassion, is our challenge. Open our minds and hearts, our ears and our hands, that we might see and feel you in the strengths and needs of others and your world. Transform our self-centered ways into self-giving lives settled on faithfulness, service, and joy. Then, may your love blossom in our lives and in the lives of those with whom we share this life. In the name and spirit of Jesus Christ, may it be so. Amen.

Prayer of Dedication of Gifts and Self

Touch these gifts and our giving with your love, O God. Then, may the same spirit that was in Christ Jesus be served through them in our world, today, now. Amen.

Sermon Summary

We can argue about it, disagree about it, ignore it, affirm it. But unless we do it, loving God and our neighbor is meaningless.

Hymn of the Day
"Christian, Rise and Act Your Creed"

Asked about which commandment is the greatest, Jesus said there were two: love God and love neighbor. Thus the inseparable link in the Christian faith between the two commandments was forged.

My recommendation for today is a hymn of uncommon directness and candor, "Christian, Rise and Act Your Creed," by Francis Albert Rollo Russell, set to a tune from *The Parish Choir*. "Christian, rise and act your creed; let your prayer be in your deed." You may also want to consider Ruth Duck's "The Call Is Clear and Simple."

Children's Time

The Most Important Rule

Preparation: Set up a checkerboard and checkers.
How many of you know how to play checkers? Can someone explain the rules? Why do we need rules to play checkers? (Accept answers.)

Another place we need rules is when we're driving in the car. What would happen if we didn't have stop signs? What would happen if we had no speed limits? What would happen if we could drive down either side of the street? (Accept answers to these.) We can't play a game without rules. When we drive, rules keep us safe. Families have rules, too. What is the most important rule in your home? (Accept answers and share one of yours.) And at school, what is the most important rule? (Accept answers.)

In today's Bible story, some important church leaders asked Jesus, "Which of God's rules is most important?" Jesus said, "You shall love the Lord your God with all your heart, and with all your soul, and with all your mind. This is the greatest and first commandment. And a second is like it: You shall love your neighbor as yourself."
Prayer: Help me, God, to find ways to love you and love others by following your rules every day. Amen.

The Sermon

The Great Debate

Hymns
>**Beginning of Worship:** "Immortal, Invisible, God Only Wise"
>**Sermon Hymn:** "O Love that Will Not Let Me Go"
>**Closing Hymn:** "Jesu, Jesu, Fill Us with Your Love"

Scripture
Matthew 22:34–46 (For additional sermon materials on this passage, see the 2005 May/June planning issue of *The Clergy Journal;* for sermon materials on 1 Thessalonians 2:1–8, see the July/August 2005 issue of *The Clergy Journal.*)

If you remember the presidential debates of 2004, you'll recall that there were four basic topics of discussion, argument, and, some would say, exaggeration – Iraq, the economy, healthcare, and the question of credibility for both candidates. There were three presidential debates and each one left the audience uncertain as to which candidate was the winner.

Our passage from Matthew today reminds me of those debates. The question, "Which is the greatest commandment?" was the third in a series of four hot topics of discussion between the Pharisees, the Sadducees, and Jesus. Hot topic number one: taxation. "Is it lawful to pay taxes to the emperor, or not?" (Mt 22:17). Hot topic number two: resurrection (v. 28), and today's topic presented by a lawyer: "Teacher, which commandment in the law is the greatest?" (v. 36).

Most of us know about Moses and the Ten Commandments. By the time Jesus lived, there were not only ten laws, but some 616 laws, which faithful Jews were expected to know and follow.

In Matthew's setting of this question, Jesus has returned to Jerusalem for the last time. Palm Sunday is past, Golgotha awaits. The Pharisees and Sadducees are plotting together on how to get him there; how to trap him into saying something or doing something that would place him in violation of Hebrew law and get him arrested. Again, I am reminded of those debates. While I watched the debates with my mind made up in terms of who I would vote for, I felt an occasional sense of compassion for whichever candidate seemed, in the moment, to be risking his political future, not on a matter of fundamental importance to our country, but on a misspoken word, a forgotten fact, a confused reference, or a wrong look on his face. Both men were under incredible pressure to think right, speak right, look right. I imagine Jesus experienced similar pressures.

"Love God above everything else," Jesus told them. "Love your neighbor as yourself." We read these verses so often that, in their familiarity, they lose power. But these answers Jesus gave were not wimpy little sound bites about "God is love." These were life-and-death times for Jesus. Each question, each sparring with the religious political machine, was a type of trap. The questions put to Jesus were intended to disarm and do harm.

Now, at least from my perspective, the question put to Jesus was not difficult. What is the greatest commandment? The answer was as ancient as Moses. Every faithful Jew knew it by heart. They wore it on their arms and foreheads. It rested by their front doors. Jesus responded to the lawyer with Deuteronomy 6:5: "You shall love the Lord your God with all your heart, and with all your soul, and with all your might." Jesus continued with Leviticus 19:18b: "you shall love your neighbor as yourself." Jesus' next words, I suspect, are where Jesus stepped out on a limb. "On these two commandments hang all the law and the prophets" (Mt 22:40).

It's interesting to consider the order of Jesus' reply. While Jesus spoke the commandment about loving God first and the commandment about loving neighbor and self second, he didn't make one more important than the other. What Jesus said was, "And a second is like it." In other words, loving God is loving your neighbor as yourself, and loving your neighbor as yourself is loving God.

We have no idea how the lawyer and the others listening reacted to Jesus' words, because Matthew doesn't report it, and immediately Jesus moves on to the fourth controversy – a question he initiates about the ancestry of the Messiah.

In the presidential debates four years ago, accusations were made and there never seemed to be enough response time for the candidates to get to the heart of the matter. In a sense it is the same with Jesus' response on love. Words are never enough. To love God, neighbor, and oneself is too often just a sound bite. Without knowing about the Good Samaritan, or the father welcoming his prodigal son, or Mary Magdalene's loyalty even in the face of crucifixion, or Jesus' steadfastness even unto death, there is no flesh-and-blood understanding of the radical nature of what Jesus was saying that day. Loving one's neighbor in the Jewish tradition of Jesus day meant loving people like oneself, loving other Jews. But Jesus broke open the understanding of neighbor. Anyone, Jesus taught, anyone who is in need, anyone who is alive, is our neighbor. That's what it means to love God.

This is where it gets messy. Yes, we have to love people we don't like. We have to love people who don't like us. We have to put ourselves in places where we aren't comfortable. And most of us, if we're honest, really don't want to do these things.

Larry was 85 years old and a member of the first church I served. He was a curmudgeon, as they say. He challenged everything I tried to do and consistently made things difficult for me. One day a rumor began circulating that he was going to leave the church. The church moderator asked me to talk with him. I did not want to. I told her of all the ways that he had been mean to me and had made my life miserable. She listened and when I was done speaking she spoke, "You know, you don't have to like him, but you do have to love him."

I hate it when church folk get you at your own game! I thought about it, called Larry, and while I never really liked him, I tried to be loving to him. He stayed at the church and I have always been grateful to that moderator who pushed me to be faithful to the story behind the words of love.

In the book *The Prophet*, Kahil Gibran puts a twist on this idea: "When you love you should not say, 'God is in my heart' but rather, 'I am in the heart of God.'" To love God above everything else and to love my neighbor as I love myself is to exist within the heart of God. I think this is precisely what Jesus wanted for us – not to win a debate on religious practices, not to become the leader of a religious movement, but to touch people with the love of God.

That, my friends, is why we're here.

– Rosemary A. Rocha

October 30, 2005

24th Sunday after Pentecost (Proper 26)
RC/Pres: 31st Sunday in Ordinary Time

Lessons

RCL	Josh 3:7–17	1 Thess 2:9–13	Mt 23:1–12
Roman Catholic	Mal 1:14b–2:2b; 8–10	1 Thess 2:7b–9, 13	Mt 23:1–12
Episcopal	Mic 3:5–12	1 Thess 2:9–13	Mt 23:1–12
Lutheran	Mic 3:5–12	1 Thess 2:9–13	Mt 23:1–12

Introduction to the Lessons

Lesson 1

(1) Joshua 3:7–17 (RCL)

The miracle parting of the Red Sea that accompanied Israel's departure from Egypt is repeated in miniature as they enter Canaan, but with a difference. It is the presence of the ark carried by the priests that stays the waters of the Jordan.

(2) Malachi 1:14b–2:2b, 8–10 (RC)

A Judean prophet of the 5th century before Christ, Malachi lived in the period after the Jews returned from exile in Babylon. Malachi is concerned with conformity to the Torah's instruction regarding the priesthood and the Temple sacrifices.

(3) Micah 3:5–12 (Epis, Luth)

Micah lived in Judah around the time of the Assyrian invasion of the Northern Kingdom of Samaria. His message is clear and simple: what happened to Samaria will also happen to Judah if its people do not repent.

Lesson 2
1 Thessalonians 2:9–13 (RCL, Epis, Luth);
1 Thessalonians 2:7b–9, 13 (RC)

First Thessalonians may be the New Testament's oldest document. Paul exhibits extraordinary tenderness toward the Thessalonians, and reminds them of how much he cares for them.

99

Gospel
Matthew 23:1–12 (RCL, RC, Epis, Luth)

Jesus' criticism is leveled at the Pharisees' behavior, not their teaching: "observe whatever they tell you, but not what they do." Service, not self–aggrandizement, is the path to greatness.

Theme

Jesus reprimanded the religious leaders of his day for reveling in the symbols of status and the trappings of their office. He reminds us that true greatness is found in service.

Thought for the day

The more you put on externally, that is, the more trappings of priestly or episcopal offices, the more you are called to take off internally through a greater intimacy with Christ.

> – Frank Griswold, Presiding Bishop of the Episcopal Church

Call to Worship

One: Be of one mind with our Lord Jesus, who emptied himself and took the form of a servant,

All: Who lived a fully human life and died a fully human death,

One: Who gave us an example of radical obedience, even to the point of dying upon the cross.

All: For God honored Christ and raised him from death to new life, so that at the name of Jesus every knee shall bow, both in heaven and on earth, and every tongue shall acknowledge that Jesus is Lord.

Pastoral Prayer

Blessing and honor and glory and power are yours, O God. In love you created the human race and called Israel to be your people. You summoned Abraham and Sarah to follow you and through their descendants all the peoples of the earth are blessed. You brought Israel through the wilderness and established them in a land flowing with milk and honey. Through prophets you spoke your word of grace and judgment. And in the fullness of time you came among us in the life, death, and resurrection of Jesus the Messiah. You call disciples in every age to follow his example of humility and service. Raise up faithful leaders to embrace the way of the cross, to stand with the weak and oppose the proud, to find life in dying to self. Guide the nations of the world into ways of freedom and give them leaders who will honor human dignity. May those who suffer in body, mind, and spirit be filled with your abundant life. And in all things, gracious God, grant that we may raise hearts and voices to you in prayer and praise; through Christ our Lord. Amen.

Prayer of Confession

O just and merciful God, we confess that we honor Christ with our words, yet seek our own glory and greatness. We prefer our own ease and comfort to the difficult way of discipleship. We have received much but returned little; we have learned many things but forgotten the great lesson of service above self. Enlarge the narrowness of our hearts with the wideness of your mercy, fill the poverty of our imaginations with the greatness of your vision, warm the coldness of our hearts with the fire of your love, and draw us out of loneliness into your fellowship; through Christ our Lord. Amen.

Prayer of Dedication of Gifts and Self

Creating God, you have set us in the midst of abundance. Redeeming God, you have brought us from death to life. Sustaining God, you are our faithful companion on life's journey. Grant us one thing more, we pray: give us hearts that break for earth's sorrow and are as generous with others as you have been with us. For Christ's sake we pray, Amen.

Sermon Summary

We misunderstand Jesus' condemnation of the religious leaders of his day for their love of titles and status if we do not also hear it as a word of judgment against us. Before he took the scribes and Pharisees to task, Jesus had already rebuked his own disciples with similar words. Jesus sets before us the path of service and humility, a path no one has followed as completely as Christ himself.

Hymn of the Day
"Lord, Whose Love in Humble Service"

What a stark contrast Jesus draws for those listening to him when he advises them to "not do as [some] do, for they do not practice what they teach," but instead live humble lives of service: "The greatest among you will be your servant." This hymn, Albert Bayly's wonderfully poetic text, admonishes us to live the life Jesus talks about here. Though set to other tunes, BEECH SPRING complements the text in such a way as to transform it into a gracious invitation to live as servants of the Servant.

Children's Time

Jesus, Our Teacher

Preparation: Bring a whole apple, a knife, a little chalkboard, and some chalk.

(Hold up the apple.) Sometimes children bring a gift of an apple to a special person in their lives. Who? (A teacher.) Today we're going to learn more about our wise teacher, Jesus. Jesus once said, "For you have one teacher and you are all students." What are some things Jesus taught us? (Write responses on the chalkboard.)

Jesus taught that everything we have belongs to God. God created an amazing world. This apple has a surprise inside. (Cut the apple in half crosswise. The seeds will be arranged in a star pattern. Hold up both halves of the apple.) What do you see? (A star, a flower, a pretty design.) Jesus taught that God's world is beautiful and filled with surprises, like this star design. One of the biggest surprises is that God sent Jesus to earth to teach us and love us. (Give each child a tidbit of apple to eat.)

Prayer: Loving God, thank you for sending your son Jesus to teach us how to love you and love others. Amen.

The Sermon

True Greatness

Hymns

Beginning of Worship: "Lord Christ, When First You Came to Earth"
Sermon Hymn: "Jesu, Jesu, Fill Us with Your Love"
Closing Hymn: "Make Me a Servant, Lord"

Scripture

Matthew 23:1–12 (For additional sermon materials on this passage, see the 2005 May/June planning issue of *The Clergy Journal*; for sermon materials on 1 Thessalonians 2:9–13, see the July/August 2005 issue of *The Clergy Journal.*)

The wealthy Quaker William Penn was ahead of his time in many ways. He intended Philadelphia, the city he founded, to be a place of tolerance not only for all Christians but also for Jews, a radical idea in the seventeenth century. Furthermore, in accordance with the Quaker idea that no human being should receive more honor than another, Philadelphia's streets are named Chestnut, Walnut, Spruce, and so on, rather than bearing the names of distinguished men and women.

In today's gospel reading Jesus denounces the scribes and Pharisees for reveling in the trappings of status. "They make their phylacteries broad and their fringes long. They love to have the place of honor at banquets and the best seats in the synagogues, and to be greeted with respect in the marketplaces, and to have people call them rabbi" (Mt 23:6–7). This is a temptation especially common to religious leaders. We might paraphrase Jesus' words thus, "Look at those pastors! They are wearing vestments imported from Europe and enjoy sitting at the head table at banquets and are overjoyed when their seminary gives them an honorary degree."

But Jesus says that such signs of status are to be avoided. "You are not to be called rabbi, for you have one teacher, and you are all students. And call no one your father on earth, for you have one Father – the one in heaven. Nor are you to be called instructors, for you have one instructor, the Messiah" (vv. 8–10).

All pastors would do well to feel a little uneasy now and then about Jesus' words in Matthew 23. Whether they call us reverend or father or pastor or some other title, congregations have a tendency to put clergy on a pedestal, and we have a tendency to enjoy it. In the sermon he preached at his installation as Presiding Bishop of the Episcopal Church, Frank Griswold said that the more you put on externally, that is, the more trappings of priestly or episcopal offices, the more you are called to take off internally through a greater intimacy with Christ.

Imagine a world that abolished all distinctions of class and even accomplishment. The French revolutionaries tried it. They abolished madame and monsieur and ordered that all individuals should be addressed as "citizen." The Soviet revolutionaries tried the same thing; tovarich or "comrade" was to be the universal form of address. The philanthropy industry would grind to a halt quickly if we had to stop handing out honorary titles!

However, these are not temptations of clergy only. Jesus' words to the scribes and Pharisees echo his words earlier in Matthew. When the "mother of the sons of Zebedee" asked Jesus if her sons could occupy places of honor in the kingdom, he replied, "You know that the rulers of the Gentiles lord it over them, and their great ones are tyrants over them. It will not be so among you; but whoever wishes to be great among you must be your servant, and whoever wishes to be first among you must be your slave; just as the Son of Man came not to be served but to serve, and to give his life a ransom for many" (Mt 20:25–28).

Jesus' point, of course, was not that it is wrong to give honor where honor is due, but that our priorities are wrong. We lift up and celebrate the wrong things. We honor the wealthy and powerful rather than those who have distinguished themselves by lives of service.

A few years ago Harvard University gave two honorary doctorates in the same year. The first was Walter Annenberg, the founder of *TV Guide*, a billionaire and friend of Presidents Ford and Reagan. For his generosity he was not only given honorary degrees but also named ambassador to Great Britain. The same year Harvard also honored Oseola McCarty. You may have heard of Annenberg, but it is extremely unlikely you've ever heard of Ms. McCarty. Oseola McCarty was a sixth grade dropout who spent 75 years as a washerwoman in rural Mississippi. During her career she saved $150,000 that she gave to the University of Southern Mississippi, saying, "I wanted to do some good for somebody else's child."

Did Walter Annenberg deserve the honors he received for his generous philanthropy? Of course he did. But when you hear Jesus say, "The greatest among you will be your servant. All who exalt themselves will be humbled, and all who humble themselves will be exalted," do you think first of Annenberg or McCarty?

We do not have to take in laundry for 75 years and then give away our life's savings to exemplify Jesus' words. Nor is it wrong to receive or give honor where it is due. But Jesus does suggest that we need to examine our priorities. Do we live lives of self-aggrandizement or service? Do we measure our lives by how much we get or how much we give?

Jesus' words in Matthew 23 hold up a standard against which all of us fall short. Yet it is a standard perfectly embodied in Jesus' own life. Jesus shows us that the way of service and humility is also the way of true greatness. Jesus is not arguing against leadership per se. On the contrary, today's reading from Joshua gives us an example of the necessity of leadership. Jesus himself showed how to exercise leadership, but he led from a position of humility and service.

Jesus' call to his disciples in all ages is "follow me." There is no place we can go where he has not already gone. The most prized title is not Doctor or Reverend or Lord or Master, but Servant. The place of honor is not the throne but the cross. And the only distinction we should seek is to be recognized as faithful disciples of the King who reigns from the cross and the Lord who kneels to wash the feet of his friends.

– J. Barry Vaughn

October 31, 2005

Reformation Day

Lessons
Lutheran   Jeremiah 31:31–34   Romans 3:19–28   John 8:31–36

Introduction to the Lessons
Lesson 1
Jeremiah 31:31–34
Jeremiah prophesies that God will make a "new covenant" that is distinctive. This covenant places the burden for sin on the individual; this covenant will be internal, rather than external; each one will know God, from the least to the greatest.

Lesson 2
Romans 3:19–28 (RCL, Epis, Luth)
Paul concludes that what the Law (Torah) had done for Israel was now accomplished by "the redemption that is in Jesus Christ" (v. 24). The new covenant revealed in Christ mediates salvation to all who have faith in Christ.

Gospel
John 8:31–36 (RCL, Epis, Luth)
Jesus' promise that the truth will make them free offends the Jews "who had believed in him" (v. 31), by implying that they are slaves. Jesus is referring not to economic slavery, but to spiritual slavery, the slavery of everyone who sins.

Theme
We can still celebrate the Reformation today if we understand the meaning of the Reformation to be not primarily about adherence to a set of propositions, but faithfulness to the One who proclaimed himself to be the very Truth itself.

Thought for the Day

There are two sorts of truth: trivialities, where opposites are obviously absurd, and profound truths, recognized by the fact that the opposite is also a profound truth.

– Physicist Niels Bohr

Call to Worship

One: You shall know the truth and the truth shall set you free.
All: Amen. Lord, have mercy.
One: All have sinned and fallen short of God's glory.
All: Amen. Christ, have mercy.
One: We are now saved by God's grace as a gift, through the redemption that is in Christ Jesus.
All: Amen. Lord, have mercy. From God, to God, and through God are all things. To God be glory forever and ever.

Pastoral Prayer

Faithful God, you have promised that your church will prevail against the forces of evil. In every age you send us holy women and men to call us back to your ways. We give you praise and thanks for Martin Luther and John Calvin, for Elizabeth I and Thomas Cranmer, for Ulrich Zwingli and Menno Simons, for Karl Barth and Martin Luther King Jr. Gracious God, we give you praise and thanks for your hand at work in our midst today and your summons to be your disciples in our time.

Give us courage to speak out against the evils and abuses that hinder the church's work and witness. Hear us as we pray for our world. Give us leaders who will honor the rights and dignity of all people; who will govern with humility and wisdom; and who will seek justice, freedom, and peace. O God, we lift our voices to you for those who cry out for freedom from want or weakness in body, mind, or spirit. We pray that your Spirit would bring healing. And in all things, we lift our prayers to you, O Lord, our mighty fortress, our hope in ages past, through Jesus Christ, the Lord of the church, in the power of the Holy Spirit who guides us into all truth. Amen.

Prayer of Confession

O God of justice and judgment, we confide in our own strength rather than your grace. We prefer the path of least resistance to the hard way of discipleship. We are more ready to celebrate the past than to follow you in our own day. Our lips sing your praise but we do not let justice roll down like a mighty stream. We celebrate your saints but our lives mock the example of their holiness. Gracious God, by the fire of your Spirit burn away all that separates us from you, from one another, and from our truest selves. Reform our lives by your living word and forgive our transgressions; for we make our confession in the name of Christ crucified and risen. Amen.

Prayer of Dedication of Gifts and Self

With hearts and hands and voices, we thank you, O God, for the bounty of our tables, for work that satisfies and delights, for the liberty to assemble in prayer and praise. And we pray for those whose tables are bare; who seek work but do not find it; and who are hindered from joining together in worship. Ever-faithful God, we offer no gift but that which you have first given us. Grant that we may give to others by the measure with which we have received from you. From the gifts that we offer, we pray that you would build the kingdom; through Christ our Lord. Amen.

Sermon Summary

We are right to give thanks for the sixteenth-century Reformers and their work, and do well to remember the truths they taught and the battles they fought. However, the churches they left behind need reformation and revival as much as the late medieval church did. The message of the reformers for our day is not so much about truth with a small *t*, but Truth with a capital *T*. The Truth that sets us free is not a thing, but our living Lord Jesus.

Hymn of the Day
"Dear Christians, One and All"

The contributions to Christian hymnody by Luther and his associates were as significant to the Sixteenth-century Protestant Reformation as were their theological insights. To involve the assembly in singing sacred texts in the vernacular was a relatively new idea that left a deep impression upon the Western church.

An alternative to the usual picks, "Dear Christians, One and All" is a hymn penned by Luther himself (translated by Richard Massie) and published in Wittenberg, 1524. For a successful introduction of the hymn, have the choir sing the odd-numbered verses and the congregation join them on the even-numbered ones.

Children's Time

The Free Gift of God's Love

Preparation: Bring red playdough and a tray.
(Give each child a small piece of red playdough.) Roll your playdough into a ball like this. (Demonstrate.) Now flatten it into a pancake. (Demonstrate.) Today we're going to learn about a big word – *reformation*. Reformation means to reshape or change something. You reformed or changed your playdough from a ball into a pancake.

Martin Luther lived over 500 years ago in Germany. He was a teacher and a preacher. He translated the Bible into German, so all of the people in Germany could read it. Luther helped people learn that God's love is a free gift for all of us. Luther was a reformer – he made changes in the church. Today is Reformation Day and we remember all the people who have made the church better.

Let's be reformers one more time. Change your clay into a heart shape. (Demonstrate.) Put your heart shape on the tray to dry, then come up after worship to take your heart home as a reminder that God's love is a free gift for you, for me, for everyone.
Prayer: Dear God, thank you for the free gift of your love. Help me to share your love with everyone. Amen.

The Sermon

Truth Is a Who

Hymns
Beginning of Worship: "God of Grace and God of Glory"
Sermon Hymn: "The Church of Christ in Every Age"
Closing Hymn: "A Mighty Fortress"

Scripture

John 8:31–36 (For sermon materials on Romans 3:19–28, see the 2005 May/June planning issue of *The Clergy Journal*; for sermon materials on Jeremiah 31:31–34, see the July/August 2005 issue of *The Clergy Journal*.)

If Reformation Day is about anything, surely it is about truth. Weren't competing truth claims at the very heart of the revolution launched by Luther and continued by Zwingli, Calvin, Cranmer, and others? Either the pope is the vicar of Christ or he is not; either the eucharistic bread and wine literally become the body of Christ or they do not; either we are saved by divine grace unaided by human effort or we participate in our salvation through good works.

But as the great writer Oscar Wilde said, "The truth is rarely pure and never simple." We know that the Reformation did not succeed on the basis of its truth claims alone; in large part it succeeded because of complex economic and political reasons. The emerging nation-states of Europe supported Luther and the other Reformers in order to gain economic and political power at the expense of the papacy.

When Protestant and Roman Catholic theologians discuss the great issues of the Reformation – the status of the papacy, justification by grace through faith, and transubstantiation – there is more agreement than disagreement. This is not to diminish the wide gulf that divided Wittenberg and Geneva from Rome in the sixteenth century and continues to divide Protestants and Catholics today, but the temptation of Reformation Day is to make that gulf far wider and deeper than it is or ever has been.

The common confession of Christ as Lord binds all Christians together, and in a post-Christian age that fundamental confession is more than enough for us to make common cause against the widespread indifference and even hostility toward all expressions of faith.

So what is Reformation Day if it is not a chance to pat ourselves on the back and congratulate one another that Luther was right and Popes Julius II and Leo X were wrong? Is Reformation Day anything more than a chance for Lutherans to sing "A Mighty Fortress" and Presbyterians to repeat some of the more exciting passages from the Westminster Confession?

I think the key to Reformation Day is in Jesus' words in today's gospel reading: "If you continue in my word, you are truly my disciples; and you will know the truth, and the truth will make you free" (vv. 31–32).

Truth is a central category in John's gospel. At the very beginning the author tells us that when the divine Word took flesh and lived among us, "we [saw] his glory full of grace and truth" (1:14). Later, Jesus declared himself to be "the way, the truth, and the life" (14:6). The great accomplishment of Luther, Calvin, Zwingli, and Cranmer was to issue a thunderous call to Western Christians to return to the Word made flesh, the Word spoken by Israel's prophets, the Word that "above all earthly powers, no thanks to them, abideth."

But if the great work of the sixteenth-century Reformers was to summon the church to return to the Word made flesh and the Word of the prophets, then that implies that the church had drifted away, that there was a great gulf between the position of the Reformers and the position of the Roman Catholic Church. Let there be no misunderstanding here: there were and are issues that separate Roman Catholics and Protestants. We do not serve the gospel well if we are not honest about our differences. But I think we are somewhat misled by the categories historians have given us. It might be better to re-christen Luther's great movement of the sixteenth century revival rather than the reformation.

Of course, Luther, Calvin, and the others did reform the church. They were convinced that the church of the sixteenth century was a different church than that of the apostles, and they believed that their work was to return the church as far as possible to the apostolic model. But that was also the goal of many who remained within the Roman Catholic Church. What Luther, Calvin, and the rest accomplished was a great revival, a movement that bore fruit not only in the Protestant churches they founded but also in the Roman Catholic Church that they left. They awakened the entire Western church to its need to "continue" in Christ's word and to let that word set them free.

Part of our problem on Reformation Day is with the word truth. If truth is a thing that is fixed, unchanging, and static, then we might as well give up all hope of reconciliation with our Roman Catholic sisters and brothers. But is that what Jesus meant by "truth"? In John's gospel truth is never a set of propositions such as mathematical formulas. The truth is always a person. The truth is the one who said, "I am the way, the truth, and the life."

Physicist Niels Bohr said, "There are two sorts of truth: trivialities, where opposites are obviously absurd, and profound truths, recognized by the fact that the opposite is also a profound truth." That sounds like it relativizes truth completely out of existence, but if the truth is not a thing but a Person, then Bohr may have been right. If Truth is a person, then perhaps both Luther and his opponents can be comprehended in Truth's embrace.

So in a post-denominational, indeed, a post-Christian age, can we continue to celebrate Reformation Day or has it become an embarrassment that we should discard? I think the Reformation still has something to say to us that should be celebrated, because what the Reformers said in the sixteenth century is just as valid today. The church of the twenty-first century – the churches that the Reformers left behind – needs reformation and revival just as badly as the late medieval church.

As Fred Pratt Green's great hymn puts it, "The church of Christ in every age / beset by change but Spirit-led, / must claim and test its heritage / and keep on rising from the dead." In every age, we need reformers to summon us to return to the truth – truth with a lowercase *t*, but even more, to Truth with an uppercase *T*. Sometimes we need to be reminded of the truths that the Reformers taught, but we always need to be reminded to return to the Truth who became flesh and dwelt among us. This Truth, whom we saw to be full of glory, invites us to abide in him and will set us free indeed.

– J. Barry Vaughn

November 1, 2005

All Saints' Day

Lessons

RCL	Rev 7:9–17	1 Jn 3:1–3	Mt 5:1–12
Roman Catholic	Rev 7:2–4, 9–14	1 Jn 3:1–3	Mt 5:1–12
Episcopal	Sir 44:1–10, 13–14	Rev 7:2–4, 9–17	Mt 5:1–12

Introduction to the Lessons

Lesson 1
(1) Revelation 7:9–17 (RCL); Revelation 7:2–4, 9–14 (RC)

These verses reveal that the destiny of the redeemed is to join the great chorus of praise that goes on eternally in the presence of God. Revelation challenges us to make our worship worthy of the One we worship.

(2) Sirach 44.1–10, 13–14 (Epis)

Sirach, or Ecclesiasticus, was written by Ben Sira, an Egyptian Jew, at the beginning of the Second century. It represents the culmination of Israel's wisdom tradition and integrates that tradition with Israel's saving history.

Lesson 2
(1) 1 John 3:1–3 (RCL, RC)

Probably written around the end of the first century, the books of 1, 2, and 3 John deal with divisive issues that had arisen in certain faith communities. The writer exhorts, "Beloved, let us love one another." God has given this love, and we are God's children. In the verses assigned for All Saints' Day the writer sounds an eschatological note: "we know that when he appears we shall be like him."

(2) Revelation 7:2–4, 9–17 (Epis)

See Lesson 1 above.

Gospel
Matthew 5:1–12 (RCL, RC, Epis)

We know this familiar section of Jesus' Sermon on the Mount as the Beatitudes. To understand it fully, it is important to keep in mind that

Jesus adapts the Jewish liturgical form of beatitude, or blessing. Jesus also adopts the perspective of Israel's prophets in placing God firmly on the side of the poor, the meek, and the persecuted.

Theme
While all Christians are saints by virtue of their relationship with Christ in Baptism, we still need those who have traditionally been called saints as examples to inspire us.

Thought for the Day
It's often been said, boldly, that the saints in heaven rejoice over their sins, because through them they have been brought to greater and greater understanding of the endless endurance of God's love, to the knowledge that beyond every failure God's creative mercy still waits.
– Rowan Williams, *A Ray of Darkness*, p. 52

Call to Worship
One: Blessed are the poor in spirit,
All: For theirs is the kingdom of heaven.
One: Blessed are those who hunger and thirst for righteousness,
All: For they will be filled.
One: Blessed are you when people revile you and persecute you for the sake of Christ,
All: For in the same way the prophets have always been perse-cuted. Blessing and glory and wisdom and thanksgiving and honor and power and might be to our God forever and ever! Amen.

Pastoral Prayer
O God of saints and sinners, we praise you for those whose lives have lighted our way – for those who have paid the cost of discipleship in lives given to serving the poor and oppressed; for faithful pastors and bold prophets; and for those who have been faithful in seen and unseen ways, even unto death.

In communion with Christ and all your saints may we, too, hunger and thirst for a world in which the hungry are fed and the homeless received with hospitality. With the saints of every age, may we show ourselves to be your children by preferring peace to violence. Following where Christ and the saints have gone before, may we take the side of the poor, the meek, and the forgotten.

With saints above and saints below, our prayers go up to you, O Lord – prayers for those in need of healing, in economic distress, in danger, and in grief. Joining our voices with the saints around your throne, we bless you, we praise you, and we acclaim you, Eternal and Mighty God, through Christ crucified and risen, in the power of the Holy Spirit. Amen.

Prayer of Confession

Holy and merciful God, often we find the cost of discipleship far too high and are more ready to admire the saints than to imitate them – to praise them than to follow where they have led. We give our lives to the pursuit of professional success, pleasure, and self-aggrandizement, rather than spending ourselves for the sake of the kingdom. We are rich in earthly things but poor in the coin of heaven; we have filled our bellies with food that perishes but have not hungered and thirsted after justice. We have sought glory and power and have given no thought to those who stumble and fall along the way. But in Christ and the saints, you have set before us, a better way. Forgive our sinful and selfish choices. Renew and inspire us that we may once again set our feet on the path of holiness and service; through Christ our Lord. Amen.

Prayer of Dedication of Gifts and Self

Blessing and honor and glory and power are yours, O God. With the saints in heaven, grant that we may honor and serve you with the praises of our lips, the service of our lives, and the gifts of our treasure. Bless all that we offer, not by the measure with which we offer, but by the grace with which you receive it, that the hungry may be fed, the homeless received with hospitality, and the gospel proclaimed with power throughout the world; through Christ, the King of the saints and the Lord of glory. Amen.

Sermon Summary

From the very beginning of Christianity, the church has recognized some women and men as examples of heroic sanctity. The heroes and heroines of the faith serve us well when they inspire us to follow their example, but we do them and ourselves a disservice when we fail to recognize that they, too, were and are frail and fallible.

Hymn of the Day
"Who Are These Like Stars Appearing"

I think of All Saints' Day as a "thematic" day, an occasion where the selection of music is driven as much, sometimes more, by the occasion as by the texts. On such days I am keenly aware of either creating or ending traditions that are important to people by the music I select, so I do so with care.

Along with How's "For All the Saints," inimitably set to Vaughan Williams' SINE NOMINE, consider Theobald Heinrich Schenck's "Who Are These Like Stars Appearing," set to ZEUCH MICH, ZEUCH MICH. The hymn keys off the lesson from Revelation and happily co-exists with the standards we love.

Children's Time

For All the Saints

Preparation: Cut white crepe paper into 24-inch lengths. Ask a musician to play a hymn for All Saint's Day that is a favorite in your church.

If you are wearing blue, stand up or raise your hand. Look at all of the people wearing blue. Did you know that saints wear blue? If you are wearing red, stand up or raise your hand. These people are saints too. (Repeat using other colors until everyone is standing or raising their hands.) Look, everyone is standing or raising their hand. Everyone is a saint. What is a saint? (Accept responses.) A saint is someone who follows God. When we are baptized, we become one of God's saints.

Today we celebrate All Saints' Day. We remember all of the saints who have followed God before us. We remember all of the people who share God's love with us today.

(Give each child a white creepe paper streamer. Invite the children to wave their streamers as you lead them through the sanctuary while a musician plays an All Saint's Day hymn.)

Prayer: Dear God, thank you for sending faithful people to teach us about your love. Amen

The Sermon

Saints and Sinners

Hymns
> **Beginning of Worship:** "Let Saints on Earth in Concert Sing"
> **Sermon Hymn:** "O What Their Joy and Their Glory Must Be"
> **Closing Hymn:** "For All the Saints"

Scripture
Matthew 5:1–12 (For additional sermon materials on this passage, see the 2005 May/June planning issue and the July/August 2005 issue of *The Clergy Journal.*)

All Saints' Day begs the question, "What is a saint?" There are a number of ways we could define saint. The simplest and earliest definition of *saint* is found in the New Testament. Paul begins most of his letters by greeting the saints – the saints at Corinth, at Ephesus, at Galatia, and so on. In the New Testament, *saint* means simply any baptized person, any Christian. The word translated as *saint* in the New Testament is *hagios* or its plural *hagioi*, a Greek word that means "holy." The saints are the holy ones, not holy because of anything intrinsic to them, but holy because of the holy presence of Christ within them.

A second, more common, use of the word *saint* is to denote one of the heroes or heroines of the Christian faith. Thus, we speak of St. Peter or St. Francis, St. Mary Magdalene or St. Clare.

For a long time I was puzzled about why the gospel reading for All Saints' Day is the Beatitudes from Luke or Matthew. However, I think I know now why that is. The Beatitudes are, if you will, Jesus' definition of a saint. Let's look at a few of the characteristics of the saints as defined by Jesus.

First of all, "Blessed are the poor in spirit, for theirs is the kingdom of heaven" (v. 3). We are a society obsessed by money, financial success, and the accumulation of things. For Jesus, wealth was not a sin, but it was a problem.

The wealthy person, Jesus warned, was likely to have her or his priorities in the wrong place. The saints are those persons who have their hearts fixed upon God's kingdom, not earthy riches. The saints do not determine their own worth or the worth of others on the basis of financial success.

Second, "Blessed are those who mourn, for they will be comforted" (v. 4). We live in a world where feelings, in general – and sadness and depression, in particular – are suspect and not exhibited in public. Men, especially, are schooled to show little expression and feeling. We also live in a "feel good" culture. "Drink this, eat that, smoke a certain brand of cigarette and you will feel good and be happy." Fairy tales end "and they all lived happily ever after," but that isn't the way life works. But what if the ability to feel deep sadness is a prerequisite for feeling great joy? The saints are complete persons who feel the full range of human emotions. Saints "rejoice with those who rejoice" and "weep with those who weep" (Rom 12:15).

Third, "Blessed are the meek for they shall inherit the earth" (v. 5). A popular bumper sticker back in Alabama where I grew up reads, "If you can't run with the big dogs, stay on the porch." As a culture we exalt the big dogs, the hot shots, the powerful. Assertiveness, even aggressiveness, is highly valued. But what if the race is not to the swift, nor the contest to the strong? What if the truly great in the world are not the Donald Trumps, but the Mother Teresas? The saints are those who choose service above self-aggrandizement.

Finally, the saints are those who long for righteousness. "Blessed are those who hunger and thirst for righteousness, for they shall be satisfied" (v. 6). Jesus was a Jew, and to a Jew, righteousness, *zedeqah*, meant something very specific. Righteousness was literally "to do right by," especially to do right by the poor and hungry, widows and orphans. So when Jesus said, "Blessed are those who . hunger and thirst for righteousness," he was literally saying, "Blessed are those who long for the hungry to be fed and the homeless to be housed, for in the end, they will not be disappointed." Of all Jesus' claims, this may be the most extraordinary. Righteousness is not at home in the world in which you and I live, but Jesus announces the coming of a new world of righteousness and justice. The saints are those who long for the appearing of such a kingdom, who never lose heart and are never satisfied with anything less.

Another definition for saint that I want to offer involves a concrete example of holiness. In the early part of this century, Henry Joel Cadbury came to teach New Testament at Harvard Divinity School. Cadbury was one of the great New Testament scholars of our century and was at work on what became the Revised Standard Version of the Bible when World War I broke out. A pacifist, Cadbury would not fight in the war, but instead volunteered to work with the Quakers caring for the wounded and dying on the battlefields of Europe. In the midst of the war, one of Cadbury's students came across his professor bandaging a wounded soldier. "Dr. Cadbury," the student exclaimed, "Why aren't you back at Harvard translating the New Testament?" "I am translating the New Testament," Cadbury replied. He was translating the New Testament not from Greek into English but from the printed page into human life. I think that may be the best definition of saint. A saint is one who translates the New Testament into a life of love and service.

In conclusion, I want to offer you the devil's definition of *saint*. American humorist Ambrose Bierce once wrote a book entitled *The Devil's Dictionary*. In it he defined *saint* as "a dead sinner, revised and edited." To give the devil (or at least Ambrose Bierce) his due, there's much to be said for that definition.

A few years ago A. N. Wilson wrote a biography of C. S. Lewis, a man who is a saint to me and to many others. Wilson's biography shocked some C. S. Lewis fans by painting a revealing picture of Lewis, warts and all, but I came away appreciating Lewis more, not less, for knowing that he struggled and fought against many weaknesses and temptations. Sometimes he battled them successfully; sometimes he did not. But I think that a saint's light shines more brightly, not less, for her or his struggles.

All Saints' Day exhausts and unsettles me. However we define saint, I find it difficult to imagine myself among those "saints triumphant [who] rise in bright array." More often than not, I choose self-aggrandizement over service; my heart and mind go in a thousand different directions, rather than being fixed on God's kingdom; and if my life is a translation of the New Testament, then it must be in an unknown tongue. But I have to keep reminding myself and keep reminding you that sainthood is not our accomplishment; it is God's gift. We follow where Christ and the saints lead, knowing all the while that we will stumble and fall. All saints are forgiven sinners, just like us. The saints remind us of what we are capable of if we will only open ourselves to the power of God, who makes all things new and raises us from death to life abundant and everlasting.

– J. Barry Vaughn

November 6, 2005

25th Sunday after Pentecost (Proper 27)
RC/Pres: 32nd Sunday in Ordinary Time

Lessons

RCL	Josh 24:1–3a, 14–25	1 Thess 4:13–18	Mt 25:1–13
Roman Catholic	Wis 6:12–16	1 Thess 4:13–18 or 4:13–14	Mt 25:1–13
Episcopal	Amos 5:18–24	1 Thess 4:13–18	Mt 25:1–13
Lutheran	Amos 5:18–24 or Wis 6:12–16	1 Thess 4:13–18	Mt 25:1–13

Introduction to the Lessons
Lesson 1
(1) Joshua 24:1–3a, 14–25 (RCL)

Joshua rehearses Israel's saving history from before the time of Abraham to their arrival in the Promised Land. His narrative moves from gift to demand. The Israelites respond by echoing Joshua's narrative and reaffirming their allegiance to the Lord.

(2) Wisdom 6:12–16 (RC, Luth)

Ascribing one's work to a great figure of the past was thought to be a way of honoring that person; thus the author of Wisdom has ascribed his book to King Solomon. In personifying Wisdom as a feminine figure, the author is drawing on a tradition also seen in Proverbs 8.

(3) Amos 5:18–24 (Epis, Luth)

The heart of Amos' message was that the indifference of Israel's wealthy to the plight of the poor rendered their worship unacceptable to God. The people of Israel believed that if they called upon the Lord, they would be saved from the Assyrian threat. Amos cautions them not to presume upon God's mercy.

Lesson 2
1 Thessalonians 4:13–18 (RCL, RC, Epis, Luth)
The people of Thessalonica are concerned about the situation of those who died before Christ's Second Coming. Paul addresses the suddenness of the Lord's return and how it is an occasion of hope and encouragement, not fear.

Gospel
Matthew 25:1–13 (RCL, RC, Epis, Luth)
The parable of the wise and foolish maidens elaborates on the image of the bridegroom as an image of the Messiah and the wedding feast as an image of the kingdom of God.

Thought for the Day
Choose this day whom you will serve.

– Joshua 24:15

Theme
Are we worshiping the God who brought Israel out of Egypt and raised our Lord Jesus from the dead, or do we worship gods of power and success?

Call to Worship
One: O God of Joshua and Moses, we bless you for leading us through the wilderness.
All: Great is your faithfulness, O Lord.
One: Faithful God, we have turned from your ways and served strange gods.
All: Forgive us and turn our feet again toward your kingdom. This day we choose again to serve the Lord. May God have mercy upon us and give us grace to serve faithfully.

Pastoral Prayer
O God of wilderness and promised land, you brought Israel out of Egypt with signs and wonders. You provided them food and water in the wilderness; you brought them into a land flowing with milk and honey. We

praise you for leading us through dangers, toils, and snares. We praise you for the pillar of light that shines in the darkness of our doubt and despair. We praise you for staying the floods of trouble when they rise to overwhelm us.

Faithful God, we pray that you would send faithful shepherds to guide your pilgrim people. Give our pastors the boldness of Joshua to challenge our complacent ways. As you raised up Moses and Joshua to lead your people, so raise up leaders who will seek justice and pursue peace. Bring wholeness to those in pain and weakness. Comfort the broken-hearted. In all things we raise our hearts and voices in prayer and praise to you, Holy One, through Christ our Lord. Amen.

Prayer of Confession

True and living God, we have worshiped false gods and offered the sacrifices of our hearts and lives upon strange altars. We have worshiped power and success, riches and pleasure, and have turned from your ways. Our hearts are wayward and unsteady, O God, and we dare not trust them to guide us. Forgive us for expecting your blessing even when our worship is false. Turn our hearts again to you, set our feet upon firm ground, and make us steadfast in your service; through Christ our Lord. Amen.

Prayer of Dedication of Gifts and Self

Holy One, you give us more than our hearts can desire or our minds can conceive, and yet our gifts to others often are miserly and mean. Shame our selfishness with your generosity; enlarge our imaginations with visions of your reign; and make us as glad to give to others as we are to receive your bounty; through Christ our Lord. Amen.

Sermon Summary

Joshua reminded the Israelites of God's faithfulness in leading them through the wilderness, and challenged them to put away false gods and worship the Lord alone. Today we are tempted to give our hearts and lives to the false gods of power and success, rather than to the true God.

Hymn of the Day
"Wake, Awake, for Night Is Flying"

"Wachet auf, ruft uns die Stimme" (the German title) is from *A Mirror of Joy,* a book of meditations written by Philipp Nicolai when he was a young pastor at Unna. A terrible plague hit his city in 1597, killing over 1,300 people in six months; during this time, Nicolai often presided at up to 30 funerals a day.

Although a staple in Advent, both the content of this hymn and the circumstances under which Nicolai composed it make this an appropriate choice for today. Nicolai also composed the tune WACHET AUF, a melody that both Bach and Mendelssohn later utilized.

Children's Time

Jesus' Strong Love

Preparation: Bring in hand weights.

(Roll up your shirtsleeves and lift the hand weights. Have the children count with you for each time you lift the weights.) Why do we lift weights? (To get stronger.) Can you show me your muscles? (Have the children bend their arms and flex their biceps.) Look at all of those strong muscles! Who is the strongest person you know? (Accept responses.) Who is the strongest person in the world? (Accept responses, including fictional ones.)

In today's Bible story we learn about someone whose love is strong, even stronger than death. That someone is Jesus. Jesus loves us so much that after we die we will be with him in heaven forever. What a wonderful promise.

(Sing the first stanza of "Jesus Loves Me" with the children.) Whenever you sing this song you can remember Jesus' strong love for you – the strongest love in the whole world.

Prayer: Dear Jesus, it's good to know that your love is with us every day. It's good to know that your love will be with us forever, too. Thanks, Jesus. Amen.

The Sermon

A Factory of Idols

Hymns
Beginning of Worship: "The God of Abram Praise"
Sermon Hymn: "Guide Me, O Thou Great Jehovah"
Closing Hymn: "Amazing Grace"

Scripture
Joshua 24:1–3a, 14–25 (For sermon materials on 1 Thessalonians 4:13–18, see the 2005 May/June planning issue of *The Clergy Journal*; for sermon materials on Matthew 25:1–13, see the July/August 2005 issue of *The Clergy Journal*.)

Monotheism is the belief in and worship of only one all powerful, all knowing, all present God. I don't think this is natural for human beings. I think it's much more natural to believe in many gods – one god of the sun, another of the moon; one god of water, another of dry land; gods of trees, and animals, and plants. Sixteenth-century reformer John Calvin observed that the human mind is a "factory of idols."

If you read through the Old Testament carefully from beginning to end, you will see that the people of Israel moved from a belief in many gods to a belief in one God. The Ten Commandments directs Israel to have no other gods "before" the God who brought them out of Egypt. They are not to worship other gods. In other words, the Ten Commandments reflects a time in Israel's history when Israelites believed that there were many gods. If they had believed that there was only one God, why would the Ten Commandments tell Israel only to worship one God?

Knowing that the temptation to worship other gods was an ever-present temptation for Israel, Joshua's emphatic command, "Choose this day whom you will serve" (v. 15) makes more sense. Joshua set a choice before the people of Israel: "If you are unwilling to serve the Lord, choose this day whom you will serve, whether the gods your ancestors served in the region beyond the River, or the gods of the Amorites in whose land you are living; but as for me and my household, we will serve the Lord" (v. 15). The people of Israel deny that they serve other gods and insist that they will serve the God of Israel: "Far be it from us that we should forsake the Lord, to serve other gods"
(v. 16). Then Joshua asks them again and cautions them that they cannot serve

other gods: "You cannot serve the Lord; for he is a holy God. He is a jealous God. If you forsake the Lord and serve foreign gods, then he will turn and do you harm, and consume you." (v. 20). Again, the people of Israel insist that they will serve the Lord.

After the second time that the Israelites say that they will serve God, Joshua commands them to "put away the foreign gods that are among you, and incline your hearts to the Lord, the God of Israel" (v. 23). What is remarkable is that after God had brought them out of Egypt and led them across the wilderness, they still were carrying around the idols that their neighbors worshiped. How could the people of Israel have done this? How could they have seen God's mighty acts and still want to worship and serve other gods?

It may be that there is something in human nature that makes us want to hedge our bets, something that says, "OK, worship God, but just in case, it might be a good idea to honor Baal or Astarte or another deity. You can never be too careful."

Or, do you remember the story of St. Paul in Athens? He encountered a temple to an "unknown god." Presumably, the Athenians had put up a temple to an unknown god on the off-chance that there might be some god to whom they were not offering sacrifices who might become angry and do them harm.

Are we really all that different from the Israelites of Joshua's day or the Athenians of Paul's day? Is the temptation to serve other gods any less real today than it was two thousand or three thousand years ago? How many of us have constructed an idol and put it in the place of the real God? I doubt that anyone actually has a gold or silver statue to which they offer sacrifices, but an idol or false god can be a career or loved one or a bank account.

The thing about gods, even false ones, is that they really do reward their worshipers. People who worship financial success often achieve financial success. A person whose single goal in life is to amass a large amount of money stands a reasonable chance of achieving it. In other words, if one offers enough of the right kind of sacrifices at the altar of financial success, then the god of financial success may in fact give you your heart's desire. Similarly, if you sacrifice at the altar of professional success and offer that god the right offerings, you may in fact achieve professional success.

False gods sometimes give us what we want, but they rarely give us what we need. Today's readings from 1 Thessalonians and Matthew remind us of a difficult and solemn truth: We are only given so much time. Both Paul and

Matthew employ the language of apocalyptic, that is, they speak of the Second Coming of Christ and the end of the world. Their message is simple and sensible: time will run out for you and for me and what then? Will we find that we have put our faith in false gods? That there is no oil in our lamps?

Joshua's challenge is as pertinent today as it was when Israel crossed from the wilderness to the Promised Land: "Choose this day whom you will serve, whether the gods your fathers served in the region beyond the River, or the gods of the Amorites in whose land you dwell; but as for me and my house, we will serve the Lord." The gods of the Amorites are long forgotten, but every day false gods attempt to seduce us with empty promises of wealth, power, and pleasure. The One who led us through the wilderness leads us still, and beckons us into an everlasting land flowing with milk and honey.

– J. Barry Vaughn

November 13, 2005

26th Sunday after Pentecost (Proper 28)
RC/Pres: 33rd Sunday in Ordinary Time

Lessons

RCL	Judg 4:1–7	1 Thess 5:1–11	Mt 25:14–30
Roman Catholic	Prov 31:10–13,	1 Thess 5:1–6	Mt 25:14–30
	19–20,30–31		or 25:14-15, 19-21
Episcopal	Zeph 1:7, 12–18	1 Thess 5:1–10	Mt 25:14–15, 19–29
Lutheran	Zeph 1:7, 12–18	1 Thess 5:1–11	Mt 25:14

Introduction to the Lessons
Lesson 1
(1) Judges 4:1–7 (RCL)
Despite the evil nature of God's people, God responds in love to their needs through the prophet and judge Deborah.

(2) Proverbs 31:10–13, 19–20, 30–31 (RC)
A God-fearing woman is a blessing to her husband, through the work of her hands and her love for the needy.

(3) Zephaniah 1:7, 12–18 (Epis/Luth)
The Lord's wrath is not to be taken lightly; therefore live as much as possible without sinning.

Lesson 2
1 Thessalonians 5:1–11 (RCL/Luth);
1 Thessalonians 5:1–6 (RC);
1 Thessalonians 5:1–10 (Epis)
Those who know the Lord – children of light and of the day – live confidently in the knowledge that their salvation is assured through the death and resurrection of our Lord Jesus Christ.

Gospel
Matthew 25:14–30 (RCL/RC/Luth);
Matthew 25:14–15, 19–29 (Epis)
God blesses us with skills and abilities, and expects us to use them for the good of others and the glory of God.

Theme
God provides for our lives now as well as in the life to come.

Thought for the Day
Do not be afraid of death, for our salvation is assured through our Lord Jesus Christ. Therefore, we live with God in this life and in the next. Praise the Lord!

Call to Worship (in unison)
O Lord, we give you thanks and praise, that you have destined us for salvation. Therefore let us live in the confident hope of your promise.

Pastoral Prayer
Thank you, gracious Lord, for the hope in which we live – that despite the lack of peace and security in the world, we know that you provide us with a peace that surpasses our understanding. Enlighten us with the confidence we seek, that our salvation is secure through our Lord Jesus Christ. Bless us with certainty, so that we may be ambassadors of your love and caretakers of our brothers and sisters in Christ. We pray in your name, Amen.

Prayer of Confession
O God, how quickly we forget your promises. Restore our faith, that we might live in the assurance of our salvation. Help us not to be haughty and arrogant in our hope, but grant us a willingness to listen to your Holy Spirit and to comfort those who mourn. In the name of Jesus, we pray. Amen.

Prayer of Dedication of Gifts and Self
Lord Jesus Christ, as children of light and of the day, we present to you our gifts of time, talents, treasures, and self. Use them for the good of others and the glory of God. Amen.

Sermon Summary

The time and manner of death is uncertain, but as children of God, we live enlightened lives in the sure and certain hope of our resurrection. Such confidence propels us to care for others.

Hymn of the Day
"God of Love and God of Power"

The New Testament parables provide a seemingly endless number of ways to envision and imagine God. In today's gospel reading, God is like an investment banker who demands high returns on his investments and is more than willing to terminate an employee who plays it safe and doesn't deliver. Not surprisingly, there is a dearth of hymns inspired by this text. However, Gerald H. Kennedy's "God of Love and God of Power," set to the music of Joachim Neander, pairs well with it: "All our lives belong to thee, thou our final loyalty." Today both preacher and musician do their best and trust God for the rest.

Children's Time

Children of Light

Preparation: Bring a large mirror and a bright flashlight.

We're going to be scientists and do an experiment with light and reflection. What happens when you look into a mirror? (Pass the mirror around and let the children look at their reflections.) We see a reflection of ourselves. Can we see ourselves in the mirror if it is dark? (No.) What do we need besides a mirror to make a reflection? (Light.) When light hits a mirror it bounces back or is reflected. (Turn on the flashlight and position the mirror so the light is reflected onto several different children.)

In the Bible, Paul, one of Jesus' followers, writes: "You are all children of light and children of the day. Encourage one another and build up each other." God's love is like a bright light shining on us. (Shine the flashlight on the children.) And God wants us to share this love, to let God's love bounce off us and shine on others. We are like mirrors for God's love. When God's love comes to us, we can be mirrors and let God's love bounce off us and shine on others. (Turn on the flashlight again and position the mirror so that light is reflected onto several children.) How can we share God's love? (Help others, care for them, invite them to Sunday school, pray for them are possible responses.)

Prayer: Dear God, help us to be mirrors of your love, letting your love bounce off us onto others every day. Amen.

The Sermon

Living in Confidence

Hymns

Beginning of Worship: "We Praise, You O God"
Sermon Hymn: "Blessed Assurance"
Closing Hymn: "My Life Flows On in Endless Song"

Scripture

1 Thessalonians 5:1–11 (For additional sermon materials on this passage, see the 2005 May/June planning issue of *The Clergy Journal*; for sermon materials on Matthew 25:14–30, see the July/August 2005 issue of *The Clergy Journal*.)

Surely the events of September 11, 2001, have awakened all of us to some of the dangers of this world. We do not know when or where death stalks us. We do know that death is inevitable. But, despite that fact, we need not live in fear. For despite death's intrusion in our lives, we cling to the realization that we are children of light and of the day. We know that our salvation through our Lord Jesus Christ is a certainty. We have nothing to fear.

That does not mean that we should become lazy or complacent in our faith. Paul admonishes us in this first letter to the Thessalonians to be sober, stay awake. We are urged to equip ourselves with a shield of faith and love. Keep the hope of salvation prominent; use it as a helmet. Do this not only for yourself, but for others. "Encourage one another and build up each other," Paul reminds us.

Sometimes death is a blessing. For the one who is terminally ill or the one whose quality of life has been exhausted, death can be a welcome reprieve. But more often than not, death is the enemy – the one who comes unexpectedly, like the thief in the night, and plunders life as we know it. Death usually brings with it great sadness and pain. Death is a time of sadness, a season of grief. And those times are usually different for each one of us. The season of grief may be a short period of time. It may be a year. It may be longer. Grief is like a series of waves that wash the shores of our hearts, then recede, only to reappear. The writer of Ecclesiastes reminds us there is "a time to weep and a time to laugh; a time to mourn and a time to dance" (Ecc 3:4). And so, we weep and mourn.

But as Paul reminded the Thessalonians in the paragraph preceding our text for today, we do not grieve as those who have no hope. Hope is the foundation of our faith. We have been destined not for wrath but for obtaining salvation through our Lord Jesus Christ. That assurance is the bedrock upon which the foundation of all faith rests.

Paul's message to us is threefold. First of all, be prepared. Stay awake. Be ready for death's sudden appearance. In the days before the Protestant Reformation, the church taught that unless one had received the benefits of last rites, that person was believed to be denied access to heaven. While the Reformation changed that teaching, keeping "short accounts" oozes wisdom. Holding grudges, for example, helps no one. Comedian Buddy Hackett is reported to have said, "I don't hold grudges. Know why? Because while you're holding that grudge, the other guy's out dancing!"

We are a forgiven people. As we pray the Lord's Prayer, we seek the Lord's forgiveness to the same degree we are willing to forgive others. Being prepared and ready for death is to keep our heart clean of transgressions. "Create in me a clean heart, O God," the Psalmist prays, "and put a new and right spirit within me" (Ps 51:10).

Second, rest assured that our salvation is in the hands of our Lord Jesus Christ who has prepared the way for us. God has clothed us with the robe of righteousness through Jesus' death on the cross. Jesus has prepared a place for us. So there is no reason to be afraid. Our salvation is not in doubt. Trust God. God has promised to provide us with all that we need. Remember your baptism! God has claimed each of us as God's own. What is more certain than the Word of God? Salvation is not something we have to – or even can – achieve. Salvation is something we receive. A gift.

Finally, be a help to one another. Encourage rather than discourage. Build up one another rather than tear down. The world is full of people who espouse a critical nature. Don't be one of them. Smile frequently, speak well of others, and give compliments in abundance. (Remember that what we sow, we reap.)

Especially, keep today's youth close to your hearts. These are scary times in which to grow up. Danger lurks everywhere it seems. Doubts of many kinds pursue our young people. Fears creep in where certainty should live. What stories can we tell that will help them live more confidently and sleep more peacefully? Violent deaths plague our youth. (The leading causes of death among youth ages 14–24 are first, accidents; second, homicides; third, suicides.) When a young person's life is touched by death, offer a listening ear and a word of comfort to those who are bewildered and in pain.

Are there widows and widowers who are lonely and grieving? Single parents who need a word of encouragement and an offer of assistance? Those who are divorced or separated from a partner? Can you discover those at the edge of poverty's door? What hope can you offer?

Regardless of our worldly circumstances, we live in the confidence that nothing can separate us from the love of God in Christ Jesus (Rom 8:38–39). When death invades our lives, we grieve, but we grieve in hope. And knowing the chaos death can bring, we offer care and condolence to those around us who suffer the pangs of death.

Do not retreat or avoid those ministries. God will equip us to be "little Christs" to those who fear, to those who doubt, to those who live with little or no hope. As children of light and of the day, we can reflect the love of Christ in those whose paths we cross. Go in peace! Serve the Lord!

– Rod Broding

November 20, 2005

Reign of Christ/Christ the King

Lessons

RCL/Luth	Ezek 34:11–26, 20–24	Eph 1:15–23	Mt 25:31–46
Roman Catholic	Ezek 34:11–12, 15–17	1 Cor 15:20–26, 28	Mt 25:31–46
Episcopal	Ezek 34:11–17	1 Cor 15:20–28	Mt 25:31–46

Introduction to the Lessons

Lesson 1

Ezekiel 34:11–16, 20–24 (RCL/Luth);
Ezekiel 34:11–12, 15–17 (RC);
Ezekiel 34:11–17 (Epis)

God's takeover of the flock is in response to the inefficient and corrupt leadership on the part of human shepherds. God's sovereignty reveals a divine right to assume total care for God's flock. The image of shepherd also reveals the relationship of God to God's people.

Lesson 2
(1) Ephesians 1:15–23 (RCL/Luth)

In words of glowing praise, Paul lauds the Ephesians for their faith in God and love for others. Then he encourages them to grow in hope and insight. Paul ends this passage with a succinct but powerful assessment of Jesus as Christ.

(2) 1 Corinthians 15:20–26, 28 (RC);
1 Corinthians 15:20–28 (Epis)

Beginning his assertion of Christ's resurrection from the previous verses, Paul continues that proclamation in a chronological format indicating aspects of the "end times" in specific references. The resurrection of the dead will accompany the triumphal subjugation of Christ's victory over death as well as all things.

Gospel
Matthew 25:31–46 (RCL/RC/Luth/Epis)

This passage offers both a warning and an opportunity. A time of judgment will occur when Christ returns. Mercy will be unavailable. But before that event, a time of opportunity to care for the needy will be ours.

Theme

Lord God, the good shepherd, owns, tends, and protects the people of God.

Thought for the Day

If ever one doubted God's care and concern for God's people, doubt no longer! Count the number of "I wills" in this text. God is the good shepherd.

Call to Worship

One:	I myself will search for my sheep and seek them out.
All:	Thus says the Lord God.
One:	I will rescue the scattered from all places.
All:	Thus says the Lord God.
One:	I will seek the lost and bring back the strayed.
All:	Thus says the Lord God.
One:	I will judge between sheep and sheep.
All:	Thus says the Lord.

Pastoral Prayer

Lord God, you are the great and good shepherd. You tend and nourish your flock. You protect us as a mother hen protects her little chicks. You seek the lost and the strayed. You gather together those who call your name. You bind up the injured and feed your flock with justice.

What are we to say to this? Our refrain is one of praise and thanksgiving. Our recall is one of gratitude and comfort. Our response is to welcome the stranger, visit the sick and the imprisoned, clothe the naked, and feed the hungry and thirsty. Our resolution is to trust your judgment and claim our righteousness through our Lord Jesus Christ. We pray that we are able to hear your voice amidst the noise of our world. Give us the will to follow your voice. Amen.

Prayer of Confession

Lord God, we have strayed from your flock by doing the things that should not have been done and by not doing the things that should have been done. We have ignored the needy. We have trampled on the rights of others. We have stolen the first fruits of the earth for ourselves at the expense of others. We are of a corrupt mind.

But our faith is restored through our hope in you! We ask for your forgiveness, and seek your grace. We plead for mercy, knowing we deserve only your wrath. We trust that our hope is not in vain, for we know you are our good shepherd and in your love you will set aside our transgressions. In the covenant of your love, and in the name of Jesus, we beg your forgiveness. Amen.

Prayer of Dedication of Gifts and Self

Lord God, you have blessed us beyond measure. You have cared for us in every way possible. You have called our names and gathered us to your side. We know who we are and whose we are. And now, in return for your gracious love, we offer our gifts, not only to you, but to the world.

We pledge our concern for your creation. We pledge our care of your people. We pledge our dependence upon your great mercy. We offer ourselves, trusting your goodness. Receive what we humbly offer, and in your power multiply it for the benefit of your kingdom. Teach us to appreciate what is given to us that we might share liberally with others. In the name of our good shepherd, Jesus Christ, we pray. Amen.

Sermon Summary

Shepherding was a difficult and lonely job. Many shepherds of Ezekiel's day were irresponsible. God becomes disgusted with the shepherds of Israel and assumes authority to shepherd the sheep. God's love encompasses all people. We are called to view all people of the world as God's sheep, consisting of one flock.

Hymn of the Day
"Lord of Glory, You Have Bought Us"

There are two ideas in the gospel text that surprise me. The first is how unmeritorious were the deeds the righteous did: they gave food, drink, a welcome, clothing, caring, a visit. The second is Jesus' declaration, "Just as you did it to one of the least of these, you did it to me."

In this hymn, Eliza Alderson captures well this bedrock Christian idea, an idea that obliterates – as Jesus himself did – the false dichotomy between material and spiritual, divine and human: "Wondrous honor you have given, to our humblest charity. In your own mysterious sentence, 'You have done it all to me.'"

Children's Time

Jesus, the King of Love

Preparation: Bring a crown, big fancy necklace, and a chair.
Let's try some riddles today. What's black and white and red all over? (A newspaper.) What has four wheels and flies? (A garbage truck.) Why did the chicken cross the road? (To get to the other side.) Who is the strongest king in the world? (Accept all answers).

(Put on the crown, the necklace, and sit in the chair.) Today we celebrate Christ the King Sunday. But Jesus was a surprising king to the people of his day. What do you think most people looked for in a king? (Highlight responses such as wears a crown and rich robes, lives in a palace, sits on a throne, has an army and many guards, rules over many lands, is rich, is powerful.) Did Jesus sit on a throne? (No. Sit on the floor.) Did Jesus wear rich robes and fancy jewels? (No. Remove the necklace.) Did Jesus wear a fancy crown? (No. Remove crown.) So why do we call Jesus our King? Jesus is the most powerful king in the whole world because Jesus is God's Son. When Jesus lived on earth he didn't use his power to rule others and become wealthy. Jesus used his power to serve others by healing, teaching, preaching, and sharing God's love. Jesus is the king of love.
Prayer: Close by praying the Lord's Prayer, the prayer Jesus taught his disciples to pray.

The Sermon

Thus Says the Lord God

Hymns

Beginning of Worship: "Savior Like a Shepherd Lead Us"
Sermon Hymn: "The King of Love My Shepherd Is"
Closing Hymn: "Go My Children, with My Blessing"

Scripture

Ezekiel 34:11–16, 20–24 (For additional sermon materials on this passage, see the July/August 2005 issue of *The Clergy Journal*; for sermon materials on Matthew 25:31–46, see the 2005 May/June planning issue of *The Clergy Journal*.)

Shepherding was not an easy life. In the first place, the sheep did not usually belong to the shepherd. He was there simply to protect the interests of the owner. The shepherd was just a laborer, a worker. The task was not some mission or vocation. It was just a job, a menial one at that. The pay was poor, and the working conditions were horrendous. It was a dirty job, a 24/7 job that few wanted. The shepherd was expected to care for all the sheep: the sick, the injured, the dumb, the bull-headed. Caring for the sheep demanded that a shepherd sleep lightly, lest some human predator sneak in and steal the sheep or some animal predator sneak in and devour them.

Shepherding was a lonely life. The shepherd would leave family to take the sheep high up into the hills to graze. He had no companion for conversation, no associate to help, no partner for comfort if ill or injured. The shepherd was subject to the weather, enduring heat or cold, wind or rain. Sheep required constant attention so they didn't wander off and become lost. And because sheep are so dumb, they would frequently follow another with little or no regard as to where they were going. Being a shepherd would not rank high on anyone's list of job preferences.

Consequently, most shepherds were not that reliable. After all, what was in it for him? The hard work required of the shepherd brought little gain, little or no recognition – even from the owner. The shepherd's attitude was not likely to be very positive. So what if a few sheep wander off? So what if a few become injured or die? So what if the grazing is poor and the sheep become malnourished? Why should the shepherd care?

The leaders of Israel were shepherds as well. These kings were appointed to care for God's "livestock," the people of Israel, "my sheep" as God called them. But these earthly shepherds cared little for their people, allowing them to be overrun by enemies and scattered throughout the land. These shepherds cared greatly for themselves, dining on scrumptious buffets and ignoring their flock, which had been entrusted to them. They treated their people harshly, impatiently, and with great force. They ignored the sick, the injured, and the impoverished. Israel was a land of ruins.

Enter Ezekiel, the prophet, God's spokesperson. In the passages preceding our text, God condemns these leaders through Ezekiel and reclaims the authority to care for Israel. Speaking for God, Ezekiel says, "You have not strengthened the weak, you have not healed the sick, you have not bound up the injured, you have not brought back the strayed, you have not sought the lost, but with force and harshness you have ruled them" (v. 4). Therefore, says God, because my sheep have become prey and because there were no shepherds, I am against the shepherds, and I will rescue my sheep.

"For thus says the Lord God," our lesson begins, "I myself will search for my sheep" (v. 2). And with that proclamation, God begins a litany of promises of how that care will be initiated and undertaken. God leaves no room for doubt as to intentions. God is no mere "hired hand." In a series of statements that start with "I will" God promises to keep and care for Israel, the people of God – the sheep of God, if you will.

God's love for Israel (as it is for us) is extravagant. The care of God will include seeking and finding the lost. God will bring them all together and gather them into one entity. God will feed them the very best, feeding on rich pastures and pure water. God will bind up the injured and strengthen the weak. God will judge the sheep and feed them with justice. Now, a question arises that we need to explore.

Who are the people of God? Is it only Israel? Is it only the people of the New Covenant, the Christian church? Are the people of Islamic faith also the people of God? Hindus and Buddhists? Atheists and agnostics? Gay and straight? Is God the good shepherd of some particular group of people, or is God the good shepherd of everyone – believers and unbelievers, the doubters and the uncertain?

In John 10, Jesus tells his followers that he is the good shepherd and then goes on to tell them what that means in terms of who are defined as the people of God. "I have other sheep that do not belong to this fold. I must bring them also, and they will listen to my voice" (Jn 10:16).

Does not that proclamation indicate the wide expanse of God's people? I think so. Does not that proclamation also indicate the universal nature of God's people? Again, I think so. We have a very inclusive God, which means that the good news in Jesus Christ is not just for a select few, but for all of humanity. Not just for a select few of like-minded "sheep," but even for those who hear God's voice in a way different from our own. What does that mean to us? It means that we have no exclusive claim as the people of God. It means that we treat everyone as God's chosen ones. It means that we refrain from judging others; rather, we love one another as Jesus loves us.

Based on the conflict and tension that exists in our world (as well as our own human nature), we know that the unity of all is not from us, but from God, the good shepherd, who speaks a word of unity. "I will save my flock, and they will no longer be ravaged" (Ezek 34:22). God, the good shepherd, will gather the scattered, seek the lost, and bring back the strayed. Thus says the Lord God!

– Rod Broding

November 24, 2005

Thanksgiving Day (U.S.)

Lessons

RCL	Deut 8:7–18	2 Cor 9:6–15	Lk 17:11–19
Roman Catholic	Sir 50:22–24	1 Cor 1:3–9	Lk 17:11–19
Episcopal	Deut 8:1–3, 6–10 (17–20)	Jas 1:17–18, 21–27	Mt 6:25–33
Lutheran	Deut 8:7–18	2 Cor 9:6–15	Lk 17:11–19

Introduction to the Lessons

Lesson 1
(1) Deuteronomy 8:7–18 (RCL);
Deuteronomy 8:1–3, 6–10 (17–20) (Epis)

God's people lack nothing for their sustenance because God is lavish in providing for them. Therefore the command to us is twofold. Do not forget the Lord your God, but remember the Lord for the goodness expressed to you. Keep the Lord's commandments.

(2) Sirach 50:22–24 (RC)

A prayer of blessing and thanksgiving for all God has done should include a prayer for deliverance as well.

Lesson 2
(1) 2 Corinthians 9:6–15 (RCL/Luth)

The amounts we reap are determined by the amounts we sow. We choose the amount of our giving, but God loves a cheerful giver, and we will be blessed with righteousness based on our generosity or lack thereof.

(2) 1 Corinthians 1:3–9 (RC)

God's faithfulness manifests itself in spiritual gifts and in strengthening us until the end. God is faithful.

(3) James 1:17–18, 21–27 (Epis)

All our generous acts of giving begin with God and result in our becoming a type of "first fruits." So, rid yourselves of wickedness and be doers of the word, for that will result in blessings. Caring for others will demonstrate the purity of your religion.

Gospel
(1) Luke 17:11–19 (RCL/RC/Lutheran)

Of the ten lepers who were healed, only one, a Samaritan, returned to Jesus to give thanks. Jesus said the leper's faith made him well.

(2) Matthew 6:25–33 (Epis)

Do not be anxious about our lives. God will provide all we need. Seek first the kingdom and righteousness of God, and all else will follow.

Theme

God bestows riches upon us to the extent that we lack nothing. Therefore, it is incumbent upon us to remember God as the giver of our wealth, not ourselves. That remembrance should motivate us to keep God's commandments.

Thought for the Day

We are blessed so that we might be blessings to others.

Call to Worship

One:	God has provided us with good land and a bountiful harvest.
All:	We remember the Lord's goodness.
One:	God has provided and we lack nothing.
All:	We remember the Lord's goodness.
One:	God has provided us with helpful commandments.
All:	We remember the Lord's goodness.
One:	God asks us to remember.
All:	We remember the Lord our God.

Pastoral Prayer

Creator God, from the time of your creation, you have blessed us in abundance. You have made our entire world a garden of plenty. Your desire is to give, and to give lavishly and extravagantly.

Help us to remember you, our creator, who has supplied us with more than we could ever hope for. Help us to care for your creation so we do not squander what you have offered to us. Help us to appreciate your creation so that in its use, we do not destroy that which you have told us to keep and manage. Guide us to make wise decisions in the use of our natural resources. Grant us wisdom so that our vision is not shortsighted. Help us to remember that our world is not so much what we have inherited from our ancestors as it is what we have borrowed from our grandchildren. Send us your Spirit, that we might acknowledge your goodness and serve you in willing obedience. We pray in the name of your Son, Jesus Christ our Lord. Amen.

Prayer of Confession

Gracious God, we confess that we have abused your creation, using more than we need, and not caring how we treat what your hands have made. We have robbed other cultures and generations by taking more than our share. Forgive us. Grant us wisdom and self-control in the use of your creation. Teach us to appreciate what you have given us. Call us to account when we overuse or abuse your world.

O God, we also fail to remember that the world belongs to you. You are author of all that is good. You are the creator. It is you who has supplied us with measure upon measure, cups that overflow. Forgive us. Amen.

Prayer of Dedication of Gifts and Self

God of all creation, you have made us rich in things. Give us hearts of gratitude, that we might return to you your fair share. Give us hearts of generosity, that we might share with others that which belongs to them as well as to us.

God of all creation, you have made us rich in people, giving us a diversity of cultures and values. Teach us to appreciate those who are different from ourselves. Help us to see the richness of other cultures and individuals.

God of all creation, you have loaned us your world. You have blessed us with a number of days. You have provided us with fruitful lands and bountiful harvests. For that we thank you and offer gifts of thanksgiving. And all God's people say, "Amen!"

Sermon Summary

Thanksgiving begins with an attitude of thankfulness for all things. Thanksgiving continues as we remember God's generosity to us. Finally, thanksgiving culminates in our behaviors that demonstrate a concern for our earth and a love for one another.

Hymn of the Day
"God of the Sparrow, God of the Whale"

There are a number of hymns appropriate to Thanksgiving Day. Some favorites of mine since childhood are: Pierpoint's "For the Beauty of the Earth"; Alford's "Come, You Thankful People, Come"; Rinkhart's "Nun Danket Alle Gott."

A new alternative to consider is Jaroslav Vajda's "God of the Sparrow, God of the Whale," set to a tune by Carl Schalk. Through the soft text and gentle melody, we are invited to consider a wide variety of things to be thankful for. I particularly appreciate mention of the natural world, the care of which the twenty-first-century church must further encourage.

Children's Time

Giving Thanks

Preparation: Bring in a bag of popped popcorn and small paper cups. What do you like about popcorn? The way it sounds when it's popping? The smell? The taste? Does anyone know who first discovered how to make popcorn? (Native Americans.) (Give each child a small cup of popcorn to eat.)

On the first Thanksgiving in 1621 – hundreds of years ago – the Pilgrims enjoyed a treat of popcorn with maple syrup prepared by the Wampanoag Indians. The Pilgrims and the Indians gathered together to celebrate the gift of a good harvest. They feasted on turkey, squash, corn, berries, apples, beans, bread, and popcorn.

Today we celebrate Thanksgiving as a time to give thanks to God for the wonderful friends and foods God has given us. We gather with family and friends, just like the Pilgrims and Indians did hundreds of years ago.

How many of you eat popcorn on Thanksgiving? What is your favorite Thanksgiving food? (Accept answers and share yours.) Who eats Thanksgiving dinner with you?

Prayer: Dear God, thank you for blessing us with many kinds of loving people and all kinds of tasty foods. Amen.

The Sermon

Remember!

Hymns

Beginning of Worship: "Earth and All Stars"
Sermon Hymn: "I Was There to Hear Your Borning Cry"
Closing Hymn: "Lord, Dismiss Us with Your Blessing"

Scripture

Deuteronomy 8:7–18 (For additional sermon materials on this passage, see the 2005 May/June planning issue and the 2005 July/August 2005 issue of *The Clergy Journal*.)

Our government has deemed it appropriate to set aside a day of Thanksgiving, making it a national holiday. Thanksgiving, however, is not a holiday of the church year. Thanksgiving for Christians is not a one-day event, but a continual prayer and way of life.

Thanksgiving begins with a state of mind, an attitude. If someone were to ask us, "What are you thankful for?" our first thoughts would probably center on the physical aspects of our lives. We are thankful for our possessions: our homes, vehicles, family heirlooms, our toys. Then, realizing how transient these items are, we shift our thankfulness to nontangible things for which we are grateful: our health, security, freedoms, faith, prosperity, our ability to earn a living. Then, at some point we begin to think about the people in our lives: our families, friends, teachers, colleagues, and associates. We remember those who have served us in times of need: medical and emergency personnel, soldiers, pastors, and teachers. We remember those who have served us as mentors and counselors.

And, perhaps finally, we remember God. Ah, yes, God. God, from whom all this goodness comes. God, who created the heavens and the earth. God, who fills the lands and oceans with food in abundance. God, who led the people of the past and continues to lead us today into lands of plenty, "where you may eat bread without scarcity, where you will lack nothing" (Deut 8:9).

We remember God who has helped us realize that we do not live by bread alone, but are nourished by a faith in our creator. Nourished by a faith that is, itself, a gift from our creator. Nourished by a faith that reminds us not to worry about our lives; what we should eat or what we should drink; what we should wear or how long we shall live.

We are nourished not by bread alone, but by a faith that teaches us to seek the kingdom of God and God's righteousness before seeking anything else. We remember a God who has called us by name; who has made us children of God in baptism; who has called us to God's table to eat and drink of God's forgiveness.

We remember our God who has given us the commandments by which we can live our lives in harmony with God and in peace with one another. Our weakness and disobedience have prevailed, and we transgress those commandments. We remember our God who loved us so deeply and completely that God's own son, Jesus Christ, was sent to die for us, thereby blotting out our sins and restoring us to a relationship with God. We remember as well (though we'd prefer to forget) not only our sins, but also our sinful nature.

Despite our tendency to forget, we remember our God whose promise of eternal life far exceeds the shortness of days we have on this earth. We remember the promise of a life where we will sup with angels and enjoy a feast that defies our comprehension. As we experience death among us, we remember the uncertainty of this life, and we remember with confidence our favor with God.

We remember that we have not achieved our status, power, and wealth by our own doing, but rather through the love and grace of God. Sometimes we fool ourselves, thinking we have made wise investments of our time and wealth without remembering the Lord our God. But we remember also the rich fool who instigated Jesus' warning that a person's life does not consist in the abundance of one's possessions, but rather in remembering the One who provides all abundance.

Our remembrance is a wonderful blessing to us, for it takes our eyes off creation and directs our vision to our creator. Our wealth and power, our prosperity and health, our friends and family, our fresh air and clean water – all are gifts of our creator. Our faith – another gift!

So, now, the question becomes, "What does it mean to be thankful? How does thankfulness exhibit itself?" First of all, it is to remember God who is the author and provider of all our blessings. Remember God in thanks and praise. Remember God, and do so often! Second, it means to be thankful for what we have received as well as what is promised to be.

Finally, that thankfulness leads to action. We take obvious and deliberate steps to care for the earth. We support legislation that reflects that value. We support political candidates who espouse a concern for our environment. We use our resources wisely and conservatively. We reuse and recycle. We do not waste. We care for others. We take action to support the poor and the needy. We care for the "least of these" in the name of Christ. We do not pretend to cure the world of all ills, but pledge to care to the extent of our skills, abilities, and resources.

We remember that once we were a people without God. Once we were no more than wanderers. Once we were required to live by a law we could not uphold. But now as God's people, we live by the words of Jesus to "love one another as I have loved you." Now we live under a new covenant, sowing bountifully seeds of love. Now we are cheerful givers. In the words of Paul, we "will be enriched in every way for your great generosity, which will produce thanksgiving to God through us; for the rendering of this ministry not only supplies the needs of the saints but also overflows with many thanksgivings to God" (2 Cor 9:11–12). Now, that's worth remembering!

– Rod Broding

November 27, 2005

1st Sunday in Advent

Lessons

RCL	Isa 64:1–9	1 Cor 1:3–9	Mk 13:24–37
Roman Catholic	Isa 63:16–17, 19; 64:2–7	1 Cor 1:3–9	Mk 13:33–37
Episcopal	Isa 64:1–9a	1 Cor 1:1–9	Mk 13:(24–32) 33–37

Introduction to the Lessons

Lesson 1

Isaiah 64:1–9a (RCL/Epis); Isaiah 63:16–17, 19; 64:2–7 (RC)
Israel's prayer for God's intervention can be summarized as a prayer of desperation, as well as a call to wait for God's action. An affirming and confident trust in the power of God, expressed in strong language, yields to a prayer of confession regarding Israel's sinful ways. The final verses reaffirm Israel's dependence upon God and include an appeal for mercy.

Lesson 2

1 Corinthians 1:3–9 (RCL/RC); 1 Corinthians 1:1–9 (Epis)
Paul's salutation is a subtle indication to the Corinthians of their divided church. Nevertheless, Paul's appreciation of the congregation reminds them of the many spiritual gifts they possess. Their assurance of salvation is due to the faithfulness of God expressed in fellowship with Jesus Christ.

Gospel

Mark 13:24–37 (RCL);
Mark 13:33–37 (RC);
Mark 13:(24–32) 33–37 (Epis)
Stay awake! Signs of the end times will be apparent. Yet despite those signs, no one but God the Father knows at what point this cataclysmic event will take place. Just be ready!

Theme

Your spiritual gifts abound as you await the Second Coming of Christ.

Thought for the Day

God's grace and peace – blessings to you from God – reveal themselves in spiritual gifts, which will strengthen you until of the day of our Lord Jesus Christ.

Call to Worship

One: We await the day of our Lord's coming.
All: God is faithful.
One: We ask for strength and endurance in waiting.
All: God is faithful.
One: We give thanks for spiritual gifts.
All: God is faithful.
One: Grace to you and peace, from God our Father and the Lord Jesus Christ.
All: God is faithful.

Pastoral Prayer

O God, our hope rests in you. We praise your name and give you thanks for your reassuring word of the coming of our Lord Jesus Christ. Lord, in your mercy,
All: hear our prayer.
We wait in hope. Strengthen our resolve that we might not weaken in our faith. Lord, in your mercy,
All: hear our prayer.
We acknowledge with thanks your gifts to your church. Teach us to use them wisely for the benefit of all. Lord, in your mercy,
All: hear our prayer.
From your blessing of grace and peace, give us a unity of spirit, that your church may speak with one voice; that we may proclaim the day of our Lord Jesus Christ. Lord, in your mercy,
All: hear our prayer.

Prayer of Confession

Heavenly Father, we find it difficult to wait for anything. We are an impatient people. Give us the patience and perseverance to accept your timing rather than our own.

Lord Jesus Christ, you demonstrated an abundance of spiritual gifts and have made them ours as well. Often we do not recognize them. Often we do not know how to use them for your glory. Give us your wisdom.

Holy Spirit, you came to be our comforter and advocate. Sometimes we ignore you, relying instead on ourselves. Give us a faith that depends on your guidance and direction through this life. We pray in the name of Christ. Amen.

Prayer of Dedication of Gifts and Self

Graceful God, giver of peace, bestower of gifts: we know that you are the author of all that is good. We know that you have made us your people. We know that you have endowed us with spiritual gifts. We know that you are faithful. Because of the many blessings you have showered upon us, we are moved to respond with gifts of love. We offer ourselves to you in gifts of time, treasury, and talents. Receive our offerings as our gifts to you, that you might use them to further your kingdom. In your almighty name, we pray. Amen.

Sermon Summary

We are a people of grace and peace, a people richly endowed with spiritual gifts, a people strengthened to the end of this time. We claim our name as God's children through God's faithfulness.

Hymn of the Day
"The King Shall Come"

This Sunday is one when both preacher and musician should be of one mind by deciding whether the theme is the coming of Christmas or the Second Coming of Christ. The calendar virtually insists that it be about the former, while the biblical texts endorse the latter.

John Brownlie's "The King Shall Come," set to Davisson's CONSO-LATION, speaks unambiguously of the Second Coming, and does so in vigorous, thrilling terms: "The King shall come when morning dawns, and light and beauty brings; Hail, Christ the Lord! Your people pray: Come quickly, King of kings."

Children's Time

A Season of Waiting

Preparation: Light the first candle on the Advent wreath and plan to gather near it. Bring a kitchen timer or alarm clock and a large calendar.

(After the children have gathered, set the timer or alarm clock to go off in one minute.) While we're waiting for the timer to ring, let's name some other things that we wait for. (A bus, a friend to come over to play, a birthday, a wedding, and a vacation are some possible responses.) How do you feel when you wait? (Eager, nervous, excited, happy.) Sometimes we only wait a short time. And sometimes we have to wait longer. (Turn off the timer when it rings.)

Today we are beginning a season of waiting in the church year. It's called Advent. Advent means "coming." During Advent we wait for Christ to come. We prepare for Jesus' birthday. The Advent season runs through the four Sundays before Christmas. (Show the children the actual dates on the calendar.) During Advent we dress the church in blue (or purple). Look at all the blues (or purples) in our sanctuary today.

We also light candles on an Advent wreath as we wait for Christ's birthday. The four candles on the outer ring mark the four Sundays of waiting. What shape is the wreath? (A circle.) Does a circle have a begin-ning or an ending? (No.) The circle reminds us of God's never-ending love.

Prayer: Dear God, be with us as we prepare for the birth of your Son, Jesus. During this time of waiting, help us to find ways to make this a joyful season for all people. Amen.

The Sermon

Grace and Peace to You

Hymns
Beginning of Worship: "My Hope Is Built on Nothing Less"
Sermon Hymn: "God of Grace and God of Glory"
Closing Hymn: "I, the Lord of Sea and Sky"

Scripture
1 Corinthians 1:3–9 (For additional sermon materials on this passage, see the July/August 2005 issue of *The Clergy Journal*; for sermon materials on Mark 13:24–37, see the 2005 planning issue of *The Clergy Journal*.)

On a small strip of land (only four miles across) in the southern end of Greece stood the city of Corinth. Originally built by the Greeks, the city was destroyed by the Romans. The devastation was so severe that the city was reduced to a desolate heap of ruins. During the reign of Julius Caesar, Corinth was rebuilt by the Romans and used as a "dumping ground" for its undesirable citizens.

In the second of Paul's missionary journeys, he stopped in Corinth and stayed there for a year and a half. (The account of that stay is summarized in Acts 18:1–17.) Paul's missionary journey to this area is the first one of which we have a record. In his previous journey, Paul's mission had been to both Jews and Gentiles. Much of his emphasis had been that of contrasting life under the law with life under the grace of the new covenant. With the diversity of cultures in Corinth, this was a logical place for an extensive missionary stop.

Paul's ministry appears to be among the lower echelon of society (1 Cor 1:26–31). While Paul names a few people who were prosperous, the majority of his converts seemed to be common, ordinary folk. In this city of debauchery, in this city of perverted values, in this city of divisiveness, Paul established a small congregation. With such differing values and behaviors inherent in the city, it is no wonder that the early Christian church in Corinth experienced considerable conflict and division.

Later, when Paul journeyed from Corinth to Ephesus, he learned of the turmoil and trouble in the Corinthian congregation and began a series of letters to them. In 1 Corinthians 5:9 Paul refers to an earlier letter. Scholars differ as to the existence or location of this letter. Some believe it can be found 2 Corinthians 6:14–7:1. Others contend that the letter has been incorporated within the two Corinthian letters we now have. Still others believe it has been lost entirely.

As the news came to Paul of dissension within the Corinthian congregation, Paul initiates his series of correspondences. Paul begins this letter with an assertion of his discipleship in order to claim his authority and then directs his comments to a select, yet wide range of believers "to those who are sanctified in Christ Jesus, called to be saints, together with all those who in every place call on the name of our Lord Jesus Christ, both their Lord and ours" (1 Cor 1:2).

Having made this declaration, Paul is ready to address the congregation at Corinth. "Grace to you and peace from God our Father and the Lord Jesus Christ" (v. 3).

"Grace to you." Grace because these were a people who knew little of grace. These were a people who had lived by the law. Either the law of God or the law of leaders, employers, despots, and kings. They needed to be reminded that they were now a people of grace.

And peace – "peace from God our Father and the Lord Jesus Christ." Just as the Christians in Corinth had not known much grace, neither had these people known much peace. Political unrest and societal turmoil had obliterated any sense of peace for these Corinthians. Paul's obvious intent is cast in this subtle, but powerful greeting. Calling this strife-ridden congregation a people of peace defies the reality of their existence. In a self-fulfilling prophecy, Paul names them as people of grace and a people of peace.

Paul commends them, "because of the grace of God that has been given you in Christ Jesus" (v. 4). Paul is careful to remind them that the grace they can claim is a gift from God, exhibited in the person of Jesus whom Paul names as "Christ Jesus." Such wording is surely intentional.

Paul reminds them of how they have been enriched in Christ Jesus, enriched "in speech and knowledge of every kind" (v. 5). Enriched, in fact, with spiritual gifts and enriched to the point where they were not lacking in any spiritual gift. Can we imagine the depth and power of such a blessing to these previous "down and outers"? Can we own this same blessing and identify ourselves as people who do not lack any spiritual gift? Can we claim our status as a people of grace and peace who wait expectantly for Christ to come again? As people who will be strengthened to the end and found blameless on the day of our Lord Jesus Christ?

The people of that tiny, volatile congregation in the midst of that wicked city could lay claim to all that Paul said. And so can the people of this congregation! "Grace to you and peace from God our Father and the Lord Jesus Christ" is God's greeting to us. Not because of our wonderful qualities and pleasant personalities, but because we have been the recipients of God's grace. We have been enriched and endowed with numerous spiritual gifts, not because of our own diligence and intelligence, but through the powers of the Holy Spirit. We are ones who have been strengthened in faith, not of our own doing, but by the grace of God.

For it is God who is faithful! It is God who has called us into "the fellowship of his Son, Jesus Christ our Lord" (v. 9). It is God who has claimed us as God's people and blessed us with grace and peace. For that, we thank God, and, like Paul, we give thanks always for one another. Amen.

– Rod Broding

December 4, 2005

2nd Sunday in Advent

Lessons

RCL	Isa 40:1–11	2 Pet 3:8–15a	Mk 1:1–8
Roman Catholic	Isa 40:1–5, 9–11	2 Pet 3:8–14	Mk 1:1–8
Episcopal	Isa 40:1–11	2 Pet 3:8–15a, 18	Mk 1:1–8

Introduction to the Lessons

Lesson 1
Isaiah 40:1–11 (RCL/Epis); Isaiah 40:1–5, 9–11 (RC)

This reading from Isaiah's prophecy begins what is sometimes called "The Servant Song." In this section, the great and mighty God of Israel's history uses power to serve. God comes to the people and meets their needs just as a shepherd holds lambs lovingly.

Lesson 2
2 Peter 3:8–15a (RCL);
2 Peter 3:8–14 (RC);
2 Peter 3:8–15a, 18 (Epis)

The writer of 2 Peter balances two seemingly contradictory topics: the imminent return of the Lord to redeem the faithful, and the patience that the faithful must demonstrate as they wait. The writer stresses that God will come at just the right time.

Gospel
Mark 1:1–8 (RCL/RC/Epis)

Mark's gospel begins in a rush of words and the urgency of John the Baptizer's preaching. This section is "the beginning of the good news of Jesus Christ, the Son of God," and John stresses that a new baptism of the Holy Spirit will release a rush of renewal.

Theme

As we wait patiently for God's presence and power, we are reminded that God's power is all about timing.

Thought for the Day

The great teacher and disciple Andrew Murray observed, "If we are faithful a day at a time, the long years will take care of themselves."

Call to Worship

One:	Comfort, comfort ye, my people.
All:	We find comfort in the midst of daily struggle.
One:	Comfort, comfort ye, my people.
All:	We find comfort in the promise of daily blessing.
One:	Comfort, comfort ye, my people.
All:	We find comfort in the grace of daily service.
One:	Comfort, comfort ye, my people.
All:	We find comfort in God's perfect timing.
One:	Comfort, comfort ye, my people.
All:	We find comfort in the gospel of Jesus Christ, the Son of God.

Pastoral Prayer

Almighty God, we rejoice in your power, which you extend in grace, and your might, which you use to bless and sustain those in need. We thank you for your perfect timing in our lives, and in this world. Increase in us patience and anticipation, as we bring to you our needs and the needs of others.

We pray for our national and international leaders, for patience and forbearance as they handle matters of vital importance to world peace. We pray for this church, for the patience and discernment of perfect timing to accomplish your will and work in ministry. We pray for those in special need, those known to us and those unknown to us, and pray for sustenance for them. We ask these things in the name of our Servant Savior, Jesus the Christ. Amen.

Prayer of Confession

Loving God, we come before you today with the burden of sin as we fall short of your call and commission in our lives. We confess to you the impatience of our lives: the impulses causing us to do those things we ought not to do, and to fail at those things we ought to do. We confess the impertinence that causes us to think and say those things that hurt others and rupture relationships. We confess the impiousness that causes us to turn away from you and exalt ourselves.

We pray for your forgiveness to fill our lives with peace and renewal. We pray for patience for your will to be done, for perspective to strengthen relationships, and for your holiness to fill every part of our lives. Release your healing grace in our lives every day. Draw us nearer to you, through Jesus Christ our Savior. Amen.

Prayer of Dedication of Gifts and Self

Bounteous God, you provide us with all we need to accomplish your will. Thank you for pouring your grace into our lives on a daily basis to sustain us and empower us. Thank you for giving us patience to seek out your blessings with diligence and to await your blessings with anticipation. We come before you today to share of ourselves – our souls, our bodies, our money, and our material things. Consecrate these things for your use in your good time. As we share who we are and what we have, continue to bless us and to release us to encourage others and, through grace, to enable them to share in your goodness. We ask this through Jesus Christ, who gave his all to you and for you, and who gave himself for us. Amen.

Sermon Summary

In an "instant" world, we struggle with impatience that causes us to say things and to take action at the wrong time. The Lord works things out in perfect timing and calls us to wait patiently for God's will to be done.

Hymn of the Day
"On Jordan's Bank the Baptist's Cry"

This is another Sunday where thematic clarity on the part of clergy and musicians will help focus the worship experience. Again, the choice is between the biblical context of John announcing the beginning of Jesus' ministry and the calendar context of the coming of Christmas.

This hymn is one of Charles Coffin's more than 100 Latin hymns. One needs look no farther to see that traditional church music "rocks" with the best of "contemporary"; Praetorius' tune makes Coffin's text dance, bringing to life the Voice in the Wilderness.

Children's Time

Decorating with Evergreens

Preparation: Bring in a fresh evergreen branch.
How are you getting ready for Christmas in your home? (Accept responses.) One way we will get ready in the church and at home is by decorating with evergreens. What is an evergreen? (A pine tree.) What do the leaves of an evergreen look like? (Green needles.) Do evergreens drop their leaves in the fall? (No.) Evergreens stay green through all seasons – spring, summer, autumn, and winter. They remind us that God's love is with us in all seasons.

(Bend some pine needles. Invite the children to smell their fragrance.) This wonderful pine fragrance reminds us of Christmas preparations. Christmas trees fill rooms with this fresh smell. The smell of pine, scented candles, and Christmas cookies baking are some smells that remind us that Jesus' birthday is coming.

Prayer: Dear God, thank you for the wonderful smells of Advent. Remind us that Christmas trees, bright lights, and joyful music are all ways that we prepare for the birth of your Son, Jesus Christ. Amen.

The Sermon

The Power of Patience, the Miracle of Timing

Hymns
Beginning of Worship: "Hark! A Thrilling Voice Is Sounding"
Sermon Hymn: "The Lord Will Come and Not Be Slow"
Closing Hymn: "O God, Our Help in Ages Past"

Scripture

2 Peter 3:8–15a (For sermon materials on Mark 1:1–8, see the 2005 May/June planning issue of *The Clergy Journal*; for sermon materials on Isaiah 40:1–11, see the September 2005 issue of *The Clergy Journal*.)

We live in an instant world. All of us feel the pressures, but also enjoy the pleasures, of the instant and the immediate. Some of us can remember when the world was not instant. When you ordered something, it came in a couple of weeks, which was pretty good time. Dinner took hours to cook. Restaurants served promptly, but not fast. Time was measured in hours.

Many of us can remember the arrival of "instant coffee" in the 1960s and fast food service in the 1970s. We started to expect that answers to our questions would come more quickly, and services would be delivered more promptly. The microwave arrived, and dinner was ready in minutes. Restaurants turned out lunches in two minutes or less. Time was measured in minutes.

In the 1990s, with the arrival of personal computers and the explosion of the Internet, we began to measure time in seconds. Through computing and Internet access, we get what we need in the virtual world in seconds. News networks bring information immediately from everywhere on the globe, 24 hours a day. Culturally, we promote "instant gratification." When we want something, we expect our wants to be fulfilled right now.

While technology has changed our expectations about time, we find that relationships do not work in seconds. Love and compassion are not achieved in an instant. The same thing is true in our walk with God. From our side, building an intimate relationship with God takes time, probably a lifetime. We have to confront our unhappiness when God does not answer our requests or fulfill our needs (at least as we understand them) immediately.

The prayer of the modern American is, "Dear God, grant me patience. And I want it right now!" Perhaps it always has been a part of human nature to be impatient with the passage of time. It was so in the early church. Jesus had died, risen from the dead, and ascended into the presence of God. The persistent promise that people in the early church heard was that Jesus was coming again in power and great triumph to judge the living and the dead, and to claim his people for all eternity.

The letter of 2 Peter addresses the impatience that people expressed when Jesus had not yet come again. Years had passed, the believers still toiled and struggled and faced persecution, and the promise of Christ still had not been fulfilled. To that end, this letter tells readers and hearers, "But do not ignore this one fact, beloved, that with the Lord one day is like a thousand years, and a thousand years are like one day" (3:8).

At the same time, God can intervene faster than we can imagine – and this letter claims "But the day of the Lord will come like a thief in the night" (v. 10). The coming of the Lord will be sudden and amazing.

While we may work hard and efficiently, and strive for instant results by getting all of the right pieces into place, we cannot control how and when God works. God is in charge of timing. We may pray diligently and want instant answers, but God will provide them in God's own time and God's own way. God will come when the time is right, and that likely will not be on the schedule we have created.

In the mid-twentieth century, the great evangelical teacher A. W. Tozer said, "The faith of Christ offers no buttons to push for quick service. The new order must wait the Lord's own time, and that is too much for the man in a hurry. He just gives up and becomes interested in something else." That is the temptation we face: when God does not work on our schedule, we may become interested in something else. We may try to take the responsibility for trying to make things happen right now. We have limited power to make anything holy or right happen in our time, or in our way, or to our preferences. This is a hard lesson to learn, and one that we must learn early in life.

A child was working with a parent to put up a swing set in the backyard of the house. Since the instructions came in pictures, the child started to put some of the pieces together, and the parent helped. As the child worked with the tools, the pieces did not fit together too well, and the child worked harder and harder and with greater and greater frustration to make things fit. And the child wanted to do the work quickly so that the swingset could be used right away. It was then that the parent uttered words that the child never forgot: "Don't force it!"

This is an ongoing lesson in life. We can help things to move along, we can receive answers to questions, we can obtain the information we need, and we can enjoy all that life has to offer. The parent's words must ring in our ears, though: Don't force it. We have to learn patience to wait for God to move in life, and we have to develop spiritual depth to discern God's perfect timing.

In this Advent season, we can learn a lot about God's timing in our lives. Just as the believers in the early church had to learn new lessons about Christ's coming, so we also have this same lesson to learn today. We need to trust that God will bring about the best results in the perfect moment.

Some of us have Advent calendars – the kind that have little doors and flaps that open for each of the days leading up to Christmas. Most of us find it hard to open one day at a time to see what is behind that specific door or flap. We long to open all the flaps or go to the last window, Christmas Day, to see the end of the season. God's timing is such that we have to learn the spiritual discipline of opening the doors of our lives one day at a time to discern God's perfect plan for us. In this season, let us move away from the human "instant" and focus on the divine "eternal," and find peace and joy as we wait with patience.

– John R. Throop

December 11, 2005

3rd Sunday in Advent

Lessons

RCL	Isa 61:1–4, 8–11	1 Thess 5:16–24	Jn 1:6–8, 19–28
Roman Catholic	Isa 61:1–2, 10–11	1 Thess 5:16–24	Jn 1:6–8, 19–28
Episcopal	Isa 65:17–25	1 Thess 5:(12–15) 16–28	Jn 1:6–8, 19–28
			or Jn 3:23-30

Introduction to the Lessons

Lesson 1
(1) Isaiah 61:1–4, 8–11 (RCL); Isaiah 61:1–2, 10–11 (RC)

In this section, sometimes called Reconciliation and Renewal, Isaiah proclaims God's peace and restoration of post-exilic Israel. God's people will dwell in peace and show God's blessing to surrounding nations and peoples.

(2) Isaiah 65:17–25 (Epis)

In this section, sometimes called Reconciliation and Renewal, Isaiah proclaims God's peace and restoration of post-exilic Israel, not only as a renewed nation, but the beginning of a new creation.

Lesson 2
1 Thessalonians 5:16–24 (RCL/RC);
1 Thessalonians 5:(12–15) 16–28 (Epis)

Paul stresses to the Thessalonians that they must give thanks and rejoice in all circumstances, demonstrating Paul's experiences in prison – in the midst of adversity there is blessing and peace.

Gospel
John 1:6–8, 19–28 (RCL/RC/Epis)

In this section of John's gospel, John the Baptizer tells listeners that he is not the one whom they seek. The one who is to come will be greater than anyone or anything they can imagine.

Theme

We proclaim the gospel in the power of peace.

Thought for the Day

Our words and our lives proclaim the true nature of God in the world. Just as John the Baptizer proclaimed, we bring the gospel with power – the power of peace.

Call to Worship

One: Who is the One whom we seek?

All: The One who will come to restore us and renew us in the midst of joy and despair.

One: Who is the One whom we seek?

All: The One who will come to help us rejoice and give thanks in all circumstances.

One: Who is the One whom we seek?

All: The One whose sandals we are not worthy to untie.

One: Who is the One whom we seek?

All: Jesus Christ, who will restore, heal, and unite us in the midst of God's glory.

Pastoral Prayer

God of grace and God of glory, you reach into our lives and into the very heart of this world to bring peace and restoration into places of conflict and brokenness. Thank you for releasing your healing grace into the world even now, making human lives whole and the heavens and the earth new.

This day, reach into the hearts and minds of those who are gathered, and those who are absent, to comfort and strengthen all who draw near you. We bring before you today those in our congregation who struggle in body and spirit, and pray for your renewing Spirit to be in their midst. We pray for our international, national, and local leaders, that they will turn to you for wisdom when making difficult choices. We pray that, through Jesus Christ our Savior, we will find wholeness and holiness. Amen.

Prayer of Confession

Renewing and restoring God, we come today confessing our sense of separation from you, from those who surround us, and from the world that you have made. While we strive and struggle with the ability and the authority we may have, we confess that we fail when we rely on our strength and our knowledge alone.

We turn to you this day, seeking your forgiveness and longing for the renewal and restoration that you have promised through apostles and prophets, and through the very work of Jesus Christ our Redeemer. Send your Spirit to mend and amend our lives so that we may be released into the world to bring your message of renewal and restoration to a hurting world, knowing that, in spite of our willfulness, your will is done on earth as in heaven. We ask for this healing grace in Jesus' name. Amen.

Prayer of Dedication of Gifts and Self

God of abundant grace and boundless love, we come before you today with all that we are and all that we have, so that we may help to accomplish your will and further your blessing in our broken and needy world. Transform our souls and bodies by your grace, so that we can be released to proclaim the gospel of peace. Do wondrous things with these tangible and intangible gifts we now present before you. Strengthen us to bring restoration and renewal to all whose lives we touch – providing for their needs and drawing them nearer to you. Throughout each day, help us to see your hand at work as you draw near. Amen.

Sermon Summary

John the Baptizer proclaimed the certain coming of Christ in holiness and peace. We each have unique and dynamic proclamations to make as God's children, and our aim is for people to see through us to find Christ. We proclaim not just in word, but also in deed.

Hymn of the Day
"Blessed Be the God of Israel"

Even more than Mark's introduction of John the Baptist last week, today's gospel seems to turn on the question of identity. Is John the Messiah?

Elijah? A prophet? None of these, the Baptist says. Instead, he is the voice in the wilderness, the one preparing the way.

"Blessed Be the God of Israel," a hymn by Michael Perry set to the music of Hal Hopson, is a good choice for today. The second verse answers the identity question the gospel writer thought so significant; what's more, like the Baptist himself, the hymn's text points to the One whose sandals John claimed to be unworthy of untying.

Children's Time

John the Baptist

Preparation: Bring in "gummy worms" candy to share.

Did you know that God sent someone long ago to help people get ready for Jesus' coming? His name was John the Baptist. John the Baptist was a wild and crazy guy. He lived in the desert wilderness. He wore clothes made of camel skin with a leather belt tied around his waist. John ate wild honey and locusts. Locusts are like grasshoppers. John ate bugs. How many of you have eaten a bug?

John the Baptist's message was this: Prepare the way for the Lord. John told people to prepare by sharing what they had with people who were hungry or who needed clothes. John's message is for us, too. One way we can prepare the way for Jesus is by sharing what we have with others – our time, our food, and our money.

I'm going to share some worms with you. (Give each child a gummy worm.) Yes, you may eat these worms. Whenever you make Christmas cookies or other treats this month, why not share a plate with a neighbor or give some food to the food bank? This is one way to share your Advent joy.

Prayer: Dear God, thank you for our many blessings. Help us share our joy, our time, and our things with others during this time of Advent. Amen.

The Sermon

Proclaiming the Peace of God in Person

Hymns
Beginning of Worship: On Jordan's Bank the Baptist's Cry
Sermon Hymn: Rise Up, Ye Saints of God
Closing Hymn: Watchman, Tell Us of the Night

Scripture
John 1:6–8, 19–28 (For additional sermon materials on this passage, see the September 2005 issue of *The Clergy Journal*; for sermon materials on 1 Thessalonians 5:16–24, see the 2005 May/June planning issue of *The Clergy Journal*.)

Most of us don't like people who are "windbags." These people simply speak and speak until they run out of air. Then they inhale and speak and speak some more. Perhaps you know a windbag. No one here this morning, of course, is a windbag, but if you were, you would tell us at length about what a windbag is and what a windbag does. Some windbags hold forth on matters they know little about, some have wrong information to tell, and some have prejudices that skew their point of view.

There are religious windbags, and they may be the worst kind. They may speak at length and with great authority about sin and righteousness, about the Bible and its contents, and about the will of God for other people's lives or for this world. People can deflate such windbags by asking them how perfectly they live out the will of God, or how they deal with people in need, or if they themselves are free from sin. Their actions may speak louder than their words, and others may find their religious pronouncements offensive and damaging.

All of us have the potential of being windbags. The challenge is to be able to proclaim the will and purpose of God – to call people to return to God. We may find a challenge to proclaim peace and justice to people who like their own great idea of peace and justice – which often means a world filled with winners and losers.

John the Baptizer faced this challenge as he came forth from the wilderness to proclaim the coming of the Messiah into the world. He spoke directly and dynamically to reach his hearers. Many who listened to John had had dealings with religious leaders who were windbags. John was clear and to the point: the Messiah will be in your midst. Be ready for him. He claims for himself the words of the prophet Isaiah: "I am the voice of one crying out in the wilderness, 'Make straight the way of the Lord.'"

John was clear that he had a responsibility to proclaim God's will, and also that he was only the mouthpiece for what God wanted to declare to the people. We have the same role as John in our families, our neighborhoods, our social networks, and our workplaces. We, like John, need to be able to cultivate a sense of humility as we proclaim the coming of the Lord. John Calvin, the great leader of the Reformation in the city of Geneva, said long ago, "God deigns to consecrate to himself the mouths and tongues of men in order that his voice may resound in them." As God did with John, so God wants to work through us so that God's voice may resound in us.

Like John, we are proclaimers. We think about proclaiming mostly through the use of the words. But if we really consider what John Calvin said, we have to ask ourselves honestly whether God's voice truly resounds in us, or whether we offer only a hollow echo because our actions speak louder than our words. Or as Ralph Waldo Emerson said in a quote familiar to us, "What you do speaks so loudly that I cannot hear what you say." God's voice may resound in what we say. Does God's voice also resound in our actions? Do others hear God's word in what we do?

Sometimes being a proclaimer means not saying or doing anything, but being quiet and listening to the world. We need to let the voices we hear reverberate through us to call people to account for oppression, violence, or neglect. We are called, to give voice to those who are oppressed and to those who struggle, so that they, too, can find peace and strength in the living God.

French theologian Jacques Ellul observed so eloquently, "Until we have struggled to the utmost limits of our strength, and known the despair of defeat; until we have really understood the actual plight of our contemporaries, when we have heard their cry of anguish; until we have shared their suffering, both physical and spiritual, and their despair and desolation; then we shall be able to proclaim the Word of God – but not till then!"

So perhaps that is the point of all proclamation. We need to speak God's word to bring people perspective and to help them come to terms with what God wants from them. But our actions testify even more clearly to the truthfulness and power of God's word. In the consistency of word and action, God's purpose becomes real.

John the Baptizer is clear about who he is in relation to who God is. What he does is consistent with God's word. In the end, John is a great mentor and a great example of God's coming into the world with an important word. How many of us can say of ourselves, with all humility and all honesty, that we are mentors to others who seek a deeper knowledge of God?

Perhaps that is what God really wants from us. God wants us to proclaim by being mentors to others. Those who are learning and growing seek out mentors to help them know what choices to make and what skills to develop. A mentor is one who helps us become more real and to grow more transparent, so that what we say and what we do are in sync.

So perhaps the best evangelism and the best ministry is to serve as a mentor to others. How is God calling you to mentor those around you? Do you need a mentor to guide you and to reflect with you? Maybe this is the best opportunity we have to be the proclaimers of peace that God wants us to be. In word and deed, we can demonstrate the peace of authentic well-being in sync with a living and a loving God.

Think about mentoring this way. These words came from a banner hanging in a church Sunday school room: "You may be the only Bible that some people ever read." May they read and understand, and find peace as you have found it and proclaim it in Jesus Christ. No longer are you a windbag then. You are, instead, a gentle breeze of the Spirit.

– John R. Throop

December 18, 2005

4th Sunday in Advent

Lessons

RCL	2 Sam 7:1–11, 16	Rom 16:25–27	Lk 1:26–38
Roman Catholic	2 Sam 7:1–5, 8–12, 14, 16	Rom 16:25–27	Lk 1:26–38
Episcopal	2 Sam 7:4, 8–16	Rom 16:25–27	Lk 1:26–38

Introduction to the Lessons

Lesson 1
2 Samuel 7:1–11, 16 (RCL);
2 Samuel 7:1–5, 8–12, 14, 16 (RC);
2 Samuel 7:4, 8–16 (Epis)

At last, King David ruled over a secure, peaceful kingdom. He lived in a beautiful palace, and was troubled that the Lord lived in a tabernacle in tents. Nathan the prophet tells David to go forward in building a temple, but then hears God saying that David's successor will build the Lord's house.

Lesson 2
Romans 16:25–27 (RCL/RC/Epis)

At the end of his letter to the Romans, Paul blesses the community of faith and prays that they may be strengthened by his proclamation of the gospel. Paul celebrates Jesus Christ's coming into the world. The Gentiles must hear this good news also.

Gospel
Luke 1:26–38 (RCL/RC/Epis)

Through an angel, God announces to Mary that she will conceive a child, the very Son of God, by the Holy Spirit. Mary wrestles with the announcement and the call, but the angel declares an essential message of Scripture: with God, nothing is impossible.

Theme

We are called to be prophetic in every season.

Thought for the Day

When we speak of God's work in the world, we are being prophetic. We confront the active or passive claims that God does not exist, and declare God's loving reality.

Call to Worship

One: God meets us in the power of the gospel.
All: In the gospel, we find hope.
One: God moves us by the power of the gospel.
All: God moves us to bring hope into a despairing world.
One: God sends us to proclaim the gospel.
All: God sends us to friends and strangers to proclaim reconciling love.
One: God reveals love and grace in the gospel.
All: God gives us opportunities to reveal divine love to others.
One: God calls us to obedience in the gospel.
All: We are joyfully obedient as we call others into God's love.

Pastoral Prayer

O God, in this Advent season, you reveal again your coming into the world. In this busy time, thank you for being right here with us. Thank you for revealing yourself afresh in the midst of our distractions. Give us attentive hearts and spirits to discern your presence in our midst. We pray for those suffering or struggling in mind, body, or spirit, and for those who may feel that you are far away. Reveal yourself to them, that they may know your love. Strengthen us to be fully present with them in their time of need, as effective ministers of your grace and mercy. In the holy name of the Savior who is coming, even Jesus Christ. Amen.

Prayer of Confession

Gracious God, we know that you are here with us, but too often we fail to see, hear, or feel your presence because of the many distractions and demands of the holiday season. We confess our weariness and our anxiety, our worries and fears.

We know, gracious God, that in our busyness, we do stumble and fall. We find ourselves hurting and in distress. We come before you now confessing our faults and all the ways we fall short of your call to us. Embolden our hearts to seek a change in our lives – a surrender to your loving will and to your perfect purposes for us. As we seek renewed life and love, empower us to bring your reconciling love to those who are hurting and far from you. We ask this in Jesus' name. Amen.

Prayer of Dedication of Gifts and Self

Gracious and generous God, we thank you that we are strengthened daily through the grace of Jesus Christ in the power of the Holy Spirit. Continue to bless us with all that we need tangibly and spiritually so that, through our stewardship of your good gifts, we may further your purpose as obedient and faithful servants. Receive these gifts of time and treasure from our hands and from our hearts. Use these gifts to bless others and to help make possible what seems impossible, locally and globally. Especially in this season, we pray for an outpouring of abundant giving to those in greatest need, and for opportunities as individuals and as a church to serve others. We pray these things in the name of Jesus Christ, your Divine Gift. Amen.

Sermon Summary

The Bible presents a great deal of prophecy about the coming of Christ, and the results of his coming. We, too, are called to be prophetic, and to present the gospel of Jesus Christ in word and in deed – to be "practically prophetic" on a daily basis.

Hymn of the Day
"The Angel Gabriel from Heaven Came"

In Luke's familiar birth narrative, church musicians receive the blessing of being able to program some of the best-loved sacred music ever written – and also the responsibility of honoring tradition while creating it.

An excellent choice is "The Angel Gabriel from Heaven Came," a Basque carol paraphrased by Sabine Baring-Gould. Summarizing Luke's touching story of the Annunciation, the text also foreshadows the miraculous birth to come. A piece that underscores Mary's role in salvation history is M. D. Ridge's "I Sing a Maid," set to a Celtic melody harmonized by Michael Joncas.

Children's Time

Meet Jesus' Family

Preparation: Bring the Mary, Joseph, and angel figures from a nativity scene. One way we can get ready for Christmas is by learning about Jesus' family. Who was Jesus' mother? (Mary. Pass around the figure of Mary.) Mary was a young woman when she found out she would be the mother of God's son, Jesus. How did Mary find out she would be Jesus' mother? (An angel told her. Pass around the angel figure.) Angels are God's messengers. One day an angel named Gabriel visited Mary. The angel told Mary that she would be the mother of God's son. And that she would name her baby Jesus.

Jesus had a father on earth who cared for him. What was his name? (Joseph. Pass around the figure of Joseph.) In a dream, God sent an angel to Joseph, too. The angel told Joseph that Mary would have a baby boy and he was to name the baby Jesus. The angel said that Jesus was God's son and that Jesus means Emmanuel, or God with us. Joseph told Mary all about his message from the angel. Then they waited for the birth of this wonderful gift from God.

Prayer: Dear God, thank you for Mary and Joseph who took care of baby Jesus. Thank you for everyone who takes care for us. Amen.

The Sermon

Practically Prophetic: Our Lives as Servant Leaders

Hymns
Beginning of Worship:	"Blest Be the King Whose Coming"
Sermon Hymn:	"O Come, O Come Emmanuel"
Closing Hymn:	"Come, Thou Long-Expected Jesus"

Scripture

Romans 16:25–27 (For sermon materials on 2 Samuel 7:1–11, 16, see the 2005 May/June planning issue of *The Clergy Journal*; for sermon materials on Luke 1:26–38, see the September 2005 issue of *The Clergy Journal*.)

Have you met any prophets lately? They are pretty hard to find here at the start of the twenty-first century in North America and Europe, in the church or in the larger culture. Prophets do not work well in a tolerant society. They cause too much anger and division. Speaking prophetically can put any person out of favor with the dominant culture, whether it is religious or secular.

Who are the prophets today? We do not know. Prophets are out of favor and out of style. But culture bashers or religious bashers are in style. These people attack certain specific practices or belief systems. But they typically do not challenge the facts or argue against a point of view using sacred texts. Instead, they attack other people.

Prophets and prophetic ministry are rare in the West because all ideas have equal footing. So perhaps we need to speak prophetically and act prophetically, but serve in another capacity – just as the apostle Paul did.

We hear today a short passage from the end of Paul's letter to the Romans. Paul wrote part of the letter as theology and part of the letter as practical advice for people living in Rome, the center of power and authority at that time in the ancient world. This passage is a summary of all that he has said. It's also a commission to the Roman Christians to reach out to the world around them and build the church.

Paul's message is powerful and practical. First, Paul shows that God strengthens us according to his gospel and the proclamation of Jesus Christ. Notice that Paul was not abstract in his words. Paul did not say that God strengthens people according to the gospel, but his gospel. Certainly, the gospel truth was rooted deeply in all that Paul said about God's work in Jesus Christ by the power of the Holy Spirit. But it was his gospel in the sense that he spoke out of his own life and own example to convict unbelievers and to support believers. Paul's words were prophetic because they called people to account.

Can others say that about you and about me? Would we be able to say that people respond to our gospel? Note that our gospel is not a narrow reflection of your point of view or my point of view. It is the gospel that has come alive in us through words and deeds. We all can declare the same essential truths. But each of us has a different set of examples and a different approach to living out the gospel. Whatever we say and whatever we do, we must proclaim clearly that Christ is alive and active in the world even now.

But to whom do we speak and with whom do we share? Paul shows us that the gospel proclamation is now for the Gentiles to receive. He says, that the gospel "is now disclosed, and through the prophetic writing is made known to all the Gentiles" (v. 25). What does that mean in our day? It means that we need to present the gospel to those who do not know Jesus Christ and who are unaware of God's love for them in Christ.

Most of us who are involved in a church have friends who also are involved in a church or who share our interest in spirituality and faith. As vaudeville performers used to say, "It's great to play to a friendly house!" One of the outcomes of taking faith seriously is that we surround ourselves with friends who are of like mind and, often, like faith. It is difficult to surround ourselves with friends who are what Paul would define as Gentiles – people who are not connected with a church and who know little if anything about God in Christ. While we may have coworkers who fit that description, we probably do not spend much time in deep conversation with them.

So it is a choice to become involved with the Gentiles of our time and, through word and deed and in a gentle and compassionate way, proclaim the gospel of Jesus Christ. One time when this kind of approach may work is around Christmas, for people are looking for some other reason for the season than spending a lot of money and dealing with crowds and traffic. People are coming to grips with greed in themselves and in their families and friends. They may be asking about their purpose and direction in life. Are we ready to proclaim a living and loving gospel of Jesus Christ to these Gentiles?

Finally, Paul says that proclamation brings about obedience of faith. We not only are trying to invite others to belief. Through proclamation we also are honing our own obedience to the call of Christ. Through our own proclamation we find greater clarity in what we believe, greater depth in our prayer life, greater conviction of the injustices that surround us, and a greater call to confront those injustices. We have a greater anticipation of Jesus Christ at work in the world in new and wonderful ways. In short, our own obedience is made more complete.

As retired pastor and Regent College theologian Eugene Peterson has written in *A Long Obedience in the Same Direction*, we are on the move as Christians. At each stage of our journey, we strive to demonstrate obedience though the road can be long and arduous. Just like the ancient Hebrews, we move forward to Jerusalem proclaiming God's love and singing of God's glory all along the way. And God can strengthen us in that daily journey so that we move forward "in the conscious and continuous effort that develops into maturity in Christ."

In our own forward movement, we must be "practically prophetic" just as Paul was. We must invite people to respond to our gospel just as Paul invited people to respond to his. In the end people respond to the gospel through us. We are the prophets who can make the gospel come alive today and bring people into the knowledge and love of Jesus Christ.

– John R. Throop

December 24, 2005

Christmas Eve

Lessons

RCL	Isa 9:2–7	Titus 2:11–14	Lk 2:1–14 (15–20)
Roman Catholic	Isa 9:1–6	Titus 2:11–14	Lk 2:1–14
Episcopal	Isa 9:2–4, 6–7	Titus 2:11–14	Lk 2:1–14 (15–20)

Introduction to the Lessons

Lesson 1
Isaiah 9:2–7 (RCL);
Isaiah 9:1–6 (RC);
Isaiah 9:2–4, 6–7 (Epis)

Isaiah continues to prophesy regarding the birth of Israel's savior. Isaiah describes the impact of this savior – one who brings light, hope, release from bondage, and loving authority and direction. Isaiah emphasizes permanence in the change this child will bring into the world.

Lesson 2
Titus 2:11–14 (RCL/RC/Epis)

In this pastoral epistle, we hear of the perfect timing of "the appearance" of God's grace in the coming of Jesus Christ into the world. Jesus' appearance on earth had an impact then, as well as an eternal and positive consequence for humankind.

Gospel
Luke 2:1–14 (15–20) (RCL/Epis); Luke 2:1–14 (RC)

Luke's gospel places the birth of Jesus Christ into the context of human history. He describes the angelic announcement of Christ's birth to the shepherds, the outcasts of that time. They are the first to see Jesus. This reflects Luke's point of view that God sent Jesus to outcasts first.

Theme
God's work in the world makes a difference for all eternity.

Thought for the Day
Billy Graham said, "Bethlehem's manger crib became the link that bound a lost world to a loving God." God worked this miracle 2,000 years ago, and it still happens today.

Call to Worship

One: We gather this night to celebrate the Savior's birth.

All: O come, all ye faithful!

One: We gather as the holy family gathered in Bethlehem.

All: O come, all ye faithful!

One: We gather as the shepherds came from the fields, keeping watch over their flocks by night.

All: O come, all ye faithful!

One: We gather to celebrate as faithful Christian saints have done for centuries.

All: O come, all ye faithful!

One: We gather with people around the world to worship the newborn King.

All: O come, all ye faithful!

Pastoral Prayer
Almighty God, we praise you this night for entering into the world that you have made so that you can draw us near to you. We give thanks that, as you have come in great humility in the baby Jesus in the manger, you also have made him to be the Messiah, the Christ, for the salvation of the world. Thank you for love and grace in the birth of Christ. This night we bring before you the hopes and fears of the entire world, especially for those places and people in conflict. In this holy season we pray for families, churches, and communities suffering division and pain. Hear our prayer for those who are ill or in need; provide for them. We pray all of these things in the name of Jesus Christ our newborn King. Amen.

Prayer of Confession

Loving God, on this holy night we have gathered to express once again our wonder and our joy at the birth of your Son, Jesus Christ. You have sent him to bring healing and peace into our midst. That healing and that peace are available to us again on this Christmas Eve. We confess that we are not deserving of the gifts of Jesus Christ, and that there is nothing we can do to achieve them. We confess those things both large and small in life that keep us from sharing in the grace of Christ. On this holy night we bring open hearts and open minds to receive the grace and forgiveness that you give us through Jesus Christ. We pledge to amend our lives and turn once again to Christ the newborn King, in whose holy name we pray. Amen.

Prayer of Dedication of Gifts and Self

Loving God, we thank you for providing for our every spiritual need in the birth of Jesus Christ the Savior. We thank you for the gift of salvation that you have brought to us through his birth, life, death, and resurrection. Your gifts lead us to provide and support the ministry of salvation and reconciliation through Christ's presence. We bring before you this night our offerings of time, talent, and treasure. May the celebration of Jesus' birth empower in us a renewed desire to share the gifts that we have been given so that we may glorify you and advance your Kingdom. We ask these things in the name of our newborn King, Jesus Christ. Amen.

Sermon Summary

At Christmas, God comes into the world in amazing ways in Jesus Christ – through a powerful light that enlightens our paths to God; a profound joy that changes our attitudes and fills our lives; and through the newborn King's authority to shape human history. God continues to do so today.

Hymn of the Day
"The Hills Are Bare at Bethlehem"

In my home congregation this worship service is the year's most special. Strings and brass sound before the service; choirs bring out their best; hundreds of people – friends old and new – fill the sanctuary with carols.

Here are several picks to enrich your Christmas Eve: "'Twas in the Moon of Wintertime," by J. E. Middleton, to a French melody; "The Hills Are Bare at Bethlehem," a quietly hopeful hymn by Royce Scherf to a tune by W. Walker; and Haugen's "Holy Child within the Manger," accompanied by guitar.

Children's Time

The Journey to Bethlehem

Preparation: On a low table, set up the stable, empty manger, and animals from a nativity scene. Bring Mary, Joseph, and the donkey with you.

Tonight our Christmas story begins in Nazareth, the home of Mary and Joseph. (Hold up Mary and Joseph figures.) Mary and Joseph had been preparing for the birth of Jesus for months. It was almost time for the baby to be born.

Then came an order from the King: all people had to return to their hometowns to be counted in the King's census. Joseph's hometown was in Bethlehem. So Joseph tenderly placed Mary on a donkey, because she could not walk all the way from Nazareth to Bethlehem. And they set out for Bethlehem. (Move donkey, Mary, and Joseph figures slowly toward the stable.)

Eventually, Mary and Joseph arrived in Bethlehem. The town was crowded with people. The innkeeper said, "No room!" Then the innkeeper saw that Mary was going to have a baby. "You may stay in my stable for the night." So Joseph led the donkey carrying Mary into the stable. He prepared a bed for her in the hay. (Move the figures into the stable.)

I think everyone knows what happened next. But we'll have to wait until tomorrow to finish the story!

Prayer: Dear God, thank you for keeping your promises. We look forward to celebrating Jesus' birth. Amen.

The Sermon

What in the World Is God Doing?

Hymns

Beginning of Worship: "O Come, All Ye Faithful"
Sermon Hymn: "What Child Is This"
Closing Hymn: "Silent Night, Holy Night"

Scripture

Isaiah 9:2–7 (For sermon materials on Luke 1:1–14 (15–20), see the 2005 May/June planning issue of *The Clergy Journal*; for sermon materials on Titus 2:11–14, see the September 2005 issue of *The Clergy Journal*.)

One of the amazing assertions about Christmas is that God took human form and came into the world. If you had been a faithful Jew at the time of Jesus' birth, the idea would have been inconceivable. You would have been asking, "What in the world is God doing?"

After all, the last time that God actually came into the world was, according to Genesis, when he walked through the Garden of Eden in the cool of the evening. Certainly God spoke to the earliest figures of the Hebrew Scriptures – people like Abraham, Jacob, and Moses. God also made pronouncements and proclamations through angels and prophets. These words assured God's people that God really was there and was mindful of their life situation.

But that dark and cold night in Bethlehem over 2,000 years ago, God once again came into the world in human form and flesh, in the person of Jesus. The evangelist Billy Graham once said, "Bethlehem's manger crib became the link that bound a lost world to a loving God."

When we hear the words of the prophet Isaiah this night, we hear how the people of Israel were walking in darkness. Have you had occasion to walk in darkness? We're surrounded by what is known as ambient light in most of the United States. The lights that come on at night in cities and towns put out a glow that is hard to escape.

But perhaps some of you have walked in darkness, without artificial light or natural light like the moon. It's easy to lose one's way and become disoriented. It's easy to stumble even on familiar paths. One may even find it hard to take another step, not knowing where it may lead. The people of Israel experienced this kind of physical darkness at night.

Isaiah, however, understood the people's darkness in a spiritual sense. They had lost their way. They were unable to move forward spiritually and they stumbled in sin and alienation from God and one another too easily. So, Isaiah prophesies that God will come into the world.

What did Isaiah stress as he spoke the prophetic word? First, he said that God comes into the world in a powerful light that enlightens our paths to God. "The people who walked in darkness have seen a great light," he proclaims. "Those who lived in a land of deep darkness – on them has light shined" (Isa 9:2). What does this mean? It means that God comes as a light-bearer. Human enlightenment will not be enough to see the very presence of God in the world.

Sometimes we do not want light in our lives. We are afraid that we will be revealed for who we really are. Once an important person came to a home and the family welcomed that visitor. "What a wonderful house," the visitor declared. "May I see more of it?"

"Of course," said the wife, "please come in and let us show you the family room." It was comfortable and well-used, but tidy.

"Very nice," replied the mysterious visitor.

"Now come and see the kitchen," said the husband, who showed off the appliances and the countertops – again, well-used but relatively clean. The visitor nodded approval.

The family took the visitor to the bedrooms, where there was a bit more clutter, but a real sense of warmth. The bathroom – well, it needed some work, but it, too, met with the visitor's approval.

"So, do you like our home?" the family members asked with a sense of hope.

"Oh, yes I do," said the visitor. "But there is one more place I want to see: your basement."

A horrified look came over the faces of the family members. "Uh, gee," the husband stammered, "could you come back another time? We need to do some work there to get it into shape."

"No, I shall see it today," the visitor declared as he made his way to the basement stairs. He flipped the light switch and the entire basement became illuminated – revealing clutter and grime and piles of papers and all kinds of things of which the family was ashamed. "Now," said the mysterious visitor, "I shall help you get this part of your house in shape, too."

So it was with Isaiah's prophecy. The people had been walking in darkness, and now a light shone on them, not to reveal shame but to bring about healing. And so it is as God comes into the world this Christmas – God brings light and healing into our lives. This is the great and wonderful gift that God brings in Jesus Christ.

Isaiah also prophesies another amazing change that God fulfilled on that Bethlehem night at the stable: God inspires a profound joy that changes our attitudes and fills our lives. Isaiah says, "You have multiplied the nation, you have increased its joy; they rejoice before you as with joy at the harvest, as people exult when dividing plunder" (v. 3). Maybe the parallel of the typical plunder under the Christmas tree is not a good analogy, but you can bet that in most households, as the gifts are opened, there is joy and love and gratitude. So it was in Isaiah's time, and so it is in ours.

Joy is not a plentiful commodity. Someone once said, "I have not been able to find joy in life. Nor have I found happiness. So I guess I'll work at being cheerful!" That's not what God has come into the world to do – to bring about a lot of cheer. No, God has come into the world in Jesus Christ to bring a profound sense of joy – a deep and abiding sense of contentment mixed with excitement. Only through faith in Jesus Christ, God in the world, can we find real and permanent joy.

Finally, Isaiah proclaims another result of God's promised coming into the world. God demonstrates the newborn King's authority and releases God's reign of justice, love, and peace. Isaiah proclaims, "For a child has been born for us, a son given to us; authority rests upon his shoulders" (v. 6). Jesus uses this authority to bring justice, righteousness, and "endless peace." God chose this way to enter our world – not in power or triumph, but in simplicity and vulnerability.

So this night we celebrate God coming into the world. God came into the world in a moment of history, at just the right time, and fulfilled all that Isaiah said centuries earlier. And God comes into your world and mine this night as we celebrate Christmas. I pray that you will know the light of Christ, the joy of salvation, and the compassionate authority that God brings into our lives through Jesus.

– John R. Throop

December 25, 2005

Christmas Day

Lessons

RCL	Isa 52:7–10	Heb 1:1–4 (5–12)	Jn 1:1–14
Roman Catholic	Isa 52:7–10	Heb 1:1–6	Jn 1:1–18
			or 1:5, 9-14
Episcopal	Isa 52:7–10	Heb 1:1–12	Jn 1:1–14

Introduction to the Lessons

Lesson 1

Isaiah 52:7–10 (RCL/RC/Epis)

This section of Isaiah's prophecy calls Israel to anticipate and expect those who bring the good news that God has returned to Zion. God promises that, in due time, all will see and know salvation.

Lesson 2

Hebrews 1:1–4 (5–12) (RCL);
Hebrews 1:1–6 (RC);
Hebrews 1:1–12 (Epis)

The writer of Hebrews introduces his communication to fellow Jews by stressing that, in the coming of Jesus into the world, God fulfilled the prophetic promises. Jesus is God's Son, revealing God's very nature and being. Jesus Christ has the fullness of divine authority.

Gospel

John 1:1–14 (RCL/Epis); John 1:1–18 (RC)

John's gospel begins by establishing the divine nature of Jesus who came into the world. Jesus possesses the fullness of God's being. Jesus reveals God's nature and proclaims God's call.

Theme

As God gives us the gift of Jesus Christ, so we give this gift to all.

Thought for the Day

Evangelist George Truett said, "Christ was born in the first century, yet He belongs to all centuries. He was born a Jew, yet He belongs to all races. He was born in Bethlehem, yet He belongs to all countries."

Call to Worship

One: We worship today with a joy that fills our hearts;
All: The good news is that Christ is born.
One: We worship today with a longing that fills our lives;
All: The good news is that Christ is born.
One: We worship today with a hope that heightens our
expectations;
All: The good news is that Christ is born.
One: We worship today with a love that transcends all time;
All: The good news is that Christ is born.

Pastoral Prayer

Almighty God, today we celebrate how, at one point in time, you came into this world to redeem it for all time. Today we celebrate how, in one person in time, you came into the world to reconcile all persons to you. We thank you that in your son, Jesus Christ, we behold your love and grace.

We pray for all members of our congregation, that we may grow as witnesses of your love to those around us. Lead us to those who feel separated from you and one another, that we may draw them back to the newborn King. Be with those who are ill or infirm, and deliver to them your gift of healing. We pray these things in the name of Jesus Christ, the newborn Savior. Amen.

Prayer of Confession

Gracious and loving God, you sent Jesus Christ to take our nature upon him. He knew the joys and the struggles of being human, yet he did not sin. In his life, death, and resurrection, Jesus demonstrated the extent to which you are willing to go to draw us back to you. Our forgiveness was born in Jesus' cradle that first Christmas Day. Help us to know that the sins we confess and also those we fail to recognize will be swept away in the all–surpassing love of Jesus Christ, our newborn Savior. Amend our lives so that we can be faithful servants, extending your love to a broken world. We ask these things through our newborn King, Jesus Christ. Amen.

Prayer of Dedication of Gifts and Self

Generous and loving God, we come with gratitude for the gift of life and love that you have bestowed upon us in Jesus Christ. Give us a deeper sense of your purpose for our lives in the gifts you have given us. As you have come in humility through Jesus Christ, so may we with humble hearts and open minds bring your gifts of love and life to those who surround us. We pray this in the name of the newborn King, Jesus Christ. Amen.

Sermon Summary

We have been given a great gift in Christ's coming – the very presence of God in the world. We have gifts to share at Christmas and through-out the year: the gift of good news; the gift of a clear path to God; and the gift of salvation for all eternity.

Hymn of the Day
"See Amid the Winter's Snow"

Whereas Luke's gospel reports the sights and sounds of Jesus' birth, John's prologue gives a theological appraisal of the event. Jesus is the light of the world – indeed, its very life – which came into the world, was rejected, and yet gives all "grace upon grace."

A fitting hymn is Edward Caswall's "See Amid the Winter's Snow," set to music by John Goss, a nineteenth-century English composer noted for his sacred vocal works. Because both hymn and tune are in the public domain, a simple search will turn up a copy for congregational use. Another seldom sung gem is "Of the Father's Love Begotten."

Children's Time

The Christ Child Is Born!

Preparation: Set up the nativity scene like you did for Christmas Eve. Have all figures present, except baby Jesus. Place this figure nearby. Plan for the church musician to play the first verse of "Away in a Manger." What day is today? Let's go into the congregation and wish everyone a "Merry Christmas." (Spend a few moments doing this.) Now let's gather around the scene of the first Christmas. (Gather at the nativity scene.) Oh, no. Someone is missing. Who is it? (Baby Jesus.) Here's baby Jesus. Let's place him in the manger. What is a manger? (A feeding box for animals.) Why was Jesus' first bed a manger? (There was no room in the inn, so he was born in a stable.)

When Jesus was born, the angels sang a beautiful song to thank and praise God. They sang, "Glory to God in the highest and peace to all the earth." We also can sing a song to thank and praise God for sending baby Jesus. (Sing "Away in a Manger" with the children and the congregation.)
Prayer: Dear God, thank you for sending Jesus to earth, the very best Christmas gift of all. Amen.

The Sermon

The Real Gifts at Christmas

Hymns
Beginning of Worship: "Joy to the World"
Sermon Hymn: "Good Christian Friends, Rejoice"
Closing Hymn: "Hark! The Herald Angels Sing"

Scripture
Isaiah 52:7–10 (For sermon material on John 1:1–14, see the 2005 May/June planning issue of *The Clergy Journal*; for sermon materials on Hebrews 1:1–4 (5–12), see the September 2005 issue of *The Clergy Journal*.)

Here's a question you'll probably hear around school or the office in the coming week: "What did you get for Christmas?" Sometimes a wise person will say, "I had my family around me and we were able to have some fun together – the best gift I ever could receive." Most people, however, will start a list of goods like toys, clothes, electronics, jewelry, or DVDs.

Some people think that Christmas is all about receiving gifts. Certainly the advertisers and retailers are excited by that prospect. We live in such a materialistic culture that one measure of love and care in a relationship is whether others give us what we want.

We move to more of an emotional or spiritual level when we talk about the opportunity to give gifts to others. As we hand brightly-wrapped presents to those we love, we communicate our love to them and that we have done our best to think about what would fill a need they have or bring them joy.

In the midst of the secular celebration in our society, we need to pause and remember that Christmas is about receiving the ultimate gift. We have been given the ultimate gift in Jesus' birth – the very presence of God coming into the world. John begins his gospel by declaring that, even before creation, God intends to come into the world and to be among us in the most complete and intimate way – in our souls and in our spirits.

Centuries before the fulfillment of God's intention and promise in Jesus, Isaiah prophesied that God would come among us in this way. Isaiah's proclamation brought hope to the people of Israel when they really needed it. The greatest gift they could receive was the good news that God really was among them and would bring healing.

There is a lot packed into this brief four-verse reading from Isaiah, much that we can take into our lives in the coming year and for the rest of our days. We have gifts to share at Christmas and throughout the year. Isaiah shows us that the gifts we have address the most profound universal spiritual needs that we have as human beings.

What gifts does Isaiah tell us that we are able to share with those around us? First, we have the gift of good news. He proclaims, "How beautiful upon the mountains are the feet of the messenger who announces peace, who brings good news, who announces salvation, who says to Zion, 'Your God reigns'" (Isa 52:7). In those days, the people of Israel would welcome this message, because it seemed like other forces were in control of their destiny. They found great comfort in the message that God was bringing peace into their lives.

In those days, a messenger deployed by the king spoke with tremendous authority and hurried to share the message. You and I are the messengers today. We have good news to share with others because of the gift of Christ at Christmas. But do we have a sense of urgency to share this good news with those we know and with those who are not known to us? Christmas offers a wonderful opportunity to share stories of personal faith with others and to give them a gift of hope. Faith is one of the greatest gifts we can share.

Isaiah shows us that, with the child born to us, we also have the gift of a clear path to God. Isaiah says that the sentinels guarding the city lift up their voices in joy, "for in plain sight they see the return of the Lord to Zion" (v. 8). Sentinels then were like the guards that we see around buildings now. Sentinels could tell if invading armies were coming, and then warn the city and mobilize the defenders. They could see if tradespeople were coming with their wares to sell. Isaiah declares that the sentinels would cry out with good news to the people: the Lord is returning! As God comes to the people, God shows them the path to greater life and to heaven itself. One of the great gifts of Christmas is that God gives us, in Jesus, a clear path to God.

Finally the coming of God in the world in Jesus Christ bestows on us the gift of salvation for all eternity. As Isaiah proclaims, the Lord has bared his holy arm in front of all. In human terms, those words suggest an attack out of hostility or revenge. But God's holy arm reaches out to the lost and the brokenhearted with love and compassion. Isaiah says, "all the ends of the earth shall see the salvation of our God" (v. 10). This is the greatest gift that God gives in Jesus Christ: God becomes human to save us from ourselves. Some will welcome this good news and others will be apathetic. Some will reject the gift. But this longed-for gift of salvation is before us now.

So how shall we respond to all these Christmas gifts? We can rejoice at the gifts we receive in this holiday season, and express our gratitude for the thoughtfulness of others. Most importantly, though, we can express our profound joy at God's gift to us of Jesus Christ, the Son of God. We will discover that we spend our lives – and all of eternity – unwrapping and sharing this ultimate Christmas gift.

– John R. Throop

January 1, 2006

1st Sunday after Christmas

Lessons

RCL	Isa 61:10–62:3	Gal 4:4–7	Lk 2:22–40
Roman Catholic	Sir 3:2–6, 12–14	Col 3:12–21	Lk 2:22–40
			or 2:22, 39–40
Episcopal (BCP)	Isa 61:10–62:3	Gal 3:23–25; 4:4–7	Jn 1:1–18

Introduction to the Lessons

Lesson 1
(1) Isaiah 61:10–62:3 (RCL/Epis)

After the exile, the people of Israel take on renewed position with their God. The prophet uses the language of weddings and royalty to remind the people that they will have a new status in the world.

(2) Sirach 3:2–6, 12–14 (RC)

This reading is essentially an explication of the commandment, "Honor your father and your mother."

Lesson 2
(1) Galatians 3:23–25; 4:4–7 (Epis)

The longer Episcopal reading, including the three verses from the third chapter sets up the juxtaposition of our slavery under the law with the subsequent section (3:26–4:7) in which Paul declares that we are children of God through the sending of a son.

(2) Colossians 3:12–21 (RC)

So many gifts; so many responsibilities. While the writer lists many of God's gifts to us – above all, love – so the writer admonishes God's people to use the gifts accordingly, including wives, husbands, and children.

Gospel
(1) Luke 2:22–40 (RCL/RC)
Jesus' birth is acclaimed by shepherds and angels, by parents and animals. Shortly into his life, Jesus is acclaimed by the devout Simeon and the prophet, Anna. Five times in these verses we read of the "child" – one who is blessed by God.

(2) John 1:1–18 (Epis)
This is the first day of a new year. John reports the new thing that God has done in the "Word become flesh." As we move toward the season of light, the Light of the world has come to shatter the darkness.

Theme
Israel was looking for restoration to prominence. But would restoration come in the way they had hoped or expected?

Thought for the Day
While continuing in the Christmas season, the world celebrates this day as the start to a new year. Israel was looking for a new start in the Lord. Is there a new start today for you?

Call to Worship

One: O my God, do not take me away at the mid-point of my life,

All: You whose years endure throughout all generations.

One: Long ago you laid the foundation of the earth,

All: And the heavens are the work of your hands.

One: They will perish, but you endure.

All: They will all wear out like a garment;

One: You change them like clothing, and they pass away;

All: But you are the same, and your years have no end.

One: The children of your servants shall live secure;

All: Their offspring shall be established in your presence.

– Based on Psalm 102:24–28

Pastoral Prayer

Eternal God, you have set us in your creation, and you bless us with your love through the events of our lives. In this new year, open our hearts and minds to know your presence and see your love at work. Give us faith and grace to live in the light of your Son, Jesus Christ our Lord, our source of joy forever. Amen.

Prayer of Confession

Merciful God, a year has past; a new year beckons. We recognize our failures over the past 12 months. Even in the past days we have indulged ourselves in ways that do not bring honor to you or physical or spiritual health to ourselves. For some it is an excess of goods at Christmas. For some it is an excess of food or drink. For some it is a willful disregard for sharing the many goods and gifts that we have. In the joy of celebrating a baby born in a manger, we celebrate also the forgiveness offered through that baby's life, death, and resurrection. Bring us newness of life in this year and always. Amen.

Prayer of Dedication of Gifts and Self

O God of ages past, God of the present, and God of years to come, we ask you to help us use this coming year in ways that bring honor to you and all people to faith in your Son. We look out over 365 days of possibility. We anticipate opportunities to give of our time, our talent, and our financial resources. Make this a year of growth for us, both as individuals and as a congregation, that we may serve those who are the least of our brothers and sisters. Bless our offerings of this day, that they may be only a foretaste of what we will offer to you. In Jesus we pray. Amen.

Sermon Summary

Sometimes things don't appear very positive for God's people, even as they were not positive upon their return from exile. God sometimes can vindicate the people in ways that they don't expect, even decades or hundreds of years in the future. It is without doubt that God's children will be restored. Will it necessarily be in this kingdom?

Hymn of the Day
"Break Forth, O Beauteous Heavenly Light"

Simeon's song is typically set as a piece of service music that conveys a sense of closure. This approach, however, does not yield a satisfying hymn of the day on the only Sunday of this Christmas season.

Instead, I keyed off Simeon calling Jesus a "light" in order to select "Break Forth, O Beauteous Heavenly Light." In this hymn, Johann Rist portrays the news of Jesus' birth as the first brilliant flicker of a life and ministry that still shines upon and beyond us to eternity. A rousing contemporary choice for hymn of the day is Marty Haugen's "Arise, Shine."

Children's Time

The Shepherds Rejoice

Preparation: Bring small candy canes, enough for each child to have two. Merry Christmas! (Encourage the children to return your greeting.) Did you know that the church celebrates Christmas for 12 days?

After Baby Jesus was born, who first heard the message of Jesus' birth? (The shepherds.) On the night of Jesus' birth, shepherds were watching their sheep on the hillsides around Bethlehem. Suddenly the sky was filled with a light so bright that the shepherds were scared to death. The bright light was an angel. "Do not be afraid; for I am bringing you good news of great joy for all the people; to you is born this day in the city of David a Savior, who is the Messiah, the Lord."

I bet Mary was surprised when a group of shepherds ran into the stable to see baby Jesus! They fell on their knees and worshiped Baby Jesus. They told Mary about the angel's message.

(Hold up a candy cane.) Shepherds in Jesus' time used canes to rescue sheep who were caught in thorny bushes or who had fallen down into holes. When you eat a candy cane, remember the shepherds, the first people to hear the good news of Jesus' birth. Like the shepherds, you can share the good news of Jesus, too. (Give each child two candy canes.) Give one candy cane to a friend and tell her or him the story of Jesus' birth. Keep the second one for yourself. Merry Christmas!

Prayer: Dear God, thank you for sending your Son Jesus to earth to teach us about your love. Help us to spread this good news to others. Amen.

The Sermon

Restoration and Vindication

Hymns

Beginning of Worship: "Joy to the World"
Sermon Hymn: "The Lord Is My Light"
Closing Hymn: "Greet Now the Swiftly Changing Year"

Scripture

Isaiah 61:10—62:3 (For additional sermon materials on this passage, see the 2005 May/June planning issue and the September 2005 issue of *The Clergy Journal.*)

It didn't look so good for the Nelson family. The parents both worked hard at modest, low-paying jobs. Their two girls were in seventh grade and fourth grade. They lived in a house that didn't look too bad if one didn't look too closely. But the builder had shaved every corner possible in order to make it affordable for people with lower incomes.

The Nelsons had celebrated Christmas, and had gone to their grandparents' home for a couple more days of celebration. They could not have anticipated the disaster that awaited them. In their absence, a substandard wire in the basement of their home chose the dark of the night to unleash its power in a destructive way. The fire smoldered for a long while, and ultimately only a quarter of the home was actually burned. But there was smoke and soot everywhere. Even the insides of the girls' jewelry boxes were soiled.

Bob was dispirited, but he had insurance. This is what insurance was for, right? The house would be rebuilt, the soot and smoke would be cleaned. It would be better than ever. But it wasn't better than ever. Insurance did cover the major part of the damage, But it couldn't replace everything that was damaged. The pictures and special clothing couldn't be replaced adequately. The deductible the Nelsons had to pay was considerable, and the house always had a bit of a smell of smoke. The Nelsons had hoped that everything would be restored, but their home never got back to the way it was before the fire.

It didn't look so good for the people of Israel in their return from their forced exile. They had lived under the rule of Assyrians and Babylonians. They were away from their homeland for generations. They were looking forward to a new beginning. There had been promises that Israel would be restored. Jerusalem again would be a capital to which princes and kings would come. God's people would be restored to a place of prominence in the world. The restored temple would again be the centerpiece of worship.

It didn't quite work out that way. Upon their return to their former land, they found that everything couldn't go back to the way it once was under David and Solomon. Others were living in their towns and cities. Rebuilding the temple and Jerusalem was hard work. And we know that outside a glimmer of prominence, Israel never was a world or regional power. Persia was flexing its muscle, and Rome was ramping up to become the power broker of the world.

Yet there is no equivocation in Isaiah's proclamation in our lesson today. Isaiah doesn't lay out the possibility of Israel's restoration. He lays it out as a matter of certain expectation. Isaiah uses the imagery of a bridegroom and a bride. They are decked with the adornments of celebration. Isaiah uses the imagery of agriculture – the earth and garden bringing forth shoots and fruits. So shall Israel be adorned and so shall Israel bear fruit.

But how can that be the case? The days of David and Solomon were long gone. More powerful nations treated Israel like third class citizens. How was Israel to be vindicated? Perhaps Israel's vindication was to come in a way that the people did not expect. At the time of Jesus, there were some who wanted to make Jesus a king to usher in the new age for Israel. Even today, there are some who still expect Israel to return to world prominence under the direction of a Messiah.

Isaiah was right, but in a way not anticipated by God's people. Nations would see Israel's vindication, and kings would see the glory of Israel. We stand about halfway between two festivals in the church. Christmas, of course, is celebrated by both church and culture. Even most non-Christians in America celebrate Christmas in some way. In these 12 days of Christmas, the church seeks to point not to gifts and trees, but to the baby in the manger.

The next festival comes in five days – Epiphany – a festival absolutely ignored by our culture even though it is a day on which important gifts are given. It is the day we mark as the visit of the Magi or Wise Men or

Kings to the boy, Jesus. Kings, you say? Kings will see the glory of Israel? And would that glory be a boy? That boy would wear a crown of beauty one day – made of thorns. That boy would hold a royal diadem in his hand – a shepherd's staff.

Well, how does it look for you on this first day of a new year? Is this the fresh start for which you have been looking? Perhaps you have big plans for the year. This is the year that you will lose those 25 pounds. This is the year you will start your new business. This is the year that you will begin daily devotions and volunteer more often in the church.

All of those things are great. Humans being what we are, though, most of our resolutions will come to nothing. We fail to rebuild ourselves or our lives, even as Israel was not able to rebuild the temple or Jerusalem to their satisfaction.

Even so, none of that negates the promises of Isaiah and the promises of God. While things may not be just as we might like them in this world, there is going to be a vindication for God's people. That vindication has just been celebrated as God's Son born in a manger. And we can rejoice, for we have been clothed with that one's garments of salvation.

Happy New Year! Happy? Maybe. Probably. As most of us count our blessings, we have more than we deserve, and we certainly have more than did the people returning from exile. We are not starting from the poverty of slavery and the lack of goods. To the contrary, most of us have far too much and find it difficult to move because we are over-burdened. Or perhaps over-blessed.

We are very blessed. But we will be even more blessed as we await final vindication and restoration. For Christians, this will not be a rebuilt Jerusalem or temple. It probably will not be in the next 12 months, save for the few of us whose earthly lives will come to an end. Instead, the final vindication comes in God's good time. So let us rejoice and exult in God's promise this New Year. Amen.

– Norman W. Wahl

January 6, 2006

Epiphany

Lessons

RCL	Isa 60:1–6	Eph 3:1–12	Mt 2:1–12
Roman Catholic	Isa 60:1–6	Eph 3:2–3, 5–6	Mt 2:1–12
Episcopal	Isa 60:1–6,9	Eph 3:1–12	Mt 2:1–12

Introduction to the Lessons

Lesson 1
Isaiah 60:1–6 (RCL/RC)
Isaiah 60:1–6, 9 (Epis)

The nations will come to worship the light and the glory of the Lord in Israel. Isaiah reveals that everyone will come bearing gifts of gold and silver and frankincense. Even kings will attend to the brightness that is Israel.

Lesson 2
Ephesians 3:1–12 (RCL/Epis)
Ephesians 3:2–3, 5–6 (RC)

The grace of Christ Jesus is not for Jews only; it is also for Gentiles – perhaps even Magi from afar. Paul refers to the "mystery" made known by "revelation"– even as the Magi had had revealed to them the mystery of the King of the Jews through a star.

Gospel
Matthew 2:1–12 (RCL/RC/Epis)

They were given a sign. They looked, they found, and they worshiped. Overwhelmed with joy, they offered the King what they had. God's people today are given a sign. We also look, find, worship, and offer our gifts.

Theme

We live in a world that threatens us with darkness; but the God of light shines brightly.

Thought for the Day

In the movies, threatening scenes are often filmed in the dark while scenes of joy and happiness are filmed in bright light. What movie scene captures your spirit this day? Whether you begin in darkness, an early dawn, bright light, or dusk, our God seeks to bring light to your life this day.

Call to Worship

One: Give the king your justice, O God, and your righteousness to the king's son;

All: That the king may rule your people righteously and the poor with justice.

One: The kings of Tarshish and of the isles shall pay tribute, and the kings of Arabia and Saba offer gifts.

All: All kings shall bow down before him, and all the nations do him service.

One: For the king shall deliver the poor who cry out in distress, and the oppressed who have no helper.

All: The king shall have pity on the lowly and poor; he shall preserve the lives of the needy.

– Based on Psalm 72:1–2,10–13

Pastoral Prayer

We rejoice, O God, in this festival of Epiphany. It is a day ignored by the culture, and a day even ignored by many of your people. But for those of us gathered in this place, may your light burst upon us in a new way.

We have spent 12 days celebrating the birth of the Christ Child. We now spend a season celebrating Christ's great work among us, great bursts of light in the world.

Even as the Magi were overjoyed upon seeing the star, may we be overjoyed in the light of the Christ. Even as the Magi bowed down and worshiped the Christ, may we bow in reverence and love this day. Let us arise and shine, for our light has come. Amen.

Prayer of Confession

Too often, God, we are people of the dark. We choose to live in darkness and move under the cover of darkness. We believe that our deeds are secret and
that we can do deeds that adversely affect the lives of others without our complicity being known.

But most of our dark deeds come to the light. Most of what we do in secret is brought into the open. And all of our deeds are known to you – the one whom we hurt most by living outside your will for us.

Forgive our frequent slipping into the darkness. Forgive the darkness that we visit on others. And forgive the grief we bring to you, the author of all that is light and true and good. Amen.

Prayer of Dedication of Gifts and Self

This day of Epiphany, Lord, we celebrate gifts of inestimable value – gold, frank incense, myrrh, silver, camels, and other riches. We call to mind nations and kings who have lavished you with gifts. We consider Magi who traveled great distances, led by a light, to give gifts to the Christ child.

Our gifts may not have the worldly value of royal gifts, but they come with no less dedication. May we bow before the child Jesus, as we give not only of our resources, but also as we give ourselves to the light of the world. Make us to be epiphanies of the Christ child as we let our lights shine before others. In the name of "I am the Light," we pray. Amen.

Sermon Summary

It is the darkest time of the year for those who live north of the equator. But darkness pervades not just the hours of the day and night, but our souls as well. Into that darkness a light comes forth – a light for all nations!

Hymn of the Day
"As with Gladness Men of Old"

This year the Christmas season consists of only one Sunday after Christmas. Perhaps you feel a little like I do: there's so much great Christmas music, yet only time to give folks a taste of it. Making matters worse, the Sunday following Christmas is usually sparsely attended.

Especially because of the short season, an apt choice for today is "As with Gladness Men of Old," a hymn by William Dix that both recollects the narrative from Matthew and places us in the Christmas story. The only melody I've known this hymn to be sung to, by Conrad Kocher, links the text musically to the Christmas story.

Children's Time

Follow the Star

Preparation: Set up the figures of Mary, Joseph, and Jesus from the Christmas nativity scene. In the background add a big shiny star – a Christmas tree topper star would work well. Choose children to carry the figures of the wise men from different points in your sanctuary. These children may sit with their families until the story begins.

The night that Jesus was born, God placed a bright star in the sky, brighter than any star the people had ever seen. People all around the world could see this star. During that time, people studied the stars. These star teachers knew that the appearance of a very bright star meant that a great king had been born.

In a different country, star teachers or Magi wanted to find this great king. So they set off, following the star. (Motion for the children carrying the Magi figures to move slowly toward the star.) It took them about two years to finally arrive in Bethlehem, where they found the child Jesus. The Magi fell to their knees to worship the child king. They presented Jesus with three precious gifts: gold, frankincense, and myrrh. And then they returned home.

Prayer: Dear God, thank you for sending your son, Jesus, to light up the world with the brightness of your love. Amen.

The Sermon

The Light of Epiphany

Hymns
Beginning of Worship: "Bright and Glorious Is the Sky"
Sermon Hymn: "O Morning Star, How Fair and Bright"
Closing Hymn: "I Want to Walk as a Child of the Light"

Scripture
Isaiah 60:1–6, 9 (For sermon materials on Matthew 2:1–12, see the 2005 May/June planning issue of *The Clergy Journal*; for sermon materials on Ephesians 3:1–12, see the October 2005 issue of *The Clergy Journal*.)

Imagine yourself in the largest open building you have ever visited. If you are a sports fan, it may be one of the large covered stadiums. When one enters one of these stadiums, one is astounded at the size of the place and the volume contained by the walls and roof.

Further imagine that all the lights are turned off in this building. Just imagine that this place is completely and utterly dark. It is as if you are in a cave one hundred feet below the surface of the earth and no light is present. You cannot even see the shadow of your fingers if you hold your hand two inches in front of your eyes. Darkness. Absolute darkness.

Now watch as a single match is struck and burns in the middle of that ball field. If that match is held high, the light of that single match will be seen from any seat in the ballpark. Think of the volume of darkness – the largest volume of darkness you have ever witnessed. And a single match of almost insignificant volume conquers the darkness.

Or imagine how important a light in the storm might be to a ship. The largest and most dangerous of the Great Lakes is Lake Superior. The north shore of Minnesota is particularly inhospitable as freighters come close to the Duluth harbor. A single storm on November 28, 1905, damaged 29 ships. That put Congress into action, and they appropriated $75,000 for construction of the Split Rock Lighthouse in 1910. The Split Rock Lighthouse has been called the most visited lighthouse in the

United States. It is still open for tours, though it hasn't been used as a lighthouse since 1969, succumbing to modern navigational equipment.

But imagine the welcome light that flashed every 10 seconds giving captains and sailors a guidepost to safety. For the first 30 years the light was a kerosene lamp, and for the last 30 years it was a 1,000 watt light bulb. Just 1,000 watts – shining through a special lens that allowed the light to be seen for 22 miles!

The people of the exile were looking for a light. In spite of the promises that had been made to them about the restoration of Israel upon their return from exile, their vision did not turn out to be the reality for which they had hoped. It probably wasn't as bad as the wilderness wanderings of Moses' time, and it certainly had to be better than slavery under the Egyptians or Assyrians or Babylonians. But it surely was no land flowing with milk and honey. It was a land of too many foreigners, too much work, and too many disappointments. They were looking for any kind of light.

Behold! Isaiah tells the people that their light has come. Darkness has covered the earth and thick darkness has overshadowed the people. Oh, the people of Israel would know that feeling of thick darkness.

We in the Northern Hemisphere labor under the greater darkness of the year. Some are even so affected by our shorter days that they are burdened physically by the darkness. These are the dark days of the year in which people start looking toward increasing light in the world.

But into that darker world, the light of the Lord comes. And, in Isaiah, it comes not just to God's people of Israel, it comes to the whole world. Nations will come to the light of Israel. Kings will be drawn to the dawn of light in Israel. Isaiah further says that the riches of the world will follow the kings – ships full of goods, camels, gold, incense, and silver. It sounds like the days of Solomon in which precious goods were brought to Jerusalem for the building of the temple.

But these honors will not go to a temple, unless it is a temple that would be rebuilt in three days. These honors would go to the Lord God, to the Holy One of Israel.

On this festival of the Epiphany, it is no large leap of prophetic logic to move to the visit of the Magi to the boy Jesus. There has been much speculation about these Magi – were they kings, astrologers, or some other world travelers? They were from the East, perhaps from Persia or Arabia, or both. It is likely that they represented the privileged of society, illustrative by their ability to travel, by their ability to command an audience with King Herod, and by the gifts that they offer to the child.

But do you hear a fulfilling of the prophecy in Isaiah? King and nations would come to the light of Israel – they were led by a heavenly light which "stopped" over the place where the child was. Do you hear that these kings or leaders would come with camels bearing riches? Do you hear that they are bearing gold and incense and myrrh – a gift to Jesus not only at his birth, but a gift applied to his body in death, too?

On this day the Christian church the world over comes to the light of Israel. On this day the Christian church sings praise to the dawn of light that dispels our darkness. Our darkness is not restricted to the fewer hours of the sun. Our darkness is manifest in downcast and troubled spirits. Our darkness is manifest in a world afflicted with war, hate, greed, lust for power, and a host of other ills. Our darkness is manifest in our own sins – evil deeds we have done and good deeds we have neglected.

It is as if we are in a domed stadium with darkness all about us. But a single match is struck – in Bethlehem, perhaps – and the world responds in the love and mercy of the light. For every bit of darkness by a government or business, there is a deed of mercy and love by a church. Even as crimes and ills are committed, there are acts of love in the name of Jesus Christ, the light of the world.

We live in darkness. It is true. But the light has come. Celebrate that light this Epiphany and always. Amen.

– Norman W. Wahl

January 8, 2006

1st Sunday after Epiphany/
The Baptism of Our Lord

Lessons

RCL	Gen 1:1–5	Acts 19:1–7	Mk 1:4–11
Roman Catholic	Isa 42:1–4, 6–7	Acts 10:34–38	Mk 1:7–11
Episcopal (BCP)	Isa 42:1–9	Acts 10:34–38	Mk 1:7–11

Introduction to the Lessons

Lesson 1
(1) Genesis 1:1–5 (RCL)

The season of light begins with recognition of the creator of the light. Light was separated from the darkness, yet darkness would encompass the world. There would come a day in which God's light would take human form.

(2) Isaiah 42:1–9 (Epis)

Not unlike the heavenly voice in the gospel, the voice of God reported by Isaiah proclaims the chosen nature of the Servant. Centuries later, Jesus takes the mantle of this charge upon himself as he reads from Isaiah in the temple.

Lesson 2
(1) Acts 19:1–7 (RCL)

Like the gospel, Acts tells of John's baptism – a baptism of repentance. The people hungered for more. As the Holy Spirit comes upon Jesus in baptism, so the Holy Spirit comes upon the people when baptized in the name of the Lord Jesus.

(2) Acts 10:34–38 (RC/Epis)

This is a part of Peter's sermon at the house of Cornelius, a Gentile. While Peter is speaking, the Holy Spirit comes upon the listeners. Immediately

Peter declares that they should be baptized with water in the name of the Lord Jesus.

Gospel
Mark 1:4–11 (RCL/RC/Epis)

The first epiphany of the adult Jesus is his baptism in the river Jordan. Father, Son, and Holy Spirit join together in an intimate exchange of truth. The Holy Spirit descended upon Jesus, but John the Baptizer declares that Jesus will be the one who baptizes with the Holy Spirit.

Theme

As Jesus is baptized, God calls him the beloved Son. God calls us as daughters and sons today.

Thought for the Day

As baptized children of God we are called to live in the model of Christ. We are to "let our light shine" to glorify our Father in heaven.

Call to Worship

> **One:** Your throne, O God, endures forever and ever;
> **All:** A scepter of righteousness is the scepter of your kingdom; you love righteousness and hate iniquity.
> **One:** Therefore, God, your God, has anointed you with the oil of gladness.
> **All:** All your garments are fragrant, and the music of strings from ivory palaces makes you glad.
> – Based on Psalm 45:7–9

Pastoral Prayer

Gracious God, you have manifested your mighty and loving hand through your creation and through all of time. "In the beginning" you created the heavens and the earth. You have continued in your creation to this very moment in life and health and every good. You have manifested your power and love through people that you have placed on this earth to serve you – patriarchs and matriarchs, judges, kings, and prophets. But you have primarily manifested your presence in the Word become flesh.

In this Epiphany season, may we continually be brought to a greater awareness of your love for the world through the great works done by Christ. From baptism to miracles to transfiguration, your Son is one whose sandals we are not worthy to untie. Yet he is a Savior that invites us into his very bosom. Praise to Father, Son, and Holy Spirit. Amen.

Prayer of Confession

O God, John's baptism of repentance should not be for Jesus, your sinless one, but it should be for us. We are the ones who have been baptized into your name, but find countless ways to bring dishonor to our status as your children. Forgive us for acting as those who have not heard your name or your command to love you and love our neighbor as ourselves. Help us to live lives that inspire people to the faith.

Your Son has given us forgiveness through his own death and resurrection. We celebrate our standing as redeemed and forgiven of our sins. In the grace of your Son, Jesus Christ, we pray. Amen.

Prayer of Dedication of Gifts and Self

Father in heaven, you embraced your Son with a loving proclamation upon his baptism in the Jordan. We ask you to similarly embrace us with your good pleasure on this day. Your Son offered his whole life and ministry to you. May you move us to be faithful as your forgiven children. Receive these offerings of ourselves and our resources, in order that more people may be served by the one who came to establish justice on earth. On our own we are not worthy, but because of Jesus' death and resurrection, we are restored as your children. Make us humble in our service as we go out to proclaim the message of the Christ. Amen.

Sermon Summary

Jesus was baptized with a baptism of repentance. It was not for him; it was for us that Jesus was baptized. How does Jesus' baptism translate into our own lives of faith and witness?

Hymn of the Day
"Hail to the Lord's Anointed"

The last time we encountered this gospel lesson (a mere month ago) worship leaders faced the dilemma of presenting this text as pointing to either Jesus' birth or the beginning of his ministry. Happily, both liturgical date and biblical context are in agreement here.

A fine choice for today is James Montgomery's "Hail to the Lord's Anointed," one of over 400 hymns the author composed. One stanza speaks of the compassion of Jesus' ministry, while another declares the universality of his kingship: "Kings shall bow down before him...all nations shall adore him...his kingdom still increasing, a kingdom without end."

Children's Time

Jesus Is Baptized

Preparation: Bring a plant mister bottle filled with water. Be sure there is water in the font.
(Invite the children to gather by the font. Use the mister to lightly spray the children.) What do you feel? All living things need water to live. What are some ways you use water? (Drinking, bathing, swimming, watering plants, and cooking are some answers.) How do we use water in a special way in church? (Baptism.)

[handwritten note: All living things need water]

In today's Bible story we hear about Jesus' baptism. Jesus was baptized in a river by John the Baptist. Jesus stepped into the middle of the river where John was waiting for him. John dunked Jesus under the water, and when Jesus came up, the heavens opened and the Holy Spirit came down on Jesus like a gentle dove. And God said, "You are my Son, the Beloved, with you I am well pleased."

When we are baptized, we are washed with water and God's words. Through baptism we become children of God, members of God's family, and God calls us beloved. (Have everyone dip a finger in the water in the font and mark their foreheads with the sign of the cross.)

Prayer: Loving God, thank you for washing us with water and your word so we can become your children. Amen.

The Sermon

Contradiction in Terms?

Hymns

Beginning of Worship: "When Christ's Appearing Was Made Known"
Sermon Hymn: "Baptized in Water"
Closing Hymn: "Jesus Call Us; O'er the Tumult"

Scripture

Mark 1:4–11 (For additional sermon materials on this passage, see the 2005 May/June planning issue and the October 2005 issue of *The Clergy Journal*.)

The Prince of Tides is a disturbing movie. Its opening scene sets the stage for what will follow. The scene juxtaposes violence with redemption. The voices of two shouting people sound from a ramshackle house. The fight grows in intensity and three children burst from the house. All of the children are young, one even appears to be younger than school age. They run down a pathway and onto a dock leading into a lake. Without a moment's hesitation, the three join hands and jump into the lake – clothing and all.

And that is when the voice-over of the film's major character explains what the children are doing – what he used to do with his brother and sister when he was a child. When their parents would fight, the children ran to escape the noise and the violence. Simply running away didn't silence the shouting and abuse. But jumping into the water would take away, at least momentarily, the angry voices. And in the calmness under the water, the children would bond with their hands held together. It was as if they were sheltered from the evils of the world. And when they could hold their breath no longer, they would, as the voice says, "rise to the light."

As Jesus came up out of the water following his baptism by John in the Jordan River, was there some kind of light that accompanied the descending dove and the heavenly voice? Was this some mystical experience that would prefigure the dazzling light that we will consider in a few weeks at the Transfiguration, along with a voice from the cloud that nearly repeats today's heavenly pronouncement with an additional rejoinder: "This is my Son the Beloved; listen to him!" (Mk 9:7)?

The first lesson today speaks of God creating the light, and the light was good. (From the Genesis lesson. Alternatively, the Isaiah passage also speaks of the Lord giving a light to the nations.) Jesus does rise to the light. Jesus is the light. Jesus is the light we celebrate in Epiphany.

So what of this baptism by John? Is it not a contradiction in terms? Even John seemed to know that his baptism would be superfluous for Jesus. In fact, in the account in Matthew, John attempts to prevent Jesus from being baptized.

Did Jesus need to be baptized? Probably not. A baptism of repentance for the forgiveness of sins for the Light of the World would be needless. Or perhaps a need was met after all.

Consider "contradiction in terms." A writer for the *Clarksburg Exponent Telegram* writes that "the words 'marital' and 'bliss' together is a contradiction in terms." She writes, "Some believe the perception of marriage has changed from 'until death do us part' to 'until the divorce papers are finalized.'"

Celebrity weddings may last only days or hours. Adulterous images on television and in the movies make a travesty of marriage. There seems no longer to be a commonly accepted idea of a lifetime commitment in marriage. Have we gotten to the point where marital bliss makes about as much sense as Jesus' baptism of repentance for the forgiveness of sins? Or have we gotten to a point where Jesus' baptism gives us hope in the face of our culture's throwaway concept of marriage?

Any marriage counselor will tell us that marriage requires work every day. Anyone who assumes that the excitement of a wedding day will automatically translate into exponential growth over the next 50 years is sadly deceived by romantic notions. Only 5 percent of couples in our day reach their fiftieth wedding anniversary. Those couples have all been blessed with good health; and those couples have put good work into their relationships.

As God's children, we are called to put good work into our relationships with each other and with God. Many, perhaps most, of us in this place have been baptized. Some may yet be seeking baptism.

In any case, the day of our baptism did not automatically result in some exponential growth in the faith. Either we, or others on our behalf, made some promises in Baptism, including promises to hear the Word and live among God's faithful people. It takes work – good work – every day.

Jesus is our model of that faithful journey in baptism. No, Jesus was not baptized for himself; he was baptized for us. We are not Jesus. We will never be Jesus. We cannot be faithful as Jesus was faithful. That is the point of a sacrament that forgives sin and offers eternal life. But even if we cannot be Jesus, we are still called to live in such a way that God can announce, "You are my daughters and sons; with you I am well pleased."

Kristi came to Baptism as a young adult. She had not been raised in a Christian home. She started attending a worship service for seekers. She quickly grew past that and was on fire for the faith. She was baptized, attended worship weekly, and volunteered for nearly everything, including being a chaperone for a seven-day youth trip! She was living as a child of the light.

But Kristi fell victim to the malady considered above. She stopped working on her marriage, and it fell apart. It was a source of deep hurt for everyone in the family. Today, Kristi is rebuilding her life in the church. She is not resting in what has happened but is putting good work every day into her faith and her family. She has asked forgiveness for her part in her marriage's failure. She is one who needed Jesus to be baptized and show her the way to forgiveness.

Have you ever wished that you could jump into a lake and escape life's troubles? That only happens in the movies, and doesn't last even there. But you can jump into the life-giving water of Christ and find a light that eclipses the darkness of the world. There is one calling you by name. God calls you son or daughter. God calls you beloved. Amen.

– Norman W. Wahl

January 15, 2006

2nd Sunday after Epiphany
RC/Pres: 2nd Sunday in Ordinary Time

Lessons

RCL	1 Sam 3:1–10 (11–20)	1 Cor 6:12–20	Jn 1:43–51
Roman Catholic	1 Sam 3:3–10, 19	1 Cor 6:13–15, 17–20	Jn 1:35–42
Episcopal	1 Sam 3:1–10 (11–20)	1 Cor 6:11b–20	Jn 1:43–51

Introduction to the Lessons
Lesson 1
1 Samuel 3:1–10 (11–20) (RCL/Epis)
1 Samuel 3:3–10, 19 (RC)

Samuel's leadership in Israel has an odd beginning. His mother, Hannah, begs God for a son, then gives him to the Lord's service. Still, Samuel needs to hear God's call. The persistence of the Lord leads to Samuel's servanthood.

Lesson 2
1 Corinthians 6:12–20 (RCL/Epis)
1 Corinthians 6:13–15, 17–20 (RC)

Because we are a people of the Spirit, is the body of little importance? Hardly. How we treat our bodies is an indication of how we honor God. The body is even a sacred place for the Holy Spirit.

Gospel
John 1:43–51 (RCL/Epis)
John 1:35–42 (RC)

Jesus calls to Philip, "Follow me." Philip calls to Nathanael, "Come and see." As the group of disciples grows in number, Jesus' identity is further revealed. Listen for the many titles for Jesus that are included in these verses.

Theme

God called Samuel, God called disciples, and God continues to call people today.

Thought for the Day

Have you ever felt called by God to a task in the church, to a task in the kingdom? God is calling you today in worship. Listen!

Call to Worship

One: May God be merciful to us and bless us!

All: Show us the light of your countenance, O Lord, and come to us. Let your ways be known upon earth, your saving health among all nations.

One: Let the peoples praise you, O God;

All: Let all the peoples praise you.

One: Let the nations be glad and sing for joy, for you judge the people with equity and guide all the nations upon the earth.

All: Let the peoples praise you, O God; let all the peoples praise you.

One: May God, our own God, bless us.

All: May all the ends of the earth stand in awe of God.

– Based on Psalm 67

Pastoral Prayer

We come to you, God, praying for unity among Christ's disciples and among all people in the world. Help us to answer the call of Jesus Christ, even as the original disciples were forged into effective witnesses of the gospel. Strengthen our resolve to move past our differences to the great message of hope and salvation that we share in Christ. Bless us this day as we are encouraged to examine our call to discipleship. May we join with all other Christians lifting up your name in praise and honor. Amen.

Prayer of Confession

O God, you call and call our names. There are times that we, like Moses, make excuses and ask not to serve you. There are times that we, like Jonah, say we will serve but then turn and go the other way. There are times that we, like Samuel, hear your voice but lack the knowledge to follow your call. Help us recognize your voice in our lives. Give us the eagerness of Samuel to jump up, even in the middle of the night, to respond to your call. Forgive us when we ignore you or make excuses. Work in us a willing spirit. We pray in the name of the one who calls us, Jesus Christ our Lord. Amen.

Prayer of Dedication of Gifts and Self

Lord of all things and all people, you bestow your generous gifts upon us. All about us we see evidence of our riches in comfort, in goods, and in money. Help us to be generous with those riches, even as Samuel was willing to give what he had for the good of others. Through our generosity, may we grow in wisdom and stature – more in accord with your will. Amen.

Sermon Summary

God often chooses rather ordinary people to do wonderful work. God still chooses people today. Are you too ordinary to be chosen by God?

Hymn of the Day
"Rise, Shine, You People!"

Each time I read the story of Philip telling his friend Nathanael about Jesus, I have to smile. There's no sense of Philip looking down his nose at Nathanael, no sense that he had a prepared speech to share. It's just a spontaneous, joyful, one-friend-to-another sharing: "We've found him! Come and see!"

For me, Ronald Klug's "Rise, Shine, You People!" displays the same enthusiasm Philip must have felt that day – an infectious, wonderfully natural enthusiasm. Dale Wood's bold and brassy music turns up the temperature, and the result is a blazingly good congregational hymn.

211

Children's Time

Hearing God's Message

Preparation: Bring in a cell phone, printed email message, and a Bible. Arrange to have someone with a cell phone in your congregation call you at a prearranged signal.

What are some ways we share good news with each other? (Phone calls, email, letters, and in person are possible responses.) Which of these things can we use to deliver God's message? (All of them.) We also use radio, the television, and Christian music. Who are some people who can deliver God's message? (Pastor, Sunday school teachers, musicians, parents, friends, you, anyone.) The Bible has many messages about God for us. I'd like to read one of my favorite messages about God to you.

(Open the Bible and then the cell phone rings. The person who calls you may hang up as soon as you answer.) You need to tell me something? But it's right in the middle of my children's sermon. Can I call you back later? Oh, it's very important. And you want me to share it with the children. Here's the message: "For God so loved the world that he gave his only Son, so that everyone who believes in him may not perish but may have eternal life." That's all? Bye!

That's amazing! That was the same Bible verse I was going to read to you!

Prayer: Creator God, open our ears so we can hear the good news of your love for us. Amen.

The Sermon

Called? Me?

Hymns
Beginning of Worship: "Let Us Talents and Tongues Employ"
Sermon Hymn: "Listen, God Is Calling"
Closing Hymn: "I, the Lord of Sea and Sky"

Scripture

1 Samuel 3:1–10 (11–20) (For sermon materials on John 1:43–51, see the 2005 May/June planning issue of *The Clergy Journal*; for sermon materials on 1 Corinthians 6:12–20, see the October 2005 issue of *The Clergy Journal*.)

According to an old saying, you just can't send a boy to do a man's work. Or can you? God seemed to do just that. In fact, if one were to review God's choices of prophets and leaders in the scriptures, God seemed to make many curious choices. Consider Jacob, Moses, David, Jonah, Jeremiah, Mary, Paul. And in today's lesson we learn about Samuel.

It is a dark time in the history of God's people. We read that "The word of the Lord was rare in those days" (1 Sam 3:1). Eli is getting old and feeble. His sons are pathetic failures, even blasphemers of God.

So who rides in to save the day? Young Samuel. What do we know of Samuel prior to God's call? We know he has a faithful mother, Hannah. Truly, it is Hannah's faith that places Samuel in the care of the priest, Eli. We know his mother faithfully visits him year in and year out. We know that Samuel is growing in stature and favor with God and with the people. But that's it. That is his entire resume. And this is the one who will deliver a message to the people so stunning that "it will make both ears of anyone who hears of it tingle" (v. 11)?

How old is Samuel? An ancient historian places him at about 12 years of age. Quite evidently Samuel is not used to hearing the voice of God. Would it otherwise have taken four tries and a suggestion from an old priest to get the communication started between Samuel and God? On the other hand, maybe the old priest isn't accustomed to God's voice, either, if it takes him three tries to set Samuel on the right path.

"Samuel, Samuel," the call goes out. "Here I am," responds Samuel, but to Eli, not to the one who calls.

"Samuel," the call goes out. "Here I am," responds Samuel a second time to Eli, and a second time incorrectly.

The call goes out for the third time, and Samuel responds, "Here I am." Samuel is consistent in his willingness to serve. But Samuel is still addressing the wrong party. After the third misadventure, Eli instructs the boy, if called again, to answer, "Speak, Lord, for your servant is listening" (v. 9).

Sure enough, the call comes a fourth time, "Samuel, Samuel!" And the line of communication between God and Samuel is opened as Samuel responds, "Speak, Lord, for your servant is listening."

As it happens, Samuel listens to a hard message, especially hard for his beloved Eli, whose family will be punished for their iniquity. In the morning Eli asks about the message from God, but Samuel is reluctant to speak the message for fear it will hurt Eli. Eli persists, and Samuel tells it all – his first exercise at telling the truth of God, no matter how discomfiting. Imagine, a 12-year-old boy delivering a word of judgment to a long-standing priest.

And what of today? Is God still choosing people who are young, who can't speak well, who seem even hostile to Word? Is God calling you?

Recall our gospel lesson for today in which Jesus is calling disciples. When we take a look at that group, there is nothing spectacular about them. We know that there are fishermen, a tax collector – quite ordinary people. You would think that if Jesus wanted to get something done in a hurry, he would have picked some priests and scribes and lawyers. Maybe Jesus would have included a Roman governor or even an emperor into his group of close disciples. But, no, Jesus seems satisfied to call quite ordinary people.

Most of us in this place are quite ordinary. This doesn't preclude the possibility that there could be someone who is quite extraordinary among us – a billionaire, a past or future Olympian, a politician who can touch the lives of thousands, the best cardiac surgeon in the world. Surely such people sit among the people of God. Yet most of us claim no great place in history. We do our jobs, we raise our families, we care for our homes, we go to school – whatever it is that takes us through the week.

And God is calling us. God is calling us or we wouldn't be here today! When God calls, we tend to be like Samuel and do not hear God's voice correctly. Or we may make excuses like Moses and Jeremiah. Or we may be contrary to the call like Jonah. Yet God calls and calls and calls.

God's people have been answering for thousands of years; for two thousand years we have been answering in the name of Christ. Who is it that teaches the children in our Sunday school? Quite ordinary people whom the Spirit calls and equips. Some teach Sunday school for 40 years. Others go from teaching to some other calling in the church. One pastor tells of the Spirit calling him to teach Sunday school, then things evolved to the point that he couldn't say no to seminary, and today he is serving as an ordained pastor in the church.

Who serves on the altar guild? Who provides leadership for the women's groups or the church council? Who goes on the mission trips to assist people whose lives have been touched by tornadoes or hurricanes, or trips to other lands to share good news with sisters and brothers a world away?

Aren't we all rather ordinary? And might we not even dismiss ourselves from consideration because we are nothing special? Each one of us is special in the eyes of God. We are called in baptism to let our lights shine. One is never too young or old or rich or poor to serve God. Listen, listen God is calling.

– Norman W. Wahl

January 22, 2006

3rd Sunday after Epiphany
RC/Pres: 3rd Sunday in Ordinary Time

Lessons

RCL	Jon 3:1–5, 10	1 Cor 7:29–31	Mk 1:14–20
Roman Catholic	Jon 3:1–5, 10	1 Cor 7:29–31	Mk 1:14–20
Episcopal	Jer 3:21–4:2	1 Cor 7:17–23	Mk 1:14–20

Introduction to the Lessons
Lesson 1
(1) Jonah 3:1–5, 10 (RCL/RC)
For the second time God commands Jonah to go to Nineveh, capital of ancient Assyria. Jonah complies and pleads with the people to turn from evil, warning of judgment to come within forty days. The whole city turns from their wickedness. God then shows compassion and spares them from destruction.

(2) Jeremiah 3:21–4:2 (Epis)
The late seventh century B.C.E. was a time of great stress, when the fate of many nations, including Judah, was threatened by invasion. God raises up Jeremiah to declare that the time is short to turn from their dishonoring sinfulness. If they do, many nations, including Israel, will be blessed.

Lesson 2
(1) 1 Corinthians 7:29–31 (RCL/RC)
Paul stresses to the church at Corinth that time is running out on this world and that they should not complicate life unnecessarily. In marriage, grieving, and in daily routines like shopping, keep life simple. The most important thing is to live in a way that is pleasing to God.

(2) 1 Corinthians 7:17–23 (Epis)
Paul tells the Corinthian believers not to be restless, but to continue in the same state that they were in when God called them. If married, stay

married. If single, stay single. Remain where and what they are. All's almost over. Don't let earthly responsibilities obscure your godly living.

Gospel
Mark 1:14–20 (RCL/Epis)

After John the Baptist was arrested, Jesus traversed the shores of Galilee saying, "The kingdom has come. Time's up. Stop sinning. Live right." He singled out Peter and Andrew, James and John, and said, "Follow me," and immediately they left their fishing nets to begin fishing for other human beings.

Theme

We don't have forever. God and God's work must be our top priority.

Thought for the Day

'Tis only one life and it will soon be past. Only what's done for Christ will last.

Call to Worship

One:	Lord, you have been our dwellingplace throughout all generations
All:	You turn us back to dust, and say, "Turn back, you mortals,"
One:	For a thousand years in your sight are like yesterday.
All:	So teach us to count our days so that we may gain a wise heart

– Based on Psalm 90

Pastoral Prayer

Eternal and loving God, the light of your love is from everlasting to everlasting. You are the same yesterday, today, and forever. And yet we are, so the psalmist suggests, like dust. Our days are soon gone and we fly away. How sobering that is, Lord, and yet we cannot escape the conviction that this is by your design, that what we call the human body was fashioned by you to house our souls only for a season and prepare them for eternity.

Help us to understand this, Lord, and help us to come to the life–changing awareness that this is why your Son and our Savior, Jesus

Christ, told us not to put all our time and energy into preserving and pampering the things of the flesh – but instead, to prioritize our interior being, our soul. So, Lord, please help free us from the foolish earthly preoccupations that distract us from our principal task at hand which is, as the apostle Paul expressed it, that of working out our soul's salvation with fear and trembling. Amen.

Prayer of Confession

Gracious, loving, and forgiving God, we're amazed at how easily we become distracted by the preoccupations of this world, the lusts of life. We know they're only temporary and not deserving of so much of our time and energy. And yet, time and time again, we fall into the trap of sacrificing what we know is right in your eyes in order to go after the bright lights on this earthly stage. Why do we do that, Lord? Why do we continue to do that when we know better? Like Peter, "Our soul is willing, but our flesh is weak." Please hear us as we confess the error of our ways. Renew a right spirit within us. Without you we are utterly helpless and hopeless in this matter, yet in partnership with you we can win the ultimate victory over the Prince of Darkness. Amen.

Prayer of Dedication of Gifts and Self

All that we are, all that we ever hope to be, and all that we acquire or ever hope to acquire we now offer to you, Lord. Do with us and the resources we offer whatever you deem right. They are all yours. We hold nothing back. Thank you for being so kind to us and for letting us enjoy everything that you, in your loving goodness, have made available to us. We humbly pray now that you will take our offerings, touch them, multiply them as you did the loaves and the fish, and then put them to use for the work of your kingdom. Take who we are and the gifts we bring out into the highways and byways of life to bless those who are less fortunate. Bless them in the name of Jesus. Amen.

Sermon Summary

Following Jesus means leaving our old way of life, our "nets," so to speak, as Jesus' disciples did. It's not easy. Sometimes the sacrifice can be great, but for the brief time we have here on earth, it's the right and the most rewarding thing to do

Hymn of the Day
"They Cast Their Nets in Galilee"

Mark doesn't report the emotional state of Simon and Andrew, James and John, but one imagines them feeling excitement and enthusiasm for the great adventure to which Jesus invites them. What else could explain their simply dropping their nets and following him?

Today's selection, "They Cast Their Nets in Galilee," a hymn by William Alexander Percy set to the music of David McKinley Williams, captures that excitement. But, going deeper, the text also reminds us that the call to follow Jesus is costly, at times demanding all. This penetrating hymn melds these elements together seamlessly.

Children's Time

Fishers of People

Preparation: Bring in a large piece of fabric netting. Bring in a variety of fishing lures, including artificial bait, in a small tackle box.

How many of you have gone fishing? What have you caught? Look at all of these fishing lures. Which one would you use to catch the biggest fish? Which one do you think would catch the most fish?"

Jesus' first four disciples were fishermen on the Sea of Galilee. Their names were Peter, Andrew, James, and John. What kind of bait do you think they used? (Accept responses.) Actually, they didn't use any kind of bait. They used a large net made of rope. Fishermen used a spinning motion to throw the circular net over the surface of the water. The net had weights around the outside. As the net sank it formed a dome under the water. When the fishermen pulled in the net, the sides gathered together, trapping fish inside.

When Jesus spoke to the fishermen, he said, "Follow me and I will make you fish for people." Would the fishermen use nets to catch people? (Throw the net over the children. Wait a few moments and gather it in.) Of course not! What would they do? (Tell others about Jesus, heal, be kind and helpful.)

Jesus calls you to be his disciples, too. How can you catch people? (Invite them to come to church or Sunday school, tell them stories about Jesus, be friendly, be kind, and so on.)

Prayer: Dear Jesus, help us to catch people by sharing the good news of your love with others. Amen.

The Sermon

Let Go of the Nets

Hymns

Beginning of Worship: "We've a Story to Tell to the Nations"
Sermon Hymn: "Give of Your Best to the Master"
Closing Hymn: "O God, Our Help in Ages Past"

Scripture

Mark 1:14–20 (For additional sermon materials on this passage, see the 2005 May/June planning issue and the October 2005 issue of *The Clergy Journal*.)

As we read about the calling of Peter and Andrew, James and John, we probably think to ourselves, "Wait a minute, this just doesn't seem realistic. Jesus speaks and they jump? They just leave everything and follow him? Either that's an exaggeration of what actually happened or it's some kind of divine intervention. Either way, it's not something I can relate to. There's no way I'd just walk away from my current life on a moment's notice."

And with that kind of thinking, many of us dismiss this passage as ancient history, with little or no application to our lives.

Not so fast. There was probably a fair amount of interactive history between Jesus and these men before they made their decision to leave home and take up with him. In fact, many New Testament scholars suggest that this was just the defining moment in what had been a longer process of Jesus pulling on their heartstrings. Clearly, they had met him some time earlier, and heard him teach and preach. The events of John 1 make this evident.

Perhaps what we have here is not the sudden and impulsive decision of four fishermen, nor the divine intervention of God, so much as the reasoned and deliberate choice of four individuals. These four, after a period of exposure to the compelling invitation of Jesus, chose to follow him. Viewed in this light, the calling of the disciples and their faith-filled response takes on a new and more realistic perspective, one that we should carefully explore for its application to our lives.

For most of us, the call of Jesus on our lives, his summons to discipleship, comes only after we have been sufficiently exposed to Jesus' life and teachings to understand the truth residing in his person and words. Spontaneous following is not the norm. But when the moment of truth–recognition comes, as it does in one way or another for most Christians, we then have to make a definitive decision – leave our nets and follow, or let the Lord walk away while we return to business as usual. Needless to say, Jesus and the entire witness of the New Testament declare that choosing the former is the far wiser course. Peter and Andrew, James and John chose the wiser course and the rest, so they say, is history.

But what about you? Have you heard and responded to the call of Christ in your life? Are you feeling drawn by the winsome truth of his presentation? If so, keep in mind that, unlike these first disciples, following Jesus doesn't necessarily mean we have to leave our homes and our professions. What it does mean, however, is that we must be willing to leave the nets of our old lifestyles – that is, the lifestyles of living for ourselves only – to enter the lifestyle of living for others.

If you do make the decision to fish for people, what then can you expect? Many things, no doubt. And the New Testament is clear that you can expect trouble. Or to express it more nobly, you can expect a summons to sacrifice.

Ouch! That's not something we want to hear. In fact, it sounds downright discouraging. And yet, it's the truth. As Dietrich Bonhoeffer once wrote, "When Christ calls a man he bids him come and die." Even though the first disciples may not have fully understood what they were in for at their initial moment of decision, Jesus soon made it abundantly clear that, at the very least, they were in for quite a strenuous ride.

When Mother Teresa was a young girl preparing to leave Yugoslavia to enter full-time Christ-following, her mother told her to put her hand in the hand of Jesus and go wherever he led her. She did, and it led her into the poorest sections of India for more than 30 years. Sacrifice. Trouble.

Here in America, to a large extent, we've lopped off the sacrificial aspect of following Christ and made the Christian life into something of a buddy-buddy relationship with Jesus, one that simply makes life go better. In effect, Jesus is our good luck amulet. We love him and we're devoted to the disciplines that keep us close to him, but when our Christ-following is subjected to the light of authentic gospel witness, it immediately shows itself to be a half-baked distortion of the biblical record – no pain, just pleasure. In this sense we ignore the cross of our Lord, along with his compelling words, "If any want to become my followers, let them deny themselves and take up their cross daily and follow me" (Lk 9:23).

One day in 1810, the father of Ann Hasseltine received a letter from a young man named Adoniram Judson, asking for permission to court his daughter so that she could accompany him on his mission to India. It read like this. "I have now to ask, whether you can consent to part with your daughter early next Spring, to see her no more in this world; whether you can consent to her departure for a heathen land, and her subjection to the hardships and sufferings of missionary life…to her exposure to the dangers of the ocean; to the fatal influence of the southern climate of India; to every kind of want and distress; to degradation, insult, persecution, and perhaps a violent death. Can you consent to all this for the sake of Him who left his heavenly home and died for her and for you?"

History records that the answer was "yes" and the subsequent lifestyle of trouble and sacrifice is now a matter of history.

So, where are you in this matter of choosing to follow? Is Jesus calling you to "leave your nets" and follow his lead? And are you tempted to go, just as Peter, Andrew, James, and John did? If so, don't let the price put you off. To a greater or lesser degree it will mean sacrifice, but in the end, the eternal payoff will far outweigh any temporal cost. From the very lips of our Lord come these reassuring words, "Truly I tell you, there is no one who has left house or wife or brothers or parents or children, for the sake of the kingdom of God, who will not get back very much more in this age, and in the age to come eternal life" (Lk 18:29–30).

Go. Leave your nets. Follow Jesus. It won't be easy, but you won't regret it, now or in eternity.

– David Wesley Reid

January 29, 2006

4th Sunday after Epiphany
RC/Pres: 4th Sunday in Ordinary Time

Lessons

RCL	Deut 18:15–20	1 Cor 8:1–13	Mk 1:21–28
Roman Catholic	Deut 18:15–20	1 Cor 7:32–35	Mk 1:21–28
Episcopal	Deut 18:15–20	1 Cor 8:1b–13	Mk 1:21–28

Introduction to the Lessons
Lesson 1
Deuteronomy 18:15–20 (RCL/RC/Epis)

Moses is about to die. The Israelites ask for a prophet to help them remain faithful. God promises to provide one from among their own kin. This prophet will speak on God's behalf. The people must listen.

Lesson 2
(1) 1 Corinthians 8:1–13 (RCL); 1 Corinthians 8:1b–13 (Epis)

What is to be done with meat sacrificed to idols – eat it, or not? Some arrogantly say, "I know it means nothing at all if I eat it." But they offend weaker believers by eating. God doesn't want our freedom to inhibit another person's devotion.

(2) 1 Corinthians 7:32–35 (RC)

Our lives should be as free from complications as possible. Take marriage, for example. It's not wrong to be married, but it is distracting to a complete focus on the Lord. Our relationship with God should be priority number one.

Gospel
Mark 1:21–28 (RCL/RC/Epis)

Jesus teaches in Capernaum with uncommon authority. Suddenly a man possessed by a demon recognizes Jesus and cries out, asking if Jesus has come to destroy all demons. Jesus rebukes him and commands the demon to come out of the man. The people are amazed and, as a result, Jesus' reputation spreads.

Theme
Many things can inhibit faithful living. Nothing should.

Thought for the Day
The deep disease of the human heart is a will broken loose from its center, like a planet which has left its central sun and started to revolve around some strange body from outer space which may have moved in close enough to draw it away.

– A. W. Tozer

Call to Worship
One: Search us, O God, and know our hearts.
All: Test us and know our thoughts.
One: See if there is any wicked way in us,
All: And lead us in the way everlasting.

– Based on Psalm 139:23–24

Pastoral Prayer
Eternal God, we praise you and celebrate your unfathomable love for us. Your glory is far beyond our comprehension, your majesty far beyond our reach, your goodness far beyond our capacity. We come close to you and we melt under the heat of our awareness of how far from your holiness we are. And yet, you love us. How well we can relate to the psalmist who wrote, "O Lord, our Sovereign, how majestic is your name in all the earth…When I consider your heavens, the work of your fingers, the moon and stars that you have established; what are human beings that you are mindful of them, mortals that you care for them? Yet you have made them little lower than God" (Ps 8:1, 3–5).

Everlasting God, we want to please and honor you with our lives. We want to be witnesses to the world, in word and behavior, proclaiming that you alone are worthy of praise. Please empower us for mission.

Fill us with your Holy Spirit. so that we can rise above ourselves and give others a preview of what awaits them when they entrust their lives to you, through Jesus Christ. Amen.

Prayer of Confession

O Lord, we pause now to scan our hearts because we love you and want so much to please you. But as we do we feel profound apprehension. We've looked into our souls before and what we've found is dark when compared to your light. And this recognition, O God, is what brings us again and again to the cross, mindful of the fact that only in Jesus Christ can we bridge the gap that exists between us. With that truth in hand we now come to you by way of the Way, confessing our sin and asking that you view us only through the lens of Jesus Christ's righteousness. Amen.

Prayer of Dedication of Gifts and Self

As we bow our heads, Lord, we are thankful beyond words for the privilege you have extended to us to participate in the eternal work of your kingdom. There are so many ways that we can spend our money, but we know deep down that there is no way that our money can be better spent than in the service of our Savior. You have given us all that we have; embolden us to hold back nothing from you. As we offer these gifts to you, anoint them with your Holy Spirit and cause them to be a blessing to all the people they touch. We pray that Jesus will be honored by our giving, and that broken lives will be healed through his transforming power. Amen.

Sermon Summary

It's so easy to get caught up in the things of this life, distracted by the duties of daily living. And yet the Bible says that whatever inhibits our godly devotion must go. Jesus can help us with this by cleansing our lives from within.

Hymn of the Day
"Silence, Frenzied, Unclean Spirit!"

An epiphany had already dawned upon the small band of disciples whom Jesus called; as a result they left all to follow him. Today we begin to hear how Jesus revealed himself in word and deed to the larger community. Mark reports many were "astounded" and "amazed" by Jesus – especially at his power to exorcise demons.

While not for every congregation, this is the ideal Sunday to use the striking hymn by Thomas Troeger and Carol Doran, "Silence, Frenzied, Unclean Spirit!" Though the harmonies will be jarring to many, if introduced well and used sparingly, this can be a hymn that people will grow to appreciate.

Children's Time

Jesus, a Different Kind of Teacher

Preparation: Bring in a small chalkboard and chalk or a white board and marker.

(Write "2 + 2 =" on the board.) What's the answer? (Write "3 + 1 =.") What's the answer? (Write "C A T.") What is this word? Good. Look at all that you have learned! How did you learn how to do math and how to read? (From a teacher.) Teachers help students learn many kinds of things. Who are some of your teachers? (Accept names.)

Jesus was a teacher, too. What did Jesus teach? (He taught about God's love.) Jesus taught by telling stories and telling people how to live in God's love.

But Jesus also taught in other ways that were pretty amazing – by doing things that normal teachers could not do. Jesus could change water into wine. He could walk on water. Jesus could heal people who were sick. Jesus could do these things because he was God's Son. Through his actions, Jesus taught the people that God's love is stronger than evil things in the world.

Prayer: Dear Jesus, thank you for coming to earth to teach us about God's love. Amen.

The Sermon

Putting Everything Aside

Hymns
Beginning of Worship: "Holy, Holy, Holy"
Sermon Hymn: "Take Time to Be Holy"
Closing Hymn: "Take My Life and Let It Be"

Scripture

Mark 1:21–28 (For additional sermon materials on this passage, see the October 2005 issue of *The Clergy Journal*; for sermon materials on Deuteronomy 18:15–20, see the 2005 May/June planning issue of *The Clergy Journal*.)

What do you think about demons? For most twenty-first century residents of Western civilization, casting out demons seems like a primitive enterprise, quite possibly an ancient portrayal of the healing of some kind of mental illness. But perhaps there's more to it.

Our contemporary understanding of illness in no way diminishes the two most important messages of such accounts. First, Jesus healed. Whether or not we now have a better understanding of what it was that he healed is of no real consequence. Fact is, Jesus alone had the power to heal. Second, there is at work in the universe a force, an unseen dynamic – evil, if you will – that is capable of and eager to disrupt our relationship with God by any means.

Capernaum, the town at the center of Mark's account, was set on the northwest shore of the Sea of Galilee – a small fishing village where today there has been considerable excavation of ancient sites. Jesus visited there often, especially in his first year of public ministry. Peter, Andrew, James, and John plied their fishing trade there. Jesus spent a great deal of time in Capernaum preaching, teaching and performing miracles in and around the synagogue.

On one occasion Mark reports that an extraordinary event happened. A man possessed by a demon suddenly became quite agitated in Jesus' company. The demon cried out in distress, identifying Jesus publicly as the Holy One of God and castigating him for having only one thing on his mind, namely, the destruction of all demons. It's safe to assume from the nature of his response that Jesus was angered by this outburst. He harshly rebuked the demon with the words, "Be silent, and come out of him" (Mk 1:25).

Whether we believe in demonic possession or understand it is, in one sense, not germane to the real point of the passage. The point is this: nothing should be permitted to stand between God and us. Demons not withstanding, there is much in our world that can do exactly that. Surprisingly, even such mundane things as marriage, grief, shopping, and the like can potentially present a problem in this regard. So writes Paul

in chapters 7 and 8 of his first letter to the Corinthian church. There
he suggests that nothing should be allowed to inhibit our "unhindered
devotion to the Lord" (1 Cor 7:35).

What Paul is suggesting is that even seemingly innocuous, common-
place, or mundane things can get in the way of our total devotion to God.
This should be a wakeup call to every one of us.

In his wonderful book titled *Prayer: Finding the Heart's True Home*,
Richard Foster writes about the so-called Prayer of Examen, "How very
strange," he says, "that the Prayer of Examen has been lost to we who live
in an age of obsessive introspection...what a loss!...what is the Prayer of
Examen? It has two basic aspects, like the two sides of a door. The first
is the examen of consciousness through which we discover how God has
been present to us throughout the day and how we have responded to his
loving presence. The second aspect is an examen of conscience in which we
uncover those areas that need cleansing, purifying and healing."

Examining our conscience every day to identify what needs cleansing,
purifying, and healing is crucial to the health of our connectedness to
God. A failure to engage in this internal examination will inevitably and
unavoidably result in things coming between us and God. Perhaps this is
what David had in mind when he wrote, "Search me, O God, and know
my heart; test me, and know my thoughts. See if there is any wicked way
in me, and lead me in the way everlasting" (Ps 139:23–24).

What then do we do when we scan our souls and find things that
need to be removed, demons by any other name, things that stand between
us and the Lord? Very simply, we engage in what Foster calls the "scrutiny
of love." Again, he writes, "Without apology and without defense we ask
to see what is truly in us. It is for our own sake that we ask these things."

With this scrutiny, Jesus begins to do in us what he did in the man of
Capernaum who was possessed by a demon. He commands the demon to
come out. For us the cleansing may not be so sudden or dramatic as the
man in our text today, but the result is no less freeing.

In the New Testament we're led to believe that the one thing that
most hindered Peter from a healthy closeness to God, Peter's demon so
to speak, was what Jesus once referred to as a "weak flesh." Peter's heart
was in the right place, but under pressure of opposition, he caved, perhaps
the most dramatic example of this coming in the High Priest's courtyard.
But something happened to Peter over the years. He changed. He grew.

He became strong, even to the point of martyrdom. Years after his colossal courtyard failure he was able to speak these words of confidence and exhortation, "Beloved, do not be surprised at the fiery ordeal that is taking place among you to test you...but rejoice insofar as you are sharing Christ's sufferings, so that you may also be glad and shout for joy when his glory is revealed" (1 Pet 4:12, 13).

Peter's weak-flesh "demon" was exorcised, freeing him to breathe into others what had once been absent from his own life – courage. And how did it happen? By examen, by subjecting his soul to the daily scrutiny of Christ's love, by the slow but sure exposure of his demon to the rebuking Word of Christ.

In John's gospel Jesus cautions his disciples and us with these words, "In the world you face persecution..." In other words, demons of all kinds can and will affect us, disrupting our lives and threatening our devotion to God. "But take courage!" Jesus then declares. "I have conquered the world" (Jn 16:33).

To believe in demons or not to believe in demons – either way, the fact remains that things do get between God and us. When that happens we must remember that it is Christ, and Christ alone, who has the power to heal.

– David Wesley Reid

February 5, 2006

5th Sunday after Epiphany
RC/Pres: 5th Sunday in Ordinary Time

Lessons

RCL	Isa 40:21–31	1 Cor 9:16–23	Mk 1:29–39
Roman Catholic	Job 7:1–4, 6–7	1 Cor 9:16–19, 22–23	Mk 1:29–39
Episcopal	2 Kgs 4: (8–17) 18–21, (22–31), 32–37	1 Cor 9:16–23	Mk 1:29–39

Introduction to the Lessons

Lesson 1

(1) Isaiah 40:21–31 (RCL)

Israel complains that God has abandoned them, but it isn't true. Isaiah tells them to look at creation and see God's presence. God created everything and still rules over all people and earthly authorities.

(2) Job 7:1–4, 6–7 (RC)

Job complains to God that his life is nothing. Pain and suffering are Job's companions day and night.

(3) 2 Kings 4: (8–17) 18–21, (22–31), 32–37 (Epis)

Elisha is in Shunem, staying with a family who has an only child, a boy. One day the boy's head begins to hurt, and he dies. Elisha is summoned. After praying and placing his body atop the boy's, the child is revived.

Lesson 2

1 Corinthians 9:16–23 (RCL/Epis);
1 Corinthians 9:16–19, 22–23 (RC)

Paul submits himself to the different lifestyles of persons he's trying to reach with the gospel. In this sense he makes himself weak, a slave of sorts. Paul's desire is to share with them in the blessings associated with the gospel.

Gospel
Mark 1:29–39 (RCL/RC/Epis)

One day Jesus heals Peter's mother-in-law, along with other sick persons. The next morning, while Jesus is praying alone, the disciples search him out to report that everyone is looking for him. Jesus then decides to leave for other villages where he can pursue his mission of preaching.

Theme

Life comes to those who are close to God.

Thought for the Day

What lies behind us and what lies before us are tiny matters compared to what lies within us.

– Ralph Waldo Emerson

Call to Worship

One: We are crucified with Christ.
All: It is no longer we who live, but Christ who lives in us,
One: For to live is Christ and to die is gain.
All: Come, Lord Jesus. May your loving Holy Spirit fill us in this time of worship.

Pastoral Prayer

Almighty God, we praise you as we come together in worship. As Augustine proclaimed, our hearts are restless until they find their rest in you. We come to this sanctuary because we know and believe that only in spiritual proximity to you will our lives find purpose and meaning.

Please fill us with your life-engendering Holy Spirit, not because we are worthy, but because you love us. We know that we cannot represent you in the needy and broken world in which we live unless you live inside us, empowering us for the challenge that is everywhere evident. How grateful we are, Lord, that you will enter into intimate relationship with us through Jesus Christ. How grateful we are that through the work of your Holy Spirit, Jesus can be as alive for us today as he was for the disciples who lived and served with him in the flesh.

Use us now, we pray, as mightily as you used them. May we be the loving and saving presence of the Savior to all who are imprisoned by sin and suffering. Amen.

Prayer of Confession

Eternal, loving, and forgiving God, it is difficult for us to draw close to you because such closeness makes us realize how far from you in spirit we truly are, as far as the east is from the west. There is absolutely nothing we can do of our own volition to extricate ourselves from this plight, apart from coming to you on the strength of the love and cleansing power of Jesus Christ. He alone is our confidence. He alone is our hope. He alone is our Savior. And so, desperate for your forgiveness, Lord, we come boldly to your throne of grace, confessing not only our sinful acts, but our sinful condition, knowing full well that in Jesus Christ our Lord, we can be washed clean and given a new beginning. Amen.

Prayer of Dedication of Gifts and Self

How can we thank you, O God, for the generosity you show to us, for the giving spirit you exhibit to us? We survey all that we are and all that we have, and we marvel at your beneficence. Help us count our many blessings to see what you have done. Open our hearts to give from love and gratitude, not obligation and duty. As we bring these gifts to you now, we dedicate them to the glorious work of your kingdom. May Jesus' name be praised in and through what we offer. May these gifts be a marvelous blessing to those whose lives will be touched by the good works they support. Amen.

Sermon Summary

The world is filled with broken people, but when they are touched by Jesus, life happens. Healing of mind, body, or spirit happens. The assurance that things will be all right grows. As Christians, we are the beneficiaries of this blessing, and the instruments of it as well.

Hymn of the Day
"In Solitude"
Seen as a whole, the Epiphany season is a crescendo to Transfiguration
Sunday, when we hear the voice from heaven confirm that Jesus is, indeed,
God's beloved son. Perhaps as a contrast, today could be a time to go with
Jesus to that quiet place in the heart where, in prayer, we speak to God
and God speaks to us.

Ruth Duck's "In Solitude," set to the tune LAND OF REST, is a
wonderful choice for such a journey. The sincere text and gentle tune meld
seamlessly together, resulting in a beautiful invitation to and reflection
upon prayer. Another great choice is Jay Beech's "Everybody Needs."

Children's Time

A Healing Touch

Preparation: Bring in a cotton ball, piece of satin, soft stuffed animal,
and other soft materials.
(Pass around the soft items you brought.) How are all of these items
the same? (They are soft.) Can we tell they are soft by looking at them?
Smelling, tasting, or listening to them? How can we tell whether or
not something is soft? (By touching it.) We can use our sense of touch
to tell if something is soft or rough. What are other ways we use our
sense of touch?

Jesus was a wonderful teacher. People listened to his stories for
hours. They followed Jesus wherever he went because they wanted
to learn more about God's love. Jesus had another very special way
of teaching – Jesus used the sense of touch. In today's Bible story, a
woman was sick with a high fever. Jesus gently held her hand and her
fever was gone. Jesus used his touch to heal people. When people heard
about Jesus' healing touch, people came from the whole city, bringing
their sick loved ones to be healed. Through his healing touch, Jesus
taught people about the power of God's love.
Prayer: Dear Jesus, help us to share your love through our words and
our actions. Amen.

The Sermon

When Life Comes to Life

Hymns
Beginning of Worship: "Praise to the Lord the Almighty"
Sermon Hymn: "Pass Me Not, O Gentle Savior"
Closing Hymn: "Jesus Shall Reign"

Scripture
Mark 1:29–39 (For additional sermon materials on this passage, see the October 2005 issue of *The Clergy Journal*; for sermon materials on 1 Corinthians 9:16–23, see the 2005 May/June planning issue of *The Clergy Journal*.)

A pastor was preparing to leave the congregation where he had served faithfully for seven years. Both he and his parishioners were in tears over the parting. Gifts were given, embraces shared, kind and complimentary words offered:

"Pastor, we thank you from the bottom of our hearts for your service to the Lord here."

"Pastor, your faithfulness has been an inspiration to us."

"Pastor, God has truly blessed us with your ministry."

But of all the gracious and kind comments made, the most moving, the most impressive was this: "Pastor, we knew that no matter how bad things were, no matter how difficult things became, if you were present, somehow it would be all right." No pastor could hear anything more uplifting and affirming than this.

"Pastor, we just knew that no matter how bad things were, no matter how difficult things became, if you were present, somehow it would be all right." Multiply that sense of reassuring presence a hundred-fold and it begins to convey something of the assurance that those who were sick or poor or broken by life must have felt in the presence of the Good Pastor, Jesus Christ. When Jesus was around, these people just knew that things would be all right. Healing would happen.

Life comes to life in the presence of God. Elijah breathing life into a dead boy's body. Isaiah telling us to wait upon the Lord for renewal of strength. Paul doing whatever it takes to elicit the life-giving blessings of the gospel in the churchgoers of Corinth. Jesus healing the sick and broken. Again and again, the message is the same – wherever God is, wherever Jesus is, life comes to life; things will be all right.

Mark writes, "That evening, at sundown, they brought to him all who were sick or possessed with demons. And the whole city was gathered around the door. And he cured many who were sick with various diseases" (1:32–34). What a blessing it must have been to be a beneficiary of the new life God brings through Jesus Christ.

The life-giving blessings of Jesus' touch are not limited to the narrow band of men and women who knew him in the flesh two thousand years ago. We don't have to celebrate from afar. Look within. We too have joined the ranks of those first men and women who were touched by Jesus and given new life. For us this newness of life may not have come through physical restoration from infirmity, but it surely has come through spiritual restoration from sin.

And this new life places upon each of us an obligation not just to be beneficiaries, but also conduits – individual pipelines, if you will, through which the loving and life-giving spirit of Christ can flow into the lives of others in need. Paul understood this. That's why he became, as he put it, all things to all persons, so that he could offer to others what was offered to him, namely, newness of life in Jesus Christ.

It is incumbent upon us to follow this example. Wasn't this the duty that Christ was placing upon us over and over again in the gospels? "Not everyone who says to me, 'Lord, Lord,' will enter the kingdom of heaven, but only the one who does the will of my Father in heaven" (Mt 7:21). And in one of his last parables, that of the Sheep and Goats, didn't Jesus promise God's reward to those who feed the hungry, give drink to the thirsty, welcome strangers, clothe the naked, care for the sick, and visit the imprisoned?

We can convey life to others in the name of Jesus. What we must keep in mind, however, and it is crucial for us to do so, is that we can be effective only insofar as we ourselves remain connected to the source of life, God Almighty. After Jesus poured life into those who were sick and broken in Peter's hometown, Mark tells us he withdrew to a solitary place where he could be alone with God in prayer. Why did Jesus do that? He did it to ensure that God's Spirit continued to flow unabated into his soul, from where it could be dispensed to others as the need arose.

One of the great missionaries of the twentieth century was Mary Reed. As a young woman she determined to bring life to the women of India in the name of Jesus. For eight years she worked under difficult conditions in Cawnpore, India, until her health began to collapse. She was sent to the Himalayas to recuperate, and while there she discovered a colony of five hundred lepers living without help or support. Some time later she returned to India, but within a year her health failed again, and she was sent back to America. Much to her dismay and to the confusion of the doctors, her health continued to fail until one day she realized what was happening. The pain in her finger, the spot on her face – telltale signs that she herself had contracted leprosy. Instead of decrying her plight she returned to India where she could work with a community of lepers and bring to them the life that Christ had brought to her. And so, in Chandag, India, a settlement and a hospital for lepers grew as a result of her efforts. A single woman. A soul filled to the brim with the life of Jesus Christ. A servant of the Lord who brought life to those who were broken in body and spirit by a dread disease.

A teacher of first and second graders in vacation Bible school taught the children that we are Jesus' hands and feet in the world. Then he asked the children where Jesus lives today. The response was nearly unanimous, "Jesus lives inside us." One little boy was puzzled, however. Looking at the large picture of Jesus on the wall he said, "I'm small and Jesus is big. If Jesus lives inside me why isn't he sticking out somewhere?" Good question. Truth is, if Jesus lives inside us, if we are filled with his life, he does stick out somewhere, bringing health and well-being to others.

Wherever Jesus is, all things end up all right. Healing happens. Life comes to life in the presence of God. May we be not just the beneficiaries of this blessing. May we be the instruments as well.

– David Wesley Reid

February 12, 2006

6th Sunday after Epiphany
RC/Pres: 6th Sunday in Ordinary Time

Lessons

RCL	2 Kgs 5:1–14	1 Cor 9:24–27	Mk 1:40–45
Roman Catholic	Lev 13:1–12, 44–46	1 Cor 10:31—11:1	Mk 1:40–45
Episcopal	2 Kgs 5:1–15b	1 Cor 9:24–27	Mk 1:40–45

Introduction to the Lessons
Lesson 1
(1) 2 Kings 5:1–14 (RCL); 2 Kings 5:1–15b (Epis)
Naaman, a general under the King of Aram, has leprosy. His Jewish servant girl advises him to visit the prophet Elisha to be cured. He travels to Israel and is told to bathe in the Jordan River. After initial resistance, he does so and is cured.

(2) Leviticus 13:1–12, 44–46 (RC)
God gives Moses and Aaron instructions on how to deal with people's skin ailments. If the skin problem is a rash, the person will not be declared unclean. But if the skin problem is more serious, he or she will be declared unclean and must be separated from the camp.

Lesson 2
(1) 1 Corinthians 9:24–27 (RCL/Epis)
Paul wants the Corinthian believers to give a total effort in living the Christian life. Consider the athlete who gives a wholehearted effort to win a prize that won't last. How much more then should the Christian work to win a crown of victory that is eternal.

(2) 1 Corinthians 10:31–11:1 (RC)
Do everything to the glory of God. Don't let your life inhibit anyone else's spiritual well-being. Live as though you're thinking of the interests of

others and not just your own. Follow my example, Paul tells Corinthian believers, because he himself has followed the example of Jesus Christ.

Gospel
Mark 1:40–45 (RCL/RC/Epis)
One with leprosy begs Jesus for healing. Jesus, filled with compassion, heals him. Jesus dismisses him with the warning not to tell anyone. Instead, the man tells everyone, forcing Jesus to avoid public places because of the overwhelming attention.

Theme
God calls us to excellence, in our person and our performance.

Thought for the Day
Sloth, writes Dorothy Sayers, is "the sin which believes in nothing...finds purpose in nothing, lives for nothing and only remains alive because there is nothing it would die for."

Call to Worship
One:	Finally, beloved, whatever is true, whatever is honorable, whatever is just, whatever is pure,
All:	Whatever is pleasing, whatever is commendable, if there is any excellence,
One:	And if there is anything worthy of praise, think about these things.
All:	And the God of peace will be with you.

– Based on Philippians 4:8–9

Pastoral Prayer
Almighty and ever-loving God, as we enter into your heavenly presence we fall to our knees in reverence and awe. Your glory, your perfection, your majesty, your unmitigated love – they all overwhelm us. Were we to look on your face, we would surely die, because our souls cannot comprehend the full grandeur of your being.

And yet, in the person of your son Jesus Christ, you left the glory of heaven and entered into the muck and mire of a sin-filled world. You transcended the gap between us and reached out to provide all persons, everywhere, with the chance to share in your splendor. How can we possibly comprehend the magnificence of your beneficence? We cannot. Nevertheless, having caught a glimpse of your brilliance, we are highly motivated to please you, to emulate you, and to have our lives characterized by your excellence. Oh, how we praise you, Lord. Amen.

Prayer of Confession

Gracious God, as we behold your glory, our hearts are overwhelmed with contrition. We look at ourselves honestly and recognize that there is nothing we do or say, however noble, that is not tarnished by selfish desire. For this reason we would never presume to come to you boldly in prayer, were it not for Jesus Christ. We give thanks that he died for our sin and that his righteousness is imputed to us simply by the exercise of our faith. How amazing that is, O God. Forgive us, we pray, for failing to pursue your perfection as Jesus counseled us to do. We ask, confident in the atonement that is ours through the blood of the Savior. Amen.

Prayer of Dedication of Gifts and Self

Lord, as we bring our gifts to you, examine the motives that lie behind our giving. We can hide from others, but we cannot hide from you. Burn off whatever motive we may exercise in our giving that is less than your love. Replace it, we ask, with the selflessness of Jesus who gave his all from a place of unblemished love. Let this offering be our moment of renewed dedication to you and to our pursuit of becoming all that you want us to be. Amen.

Sermon Summary

What pleases God most is not rigorous religious living, but our willingness to love selflessly. Jesus demonstrated this, especially in the cross, but also in countless other interpersonal encounters such as in his healing of the one with leprosy. So must we.

Hymn of the Day
"Here, Savior, in This Quiet Place"

Jesus' healing encounter with the anonymous man with leprosy was ever so brief. He spoke all of eight words to Jesus: "If you choose, you can make me clean," and Jesus spoke six in reply: "I do choose. Be made clean." Oh, that healing would come so quickly to us, our neighbors, our world!

Fred Pratt Green's "Here, Savior, in This Quiet Place" fashions into words the universal yearning for healing. Yet, ever so tenderly, the hymn also gives us the words to ask for faith when healing is not immediately forthcoming. A recent tune by Peter Cutts, CHATHAM, reveals the essence of Green's text.

Children's Time

Shh! It's a Secret

Preparation: Bring in some play money.

(Whisper loudly and hold up the play money.) I have a secret! I've just won 10 million dollars. I'm not supposed to tell anyone that I'm rich. But I can't help it. I just had to share my happy news with you.

(Revert to normal voice.) Today's Bible story is about someone who had something wonderful happen in his life. This man lived during Jesus' time. He had a horrible disease called leprosy. All people with this disease had to live outside of the city, away from their family and friends. They were very lonely.

This man with leprosy had heard of Jesus. When he saw Jesus, he ran to him, fell on his knees, and begged Jesus to heal him. He knew that Jesus could heal him. Jesus touched the man and immediately he was healed. Then Jesus told him, "Don't tell anyone!"

But the man was so happy – this was the best thing in the whole world that could have happened to him. He went out and told everyone he saw that Jesus had touched him and healed him. The power of God's love had healed this sick man. He couldn't keep this a secret.

Prayer: Dear Jesus, we won't keep your love a secret! Amen.

The Sermon

What Pleases God Most

Hymns

Beginning of Worship: "Be Thou My Vision"
Sermon Hymn: "I Have Decided to Follow Jesus"
Closing Hymn: "Living for Jesus"

Scripture

Mark 1:40–45 (For additional sermon materials on this passage, see the 2005 May/June planning issue and the October 2005 issue of *The Clergy Journal.*)

How do we best show that we love God? How do we best demonstrate our devotion? What does God look for in us? What brings a smile to God's face? Would sound doctrine delight God most? What about rigorous spiritual discipline? What if we prayed, studied, served, and worshiped with the passion of a monastic saint? Would God be most happy with that? Or perhaps God would be most impressed with an inner contriteness?

What does God most want to see in us? What would gladden God's heart? The only basis we have for answering these questions is Jesus Christ, who was and is God with us. In Christ, God reveals what is most pleasing. And, in simple words, it is this – a life of selfless love selflessly expressed.

Of course the cross is the best example of this in the life of Jesus, but throughout Jesus' ministry we see innumerable examples of this truth played out in vivid ways. Case in point, Jesus' healing of the unnamed man with leprosy, a story recorded in our gospel reading today and repeated in the gospels of Matthew and Luke.

Jesus was engaged in ministry around the Sea of Galilee – preaching, teaching, and healing in many different towns. On one occasion a man whom Luke describes as "covered with leprosy" approached him. This alone must have been quite startling to the onlookers, since the law strictly prohibited a leper from any kind of social contact. Moses wrote in the book of Leviticus, "The person who has the leprous disease shall wear torn clothes and let the hair of his head be disheveled; and he shall cover his upper lip and cry out, 'Unclean, unclean.' He shall remain unclean as long as he has the disease; he is unclean. He shall live alone; his dwelling shall be outside the camp" (Lev 13:45–46).

Clearly this man had no business coming close to Jesus, or anyone else for that matter. And yet he did, no doubt from a place of total desperation. "If you choose, you can make me clean," the man cried out. Notice how Jesus responded. "Moved with pity, Jesus stretched out his hand and touched him, and said to him, 'I do choose. Be made clean!'" (Mk 1:40–41).

What do we see being played out here? It's clear, we see selfless love being selflessly expressed. Jesus then commanded him with what Mark refers to as a "stern warning," to keep quiet about what had happened. "See that you say nothing to anyone; but go, show yourself to the priest, and offer for your cleansing what Moses commanded, as a testimony to them" (v. 44).

And did the man comply? Sadly, no. Instead he ran around telling everyone about what had happened, making it extremely difficult from then on for Jesus to come and go openly.

Things can be said about this man's disobedience and the sadness attached to that. Things also can be said about the point Jesus wanted to make to the priests about his authority over disease. In addition, things can be said about Jesus' lifestyle, how he had to hide from curiosity-seeking people to ensure that he could get done what he came to earth to do. But the principle point of this passage seems to be the window of insight it provides into the soul of our Savior. Jesus was "filled with pity." Selfless love selflessly expressed. If we're trying to identify what pleases God most, this is it. This is what God is all about. This is excellence in God's eyes.

Dr. Marion Boehr, now retired, was for many years an American Baptist missionary to India. As a physician she saw unimaginable suffering and in her address to the 1987 Biennial Convention of American Baptists she shared these words:

> The genius of the Christian faith is concern for the individual. Every human soul is infinitely valuable in God's sight. Statistics show that within India 10,000 children die each month of malnutrition-related infectious diseases, and three out of every twenty born this year will die before the year is over. The survivors seldom reach their physical and mental growth potential. To hundreds of millions of children, life

is little more than a vigil of death. It is certainly no banquet. As Christian missionaries we teach that Jesus came that we might have life, and have it more abundantly. The uncomfortable question is still with us – where is this abundant life in the midst of poverty, misery, sickness, and suffering? Christ Himself champions the downtrodden, the refuse of this inhuman planet. He honors every fragment of the human race, however miserable, however foul. He teaches us that if we would serve Him we must serve them, and if we would glorify Him, we must honor them…I often think of the last war, when a reporter on the front lines watched with horror and fascination as a pretty young army nurse prepared a wounded soldier for surgery. He was filthy, covered with blood and dirt. She worked skillfully and without hesitation. Finally the reporter blurted out, "Nurse, I wouldn't do what you're doing for a million dollars." Without hesitating in her work she answered quietly, "Mister, I wouldn't either! None of us would do what we do for a million dollars. We do it because the love of Christ constrains us."

It's all well and good to be spiritually disciplined. It's all well and good to nail down firmly what we believe. It's all well and good to suffer for the Savior. But if none of this is founded on a heart transformed by the love of God, of what use is it? It's nothing more than the exercise of a soul bent on selfish ambition.

What gladdens God's heart most is the excellence of selfless love selflessly expressed. Now, go and love others selflessly in the name of Jesus.

– David Wesley Reid

February 19, 2006

7th Sunday after Epiphany
RC/Pres: 7th Sunday in Ordinary Time

Lessons

RCL	Isa 43:18–25	2 Cor 1:18–22	Mk 2:1–12
Roman Catholic	Isa 43:18–19, 21–22, 24–25	2 Cor 1:18–22	Mk 2:1–12
Episcopal	Isa 43:18–25	2 Cor 1:18–22	Mk 2:1–12

Introduction to the Lessons
Lesson 1
Isaiah 43:18–25 (RCL/Epis);
Isaiah 43:18–19, 21–22, 24–25 (RC)

God is about to do a new thing for the chosen people, even though they have not honored God with appropriate sacrifices and prayers. Instead, they have burdened God with their sins.

Lesson 2
2 Corinthians 1:18–22 (RCL/RC/Epis)

The writer professes that through Jesus Christ, God has put God's seal on the people and given them the Holy Spirit. This is a sign of the eternal "yes" of God, who is faithful to all promises.

Gospel
Mark 2:1–12 (RCL/RC/Epis)

Four people who wanted to bring a friend who was paralyzed to Jesus in a crowded house went up on the roof and made a hole in it, then let the man down in front of Jesus. Jesus forgave his sins and healed him.

Theme
Paralysis occurs in many ways. We bring each other to Jesus for healing.

Thought for the Day

Jesus meets a man with paralysis, but sees that his problems run deeper. Jesus helps the man when he sees his faith and the faith of those who brought him.

Call to Worship

One: Happy are those who consider the poor;
All: The Lord delivers them in the day of trouble.
One: The Lord protects them and keeps them alive;
All: They are happy in the land.

– Based on Psalm 41:1–2b

Pastoral Prayer

For love and forgiveness and patience, we give you thanks, O Lord. For friends and family, for all those who care enough to see that we get what we need to be safe and fed, we give you thanks, O Lord.

Teach us to be that kind of friend to others, even to those we have never met. Give us faith enough to share with those for whom faith is hard to come by, or who struggle because of difficulty simply to recognize your goodness. And when we find ourselves among those who strain to find an ounce of faith, send friends our way who will let us lean on them until we can find our own way of standing. Amen.

Prayer of Confession

You see us, O holy God, as we are, and you love us still. You see our weaknesses, our foibles, our sins, the ways in which we struggle to find meaning. We come to you with problems of one sort and you are able to look deeper within to see the real trouble. Give us the ability to see ourselves as you see us. Show us what we ought to do to be more like Jesus, our Lord and Savior. Amen.

Prayer of Dedication of Gifts and Self

As we have heard your words today, O Lord, we are now drawn to offer ourselves in service to you. Give us the ability to see the gifts you have given us, and the ability to use those gifts in your world. Amen.

Sermon Summary

Jesus sees us as we are, and knows our deepest needs.

Hymn of the Day
"Oh for a Thousand Tongues"

Oh, to know the joy of being healed as the man in Capernaum did! Such an occurrence would be the turning point in one's life, an event coloring all others. The hymn "Oh for a Thousand Tongues" testifies that, for Charles Wesley, that event in his life was becoming a Christian.

Penned on the first anniversary of his 1738 conversion, Wesley's mighty hymn is comprised of eighteen stanzas from which four are generally selected. Carl Gläser's AZMON is an uplifting eight-bar melody that complements well Wesley's jubilant text.

Children's Time

Four Faithful Friends

Preparation: Identify the ways your church building is inviting to people with physical disabilities.

Churches are welcoming places, places for everyone to worship God. Some of God's people use wheelchairs or walkers or crutches. How is our church building welcoming for them? (Accept answers and point out others.)

One day four people brought their friend to see Jesus. They carried their friend on a mat because he couldn't walk. They knew that Jesus could heal their friend, if only they could reach Jesus. The house where Jesus was teaching was packed with people. They couldn't get through the crowd. The four friends climbed to the rooftop. The flat roof was made of woven plants and covered with clay. They carefully removed part of the roof and lowered their friend through the opening. Jesus looked up and watched as the man came down from the roof. Jesus said, "Stand up, take your mat and go to your home." And that's just what the man did! Jesus healed him!

These four people found a way to get their friend to Jesus. What do you think was the first thing the five friends did together?

Prayer: Dear Jesus, help us to welcome all people who want to see you. Amen.

The Sermon

Paralysis

Hymns

Beginning of Worship: "I Sing the Mighty Power of God"
Sermon Hymn: "Live into Hope"
Closing Hymn: "Come, Thou Fount of Every Blessing"

Scripture

Mark 2:1–12 (For sermon materials on 2 Corinthians 1:18–22, see the 2005 May/June planning issue of *The Clergy Journal*; for sermon materials on Isaiah 43:18–25, see the November/December 2005 issue of *The Clergy Journal*.)

Jesus was at home in Capernaum. Word got around after a few days that he was there and people came to hear him teach. There was quite a crowd, with people filling up the house and spilling out into the street.

For one man, this day was quite different. He suffered from some sort of paralysis. We don't know how long he'd been paralyzed, how often he'd prayed to be healed. We don't know if he'd grown despondent from the length of time he'd been bedridden. But one thing we know: there were people close to him who cared about what happened to him. They wanted to do something to help.

The details of the story are sketchy, but I like to imagine that someone close to this man heard that Jesus was nearby and hit upon the idea of taking the sick man to be healed. He got three other friends, and they planned to carry this man to where Jesus was. They knew he couldn't get there on his own, so they determined to take him.

This is what real friendship and love are about. When we can't do for ourselves – when our physical or spiritual or emotional health is weak – those who care about us step into the picture and provide the help we need.

These people took the man to the house where Jesus was teaching, but they couldn't get anywhere near the door because of the crowd. I imagine them talking among themselves about just how they would get Jesus to see the man. They must have discussed and discarded several possibilities before one of them tentatively said, "You know, about the only way we can get him in front of Jesus is to go up and let him down through the roof." Everyone laughed. "Yeah, right!" "No, really." And they all looked at him as though he had lost his mind. After some talking, he convinced them to give it a try.

Maybe one friend ran home to get a shovel, and they struggled up the ladder to the roof, carrying their friend. Most roofs in those days were formed by beams and rafters, then covered with matting or straw, or with tiles or a type of cement that hardened in the sun, or even a layer of dirt. Mark says that they dug through the roof in order to open up a hole.

Now imagine Jesus, in the house below, with the room absolutely filled with people. It must have been a little hot and dusty. There was some shuffling as people stirred, but mostly they were very quiet, listening. Some were listening to find things to disagree with. Others were listening for some word that would help them in their lives of faith. Both kinds of listeners had their attention focused on Jesus.

Then a little dust fell from the ceiling. A couple of people looked up but didn't see anything. Then more dust. Then the faint noise of digging, which began to get louder. Soon everyone was looking up as a man's face appeared at a hole in the roof. Jesus had stopped teaching. The hole got bigger. Though there was no room in the house, suddenly people somehow made room as a pallet was lowered through that hole in the roof down beside Jesus.

Jesus looked at the man, but also at his companions, still up on the roof, I imagine. There they rested, peering down into the room, filled with hope and prayers for their friend. Mark tells us that Jesus saw their faith. Does he include the faith of the sick man? Probably, but he also is referring to the faith of those who brought him. Jesus cared about their concerns, their prayers, their hopes.

When we pray for those we love, God sees our tears, feels our heavy hearts, understands our pleas. And when we don't have faith enough to see us through, we are buoyed by the faith of those around us. People who care about us pester us about our health, love us when we feel unloved, pray for us when we have lost all ability to pray. They can tell when we have had more than we can take, and they find ways to let us know they will share the burden with us, that they will hope for us, that they will believe for us when our faith is thin.

When Jesus saw their faith, he said to the man – and here's the surprise part of the story – "Child, your sins are forgiven." This wasn't the way it was supposed to happen! The poor guy was there to be healed, not this! Forgiveness could be granted by other means. They hadn't gone through all this for plain old forgiveness.

I have wondered, though, if the sick man might have been the only one there who wasn't troubled by Jesus' statement. Was there something Jesus could see in him that no one else could? Was there some need that even a miraculous physical healing would not touch? Were there needs unseen to all but the man and God? Jesus stepped into a different realm as he moved to heal the spirit before the body.

Mark indicates that some scribes who were there became furious. Only God had the authority to forgive sins. What was this Jesus trying to do?

Jesus confronted their anger. "Do you think it is easy to tell someone their sins are forgiven?" he asked. Of course they thought it was easy.

And so Jesus told the man to pick up his mat. He did, and walked away, and all were amazed, even (especially?) the scribes.

The signs of Jesus' ministry and the signs of the kingdom of God were often dramatic healings, as in this story. But there is a deeper sign embedded here. Not every person who was paralyzed had access to Jesus, or experienced that kind of healing. All of us, though, have access to the power of forgiveness offered to this sick man. This man's healing was indeed a sign. Jesus made it clear – "so that you may know that the Son of Man has authority on earth to forgive sins" (Mk 2:10) – that the healing of the man's paralysis pointed to a different kind of healing. The visible points us toward the invisible. Whatever the man's physical need, he also shared with all humanity hidden spiritual needs, and those needs were met by the Son of Man.

Paralysis takes different forms, and though some experience the extraordinarily difficult burden of physical paralysis, all of us know the hidden burden of the paralysis that affects the soul – when we are unable or unwilling to respond to God's gifts of mercy and grace. Often those who love or befriend us are the ones who nurture our souls and help us take the first steps back toward God. Even if we can't make those steps on our own, there are sometimes those who carry us in their prayers and their love until we are able to walk on our own. Once there, we find the spiritual healing we need, the forgiveness, the love, the grace. We find Jesus.

– Melissa Bane Sevier

February 26, 2006

Last Sunday after Epiphany/Transfiguration
RC: 8th Sunday in Ordinary Time

Lessons

RCL	2 Kgs 2:1–12	2 Cor 4:3–6	Mk 9:2–9
Roman Catholic	Hos 2:16–17, 21–22	2 Cor 3:1–6	Mk 2:18–22
Episcopal	1 Kgs 19:9–18	2 Pet 1:16–19	Mk 9:2–9
		(20–21)	

Introduction to the Readings
Lesson 1
(1) 2 Kings 2:1–12 (RCL)
Elijah is taken away from Elisha by a chariot of fire. Elisha asks for a double measure of Elijah's spirit.

(2) Hosea 2:16–17, 21–22 (RC)
The Lord promises a time when Israel will no longer worship the Baals, but will return to the Lord in faithfulness.

(3) 1 Kings 19:9–18 (Epis)
Elijah, fleeing from Jezebel, seeks shelter in a cave. There he hears the Lord pass by in the sound of sheer silence and is told to return to his mission.

Lesson 2
(1) 2 Corinthians 4:3–6 (RCL)
God has shown light in our hearts so that we may see the face of Jesus Christ. The truth is not veiled to us.

(2) 2 Corinthians 3:1–6 (RC)
Paul does not need a letter of recommendation, for the Corinthians themselves are a letter of Christ, written on the flesh of their own hearts.

(3) 2 Peter 1:16–19 (20–21) (Epis)

The author speaks of being an eyewitness to the Transfiguration, which illustrates a lamp shining in a dark place.

Gospel
(1) Mark 9:2–9 (RCL/Epis)

Jesus takes Peter, James, and John to a mountain, and is transfigured before them. They hear a voice say, "This is my Son, the Beloved; listen to him!"

(2) Mark 2:18–22 (RC)

John's disciples were criticized for not fasting. Jesus used the opportunity to say that things were changing.

Theme

There are moments of truth that change the way we see God and the world.

Thought for the Day

Sometimes we are allowed to see beyond the veil. We have a brief glimpse of God, and we take that vision with us into our daily lives.

Call to Worship

One:	The mighty one, God the Lord, speaks, and summons the earth from the rising of the sun to its setting.
All:	Out of Zion, the perfection of beauty, God shines forth.
One:	Our God comes and does not keep silence, before God is a devouring fire and a mighty tempest all around.
All:	The heavens declare God's righteousness, for the Lord is judge.

– Based on Psalm 50:1–3, 6

Pastoral Prayer

O Holy God, in Jesus Christ you lifted the veil between heaven and earth to show us your glory. In him we see love in its purest form.

Help us to look for and recognize those moments in our lives when the space between you and us is thin and we are truly in the presence of the Holy One. In our daily living, let us reflect that glory and love to those around us. May we see you in what we imagine to be the unlikely places – not just on the mountaintop, but in our homes and our schools, among our friends and at work, in our communities and in our daily circumstances. Amen.

Prayer of Confession

Gracious God, how often our vision is limited, and we do not see your glory and love. We fail to see you in those who are poor, needy, or oppressed, and therefore we do not act on their behalf. Forgive us and open our eyes, O Lord. Teach us to see with renewed vision. Teach us to act with renewed love. Amen.

Prayer of Dedication of Gifts and Self

Let us, O Lord, offer our lives, our hearts, and our gifts to serve you. As our vision is renewed, so renew our acts of kindness, our dedication to show Jesus to the world, and our desire to make our spheres of influence better reflect the glory of God. Amen.

Sermon Summary

As Jesus and the three saw the glory of God on the mountain of transfiguration, then continued the journey toward Jerusalem and the cross, so we have past experiences of God to help us move through the valleys on our way to Easter resurrection.

Hymn of the Day
"Jesus, Take Us to the Mountain"

Transfiguration Sunday is a liturgical mountaintop, capping off Epiphany like a jewel and giving us a glimpse of Jesus in his splendor. But though a high peak, it is not the highest; that honor belongs to Easter alone. Before then we sojourn the valley of Lent.

"Jesus, Take Us to the Mountain" is a splendid hymn for Transfiguration Sunday by Jaroslav Vajda and Carl Schalk. The first verses have us on the Mount of Transfiguration; the fourth verse whisks us to that sadder mount, Golgotha; the final verse leads us beyond to the point of telling Jesus' story, just as Jesus instructs his disciples to do.

Children's Time

A New View

Preparation: Bring a pair of sunglasses.
(Put on sunglasses.) Do I need to wear sunglasses in here? (No.) When do people usually wear sunglasses? (Outside on a sunny day.) Why? (The sun is very bright and it bothers our eyes.) We wear sunglasses to protect our eyes from too much bright sunlight.

In our Bible story today, three of Jesus' disciples needed sunglasses. Jesus led Peter, James, and John to the top of a mountain. When they reached the top, Jesus changed right in front of them. His clothes became dazzling white and his face shown like the sun. The disciples shielded their eyes from the bright light like this (shield your eyes with your hand). The disciples were terrified! That means they were very, very scared. Then a cloud softly floated down and covered the mountaintop. From the cloud came a voice saying, "This is my Beloved Son. Listen to him." God was giving the disciples a special message – Jesus was God's Son!

Prayer: Dear Lord, on bright sunny days remind us that your love surrounds us like the sunshine. Amen.

The Sermon

Renewing the Vision

Hymns
Beginning of Worship: "Holy, Holy, Holy"
Sermon Hymn: "O Wondrous Sight, O Vision Fair"
Closing Hymn: "Ye Watchers and Ye Holy Ones"

Scripture

Mark 9:2–9 (For additional sermon materials on this passage, see the 2005 May/June planning issue and the November/December 2005 issue of *The Clergy Journal.*)

Have you ever had a moment of truth – an experience that truly changed you or the way you looked at things for the rest of your life? Perhaps you remember a few years ago when then Secretary of State Madeleine Albright learned from a reporter that her parents, whom she'd always known as Catholics, were actually Jews who had converted to save themselves and their family from the Holocaust. How such knowledge must have re-arranged what Albright knew about her past and how she viewed her own identity.

In today's gospel reading, three disciples were confronted with the identity of Jesus. The Jesus they had known was now revealed to them in a new and incredible way.

In Mark, the passage is sandwiched between some interesting material. It comes after Peter confesses, "You are the Messiah," and Jesus' insistence that he will die and that those who follow him will also be required to give up much. Then immediately following the trip to the mountaintop, Jesus and the disciples hit the road again on the way to Jerusalem and the cross.

Wedged in between these themes of death comes this magnificent passage of exaltation. In this amazing account, Jesus was physically changed before their eyes – in a way that no one had ever seen. Peter had confessed him as Messiah, but they were unprepared for the visualization of that reality.

There is so much here that echoes themes from ancient Israel. Jesus glowed with the brightness often associated with God's presence in Exodus and elsewhere. There was a voice and a cloud, also indicators in Exodus of the eternal present with humans. Moses and Elijah were present, symbols of Law and prophecy. This was a vision for men who would understand that they were witnessing something deeply connected to their spiritual heritage. The Jesus they knew as friend, teacher, rabbi, was somehow uniquely identified with God. Even so, they did not seem to grasp the full magnitude of what they saw.

They knew, though, that it was something big – something far bigger than they had ever before witnessed. Peter, I suppose, felt as though he had to say something. He offered that the disciples might build three dwellings, like shrines, for Moses, Elijah, and Jesus. But before anyone could make an answer, a voice spoke out of a bright cloud: "This is my beloved Son, with whom I am well pleased" (Mk 9:7). These were familiar words, the same words spoken by the heavenly voice at Jesus' baptism, at the beginning of his ministry. Now as Jesus moved toward Jerusalem, the words were the same. And these words were added: "Listen to him!" (v. 7).

This account in Mark draws us in two seemingly competing directions. First, it draws us back to the past. Like the three disciples stupefied there on the mountain, we see the long history of God and Israel symbolically enacted through voice, brightness, cloud, and prophet. But also, the story draws us toward the future of change.

This event is called the Transfiguration, because Jesus was transfigured – changed – right in front of the three. But they must have been changed, also. It's impossible to imagine they could have come down the mountain and left that event behind them. They took it with them. In the future, at times when they wondered about their faith – questioned deep down what the whole experience with Jesus had meant or who he was – they could recall this event and what they had seen. As they tried to follow the teachings of Jesus, they could remember the voice from the cloud: "This is my Son…listen to him!"

Sometimes things happen to us or in us that change the way we see things, just as Madeleine Albright was changed by the information about her parents.

On a much smaller scale, this is one of the essences of worship, is it not? In our praise of and experience of God, we find ourselves changed. In worship, we remember together the events of the faith and the events of our own lives that have changed us. In communion, we are drawn to recall the self-giving love of God that has brought us this far. In the charge, we are moved to go with our changed hearts and translate them into changed lives – to make a difference in the world in which we live. Worship rearranges how we look at our past and how we imagine the future.

In addition to worship, there are other times and places where we see the glory of God. We must, though, keep our eyes open for the glory and our ears attuned to hear the voice. Can you see the glory of God in the beauty of nature – the desert at sunset or a mountain stream? Have you heard the voice of God in the cry of a newborn baby, the laughter of a child, or the developing expressions of teenagers?

It is easier to see the glory and hear the voice at the mountaintop. But what about when we return from the mountain?

Jesus and the disciples might well have asked the same question. Why wasn't the prayer of Jesus in Gethsemane answered with a change in the coming events? Why was there no glory, no voice at Golgotha? "If you are the Son of God, come down from the cross!" taunted those who passed by. If God could be made known in the glorious mountaintop experience, why not then, when a miracle was needed? Where was God when Jesus breathed his last? "My God, my God, why have you forsaken me?"

Why, indeed. None of us will ever fully comprehend the darkness of the cross, the depth of the isolation, the pain of the separation. But somehow through the darkness of that experience, we are drawn from light to light – from Transfiguration to Easter.

We need that light when we, too, traverse the darkness. We look for it. In the valley of the shadow of death, in the depth of loss, in the crisis of faith, in the loneliness of depression, in the fear of illness, we wonder about the light. Where are the glory and the voice when we need them most? Sometimes they seem to be missing, even as they were conspicuously absent at the cross. In Jesus' own experience, we can see that we are drawn through the valley from light to light. Jesus and the three went from the mountaintop of transfiguration to the valley of the cross, where it seemed the light of glory would never be seen again.

As we prepare to journey through Lent, to walk the way of the cross, the austerity of the season reminds us of the stark seasons of our lives. We also have dark periods when the light of glory is nowhere to be seen. Yet the memory of past visions of glory is somehow able to sustain us until Easter morning, when the light of the resurrection dispels the darkness, and the glory of the Lord is finally brought to full expression.

– Melissa Bane Sevier

March 1, 2006

Ash Wednesday

Lessons

RCL	Joel 2:1–2, 12–17	2 Cor 5:20b—6:10	Mt 6:1–6, 16–21
	or Isa 58:1–12		
Roman Catholic	Joel 2:12–18	2 Cor 5:20—6:2	Mt 6:1–6, 16–18
Episcopal	Joel 2:1–2, 12–17	2 Cor 5:20b—6:10	Mt 6:1–6, 16–21
	or Isa 58:1–12		

Introduction to the Lessons

Lesson 1
Joel 2:1–2, 12–17 (RCL/Epis); Joel 2:12–18 (RC)

The prophet says the day of the Lord is coming, full of darkness and gloom. Even so, there is always time to return to the Lord, who is gracious and merciful. The whole congregation shall be gathered to reconsecrate themselves to the Lord.

Lesson 2
2 Corinthians 5:20b—6:10 (RCL/Epis);
2 Corinthians 5:20—6:2 (RC)

Paul describes the truth of his work as an ambassador of Christ and urges repentance upon the Corinthians. Christ has done the work of reconciliation; the reader is entreated to respond.

Gospel
Matthew 6:1–6, 16–21 (RCL/Epis);
Matthew 6:1–6, 16–18 (RC)

Before and after the verses that give us the Lord's Prayer (vs. 9–13), Jesus gives other instructions about how to pray. He warns especially against being like hypocrites who look sad in order to show their repentance. Instead, the faithful, even while fasting, should be joyful before others.

Theme

Now is the time; do not put off being reconciled to God and neighbor.

Thought for the Day

As we enter the season of Lent, it is a time of self-examination. We remember that God has moved toward us, especially in the person and work of Jesus.

Call to Worship

One: God so loved the world that he gave his only Son, so that everyone who believes in him may not perish but may have eternal life.

All: Indeed, God did not send the Son into the world to condemn the world, but in order that the world might be saved through him.

– John 3:16–17

Pastoral Prayer

As we enter this holy season of Lent, O Lord, we prepare to walk the way of the cross with you. Make us mindful, we pray, of those for whom the valley of the shadow of death is a present reality, not just an idea. Open our eyes to see those around us who are in desperate need, whether their needs are physical, psychological, emotional, social, or spiritual. Help us to find ways to meet their needs while preserving their strength and dignity. Make of us peaceful people in our homes and in our world, because of the work and word of Jesus. Amen.

Prayer of Confession

Have mercy on us, O God, according to your steadfast love; according to your abundant mercy, blot out our transgressions. Wash us thoroughly from our iniquity, and cleanse us from our sin. Create in us clean hearts, O God, and put a new and right spirit within us. Restore to us the joy of your salvation, and sustain in us a willing spirit. The sacrifice acceptable to you, O God, is a broken spirit; a broken and contrite heart, O God, you will not despise. Amen. (Based on Psalm 51.)

Prayer of Dedication of Gifts and Self

Receive us, O giving Lord, as your willing servants. Use the gifts of our talents, money, time, and energy to bring restoration and reconciliation to this world. May this season of Lent be a time when we reassess all we have been given, and what we have to share. Amen

Sermon Summary

The time of Lent is the right time for self-examination, for recommitting ourselves to the spiritual disciplines and to a life with Christ.

Hymn of the Day
"Ashes"

Whether or not a congregation imposes ashes, Ash Wednesday is intended to be a time of penetrating self-reflection that lays the heart bare before God. Both the texts we hear and the rituals we use encourage this, yet we need to hear the promise of grace to truly go to such a vulnerable place. Tom Conroy's "Ashes" brings such a perspective to Ash Wednesday. He uses ashes as a metaphor for the repentance we show – the amends we make to our lives – that we then offer to God. Not for the purpose of appeasing God, but in order to please God. Michael Joncas' accompaniment fills out Conroy's tune beautifully.

Children's Time

Ash + Wednesday

Preparation: Bring ash mixture (ashes plus water or olive oil), a palm branch, a sheet of paper, and a marker.

(Hold up the palm branch.) Do you know what kind of tree this branch is from? (A palm.) Palm trees grew where Jesus lived. If I burned this palm branch, what would be left? (Ashes.) These are ashes from a palm branch. (Dip a fingertip in the ashes and hold it up for the children to see.)

What day of the week is it today? (Wednesday.) (Write Ash + Wednesday on the paper.) Today is Ash Wednesday. On Ash Wednesday we remember that God made us and we belong to God. We mark each person's forehead with a cross of ashes as we say, "Remember that you are dust and to dust you shall return." The ash cross tells us that the church season of Lent is beginning. During Lent we hear stories about Jesus' life. When Lent is through, it will be Easter.

(Mark each child's forehead with an ash cross as you say the words from the previous paragraph. Or mark them with the ash cross when the whole congregation comes forward.)

Prayer: Dear God, thank you for making us and loving us. It's good to know that we belong to you. Amen.

The Sermon

Now Is the Time

Hymns

Beginning of Worship: "My Song Is Love Unknown"
Sermon Hymn: "Sunday's Palms Are Wednesday's Ashes"
Closing Hymn: "Jesus Walked This Lonesome Valley"

Scripture

2 Corinthians 5:20b—6:10 (For sermon materials on Matthew 6:1-6, 16-21, see the 2005 May/June planning issue of *The Clergy Journal*; for sermon materials on Joel 2:1-2, 12-17, see the November/December 2005 issue of *The Clergy Journal.*).

"Now is the acceptable time; now is the day of salvation" (2 Cor 6:2). These are words of hope after some pretty depressing scripture readings! This is the dichotomy and the blessing of Ash Wednesday, the beginning of Lent. Tonight we come together as people who sometimes experience hopelessness. Yet with Christ we are a people with a hope that is certain.

Lent, like Advent, is a season of preparation. Where Advent prepares us for the coming of Christ, Lent prepares us to remember anew his sacrifice on our behalf. Lent originated in the Roman church around the end of the third or beginning of the fourth century. It was a time for those adults who were to be baptized at the Easter Vigil service to enter into their final preparations, culminating the three years (yes, three years) of teaching and spiritual reflection required of them before they could become full members of the church.

In those early days, Lent began with a spiritual humbling. Ash Wednesday was later given its name because the new members and other Christians who participated received ashes on their foreheads to remind them and others of their sin, mortality, and repentance. From the times of the prophets, ashes were the symbol of penitence and mortality.

Whether or not you choose to receive and wear the ashes as an outward sign of your faith and humanness, I encourage you to use this day as a time to reflect on your own relationship with God. On Ash Wednesday, we are reminded to look inward at our own hearts and outward toward Christ.

In our first reading today, the prophet Joel warns about a day of judgment, yet calls for repentance and reconciliation with God. The psalm that David wrote after his affair with Bathsheba, used for our confession, repeats the same theme: we have sinned and seemingly are without hope. Yet somehow hope remains; hope is in God.

In the epistle reading, Paul returns to a similar subject when he tells of grace and hope. He gives us reason for hoping. Whether we are burdened by sin or depression, by illness or a sense of futility, Christ is our hope. Through him we can be reconciled to God, from whom we were estranged by our sin. Everything old has passed away, says Paul. Everything has become new. Here is what the psalmist experienced. Even after his horrible acts of adultery and murder, he was eventually able to put the painful, even sinful past behind him because of the grace and mercy of God.

The message of Lent, of penitence, really is a message of peace and comfort. It is only when we recognize where we would be without God that we can understand what it means that we have been redeemed from hopelessness.

Paul calls the Corinthians not only to consider their past, and therefore their need for God, but he says that God calls them to a ministry of reconciliation. Likewise, we are called by God to help people be reconciled with God and their fellow human beings. And we are called to reconciliation in our own personal relationships.

Finally, Paul makes an emphatic statement about the present situation. "Now is the acceptable time; now is the day of salvation!" Notice that he doesn't beat the reader over the head shouting, "Now is the time of God's judgment, so get your act together or else!" No, now is the acceptable time. It is a call to reconciliation. Now. Don't wait.

Though we live in a culture of immediate gratification and response, it is often the important things we put off until a later time. We can become sluggish and lazy in matters of faith, imagining there is always more time – always some point in the future – when we can set things right with God and our neighbor.

This is not the way of the gospel. Each moment is filled with importance. Each day is a day ripe with opportunity and possibility. Each encounter is a chance to do the right thing. Each prayer is a time to start over with God.

As Lent is the time for reflection, for penitence, for self-examination, begin today. Now is the acceptable time. Search your own heart. In what areas are you far from God? Are there people from whom you need to seek forgiveness? Are there people you need to forgive? What in your life needs to be made right? Let the ashes be your symbol of mourning those shortcomings and of repentance.

Have you been putting off God's call to discipleship in some way? Now is the acceptable time.

Make this Lenten season a time when you determine to make every day count. Resolve to follow some new (for you) or renewed spiritual practice during the next weeks, so that when you celebrate the resurrection, you will see that you have indeed been changed in the time between Ash Wednesday and Easter.

Now is the time to renew your prayer and meditative practices. Perhaps there is a devotional book that you have wanted to read for some time. Pick it up and get started. Set aside five minutes a day for spiritual reading, meditation, and prayer. Maybe the time will grow into something longer, but it is best not to set goals that are so high they lead quickly to failure. For once, set a goal you know you can accomplish, and move ahead with joy, rather than with a sense of desperate obligation.

Now is the time to renew your practices of service in the name of Christ. Where have you sensed the call to serve others? Is there a place where the hungry are fed, the poor are clothed, the homeless are housed, the aged are cared for, the young are attended to, the sick are made well? What is God calling you to do? Now is the time.

Now is the time to attend to the poverty in your own soul. It is the time for searching, for self-examining, for letting God into the chambers of your heart that you prefer to keep hidden. Where have you not received or offered forgiveness? Where have you been hurtful, critical? In what ways have you disappointed yourself and God? Now is the time for change, for reconciliation.

As the season of Lent returns this year, let it return to you as a new opportunity for growth. Now is the acceptable time; now is the day of salvation. Let now be the time for you to be renewed in your faith.

— Melissa Bane Sevier

March 5, 2006

1st Sunday in Lent

Lessons

RCL	Gen 9:8–17	1 Pet 3:18–22	Mk 1:9–15
Roman Catholic	Gen 9:8–15	1 Pet 3:18–22	Mk 1:12–15
Episcopal	Gen 9:8–17	1 Pet 3:18–22	Mk 1:9–13

Introduction to the Lessons

Lesson 1
Genesis 9:8–17 (RCL/Epis); Genesis 9:8–15 (RC)
After the great flood, God establishes a covenant with Noah that never again will the earth and its inhabitants be destroyed by water. As a sign of the covenant, God places the rainbow in the clouds so that humankind may see it and know.

Lesson 2
1 Peter 3:18–22 (RCL/RC/Epis)
Christ, the righteous, suffered for the unrighteous. The writer refers to the days of Noah and the building of the ark when eight persons were saved through the waters, prefiguring the waters of our baptism.

Gospel
Mark 1:9–15 (RCL);
Mark 1:12–15 (RC);
Mark 1:9–13 (Epis)
Jesus is baptized in the Jordan River by John. Just as he is coming up out of the water, the heavens open and the Spirit like a dove descends, accompanied by a voice from heaven. Then Jesus went into the wilderness where he was tempted for 40 days.

Theme
Baptism marks us as Christ's own and leads us to righteousness.

Thought for the Day

Work for justice in the world, and relief from suffering. It is part of your calling as followers of Jesus Christ. Know that he goes with you as one who is powerful and strong.

Call to Worship

> **One:** Help us to know your ways, O Lord. Teach us your paths.
> **All:** Lead us in your truth and teach us, for you are the God of our salvation; for you we wait all the day long.
> **One:** You are good and upright, O Lord. You instruct sinners in the way.
> **All:** All your paths are steadfast love and faithfulness, for those who keep your covenant and your decrees.
>
> — Based on Psalm 25:4, 5, 8, 10

Pastoral Prayer

We give you thanks, O Lord, for all who have gone before us in the faith. We often forget the sacrifices they made and the troubles they endured. We thank you for the freedoms they secured for us.

We pray for those whose struggle continues: for those caught in religious wars; for those whose faith is subject to ridicule; for those who are treated unjustly; for those who live in dangerous places. May the waters of our baptism remind us of our calling to serve the powerful Christ, and may you give us the strength and courage to bring justice and peace to your world. Amen.

Prayer of Confession

For your name's sake, O Lord, pardon our guilt, for it is great.

O God, do not remember the sins of our youth or our transgressions; according to your steadfast love remember us, for your goodness sake, O Lord! Relieve the troubles of our hearts and bring us out of our distress. Consider our affliction and our trouble, and forgive all our sins. May integrity and uprightness preserve us, for we wait for you. Amen. (Based on Psalm 25.)

Prayer of Dedication of Gifts and Self

You, O Lord, are the author and giver of all good things. Lead us into a more perfect gratitude, through which we may also become givers of good things. Make our Lenten disciplines ones of joy and sacrifice, through Christ our Lord. Amen.

Sermon Summary

The waters of baptism are our call to righteousness and justice, and bring a sense of solidarity with those who must endure suffering for their faith.

Hymn of the Day
"O Lord, Throughout These Forty Days"

Again we encounter Mark's account of Jesus' baptism, only this time the context of the pericope is tailored to place Jesus' temptation front and center. But if the day's question is temptation, then God's good news in Jesus is the answer.

Claudia Hernamen's "O Lord, Throughout These Forty Days," found altered in various ways and set to different tunes, both highlights the theme of temptation and serves as an introduction to the season of Lent. A bolder, more assuring choice is John Rippon's "How Firm a Foundation," set to FOUNDATION.

Children's Time

Purple People

Preparation: Identify all of the purple in your sanctuary: altar cloths, banners, in stained-glass windows, and so on. Wear a purple stole. What's your favorite color? (Accept responses.) What color is the church wearing today? (Purple.) Let's go on a purple hunt. First of all, can you find someone wearing purple? (Encourage the children to go out into the congregation and find people wearing purple, ask the purple people to stand briefly, then return to you.) Now let's find purple in our church. (Lead the children to the purple altar cloth, point out purple banners, visit stained-glass windows with purple in them, and other purple items in your worship space.)

During Lent, the name of this season of the church year, the church dresses in purple, the color of kings. It's a time to learn more about our king, Jesus. During Lent, we are purple people, people who love and worship Jesus Christ, God's Son, our King.

Prayer: Dear God, today we give you special thanks for purple, the color of kings. Thank you for our King, Jesus. Amen.

The Sermon

Through the Waters

Hymns

Beginning of Worship: "O Love, How Deep, How Broad, How High"
Sermon Hymn: "What Wondrous Love Is This"
Closing Hymn: "All Hail the Power of Jesus' Name!"

Scripture

1 Peter 3:18–22 (For sermon materials on Mark 1:9–15, see the 2005 May/June planning issue of *The Clergy Journal*; for sermon materials on Genesis 9:8–17, see the November/December 2005 issue of *The Clergy Journal*.)

If I maintained a list of Bible passages I wish would never appear in the lectionary, this one would sit very near the top. And, though it does appear once every three years, I have steadfastly avoided preaching it until now. Perhaps this is part of my Lenten discipline – to remove myself from the security of comfortable texts and delve into something new and challenging.

I take some solace in knowing I am not alone. Much better scholars than I have confessed to an incomplete understanding of what our biblical author had in mind with some of these statements. There are some of the sentences in this passage we may have to touch on and then let go of because their meaning remains obscure to the modern reader. Even so, I believe the text as a whole is indeed worth wrestling with on this first Sunday of Lent.

Lent is a season that belongs to Christians alone. We share with much of the world our major holidays of Christmas and Easter, perverted as they have been by materialism and secular interests. Even Advent, with its themes of preparation, has been co-opted in a general way as a shopping season. Lent is one season the secular world has left alone, and you can certainly see why. Who wants to celebrate the season of fasting and repentance? For Christians, even, the word celebrate hardly applies. "Observe" is a more accurate way of describing our relationship with this time of year. In this season we observe, meditate, and contemplate our own hearts and our relationship with God.

We mentioned on Ash Wednesday that Lent originated as a period of final preparation for converts who would be baptized on Easter. This passage, then, with its focus on redemption and baptism follows naturally in the lectionary. We begin the observance of Lent this first Sunday with a reflection on the character of Jesus' sacrificial redemption.

Verses 18-20, of course, contain the problematic parts of the text. What in the world are we to do with Christ preaching "to the spirits in prison, who in former times did not obey"? After some study on these verses in various sources, I have reached the conclusion (along with many others) that the original meaning of the text has been lost to us. I lean toward the interpretation of many who see this as part of an early hymn of praise to Christ. The crucified and risen Christ was powerful enough to reach those who were far away from God by their own disobedience, and also to have "angels, authorities, and powers made subject to him" (v. 22).

In the middle of this (possible) hymn, there is a discussion of baptism. It begins, improbably, with Noah. (The "spirits in prison" may refer, as many believe, to the beings of Genesis 6:1ff seen as evil influences on the people of earth, whose disobedience led to the flood.)

Noah's family of eight survived the evil and turmoil that had encompassed the earth by going through the flood. It's not as though they were washed by it. But what they experienced before, during, and after the flood should have made them want to live righteous lives with God and each other. We normally portray the flood and the ark as a lovely Bible story, complete with animals, water, and rainbow. What a terrifying and horrible event the story truly reveals. Those who were saved were witnesses to the perishing of their friends and neighbors. It was through torrential rains that lasted 40 days and nights that they came out safely and eventually. This method of salvation was not a pleasant one. They rocked and waited and were wet for many months. Finally, they were able once again to put their feet upon dry land, when they received the promise of God and started anew to plant and harvest – returning to life as they knew it.

First Peter, scholars tell us, was written to a people who were suffering on account of their faith. If they can picture their own baptism as not just a lovely ceremony, not a nice bath to wash dirt from the body, but also as a symbolic transition through trials to reach a new place, then they may have some hope that their suffering is not in vain. Jesus' suffering, the author says, was meaningful. The suffering of the righteous can also bear meaning if one allows it to be borne in and by faith.

Baptism is "the appeal to God for a good conscience, through the resurrection of Jesus Christ" (v. 21). Baptism, too, has real meaning, not just symbolic significance. Those who were baptized in the time of 1 Peter's writing knew they would likely be persecuted for their faith. Being baptized with the faith community meant they would support one another through the coming "flood." They were bound to Christ, whose redemptive strength was shown in his preaching to the spirits and the subjection of the angels and other powers. And these individuals would have the encouragement and companionship of both Jesus Christ and the community to survive the onslaught.

Christians today, at least in the West, rarely find a reference point for the kind of suffering which gave First Peter his reason for writing. We certainly suffer, but rarely for our righteousness. We don't have to look too far into the American past, though, to find a near equal.

Americans of African descent, when enslaved in the early centuries of our country's history, found that conversion to Christianity, though often required, did not save them from persecution. If anything, those who learned to read the scriptures for themselves found there calls for justice and equity that were completely counter to the preaching they heard in white churches. To endure their suffering, they recounted Bible stories of faith, and water was essential to their storytelling.

Their spirituals taught them how to escape the dogs who were sent to hunt down escaped slaves ("Wade in the Water" where your scent cannot be picked up), and made them know that safety might be theirs on the other side of the Jordan (the Ohio River).

Deep river, my home is over Jordan.
Deep river, Lord, I want to cross over into campground.
Oh, don't you want to go, to that gospel feast,
That promised land, where all is peace?
Lord, I want to cross over into campground.

As we begin Lent, we remember the unjust suffering of those who
went before us, and of those who suffer at the hands of others today.
We walk through the waters of Lent, sharing with them in solidarity the
turmoil of persecution. And we remember our own baptism, which draws
us through the water. It's not just a washing of dirt off the body; it's a
calling, an appeal to God for a good conscience. We live righteously so that
no one ever has to suffer at the hands of another again.

– Melissa Bane Sevier

March 12, 2006

2nd Sunday in Lent

Lessons

RCL	Gen 17:1–7, 15–16	Rom 4:13–25	Mk 8:31–38 or Mk 9:2–9
Roman Catholic	Gen 22:1–2, 9, 10–13, 15–18	Rom 8:31–34	Mk 9:2–10
Episcopal	Gen 22:1–14	Rom 8:31–39	Mk 8:31–38

Introduction to the Lessons

Lesson 1
(1) Genesis 17:1–7, 15–16 (RCL)

The passage reflects God's covenant renewal to Abram and Sarai, promising that they will become the parents of a son, even in their old age. Included in this passage are their name changes to Abraham and Sarah.

(2) Genesis 22:1–2, 9, 10–13, 15–18 (RC); Genesis 22:1–14 (Epis)

The call to Abraham to sacrifice his son Isaac is the focus of these passages. About to kill Isaac, Abraham spots a ram in the bushes as the angel of the Lord instructs him not to kill his firstborn son.

Lesson 2
(1) Romans 4:13–25 (RCL)

Paul reminds us that even the promise to Abraham did not come from Abraham's ability to fulfill the law. Rather he states that Abraham received the God's covenant promise because of his faith.

(2) Romans 8:31–34 (RC); Romans 8:31–39 (Epis)

Paul is certain that because of God's gift of grace, nothing will be able to separate us from the power of God's love through Jesus Christ our Lord.

Gospel

(1) Mark 8:31–38 (RCL/Epis)

Jesus predicts his suffering and death. As he does, he not only rebukes Peter for his inability to accept the prediction, but he invites his disciples to take their crosses and follow him.

(2) Mark 9:2–10 (RC)

Jesus' transfiguration is the central focus of this passage. Not only does Jesus receive God's approval, when the experience has ended, the disciples see Jesus only.

Theme

What does it mean to distribute the weight of the cross?

Thought for the Day

As we hear Jesus' call to take up our crosses and follow him, we pray for the Spirit's help to follow willingly, and trust that as we do, Christ will help us with the burdens of our own crosses, which threaten to weigh us down or destroy us.

Call to Worship

O God, there are so many voices that call to us daily. They call to us and compete for our trust and our allegiance. As we hear those voices, help us to listen only to the voice of your son, that empowered by your Spirit we may faithfully follow him now and always.

Pastoral Prayer

Gracious God, so many people and voices cry out to us and ask us to follow. It is often more difficult than we can bear to hear your voice in the midst of the cacophony of this world.

Help us block out all the voices which would lead us astray from you. Help us to see that of all the voices in this world, we can trust and be attentive to your voice. For as your son invites us to follow, he knows our voices, he has experienced our lives, and he responds to our cries. Help us, we pray, to accept his invitation willingly and without delay, so that we might celebrate your faithfulness to us, and in turn, nurture our faithfulness in you. Amen.

Prayer of Confession

Loving God, we humbly confess that all too often we are more interested in listening to the voices of this world than we are in listening to your voice. Those voices claim us daily, and tempt us to follow them to places more destructive than we could ever imagine. Those voices would have us believe that we do not need you, or the power of your love. They would make us think that we are our own gods, and that we can provide for our needs.

Help us, we pray, to listen to you and your son as he invites us to take up our crosses and follow him. Help us to trust that as we take up our crosses, Christ goes with us – sharing our burdens, knowing our pain. For through Jesus' suffering and death we have been given new life and new hope to realize that as we carry our crosses, nothing will be able to separate us from the power of your love. Amen.

Prayer of Dedication of Gifts and Self

Loving God, you gave your son to suffer and die for the sake of our sins so we might have an abundant life. Since Jesus gave his life for us, help us in turn give our lives to him through these gifts we bring. Empower us to live our lives with joy and thanksgiving, trusting that as we take up our crosses and follow Jesus, he will be there to guide and direct us. Amen.

Sermon Summary

In the midst of our harried and busy lives, Jesus invites us to follow him. He invites us to bring along our worries and cares as we carry our own personal crosses. As we do, he will help us and walk with us along the way.

Hymn of the Day
"What Wondrous Love Is This"

As the story of Jesus' ministry approaches its mighty climax, his words to the disciples regarding his suffering and death, along with those about cross bearing, grow ominous.

A hymn that captures the purple hues of this passage is the American hymn, "What Wondrous Love Is This." Set to the haunting tune of the same name, the text profoundly captures our response to Jesus' prediction and assures us of the happy outcome of Jesus' self–giving – "And through eternity I'll sing on."

Children's Time

A Lesson on New Life

Preparation: Bring in photos or drawings of the life cycle of a butterfly. Jesus was a wonderful teacher. In our Bible story today, Jesus teaches his disciples about what would happen when he died on the cross. This is what Jesus said: "I will die on a cross. (Invite the children to make a cross with their fingers.) After three days (count to three with the children) I will rise again to a new life." This was hard for the disciples to understand.

One way we can understand Jesus' new life is through the example of a butterfly. Help me tell the story of a butterfly's life. We begin as tiny eggs. (Curl up into a ball.) Then we hatch. (Uncurl and stretch arms over head.) Now we are very hungry caterpillars. We munch on lots of leaves and get bigger and bigger. (Pat your tummy.) Finally we climb onto a sturdy branch and rest. (Pretend to sleep.) Our bodies change into chrysalises. Chrysalises are smooth little caterpillar containers. When caterpillars are inside their chrysalises they look dead. They don't move. They just hang from a branch. Then one day we break out of our chrysalises. We stretch out our wings. (Stretch out arms and flap them.) But wait. Are we still caterpillars? (No! We're butterflies now.) This is like when Jesus died. They placed his body in a cave. He was dead. But after three days God raised him to a beautiful new life.

Prayer: Dear God, thank you for raising Jesus to new life so that we can have a beautiful new life when we die. Amen.

The Sermon

Will It Ever Sell?

Hymns
Beginning of Worship: "Guide Us Ever Great Redeemer"
Sermon Hymn: "Jesus Calls Us O'er the Tumult"
Closing Hymn: "Hear I Am, Lord"

Scripture

Mark 8:31–38 (For additional sermon materials on this passage, see the 2005 May/June planning issue and the November/December 2005 issue of *The Clergy Journal*.)

She was at the county fair when she saw it – the Kitchen Miracle. As she watched the presentation, she saw how it could slice, dice, puree, make slaw, do a thousand different things that needed to be done and would take much longer to do without it. At first she hesitated. She didn't want to look too eager. Then she got caught up in the enthusiasm of the crowd. She pulled out her checkbook and a Kitchen Miracle belonged to her.

Whether we welcome them or not, we are assaulted by all sorts of people offering us the "real deal." They offer us that magic pill, that certain something that tells us we are important. They make us believe that we count, we really do. We can have it all, and have it our way as well.

It is difficult for us to believe any of it, isn't it? And we take that healthy skepticism not only into the marketplace, but into church as well. Somehow we wonder if the same old message, the power of the gospel to which we are so aligned, will still sell. Do any of us believe it? And yet even behind the skepticism, we do have the need to believe. We have the need to believe in God; we need to believe that this story that we hear day in and day out is more than a story. We want to believe that it is our story – about our eternal destiny and our eternal souls.

Then again we come to the gospel for this day and we read the words, "If any want to become my followers, let them deny themselves and take up their cross and follow me. For those who want to save their life will lose it, and those who lose their life for my sake, and for the sake of the gospel, will save it" (vv. 34-35). We hear those words, and we wonder, "Will it sell?" What would ever motivate us to follow through with what Jesus demands? Denying ourselves is something we are not sure we desire.

Even as we ask our questions and admit our skepticism, we still have an emptiness that needs to be filled. Behind our self-centeredness, we are forced to admit that somehow all the values that we have considered our values – earning a paycheck, depending on friends and families – haven't always worked. We realize we can't define ourselves by what we do, for what we do may not be there tomorrow. We can't always be confident and gain our strength from our families. So we do have a need to believe, and this gospel and this God aren't afraid to address our needs and our skepticism.

This gospel addresses our emptiness and our loneliness; it accepts our skepticism for what it is because it tells us about Jesus. It tells us about God's Son, who saved the whole world by losing his own life. It proclaims the power of Jesus, who took all our sin and suffering, placed them on the cross, and carried that cross all the way to Calvary. It proclaims the miracle of God's love for us by showing us Jesus, who became the Christ and was anointed with the oil of our suffering as well as the stench of our sin. Jesus is the only one who was able to deny himself and follow through with the charge that God had given him, namely, to suffer and die for the sins of all of humankind.

As Jesus invites us to deny ourselves and take up our crosses, he really is telling us that something is lacking in our lives and in our hearts. I need to deny my job if I think that my job gives me the ultimate meaning in my life. If I believe that I would be lacking without my marriage, then it is that attitude about my marriage that I need to deny. In other words, we become empty and lonely if we only define ourselves by whom we are, or what we do. If we let our relationships define who we are, the day will come when we will be separated from those important relationships.

Jesus, however, knows our imperfections and accepts our weaknesses. He knows how difficult it is for us to deny ourselves. Because of that, Jesus takes our burdens and imperfections with him to the cross. In so doing, he helps us carry our own crosses – those burdens that lead to loneliness and a lack of fulfillment. He puts them all to death as he dies for us. He does all of this for our benefit. As Luther wrote in his explanation to the second article of the Apostles' Creed, Christ does all of this that we may be his own, live in his kingdom, and serve him in everlasting righteousness, innocence, and blessedness. He does all of this and then he invites us to follow him.

It had been almost a week later. She came down to the kitchen for breakfast and suddenly remembered that she had left the Kitchen

Miracle in her car trunk. "Some miracle," she thought to herself. How different it is for us who are claimed by Jesus. Jesus doesn't stay on the shelf or boxed up. He comes to this earth, suffers, dies, and invites us to follow him. With the help of God's Holy Spirit, God will give us the power to do so, not only now, but always.

Thanks be to God! Amen.

– John R. Bucka

March 19, 2006

3rd Sunday in Lent

Lessons

RCL	Ex 20:1–17	1 Cor 1:18–25	Jn 2:13–22
Roman Catholic	Ex 20:1–17	1 Cor 1:22–25	Jn 2:13–15
	or Ex 20:1–3,7–8,12–17		
Episcopal	Ex 20:1–17	Rom 7:13–25	Jn 2:13–22

Introduction to the Lessons

Lesson 1
Exodus 20:1–17 (RCL,/RC/Epis)

The Ten Commandments are given by God as a necessary way to help the Israelites survive and thrive in the wilderness. The key to their survival was not allowing themselves to be tempted to worship other gods.

Lesson 2
(1) 1 Corinthians 1:18–25 (RCL); 1 Corinthians 1:22–25 (RC)

The Corinthian congregation is a group that has been torn apart by divisions not only from within, but also from the community as well. Paul firmly commits his work to the message of the gospel, a message that defies wisdom and logic.

(2) Romans 7:13–25 (Epis)

Paul comments on the power of sin as a paradox at work in his life. On the one hand, he wants to do good and not evil. On the other hand, he does just the opposite. Only Jesus can deliver him from this dilemma.

Gospel
John 2:13–22 (RCL/RC/Epis)
John 2:13–15 (RC)

Jesus enters the temple near the time of the Passover. While there he throws out the moneychangers and those who sell sacrifices, and also talks about his death and resurrection in response to the Jews asking him for a sign.

Theme

What is Jesus' ultimate sign?

Thought for the Day

Signs are all around us. In the midst of our confusion, we seek a sign that guarantees that God is with us and will neither leave us nor forsake us.

Call to Worship

Lord God, we seek some guarantee, some sign of your Holy Presence. As we begin our worship, draw us to you and let us glimpse you at work, not only here in this house, but in the world, as you bring hope and life to all your children.

Pastoral Prayer

Almighty and everlasting God, we live in an age of signs and wonders. Help us to see that these signs and wonders reflect not only the accomplishment of humankind, but also reflect the many ways in which you have blessed this earth. Help us see in these wonders not our glory, but your glory, O God. Help us to appreciate and be thankful for what you have done for us. Help us worship you, our Creator, for we gain our strength only from you. Help us to be mindful of the most powerful sign you have given to us, the death and resurrection of your son, our Lord and Savior Jesus Christ. For it is in Christ and through Christ that we have been given eternal life with you. Amen.

Prayer of Confession

Patient God, you have given us eyes to see and ears to hear, and yet when we are confronted by your goodness and surrounded by your love, we fail to see you or hear your voice. More often than not we attend to the voices of the world that create confusion for our spirits and souls, rather than tune in on the power of your word and the gift of your love. O God, we confess our struggle to hear and see. We admit that we have failed. We recognize our desire to be influenced by the voices of this world and the signs of this age. We realize how easy it is to trust those who would gratify us immediately, and yet leave us to wither and die. As we worship you today, we humbly confess our shortsightedness and our sin – all the ways in which we have gone away from you. Forgive us, O God, and restore within us a desire to see you and to listen to your voice. Amen.

Prayer of Dedication of Gifts and Self

As we gather our gifts on this day, instill within us a spirit of dedication and thanksgiving. Help us to commit our very lives to you, O God. Give us the grace to see you, to hear you, and to love you. Give us the strength to walk in the narrow path of your love and to ignore those that would lead us down a different pathway. Help us recognize your face in the faces of those who are poor, lonely, estranged, or suffering. Allow us to see your son in the faces of those around us each day. Empower us, O God, so we might commit our lives to being your faithful servants, not only now, but always, through Jesus Christ our Lord. Amen.

Sermon Summary

As we search for signs of God's presence, we want some assurance that the God whom we seek is precisely the Christ who has come to earth, to suffer and to die that we might have life and have it eternally.

Hymn of the Day
"O God, How We Have Wandered"

The tumultuous scene of Jesus driving people out of the temple is superceded by what must have sounded like the most outrageous of claims: if the great temple in Jerusalem were destroyed, Jesus would raise it up again in three days. According to John, only after Jesus' death and resurrection was some sense of these words able to be made.

A selection in line with this pericope and its Lenten context is Kevin Nichols' "O God, How We Have Wandered." Set to the great PASSION CHORALE from Bach's *St. Matthew Passion*, the text is a stark admission of our estrangement from God and a plea that God meet us with grace.

Children's Time

Marketplace

Preparation: Make a sign that says "SALE." Cut three pictures of animals from magazines and write prices on them, such as a cow for $500, a sheep for $250, and a chicken for $25.

(Hold up your sign.) What does my sign say? I'm having a big sale right now! I'm going to sell lots of animals. See, I have pictures of the animals that are for sale. (Hold up each picture and name its price.) Do any of you want to buy these?

Do you think we should sell animals in our worship space? (Accept responses.) What should we do here? (Sing, pray, praise God, baptize, and share communion are possible responses.) In today's story from the Bible, Jesus went to the temple, his worship space. And he found lots and lots of people selling animals. Jesus grew angry. He shouted at the sellers, "Stop making my Father's house a marketplace! The temple should be a house of prayer." Jesus knocked over all of the tables. He set free all of the animals.

I'm not really selling animals today. Instead I wanted you to think about what Jesus taught about how we should use our worship space.

Prayer: Dear God, thank you for places where we can worship you. Remind us to use these places to pray, sing, and praise your holy name. Amen.

The Sermon

Breaking the Code

Hymns
Beginning of Worship: "Great Is Thy Faithfulness"
Sermon Hymn: "Day by Day"
End of Worship: "Precious Lord, Take My Hand"

Scripture

John 2:13–21 (For additional sermon materials on this passage, see the November/December 2005 issue of *The Clergy Journal*; for sermon materials on Exodus 20:1–17, see the 2005 May/June planning issue of *The Clergy Journal*.)

> "The Jews then said to him, 'What sign can you show us for doing this?' Jesus answered them, 'Destroy this temple, and in three days, I will raise it up?' (vv. 18–19).

The curator of the Louvre Art Museum in Paris is murdered, and beside his body is scrawled this message:13-3-2-21-2-2-8-5 followed by these words, "O, Draconian devil! Oh, lame saint!" That's the way Dan Brown's book, *The DaVinci Code*, begins. As it does, it promises to lead the reader through a series of mysteries and codes that not only relate to the murder, but also to a conspiracy that the Christian church has allegedly covered up for many centuries.

The book is pure entertainment, nothing more, nothing less. What makes the book so intriguing is Brown's ability to hook his readers with a sense that they, too, are involved in trying to break the code, debunk the mystery, and solve the case so to speak. What captivates us about the book captivates us about life itself.

Each and every day we run into mysteries, we are surrounded by codes: we too search for the meaning of what seems to be incapable of being explained.

Ask a teenager what the word *fat* means, not f–a–t, but *phat*, and you might be surprised. Spend some time watching or observing your kids or grandkids in an Internet chat room or sending text messages and ask them about the abbreviations they're using, like "lol" or "brb". Watch two identical twins who are not yet out of diapers playing together, and you will discover that they have a language code of their own.

We're not only interested in specific particulars of behavior. The codes and the mysteries go beyond the specifics and envelop the universality of life itself. That mysterious DNA code of life continues to amaze us. The miracles of births, as well as the sanctity of death, remain mysterious as well. Confronted with life's tragedies and triumphs, don't we desire to ask God why? Why do you do things like this? Why do you allow tragedies to happen? Why do so many wars in our world involve religious differences? Why did you send your only Son to suffer and die? What causes people to marry? What makes them want to divorce?

When we read this gospel text, we usually choose to focus on Jesus' interaction with the moneychangers in the temple. For years pious preachers have used Jesus' wrath as an occasion to lambaste bake sales, raffles, or other great sins and vices promoted by well-intended parishioners. The meat of the text, however, is served in the verses that follow. The Jews look for a sign. Jesus, however, speaks about tearing down the temple in three days and building it up once again. The Jews are confused, thinking about the temple that was the replacement temple built after the exile. The writer of John breaks the code, and lets us know that Jesus is really talking about his death and resurrection.

The verses remind us of the experience that the Jews shared as they encountered Jesus. Somehow, they failed to see the obvious. They didn't recognize that the one who stood before them was the Christ, the very Son of God. They wanted more than Jesus' presence. They wanted guarantees, power, magic, something to reassure them that Jesus would be a king after the order of their great ancestor, King David. They failed to accept that Jesus' power resided in his ability to go to the cross and suffer and die for the sins of all humankind. As a result, Jesus speaks a word about the temple in a code-like way. Destroying the temple and rebuilding it in three days would be just as inconceivable to them as Jesus being crucified and being raised from the dead three days later. Jesus' mission on earth wasn't enough for them.

I sometimes wonder if we fail to see the obvious as well. I wonder if we are looking for more than what Jesus is offering. As we look for more, do we miss the opportunities Jesus gives us? Do we see him in the breaking of the bread and the sharing of the peace? Do we touch him when we clothe the poor and feed the hungry? Do we truly trust that as we worship in his name, he is in our midst? It can't be that simple can it? There must be a code to be broken to make all of this genuine.

If we follow Jesus through the Gospel of John, however, we will see that in the end the code is broken for us. Jesus is the one who says, "no one has greater love than this, to lay down one's life for one's friends" (Jn 15:13). Jesus is the one who does exactly that. Jesus goes to the cross and gives up his life so that he might make us – who had been his enemies – into his friends. The power of the story is found in the fact that it is for each one of us.

God meets us in a very personal and intimate way. God meets us in bread and wine, body and blood. And even as God meets us in the gift of Jesus, the code is broken and the mystery is revealed. This, our God, is not a God who is distant from us...but a God who is so close to us that we can taste and experience that God is good.

For some reason or another, I found *The DaVinci Code* rather slow going. In fact, I've never read 35 chapters of any book only to find that I am halfway through the book. I was half finished and I had no clue about the ending. As we continue in our daily lives, we can be confident that the ending of our story is not in doubt. God is revealed to us in Jesus Christ. We have been given a life with God that will never end.

Thanks be to God. Amen.

– John R. Bucka

March 26, 2006

4th Sunday in Lent

Lessons

RCL	Num 21:4–9	Eph 2:1–10	Jn 3:14–21
Roman Catholic	2 Chr 36:14–17, 19–23	Eph 2:4–10	Jn 3:14–21
Episcopal	2 Chr 36:14–23	Eph 2:4–10	Jn 6:4–15

Introduction to the Lessons

Lesson 1
(1) Numbers 21:4–9 (RCL)

Poisonous snakes attack the children of Israel while they are in the wilderness. Moses makes a snake out of bronze, places it on a stick, and lifts it up. When a person is bitten, he or she touches the bronze snake and is healed.

(2) 2 Chronicles 36:14–17, 19–23 (RC);
2 Chronicles 36:14–23 (Epis)

In this final chapter of the book of the Chronicler, the writer describes the destruction of the temple in Jerusalem, and reports that those who are left in Jerusalem are carried into exile.

Lesson 2
Ephesians 2:1–10 (RCL); Ephesians 2:4–10 (RC/Epis)

This passage contrasts the Christian's former life of sin and death with the new life that is given by God. Included here is the traditional verse that says we are saved by grace through faith, not by what we have done, but by what God has done for us.

Gospel
(1) John 3:14–21 (RCL/RC)

John refers to the wilderness event in the first lesson and connects it to the lifting up of the Son of Man in reference to Jesus' crucifixion. This reference is followed by the familiar John 3:16, which often has been called "the gospel in miniature."

(2) John 6:4–15 (Epis)

John's account of the feeding of the five thousand serves not only as an introduction to Jesus' discourse about the Bread of Life, but also reveals the desire of the crowd to make Jesus their bread king.

Theme

Our salvation comes to us through God's gracious action in Jesus Christ.

Thought for the Day

We live in a world that emphasizes accomplishments and glories in victory. God gives us the victory or salvation as a gift.

Call to Worship

Come, all who are weary and heavy-laden, and God will give you rest. Come all who are weighed down by the defeats of sin, and the wilderness of this world, and God will give you hope. Worship God, whose Son has defeated death, so that we might have eternal life.

Pastoral Prayer

Give us wisdom to receive what the world cannot give – oneness with you. Help us to understand that our eternal salvation does not depend on our ability to be perfect, but on the great miracle that you have accomplished through your Son's suffering and death. Give us the assurance that the lives we lead need not be lives of struggle, but rather lives of praise and thanks to you for the wonderful gifts you have given us. Make us witnesses to lead others to your Son, pointing not to what we have done, but to what you have done through Jesus Christ our Lord. Send us out with words of hope and inspiration for all, proclaiming the miracle of our salvation given by your grace, through faith. Amen.

Prayer of Confession

Patient and loving God, you have promised to never leave us or forsake us. You have given us the gift of your presence here on earth and assurance of your eternal presence when we die. You have given us every good and perfect gift, and yet we still doubt your goodness. We continue to be tempted to turn to gods who demand from us what we can never give and offer us death and destruction rather than life and resurrection. Gracious God, help us see beyond the things that are transient and focus on things that are eternal. Give us confident trust that our salvation is a gift from you, a result of your grace, given to us through Jesus Christ our Lord. Amen.

Prayer of Dedication of Gifts and Self

O God, you are the giver of all good gifts. Help us not take for granted all that you have given us. Help us see our very lives as gifts from you. Help us trust that what you have done for us is not due to any merit on our part, but purely from your divine love and mercy. Open our hearts to respond to your grace with generosity. Bless these gifts and send them into the world to proclaim your grace and salvation to all people. Amen.

Sermon Summary

The Christian life does not consist of a series of competitions, testing our fitness to enter God's kingdom. Rather, our lives are centered in the grace that God has given to us freely.

Hymn of the Day
"My Song Is Love Unknown"

With words reflecting back to the prologue of this gospel, today's lesson from John reiterates the reason for Jesus' coming: God's love for the world. And with Good Friday approaching, the great cost to God to express this love looms ever larger.

Samuel Crossman's "My Song Is Love Unknown" is a good choice for today. Narrative-like in its retelling of the passion story, Crossman's hymn emphasizes God's love. The music, composed especially for this hymn by John Ireland, splendidly carries the text to its heart felt conclusion: "This is my Friend in whose sweet praise I all my days could gladly spend."

Children's Time

God's Free Love

Preparation: Bring a paper heart in a bag. Bring a handful of coins.
How many of you like riddles? Let's try one:

I'm invisible. That means you can't see me. You can feel me whenever you get a hug, a kiss, and a kind word. You can feel me whenever someone cares for you. What am I? (Remove the paper heart from the bag.) Who made love? (God.)

(Show the money.) Do you think I would have to pay this much for God's love? How much do you think I would have to pay? (Accept responses.) Good news! God's love is free! We don't have to pay anything for God's love. How can we give thanks for God's free love? (Share it with others, pray, sing, and worship are possible responses.) We're going to say a prayer together. Whenever I hold up the heart, you pray the words, "Thank you, God."

Prayer: For warm gentle hugs. (Hold up heart.) For kind friends. (Hold up heart.) For moms and dads and grandmas and grandpas. (Hold up heart.) For sending Jesus to teach us about your love. (Hold up heart). Thank you, God, for your free gift of love. Amen.

The Sermon

What a Gift!

Hymns

Beginning of Worship: "Love Divine, All Loves Excelling"
Sermon Hymn: "A Mighty Fortress Is Our God"
Closing Hymn: "My Hope Is Built on Nothing Less"

Scripture

Ephesians 2:1–10 (For additional sermon materials on this passage, see the 2005 May/June planning issue and the November/December 2005 issue of *The Clergy Journal*.)

"For by grace you have been saved through faith, and this is not your own doing; it is the gift of God" (Eph 2: 8).

I was on my way to a meeting one day, in a hurry as usual, when I decided to stop at a gas station for some breathmints. I ran in, put my dollar on the counter, received my two cents in change, and walked back to my car. It was actually to my chagrin that I opened up the box and read these words, "Sorry, you're not a winner! Try again!" Admittedly I didn't expect great news from this box, but the problem was that I didn't even know I was a contestant in a game.

And then I wondered, "How do they know? How do they know I'm not a winner?" Maybe the breathmint makers knew that the person who bought the mints would be from Minnesota and that the Wolves would lose to the Lakers in six games. Maybe they had some personal insight into my life. They knew my history as a bench warmer on the Roosevelt High School Teddies. They saw how I struggled at racquetball. Maybe they had insight into the times that I've tried so hard, only to come up short.

On the other hand, perhaps the breathmint makers were making a more universal comment on the situation of all of humankind. Maybe they recognized that winning is only a trait that can be shared by a privileged few. Maybe they know that more often than not, our chances of losing in life are as sure as our chances of losing the Powerball.

Now all of this goes along with my pastoral perspective that anything in life can give a preacher sermon material. Yes, even breathmint boxes can take us back to the basics, back to the Bible basics. These are the basics we truly need to hear, and with which we need to be renewed. Even breathmint boxes drive us back to the Word made flesh who dwelt among us so that we could behold God's glory as of the only begotten of the Father, full of grace and truth. Even losing an inane contest can remind us of Jesus the Christ. He came into this world to defeat sin and Satan, not with power and might, not with sword and shield, not with a victory cry as he took the battlefield in full view of his cowering enemies. Rather, it reminds us of Jesus who conquered by losing, who gave up his life so that we in turn may not have to lose our lives eternally.

It is Paul who reminds us that the salvation that God has given us does not come from any contest or competition on our part. Rather, he says, "For by grace you have been saved through faith, and this is not your own doing; it is the gift of God – not the result of works so that no one may boast." Then Paul continues, "For we are what he has made us, created in Christ Jesus for good works, which God prepared beforehand to be our way of life" (v. 10).

This is powerful stuff. This is great news. This is the stuff we can tell the breathmint makers and the people who run the Powerball. We have been given something that they can never promise us. We are God's children, God's created people through faith. It is in our baptism that we have been given this promise and it is the very grace of God that has made us one with God.

Ultimately, that recognition changes us, for we have been changed. We recognize that our lives need not be filled with struggles or controlled by the contests that we perceive to be so important. It means that we don't have to live vicariously through our sports teams, and make them our modern-day messiahs, busting out with pride when they win and being totally and completely crushed when they lose. It changes us so we recognize that life itself is not a game; rather, life is a gift.

And because life is a gift, then we can treat one another as gifts as well. We can begin to look at people not as our antagonists, but as our allies. What would happen in our lives if we treated people that way? What would happen if the nations of the world treated one another that way? Time itself is a gift, given to us by the benevolent hand of God who helps us see that time is not to be wasted, it is not to be killed. Rather, time is to be used for our benefit and for God's glory. Each second, each minute is precious.

For we have great news that the Powerball can never give us. We have the best news that breathmints cannot help us achieve. We have been made winners by Christ, who gave up his life for us, so we might have life and live it abundantly.

A month later I decided to buy another box of the same brand of breathmints. I opened the cover and there was no longer any declaration of whether or not I was a winner. The slate had been wiped clean. Someone had given them the news. People of God, our slates have been wiped clean. God has given us the gift of salvation by grace through faith, and God will help us give the news to all people. Life is not a contest or struggle, but a gift to be celebrated through Jesus Christ our Lord. Amen.

– John R. Bucka

April 2, 2006

5th Sunday in Lent

Lessons

RCL	Jer 31:31–34	Heb 5:5–10	Jn 12:20–33
Roman Catholic	Jer 31:31–34	Heb 5:7–9	Jn 12:20–33
Episcopal	Jer 31:31–34	Heb 5:(1–4) 5–10	Jn 12:20–33

Introduction to the Lessons
Lesson 1
Jeremiah 31:31–34 (RCL/RC/Epis)
Jeremiah predicts a time when God's covenant with Israel and Judah will be renewed. The difference between this new covenant and the covenant given to Moses is that this covenant will be written on people's hearts.

Lesson 2
Hebrews 5:5–10 (RCL);
Hebrews 5:7–9 (RC);
Hebrews 5:(1–4) 5–10 (Epis)
The writer of Hebrews talks about Christ as the high priest. As he describes Christ's role, he says that Christ does not glorify himself, but as an obedient servant, he is similar to the ancient king of Salem, Melechizedek.

Gospel
John 12:20–33 (RCL/RC/Epis)
The passage begins with those who are Greek asking to see Jesus. It comes to a conclusion with Jesus describing not only his death, but also teaching that his death will be the occasion to draw all people to himself.

Theme
God keeps the covenant with God's people; we are to remember that covenant as well.

Thought for the Day

We live in a world that is littered with broken promises and failed relationships, but God promises a relationship with us that will never fail or be broken.

Call to Worship

God invites us this day to discover the joy of the relationship that has been given to us through Jesus Christ. As we celebrate that relationship, let us give thanks that God's promises to us are sure, and will never be broken.

Pastoral Prayer

Our world is a place of broken promises and shattered dreams. Help us look to you, O God, as the pioneer and perfecter of our faith. Open our hearts to receive the gift of your benevolence, and the strength of your promise. When relationships fail and dreams die, remind us that you gave your Son for us. Increase our trust in Christ, whose sacrifice for our sins has given us hope not only for this world, but also the world to come. Be with all who struggle to see that your promise to be our God can be trusted, and that we are your children. Amen.

Prayer of Confession

Why is it, O God, that we believe we can go it alone in life? Is it because we are enamored with our own self-reliance, ingenuity, or creativity? Is it because we truly think that in our world, filled with technological advances, we no longer need the miracle of your grace? On this day we pray that you would once again break into our world of shattered dreams and broken delusions. Shatter our own images of self-reliance. Forgive us and wake us up from our sleep. Help us trust that as hopes and dreams disappear and as human relationships are broken, your relationship with us continues throughout eternity. Amen.

Prayer of Dedication of Gifts and Self

Generous God, receive the gifts that we offer, that they may be used to your glory. Let us never underestimate your ability to take what seems small and insignificant and use it to create a glorious miracle. Create within us willing spirits to serve you and generous hearts to share the blessings that you have given. Accept what we give, so that it might be used for the benefit of your mission and the glory of your will, for the sake of Jesus, your Son, our Lord. Amen.

Sermon Summary
Broken promises are part and parcel of our existence. In contrast, God's promise to be our God is a promise that will never be broken and leads us to trust God.

Hymn of the Day
"When I Survey the Wondrous Cross"
The long shadow of the cross now colors all Jesus' words and deeds. Though there are many themes to key off of in today's gospel lesson, it is the idea of glorification that attracts my attention.

In his signature hymn, "When I Survey the Wondrous Cross," Isaac Watts uses language – "the Prince of Glory," "so rich a crown" – pointing squarely to glorification, while the hymn's closing idea reiterates Jesus' words about losing and serving: "demands my soul, my life, my all." Of great historical importance is the fact that this is the first hymn in the English language to use the personal pronoun "I."

Children's Time

Loving from the Inside Out
Preparation: Bring heart stickers, a mask, and a change of shoes.

Today we hear a message from a prophet named Jeremiah. God loved Jeremiah and chose him to give the people messages from God. Jeremiah lived long, long ago – long before Jesus did. At that time, most of the people didn't follow God's laws. So Jeremiah said to them, "God will put God's law inside of you and will write it on your hearts." Jeremiah said that God would change the people into more loving people from the inside out. I wonder what this means.

(Put on the mask.) Can I change myself into a more loving person by putting on a mask? (No.) (Put on other shoes.) Can I change myself into a more loving person by changing my shoes? (No.) Only God's love can change me into a more loving person. God's love is changing us every day. God's love starts inside us. It changes us into more loving people from the inside out.

I'm going to put a heart sticker on each one of you as a reminder that God's love is working inside of you, changing you into a more loving person from the inside out. (Place a sticker on each child's clothing.)
Prayer: Thank you, God, for sending your love to change us from the inside out. Help us to be more loving every day. Amen.

The Sermon

Remember the Promise!

Hymns
Beginning of Worship: "O Jesus I Have Promised"
Sermon Hymn: "Lord, Keep Us Steadfast in Your Word"
Closing Hymn: "Take My Life That I May Be"

Scripture
Jeremiah 31:31–34 (For sermon materials on Hebrews 5:5–10, see the 2005 May/June planning issue of *The Clergy Journal*; for sermon materials on John 12:20–33, see the January 2006 issue of *The Clergy Journal*.)

"But you promised, Dad!" eight-year-old Kyle cried out to his father. His father had come home late from the office on this hot summer day. As he pulled up the driveway, there sat Kyle, waiting with his fishing pole. When he saw Kyle, he didn't even want to get out of the car. He remembered the night before when he said to Kyle, "Be ready at noon, because I'll be home and we can go fishing!" He sat in the car and thought to himself, "He'll never understand! He won't understand that what started as a small problem at the office blew up into a major crisis! He'll never understand, but then why should he?" As he got out of the car, Kyle walked away from him in tears. His dad wondered what he could say.

It happens to all of us, doesn't it? Either we break our promises or we are on the receiving end of broken promises. It happens to children and parents. It happens at work. It happens to young married couples, and couples who have been married for 40 or 50 years. It just happens.

When we experience broken promises, it's almost as if a piece of ourselves, our trust, our integrity is chipped away. The more our trust and integrity are chipped away, the more we replace them with suspicion and mistrust, with disappointment and anger, with frustration and despair. Each broken promise we experience reminds us not only of our own failures, but also of the fact that we humans fail regularly in our attempt to be faithful – faithful to one another, faithful to God.

We're not alone in our ability to break promises. We see that dynamic at work throughout the Bible. In this Sunday's text, Jeremiah addresses the historical fact that both Judah and Israel have been unfaithful. They have broken their side of the covenant that God made with them. Jeremiah contrasts their unfaithfulness with God's faithfulness. He writes,

The days are surely coming, says the Lord, when I will make a new covenant with the house of Israel and the house of Judah…This is the covenant that I will make with the house of Israel after those days, says the Lord: I will put my law within them, and I will write it on their hearts; and I will be their God, and they shall be my people (Jer 31: 31, 34).

God, in spite of Israel's unfaithfulness, recommits to Israel. Isn't that truly amazing? If we were God for a day, would we have continued in our journey to be with Israel? My sense is that our answer would clearly be no. Long before the prophet Jeremiah, our patience would have run its course. We would have ended that relationship long before this point.

This is the wonderful thing about God. Our God continues to try to win us over. Our God continues to renew covenant promises with us. Our God desires us as God's own people. What would be impossible for us is possible for God. In fact, so great is God's commitment to us, that Jesus Christ comes to earth to suffer and die, to seal God's promise with his very blood. That is what we remember when we hear Jesus' words, "This is my blood of the covenant, which is poured out for many for the forgiveness of your sins" (Mt 26:27).

In contrast to everything we experience in our lives, God's dedication to us is a refreshing change. In the midst of our despair, there is hope. As we experience broken relationships, we are offered healing. God never gives up on us, but God walks with us as we experience the failure of relationships and tells us that the relationship given to us in Jesus Christ will never fail. In the midst of death and sin, God gives us life and forgiveness. As we experience abandonment and loneliness, God continues to be at our side. When we are mistrusting and hardened, or suspicious because of what we have experienced, God wipes those attitudes away and points us to the Son on the cross for our sakes.

In the face of all that God has done for us, God calls on us to "Remember the promise!" God calls on us to be people of this new covenant. God then sends us out into the world to be conveyors of hope, reflectors of God's love. God sends us out as people who can be trusted. For God gives us the grace and the hope that we need to make a difference in this world, not because of what we do, but because of what God can do in and through us. As we remember God's promise to us, we can face the future without fear. Even though we do not know what the future holds, we can be confident that God will continue to hold us. We have a peace that the world cannot give, and this peace is ours today and throughout eternity. Amen.

— John R. Bucka

April 9, 2006

Passion/Palm Sunday

Lessons

RCL	Isa 50:4–9a	Phil 2:5–11	Mk 14:1—15:47 or Mk 15:1–39 (40–47)
Roman Catholic	Isa 50:4–7	Phil 2:6–11	Mk 14:1—15:47 or Mk 15:1–39
Episcopal	Isa 45:21–25 or Isa 52:13–53:12	Phil 2:5–11	Mk (14:32–72) 15:1–39 (40–47)

Introduction to the Lessons
Lesson 1
(1) Isaiah 50:4–9a (RCL); Isaiah 50:4–7 (RC)

One of the Servant Songs from Isaiah, this reading emphasizes God's saving grace, even in the midst of pain and suffering. Although Christians traditionally apply the imagery to Jesus, it is a declaration of confidence that God will act in this world and the world to come to redeem all God's people.

(2) Isaiah 45:21–25 (Epis)

This reading is more appropriate for the triumphal aspect of Palm Sunday. Here God's righteousness and omnipotence are affirmed and God's glory is declared; "every knee bows" before that splendor.

Lesson 2
Philippians 2:5–11 (RCL/RC/Epis)

This hymn of the ancient church is a song of praise to Christ. In his majesty, Jesus chose servanthood; in his humility, Jesus was exalted. We worship and follow the One who responded with his whole heart to the call of God, even to his death and beyond.

Gospel
Mark 14:1—15:47 (RCL/RC);
Mark (14:32–72) 15:1–39 (40–47) (Epis)
The longer reading begins two days before the Passover and includes the story of the woman with the alabaster jar of ointment. The shorter version gives the option of entering the story at Gethsemane and concluding with Jesus' death or with the placing of his body in the tomb.

Theme
Our commitment to discipleship is challenged by fear, ambivalence, apathy, and the status quo.

Thought for the Day
To believe in something not yet proved and to underwrite it with our lives: it is the only way we can leave the future open.
– Lillian Smith ("The Journey," 1954)

Call to Worship
Leader: Let the mind of Christ be our mind.
Right Side: Let the humility of Christ humble us.
Left Side: Let the obedience of Christ teach us to obey.
Right Side: Let the service of Christ inspire our service.
Left Side: Let the humanity of Christ shape our humanity.
All: Let the glory of Christ lead us to glory.

Pastoral Prayer
Humble God of majesty, in the life of Jesus, in the life of the unnamed woman with the ointment, you showed us again and again that both majesty bending to service and humility rising to glory are part of our vocation as disciples. Grant us the humble pride that bends to serve the most needy because there – amid the oppressed, beside the suffering, enfolding the unwanted – we know the honor of serving Christ himself. Grant us the obedient majesty that uses your power in us to raise a sister or a brother to glory. Grant us the mind and the heart of Christ, that we may carry on his work until he comes again in triumph. Amen.

Prayer of Confession

All-loving God, we confess that sometimes we offer you only half our
heart. We confess that we too often hold back, willing to commit only
a limited portion of our time, our energy, our resources, our vision, and
our gifts to witnessing your goodness and your good news in the world.
We confess that the example of the woman who ministered to Jesus often
makes us uncomfortable because it is so abundant, so abandoned, so
excessive. Remind us, all-loving God, that you gave everything. Remind
us that you created us in your image and filled us with your spirit so
that we, too, can give everything. Grant us the courage to be people
whole–heartedly yours! Amen.

Prayer of Dedication of Gifts and Self

God, who pours out the abundance in which we live, receive these offerings, gleaned from that abundance. Bless us, as you blessed the unknown
woman who ministered to Jesus, with the generosity of heart to pour out
our greatest treasures in your honor. Amen.

Sermon Summary

The unnamed woman with the ointment dared to act on her belief, even
when it upset the status quo and made others uncomfortable. As disciples,
we are invited to act on our belief, on behalf of Jesus, in remembrance of
her.

Hymn of the Day
"O Sacred Head, Now Wounded"

The passion account lies at the heart of the Christian message and is
capable of bringing the strongest and most callous among us to tears. Only
a handful of hymns are both worthy and capable of being programmed
alongside this text.

Foremost among these is Paul Gerhardt's immortal "O Sacred Head,
Now Wounded," set to Hans Leo Hassler's PASSION CHORALE, a
melody the composer originally wrote for a love song and J. S. Bach
later harmonized. The best contemporary choice I know is Marty Haugen's "Tree of Life," though it embodies a theology quite different from
Gerhardt's.

Children's Time

A Royal Welcome

Preparation: Bring palm branches and three-foot lengths of colorful gift wrap ribbon. Ask a member of your congregation to portray Jesus in biblical costume.

Today we're going to pretend we lived when Jesus walked on earth. These are the colorful cloaks you wore. (Drape a ribbon around each child's neck.) And we need palm trees. (Ask people sitting along the aisle to hold and wave the palm branches you give them.) One last thing. We have to learn a special word to welcome Jesus: Hosanna! Let's say it together. Now we're ready to begin the story.

Many people in Jesus' time hoped that Jesus would be king. Oh, look! Here comes Jesus now, riding on a donkey. (Jesus stands in the back of the sanctuary, pretending to be riding a donkey.) Let's welcome him as our king. (Jesus pauses to let children prepare.) Lay down your cloaks to make a beautiful path for Jesus to follow to Jerusalem. Quickly, pick a branch from a palm tree. (Have the children line the aisle.) Here comes Jesus! Wave your palm branch up high. Let's all say "hosanna" together. (Have Jesus come up the aisle and then exit the sanctuary.) This is the Sunday that we remember how people in Jerusalem waved palm branches to welcome Jesus as their king. Take home your palm branch and streamer as a reminder that Jesus will always love us and care for us, like good kings are supposed to do.

Prayer: Dear God, thank you for sending Jesus to love us. Amen.

The Sermon

In Remembrance of Her

Hymns
Beginning of Worship: "Shadows Gather, Deep and Cold"
Sermon Hymn: "O Lord, How the Fallen Woman Wept"
Closing Hymn: "Would You Share Christ's Passion?"

Scripture

Mark 14:1–15:47 (For additional sermon materials on this passage, see the January 2006 issue of *The Clergy Journal*; for materials on Philippians 2:5–11, see the 2005 May/June planning issue of *The Clergy Journal*.)

Today is one of the hardest days of the entire church year on which to affirm the faith we claim as our own. We are invited to consider the ambivalence Christians have always shown, an ambivalence that welcomes the One who is Radiant Truth Incarnate with shouts and songs of praise one moment...and that nails him to the cross the next moment. We are asked to wrestle deeply with our own discomfort at the challenging mandate of Jesus, and with our own broken response to our discipleship.

The story of this day and this week is not about some other people in some other time. It is about us. It reveals the full reality of our own spiritual journey, which encompasses moments of abiding commitment to holiness and, at the same time, a faint-heartedness that leads us to deny our principles in the time of trial, leaving us colluding with the powers and principalities. Indeed, leaving us to deny the one we call Messiah, not once, not twice, not three times, but again and again and again. Daily.

In the midst of the story of Jesus' passion, we find a most challenging text, a snapshot of an encounter between Jesus and an unnamed woman with a jar of precious ointment. Because we are entering Holy Week, it is tempting to read quickly past these verses, seeing them as nothing more than background for the important stuff. But I would submit to you that this may be the most important part of the story, and I invite us to linger here this year to consider it with prayerful hearts.

Let us remember that all four of the gospels include stories of pivotal meetings that Jesus has with women, events that change Jesus and his ministry profoundly. Think, for instance, about the wedding in Cana and the request from his mother for Jesus to help the host out of an awkward situation. Although Jesus initially rebuffs Mary, he goes on to transform the water into wine. Think of the meeting with the persistent Canaanite woman who begs him to heal her child. Think of the meeting with the Samaritan woman at the well through whom Jesus reaches out to the villagers of Samaria, the rejected sisters and brothers of the Chosen People. Each describes a liminal moment in which Jesus himself was transformed, or changed direction, or altered or expanded his teaching.

Here, again, in this encounter, there is a transformation. Jesus is sitting at dinner in Bethany. The text suggests that he is in the home of friends. Nothing about the dinner seems particularly fraught until an unnamed woman enters the room, opens a jar of ointment, and pours it on his head. Let's not quibble about nuances of the original Greek text. The translations read, "She poured the ointment on his head." It does not read, "She dabbed a little ointment on his hair" or "She patted some ointment on his forehead." The text reads, "She poured the ointment on his head" (Mk 14:3).

Imagine, if you will, having a jar of highly scented ointment (we learn this is ointment for burial, so it is probably nard or myrrh) dumped over your head as you're eating a meal. I believe I would have been more than a little startled. Imagine the rest of the dinner party responding to this event. Notice that the story does not say that people rushed to wipe away the ointment or to clean up the mess or to express concern for Jesus. What it says is that some of the people were angry about the interruption and that others scolded the woman. Jesus, meanwhile, is sitting there with ointment spreading through his hair and down the sides of his head.

Into the noise and the babble, he says, "Stop." Then, in the silence, he makes a statement about the action of the woman, "She has performed a good service for me...She has done what she could; she has anointed my body beforehand for burial" (vv. 6, 8).

Because of the context of this story, I suspect the majority of us have never bothered to stop and think about the powerful witness of this woman. She is the first person who believes what Jesus has been saying about what is going to happen when Jesus meets the authorities. She is the first person who publicly and visibly acknowledges his imminent death. She does what she can. She cannot stop him or save him, but she can show him that she has listened to him and really, truly heard him. She can honor him and grieve him, and she can do it in such a way that Jesus knows someone cares. Jesus knows that someone is not wasting time denying what he is saying because it is too hard to hear, or it makes her anxious, or because it is uncomfortable. She dares to pay attention and she risks believing. And then she acts on what she believes.

If Jesus had any doubts; if he perhaps thought this cup might pass his lips, this unnamed woman disabuses him. In her response, she offers her own strength to match his resolve, to support him in his coming passion.

And in Mark's gospel, her action and Jesus' recognition of it set in motion the final events that lead to the crucifixion.

As we enter into the story of this many-layered week again, I would invite us to pause with this unnamed woman and ask what she can offer us as a model of discipleship. It is so easy, 2,000 years after these events, to be lulled by the narcotic of superficial piety. In truth, the shock of Jesus' crucifixion has become pretty dull. And hastily turning our mind to his divinity or to the resurrection when we become uncomfortable allows us to avoid any deep awareness of his pain.

But this unnamed woman didn't give in to any of that. She didn't sit around talking about what Jesus might mean; she didn't get deflected by plans or possibilities. She entered straight into the heart of the matter and prepared Jesus for his death.

Not only did this woman transform that day and that place for Jesus, she challenges us to remember that Jesus told us he died – and will die – every time one of the least of us is sacrificed on the cross of power. She challenges us to remember that Jesus, therefore, is dying every minute of every day...often because of our inaction, ignorance, or greed. She challenges us to believe that Jesus is dying and to dare to do what we can. She challenges us to claim our power to make a difference this year...as she made the only difference she could all those years ago. This year, I invite us to take up her challenge in remembrance of her. Amen.

– Andrea La Sonde Anastos

April 13, 2006

Maundy Thursday

Lessons

RCL	Ex 12:1–4 (5–10) 11–14	1 Cor 11:23–26	Jn 13:1–17, 31b–35
Roman Catholic	Ex 12:1–8, 11–14	1 Cor 11:23–26	Jn 13:1–15
Episcopal	Ex 12:1–14a	1 Cor 11:23–26 (27–32)	Jn 13:1–15 or Lk 22:14–30

Introduction to the Lessons

Lesson 1

Exodus 12:1–4 (5–10) 11–14 (RCL);
Exodus 12:1–8, 11–14 (RC);
Exodus 12:1–14a (Epis)

God's instructions to Moses and Aaron concern preparations for the Passover. The connection between the blood of the lamb smeared on the doorposts of the Hebrews and the blood of the Lamb shed for us on the cross is one replete with meaning.

Lesson 2

1 Corinthians 11:23–26 (RCL/RC);
1 Corinthians 11:23–26 (27–32) (Epis)

Here Paul instructs the church in Corinth in the celebrating of the Lord's Supper. The words are the age-old words, calling the church to remembrance and to covenant.

Gospel

John 13:1–17, 31b–35 (RCL); John 13:1–15 (RC/Epis)

Unlike the synoptic accounts, John does not describe the institution of the common meal in his rendition of the Last Supper, but tells of Jesus washing the feet of his disciples. The community is invited to ground itself in this example of service and humility.

Theme

As disciples, who serve as surrogate hosts, we are commissioned to act with the same unconditional love as the one who is the true Host.

Thought for the Day

We know that our heart has broken through into the Real Presence and stands at the table of God when we can turn to the enemy beside us and say, "Namaste – the Holy within me recognizes the Holy within you. We are well come together."

Call to Worship

> **One:** We come to serve God in the presence of all people.
> **All:** We come to break God's bread of life for the hungry.
> **One:** We come to pour God's cup of abundance for the thirsty.
> **All:** We come to serve God in the presence of all people.

Pastoral Prayer

Remembering God, teach us to remember you in every moment, with every breath, as we eat and drink. Remind us that we remember your Child, our beloved Teacher, not only in the prayers we offer and the words we profess, but in deeds of love and generosity. Remind us that we are filled with the wisdom of your Spirit and, therefore, we are advocates for the oppressed, guiding lights for those in darkness, sustainers of the needy. Remembering God, who never forgets us, remind us never to forget you. Amen.

Prayer of Confession

We remember that we are your people, God of the covenant. And we remember all the ways in which we have not lived as people in covenant with you. We remember that we are disciples of the Sovereign One, who came to serve rather than to be served. And we remember all the ways in which we have used our power to oppress rather than to liberate. We remember that we are temples of your Spirit, and we remember all the ways we have ignored the word of that Spirit speaking in us. Remind us to remember whose we are, and to act accordingly. Amen.

Prayer of Dedication of Gifts and Self

Receive these offerings which we return to you, God of all good gifts, that they may provide a feast of abundance for those in need, an act of hope and faithful care while we await your coming banquet. Amen.

Sermon Summary

God's table is a table of radical welcome to which the whole creation is called and at which the whole creation is blessed and fed. If the table around which we gather in our sanctuaries is closed to even one of God's creating, it is not God's table.

Hymn of the Day
"Love consecrates the Humblest Act"

Maundy Thursday is the day of the commandment ("Do this in remembrance of me") and of footwashing. It's amazing how powerful this humble act is, to watch one take hold of another's feet, to hear the water fall gently over the limbs into a basin, to see the feet being dried with a towel.

S. B. McManus' "Love Consecrates the Humblest Act," set to TWENTY-FOURTH, attributed to Lucius Chapin, is my recommendation. Love "consecrates," love "halloes," love "sheds a benediction sweet." As McManus says, "Let us now gladly do!"

Children's Time

A Special Meal

What is your favorite food? (Accept responses and share your own.) I'm going to name foods from different kinds of special occasions and you tell me what it is.

Cake and ice cream (Birthday).

Turkey and dressing, pumpkin pie (Thanksgiving).

Buttered popcorn and soda pop (movie).

In church, we have a special meal, too. The food at this meal is bread and wine. Do you know the name of this special meal? (Communion.)

Where does bread come from? (Wheat which is ground into flour.) Where does wine come from? (Grapes.) Jesus blessed these foods for his special meal. This simple meal is for all people, a meal about Jesus' love for us. Whenever we eat the meal of Holy Communion we know that Jesus is with us and forgives our sins. We remember that Jesus loves us, forever and ever.

Prayer: Thank you, Jesus, for coming to us in a special meal of bread and wine. Whenever we share this meal with God's family, help us to celebrate the good news of the new life you bring to all people. Amen.

The Sermon

In Remembrance of Me

Hymns

Beginning of Worship: "If Our God Had Simply Saved Us"
Sermon Hymn: "An Upper Room Did Our Lord Prepare"
Closing Hymn: "Now to Your Table Spread"

Scripture

1 Corinthians 11:23–26 (For sermon materials on John 13:1–17, 31b–35, see the 2005 May/June planning issue of *The Clergy Journal*; for sermon materials on Exodus 12:1–4 (5–10) 11–14, see the January 2006 issue of *The Clergy Journal*.)

Tonight, we in the community of faith around the world gather at a table of remembrance and thanksgiving. We gather around the symbols of our faith to speak words of blessing and then to break bread and to drink from a common cup. This is a table of radical welcome, a table where no differences of tradition or education or wealth or social level or gender or age or power or marital status or culture or ethnic background or length of time in the faith or anything else should separate us. This is a table from which no one, no one, is excluded. Let me say that again: This is a table from which no one, no one at all, is excluded.

Do we believe that? Do we, disciples of Jesus of Nazareth – who ate with sinners, who touched lepers, who spoke with the outcast – believe that? Do we entrust this table, this bread, this wine to God with our whole hearts, without judgment of the souls who come to eat here? Or have we ringed this table with moats of self-righteousness, with fences of pious regulations and the barbed wire of doctrinal tests? Have we demanded that people be clean and presentable, married, single or widowed...but never divorced? Have we insisted on Baptism – in spite of the fact that none of the original disciples was a baptized Christian? Have we laid down rules about bread made with wheat and fermented grape liquid...regardless of whether such bread or wine is available to the people who are gathering or can be eaten and drunk by the people present?

"Do this in remembrance of me."

This is the table of radical welcome because Jesus was a radical host.

In my first year of ordained ministry, a young woman came to see me early in November. Struggling to speak through her tears, Ellen explained that her parents and younger sister were coming 300 miles north to share Thanksgiving with Ellen and her husband of six months. Her husband's parents were also coming a substantial distance to share this "first extended-family Thanksgiving." Everyone was excited...except Ellen, who was a whisper away from a panic attack.

You see, her family was from Virginia and the traditional Thanksgiving meal included ham and sweet potatoes, pecan pie, cornbread, and okra. Her husband's family was from Vermont and had never celebrated Thanksgiving without turkey and stuffing, apple cider, cranberry sauce, and whipped squash. Her mother had sent two family recipes by mail. His mother had sent three family recipes by email. Ellen was smart enough to realize that the menu – whatever it was – had the potential to disappoint someone or, what seemed even more possible, would disappoint everyone! It was a disaster in the making.

So we prayed together for a quiet heart. We prayed that Ellen could be centered in who she was as a person of God, filled with the wisdom of the spirit. Through the calm of the prayer, Ellen realized that her table needed to be a table of radical welcome.

On Thanksgiving, she carried a pan of cornbread to the table and a pitcher of cider. After grace, but before she brought the rest of the food from the kitchen, she cut the cornbread into pieces and served it onto the bread plates as she shared a story that her grandmother had told her about being a young bride making cornbread from this same recipe. And she went around the table pouring cider in each glass while she told a story about her husband's great-uncle who had owned an apple orchard and pressed his own cider. And then she said, "Greg and I feel very honored to stand in this long line of people who celebrated the bounty of the harvest together with the produce of their land. We have such rich traditions to draw on from generations and generations. And we want to bring something to add to this table, something that is uniquely ours, to be part of what we are really celebrating, which is that we each have a larger family now who are all welcome at the same table." And then she and her husband Greg carried in the rest of the food which included roast duck (not ham or turkey) and broiled acorn squash (not whipped butternut) and sweet potato pie (not pecan).

"Do this in remembrance of me."

Tonight is not about whether the right elements are white bread and wine or matzo and grape juice. Tonight is about remembering not only with a meal of thanksgiving and memorial; it is about remembering who Jesus was and what he stood for and whom he stood with. It is not about whether the words are said this way, or a particular gesture is done now or later. It is not about testimonials or creeds or doctrines or anything else that might separate us from one another.

Tonight is about the radical, unconditional welcome that God offers us in this feast which we celebrate in remembrance of Jesus Christ, who went to his death rather than deny us. Tonight is about the challenge that Jesus offered his first disciples at that first table when he laid his hands on what happened to be there, blessed it, and gave it to everyone who was gathered – including the one who was about to betray him, the one who was about to deny him, and the ones who would run away. Jesus said, "In time to come, do this, just like this: with whoever is gathered and whatever is at hand, and remember me." May it be so tonight, tomorrow, whenever we gather at a table with friends or strangers. May it transform us each and every time until we share this feast together with the whole creation in the realm of God. Amen and amen.

– Andrea La Sonde Anastos

April 14, 2006

Good Friday

Lessons

RCL	Isa 52:13–53:12	Heb 10:16–25	Jn 18:1—19:42
		or Heb 4:14–16; 5:7–9	
Roman Catholic	Isa 52:13–53:12	Heb 4:14–16; 5:7–9	Jn 18:1—19:42
Episcopal	Isa 52:13–53:12	Heb 10:1–25	Jn (18:1–40)
			19:1–37

Introduction to the Lessons

Lesson 1
Isaiah 52:13–53:12 (RCL/RC/Epis)

The fourth Servant Song from Isaiah invites us to see the Servant in a new way: not majestic, but marred; not one who graciously stoops from divine perfection to participate in human existence, but one already wounded by life.

Lesson 2
(1) Hebrews 10:16–25 (RCL); Hebrews 10:1–25 (Epis)

This passage is a proclamation of the difference between the sacrifices of the old and the new covenants. It reminds the community that the sacrifice offered for us was "once and for all." We are invited to be in God's presence, and also invited to be changed by the sacrifice Jesus has made.

(2) Hebrews 4:14–16; 5:7–9 (RC)

The key to this passage is not in the authority in the image of high priest, but in the obedience. Here is an unequivocal declaration of the full humanity of Jesus, which draws us into his very real pain and suffering.

Gospel
John 18:1–19:42 (RCL/RC); John (18:1–40) 19:1–37 (Epis)

This is the story of the arrest, trials, crucifixion, and death of Jesus from John's perspective.

Theme

Being a disciple is not about reaping the personal benefits of Jesus' sacrifice on our behalf. It is about being willing to stand where Jesus stood on behalf of those who are suffering here and now.

Thought for the Day

Spiritual warrior's pledge: Not for myself alone, but that all the people may live.

— Brooke Medicine Eagle ("Buffalo Woman Comes Singing")

Call to Worship

Leader:	Why do I forsake Jesus, the one I call Christ?
Right Side:	Why do I shut my ears to the groaning of my sister?
Left Side:	Why do I turn my eyes from the hunger of my brother?
Right Side:	Why do I condemn my sister to the cross of injustice?
Left Side:	Why do I abandon my brother to the dogs of war?
All:	Why do I forsake – over and over – Jesus, the one I call Christ?

Pastoral Prayer

Suffering God, on this day when we seek to know what it means to stand at the cross, let us feel – however briefly – the suffering of a sister or brother who is sitting with a child mortally wounded by rocket fire, who is dying of starvation that we could have prevented, who is an unlisted prisoner expunged from our memory, who is an illiterate immigrant working in an illegal sweatshop. Teach us to see the Christ in those faces, to see his death in those deaths. May we witness your gift of salvation by giving our lives as Christ gave his, to lift the burden of death from this world. Amen.

Prayer of Confession

God, who stands with all who are crucified by lives of agony and violence, we confess that we are still responsible for raising too many crosses on too many hills. We confess that we have learned to walk by the crosses of prejudice, war, inequity, oppression, disease, illiteracy, and addiction with dead hearts and averted eyes. Remind us that the women and men and children hanging there are your living body, dying again and again for our sins. Break open our hearts to that shocking reality and receive our whole-hearted repentance. Amen.

Prayer of Dedication of Gifts and Self

When you have poured out so much for us, Abundant God, how can we withhold our hearts, our minds, our tithes, our time? We ask that you receive and bless all that we bring and all that we are, in the name of your Son. Amen.

Sermon Summary

Good Friday is not about Jesus dying once, two millennia ago; it is about our willingness to continue to subject God to suffering by our choices today.

Hymn of the Day
"When Jesus Wept"

It is my custom this night to pare the music down to the most sacred of all instruments: the human voice. No organ. No piano. Nothing to detract from the story we have come to hear with trembling hearts.

An oft-overlooked gem lying dormant at the back of most hymnals is William Billings' "When Jesus Wept," a simple round for four voices. "When Jesus wept, the falling tear in mercy flowed beyond all bound…" The gently falling minor melody portrays not only Jesus' tears, but also the utter anguish of this night.

Children's Time

A Sad Day

Preparation: Set out a processional cross or other large cross with room for the children to gather around it. Bring in several roses with thorns, and rose petals.

(Invite the children to sit at the foot of the cross.) This day is called Good Friday. On Good Friday, we remember the day that Jesus died on the cross. Jesus suffered greatly on that day. Some Roman soldiers made a crown of thorns and placed it on his head. The thorns were sharp, like these thorns. (Hold out the rose stems and invite the children to touch the tips of the thorns.) The soldiers nailed Jesus' wrists and ankles to the cross right here and here. (Have the children touch their wrists and ankles with you.) Jesus' mother, friends, and followers cried and cried on this day.

Roses have thorns, but they are beautiful too. We know that Jesus' sad story has a beautiful Easter ending. But on Good Friday, we remember the sad part of Jesus' story. Here's a rose petal. (Give each child a petal.) Smell the petal. It smells so good. Gently rub the petal across your cheek. How does it feel? (Smooth, soft.) Think of someone you love. Then whisper a thank-you prayer for that person while you place your rose petal at the bottom of the cross. (You may need to help the children begin.)
Prayer: (Whisper) Thank you, God, for sending your only son, Jesus, to die on the cross to forgive our sins and give us everlasting life with you. Amen.

The Sermon

Poured Out

Hymns
Beginning of Worship: "To Mock Your Reign"
Sermon Hymn: "There in God's Garden"
Closing Hymn: "When I Survey the Wondrous Cross"

Scripture
Isaiah 52:13—53:12 (For additional sermon materials on this passage, see the January 2006 issue of *The Clergy Journal*; for sermon materials on John 18:1–19:42, see the 2005 May/June planning issue of *The Clergy Journal*.)

On this Good Friday in the year of our Lord 2006, we open our morning papers to image after image of the broken body of Christ. Famines around the world wipe out whole populations. Violence, crossing all national borders, leaves both oppressor and oppressed dead on urban battlefields. Terrorism explodes in democracy and dictatorship alike, spraying its random shrapnel on the powerful and the powerless. Greed, lust, prejudice, and fear spew insidious, deadly fumes into the (illusory) pockets of safety we believe still exist.

The same images under the same headlines filled our papers yesterday. They will fill our papers and news reports tomorrow. Sometimes the picture is one of a person we know, and we cry out in horror or despair. More often, our eyes – inured to the daily-ness of it all – glaze ever so slightly and skim quickly by, seeking less volatile photos or the few stories that hold some hope or some humor.

Why do we do this? How it is even possible for those who call themselves disciples of Jesus of Nazareth to do this?

It is a grievous thing indeed when Christians accept the inevitability of Good Friday. It goes against all that God has taught us when we can see Jesus hanging on the cross and believe that it has to be. Surely our beloved God, who created all things and declared them gloriously good, never desired or intended the pain-wracked death of any creature...and if God never desired such death, then it is not inevitable nor does it "have to be."

As a churchgoer for over half a century, I have often heard the crucifixion described as necessary for the salvation of humanity. I've heard it described as a sacrifice planned by our Creator from before the moment of creation, a sacrifice demanded by God to pay for our sins. It seems to me that the atonement is radically other than that. Perhaps we are invited to open our hearts this year to this day of sacrifice in a way that owns it as our choice and, therefore, recognizes that we can change it, right here, right now; that we can make this the last year in which we need to remember this event.

It seems to me that there is one meaning and one alone to the crucifixion: it is God's personal self-giving intended to teach us profoundly and for all time what violence does to God. Not what brutality and fear combine to do to God's unique Son, as if that was the last time that brutality and fear affected God! No; to teach us what happens to God, what God feels like, each and every time any single unique child of God is destroyed by brutality and fear. Every time we – not someone else, not our elected officials, not a dictator is some far country – give in to our violent impulses and lash out at a sister or brother; or give in to our need to protect and maintain our status quo at the expense of someone else, whether we call that person a neighbor or an enemy; or drown out the truth about justice and mercy so that we can avoid sharing the abundance God has entrusted to us, this is what God experiences.

God has poured God's self into human form, daring to create us in God's own image and then to share that image with us in order to bring us to our full divinity, our full at-one-ment with God. Jesus clung to that at-one-ment, trusting that even death would not separate him from it. He leaned into it so far that he died rather than deny that divine image in himself. And, in dying, he showed us again how God suffers with every death.

Yes, Jesus did it to show the way of salvation. He showed us that sometimes salvation (the true oneness with God) is a way of living and sometimes it is a way of dying, but without doubt he showed us that violence is never the way. He showed us that at-one-ment means being wholly with God in God's moment of suffering, a moment in which God does not take revenge for God's own pain.

Such at-one-ment only can be claimed by each person, individually. It is not something you can do for me, something you can give to me. It is something that I am called to do each time the opportunity arises to embrace the truth, to shed the light, to speak the word of love, to lay aside the anger, to make the gesture of peace. It is something I am called to do each time the moment comes to deny hope, to spread darkness, to harm or demean another, to give way to violence, to take up arms. I choose to claim the commission of disciple or I choose to drive home the nails. I choose to claim the inner image of divinity or to deny my fullest humanity. I do. You do.

Good Friday is not inevitable unless we choose that it be so. As we come to the foot of the cross this day, this year, we have the chance again to make it the last cross in our life. We have the chance to turn our faces toward the resurrection and never again to turn back. In Christ's name, may we choose wisely. Amen.

– Andrea La Sonde Anastos

April 16, 2006

Easter

Lessons

RCL	Acts 10:34–43	1 Cor 15:1–11	Jn 20:1–18
	or Isaiah 25:6–9	or Acts 10:34–43	or Mk 16:1–8
Roman Catholic	Acts 10:34, 37–43	Col 3:1–4	Jn 20:1–9
		or 1 Cor 5:6–8	
Episcopal	Acts 10:34–43	Col 3:1–4	Mk 16:1–8
	or Isaiah 25:6–9	or Acts 10:34–43	

Introduction to the Lessons

Lesson 1
Acts 10:34–43 (RCL/Epis); Acts 10:34, 37–43 (RC)

These verses are part of the glorious Easter proclamation, which will be repeated again and again this season. Peter preaches to a group in Caesarea, witnessing to the risen Christ and Christ's continued presence among his people.

Lesson 2
(1) 1 Corinthians 15:1–11 (RCL)

Christ is the one through whom all things are made alive. By his death and resurrection, he becomes the living promise that death will not be the final word, but that God will raise all people into the abundant ongoing creation that is "all in all."

(2) Colossians 3:1–4 (RC/Epis)

Here is the declaration of our resurrection life ("hidden with Christ in God"). Through Christ, we are already raised and will be revealed when Christ is revealed in his glory.

Gospel
(1) John 20:1–18 (RCL); John 20:1–9 (RC)

This is Mary's story. Alone at the tomb after she announces the disappearance of Jesus, she is called by name into the presence of the risen Christ and lifted out of mourning into joy.

(2) Mark 16:1–8 (Epis)

This abrupt and very human conclusion invites the faithful to wrestle with the tension between the "right now" and the "not yet" of the realm of God among us.

Theme

In the resurrection, we have received God's jubilant invitation to be resurrected people, even in this life.

Thought for the Day

Eternity is not something that begins after you are dead. It is going on all the time. We are in it now.

— Charlotte Perkins Gilman ("The Forerunner")

Call to Worship

One: Alleluia! God is with us!

All: Even when we crucify all goodness, God raises goodness again.

One: Alleluia! God is with us!

All: Even when we crucify all hope, God raises hope again.

One: Alleluia! God is with us!

All: Even when we crucify all light, God raises light again.

One: Alleluia! God is with us!

All: Even when we crucify all love, God raises love again. Alleluia! God is with us!

Pastoral Prayer

God Creator, God Redeemer, God Sustainer, you call us to witness to your unending grace and power. You have given us the greatest of miracles to be our message. Send us forth to witness with all our heart, all our mind, all our spirit, all our strength. Amen.

Prayer of Confession

On this day of joy, we confess that we have not always witnessed to the joy of our faith. On this day of peace, we confess that we have not always witnessed to the peace of our faith. On this day of good news, we confess that we have not always witnessed to the good news of our faith. On this day of new life, we confess that we have not always witnessed to the new life of our faith. Forgive us when we live as meager, depressed, sullen, or anxious people. Forgive us and make us living beacons of your joy, peace, good news, and new life. Amen.

Prayer of Dedication of Gifts and Self

In joy and glory we bring these offerings, asking that you may raise them from what is merely material and temporal, transforming them into the foundation of your eternal realm of mercy and justice. Amen.

Sermon Summary

The miracle of the resurrection is not only that it raised Jesus from the dead, but that it has freed us from our slavery to death. God's Spirit is moving mightily to raise us into the glory of God's realm. Are we willing to be raised?

Hymn of the Day
"O God, beyond All Praising"

Perhaps you, too, love the familiar Easter hymns and anticipate hearing them each year. Yet there's other music – some better than the old workhorses – to share. I've come to delight in "mixing it up."

Michael Parry's "O God, beyond All Praising," set to Gustav Holst's incredible tune, THAXTED, is so good that it's become one of our Easter staples. In my congregation it is sung as the gradual hymn preceding the gospel, but it would work equally well after the sermon. For me, this is one of the greatest hymns ever written.

Children's Time

Christ the Lord Is Risen Today!

Preparation: Plan with your church musician to play one verse of a favorite Easter hymn. Cut a roll of white crepe paper streamer into 3-foot lengths.

On Easter we have a special greeting. I'll say, "Christ is risen!" You will answer, "Christ is risen indeed!" Let's practice this, getting louder each time we repeat it.

On Easter we celebrate that Jesus rose from death to a new life, like a beautiful butterfly hatches out of its chrysalis. Let's do a dance of joy for new life. (Give each child a streamer. Lead the children around your worship space, waving the streamers. Invite the congregation to sing one verse of the chosen hymn as you and the children dance.)

Christ is risen! Christ is risen indeed! I have some happy news for you. We celebrate Easter for 50 days. Take your white streamer home to decorate your room. It will remind you that our Easter joy lasts for 50 days!

Prayer: Dear God, thank you for sending your only son, Jesus Christ, to teach us about your love and to bring us forgiveness and new life. Alleluia! Amen.

The Sermon

Acceptable

Hymns

Beginning of Worship: "Christ Is Risen! Shout Hosanna!"
Sermon Hymn: "Day of Delight and Beauty Unbounded"
Closing Hymn: "At the Font We Start Our Journey"

Scripture

Acts 10:34–43 (For additional sermon materials on this passage, see the 2005 May/June planning issue and the January 2006 issue of *The Clergy Journal.*)

Alleluia! Christ is risen! Alleluia! This is the day which our God has made holy and glorious! Let us rejoice and be glad in it!

Let us claim this day and this story as the central, binding miracle of our faith, not merely because God raised Jesus from the dead, but because through that resurrection, God has shown us what God intends for us. The resurrection shows us what God is ready to do for us right here, right now, if we are willing to accept God's invitation. Peter says, "I truly believe that God shows no partiality." No partiality, none.

This sermon is Peter's declaration of faith and by any standards it is an appropriate text for Easter morning. But we don't truly appreciate how appropriate unless we put it in its wider context because, as much as the message, the context is good news.

Peter has been traveling through Palestine, preaching, teaching, and healing. He has come to Joppa and there he has a vision in which he is shown all sorts of ritually unclean animals and is invited to kill and eat. Peter refuses, saying that they are forbidden because they are unclean. A voice from heaven says, "What God has made clean (or holy), you must not call unclean (or profane)." This conversation is repeated three times.

Immediately after the vision, while Peter is still puzzling over its meaning, messengers come from a centurion named Cornelius, asking Peter to come to Cornelius' home and preach to his household. Please remember that a centurion was a Gentile. Thus, Cornelius was, by definition, unclean. A devout Jew like Peter would not stay in his home or eat at his table.

This is what God calls a "teaching moment."

Judging by some of the stories, Peter can be slow on the uptake, but he is teachable. God has just grabbed him by the scruff of the neck, so to speak, and said, "Yo! The old categories (clean, unclean; Jew, Gentile; master, slave) don't apply any more. This 'good news' is a whole-earth thing, so let's quit all the in-house schmoozing and get with the program." Or words to that effect. So Peter goes to Cornelius and preaches this sermon to Cornelius' household, a sermon that is right out on the cutting edge of his learning curve. He has just had the vision of all the animals and he is just beginning to understand the implications, which are world-shattering, folks. This new wine will not fit in old wineskins. For Peter, the idea that God shows no partiality is a major paradigm shift.

On the surface, this may be a sermon about Peter's faith in the resurrection, but in delivering it, Peter is demonstrating that God has done more than raise Jesus. God has raised Peter. All the events that surrounded the passion, death, and resurrection of Jesus cracked open Peter's illusions about the world – the way the world operates and what the defining word is in that world. Into the open space of that soul-shift, God moves powerfully to transform Peter, to lift him up, from a parochial, narrow-minded fisherman to a confident and dynamic witness of the presence of the realm of God in Peter's day and place. God showed no partiality in using Peter who, after all, was quick to deny Jesus and vanished from the scene rather than stand at the foot of the cross!

Let me say it again: the miracle of the resurrection is not that God raised Jesus, but that God is showing us as clearly as possible that God has no partiality, that the resurrection is God's intent for every single atom of God's creation. All we need to do is to say Yes.

The difference between Jesus and us is that Jesus said yes. Everything Jesus did was a living transformation of his humanity from a temporal focus to an eternal focus. He understood that he needed to die to all the earthly stuff: to grasping after worldly power rather than depending on holy power, to piling up wealth rather than sharing it, to trying to sort out the in-crowd from the out-crowd. He understood that when he got out of that zero-based mindset, God could fill him with God's own self so completely that there was no separation between them. And he understood that such divine power is so great and so abundant that there was no way death could hold him down.

The good news, dear sisters and brothers, is that today, here today, here now, we can lay hold of that miracle and commit ourselves to being transformed and raised. God, showing no partiality, is simply waiting for our acceptance. All creation is trembling with the joyful possibility of resurrection.

God's realm is like a huge power grid, pulsing with energy: ready, waiting. Each of us has a switch which allows the energy to flow and transform what is now static into life, what is now silent into song, what is now unlit into radiance. Every switch matters. Can you imagine this world with 100,000 people who care as much about the outcasts as Father Damien or Mother Teresa of Calcutta or Zackie Achmat? Can you imagine this world with 50,000 people who care as much about justice as Senal Sarihan or Nelson Mandela or Desmond Tutu or Aung San Suu Kyi?

What God said unequivocally for all time is that we (you and I) are such people. God, in raising Jesus, showed me what glory awaits the whole universe if I dare to become the transformation I long for. God has shown you. The miracle of this day is that we do not need to wait for the opportunity; it is now and here.

Alleluia! Christ is risen! Alleluia! This is the day, the hour, the second, which our God has made holy and glorious! Let us rise in joy, acceptable to meet our God who shows no partiality, that God may rejoice and be glad with us!

– Andrea La Sonde Anastos

April 23, 2006

2nd Sunday of Easter

Lessons

RCL	Acts 4:32–35	1 Jn 1:1–2:2	Jn 20:19–31
Roman Catholic	Acts 4:32–35	1 Jn 5:1–6	Jn 20:19–31
Episcopal	Acts 3:12a, 13–15,17–26	1 Jn 5:1–6	Jn 20:19–31

Introduction to the Lessons

Lesson 1

(1) Acts 4:32–35 (RCL/RC)

Convincing evidence of the resurrection of Jesus came from the amazing unity that characterized the community of those who believed in Jesus. The resurrection inspired personal compassion that found social expression in a depth of unselfish sharing.

(2) Acts 3:12a, 13–15, 17–26 (Epis)

In response to questions about the apostles' involvement in an act of physical healing, Peter delivers a sermon succinctly summarizing the Christian message.

Lesson 2

(1) 1 John 1:1—2:2 (RCL)

The writer of 1 John opens the epistle with a description of the epistle's message – Jesus provides all people with a way out of sin and an opportunity to live in forgiveness and truth.

(2) 1 John 5:1–6 (RC/Epis)

Children of God love God and love Jesus. The presence of this love is self–evident in a person's obedience to God's commandments and in a person's faith, both of which lead to a life that overcomes the world in the same manner in which Jesus overcame the world.

Gospel
John 20:19–31 (RCL/RC/Epis)
The risen Christ engaged in many acts, which are recorded in the scriptures, to help people believe in him and share in his life. He commissioned the disciples to continue his ministry.

Theme
The risen Christ, who moved into the fellowship of his first century disciples, moves into our midst today.

Thought for the Day
Through the resurrection of Jesus, God assures us that we need never be alone.

Call to Worship
One: He is risen! Jesus Christ is risen from the dead!
All: The God of Abraham, the God of Isaac, and the God of Jacob – the God of our ancestors – has glorified Jesus.
One: We gather to praise the risen Christ.
All: We gather to worship Almighty God. Amen.

– Based on Acts 3:13

Pastoral Prayer
O God, we run from the resurrection of Jesus as fast and fearfully as the disciples ran from the crucifixion of Jesus. What is wrong with us? Do we not understand the depth and breadth of good news that comes to us in this event? Do we not want Christ showing up where we are? Or, can we simply not incorporate this new reality into our view of the world? Please help us, God. We need so badly to embrace the new reality centered upon the resurrection of Christ. As we scurry in different directions, cause us to bump into the living Christ. Fill us with questions and needs that can find answers and resolutions only in daily celebrations of Christ's resurrection and moment-by-moment trust in Christ. O God, create within us a longing that cannot be satisfied until we come to you with the same kind of unrelenting fidelity with which you come to us. Amen.

Prayer of Confession

Reading a description of the early Christian community makes us more than
a little uncomfortable, O God. Those closest to the resurrected Christ shared
everything in common; selfishness seems to have vanished from their midst.
What does that say about us and about our proximity to the risen Christ? We
share only with reluctance. We hold our possessions, even as our lives, close
to the vest. God, forgive us. To read that within that early community of the
resurrection "there was not a needy person among them" inspires exalted awe
within us and evokes confessed guilt from us. So many people around us are
in need in so many ways. O God, forgive us. Loving God, teach us to translate
our belief in the risen Christ to meeting the needs of people around us, that we
may demonstrate our faith in Christ by our service to them. Amen.

Prayer of Dedication of Gifts and Self

O God, we give because we believe, we share because we love. As our predeces-
sors in the faith shared everything, we seek at least to share something – money
to finance the spread of the gospel, clothes for those without adequate dress,
and food for the many who are hungry. We dedicate who we are and what we
have to you, asking you to make us consistent, wise, and faithful as we grow in
our willingness to share everything in the name of Christ. Amen.

Sermon Summary

The risen Christ, who moved into the fellowship of his first-century disciples,
moves into our lives as well.

Hymn for the Day
"We Walk by Faith and Not by Sight"

Brimming with preaching and musical themes, it is the portrait of Thomas
drawn by John that is so memorable and inspirational here, because it puts
a human face on doubt. Who has not uttered Thomas' words in one form
or another?

Henry Alford's "We Walk by Faith, and Not by Sight" is an ideal selection
to go with this text. His hymn is pure eloquence: "We may not touch his
hands and side, nor follow where he trod; but in his promise we rejoice; and
cry, 'My Lord and God.'" Gordon Slater's ST. BOTOLPH complements the
silkiness of Alford's writing.

Children's Time

Peace Be with You

Preparation: Ask your church musician to play a peaceful, soothing piece as children come forward.

Christ is risen! (Encourage children to respond, "Christ is risen indeed!") How does this music make you feel? (Accept responses.) It makes me feel peaceful. What does peace mean? (Sense of calm, safety, and quiet are possible responses.)

Today's Bible story takes place on Easter night. Jesus' followers had gathered in a house in Jerusalem. They locked the doors. They were afraid. They were afraid that they would be arrested and killed because they loved and followed Jesus. Suddenly Jesus appeared inside their house. He didn't walk through the door. He didn't climb through a window. He just appeared. The disciples thought they were seeing a ghost. They were even more afraid. Jesus knew they were afraid so he said to them, "Peace be with you." Jesus showed his friends the nail holes through his wrists and ankles. How do you think Jesus' followers felt after Jesus appeared to them? (Happy, joyful.) Jesus was alive! They were amazed. Jesus had died, but now here he was, standing with them, sharing the peace that new life can bring.

When we share the peace during worship, we are celebrating the peace that Jesus brings to us, too.

Prayer: Dear Jesus, thank you for bringing your peace into our lives every day. Amen.

Sermon

In Our Midst

Hymns
Beginning of Worship: "O For a Thousand Tongues to Sing"
Sermon Hymn: "These Things Did Thomas Count"
Closing Hymn: "I Greet You, Sure Redeemer"

Scripture

John 20:19–31 (For additional sermon materials on this text, see the 2005 May/June planning issue and the January 2006 issue of *The Clergy Journal.*)

Reading the gospel accounts of the post–resurrection appearances of Jesus sometimes reminds me of watching old movies of the keystone cops. In virtually every narrative, the serenity of Jesus stands in sharp contrast to frenetic activity among followers of Jesus. The chronological sequence of what happened immediately following the resurrection of Jesus is as difficult to determine as is the nature of the various personal reactions to Jesus by the disciples who encountered him.

After the resurrection of Jesus, people who were as familiar with Jesus as they were with members of their own families failed to recognize him. Others saw him and knew his identity from a distance. Some individuals spoke of Jesus' physical traits – his scars, his hunger, the look in his eyes. Others told stories about his mystical nature – here one moment and gone the next, moving in and out of a room with closed doors. Participants in the same event with Jesus frequently reported different accounts of what happened.

Some people find the conflicting reports of the resurrection disturbing. Fearing that cynics may charge, "Why, the whole thing is made up – you Christians cannot even agree on one story," many believers labor tenaciously to reconcile all of the accounts, to impose order where there is confusion, to create uniformity out of diversity. Such people seem to fear that others will not believe in the resurrection of Jesus unless they can prove the resurrection by offering harmonized accounts of what Jesus said and did.

Personally, I am not of that mindset. I find the confusion and the contradictions in the resurrection stories of the gospels profoundly reassuring. Obviously, what we have in the gospels is not a carefully choreographed presentation of Jesus developed out of a studied strategy. No. What we read in the gospels are the disparate accounts of numerous individuals writing out of the excitement and wonder born of experiencing a totally new reality – the resurrection of Jesus of Nazareth, dead on Friday and alive on Sunday and in their midst during subsequent days.

Think about the dynamics here. If three people who watch a serious automobile accident cannot agree on the details of what happened when talking with a police officer only a few minutes after the accident, why should we expect hundreds of people to speak of their experiences with the resurrected Christ with words and interpretations that are exactly alike? The affirmations of the resurrection of Jesus that pervade the gospels are not the product of mob psychology, an imposed doctrinal orthodoxy, or a strategy to convince the world about this stupendous event. They are the product of hundreds of different personal experiences. In the diversity of numerous individuals' reports related to the risen Christ, resides great promise for us.

The powerful meaning of the resurrection of Jesus for our lives is lost if the resurrection is considered only a doctrine to which every individual must give a thumbs-up or thumbs-down reaction. The resurrection of Jesus is not a theory to be proven or a creedal statement to be repeated so much as an experience. And this experience is to be realized by individuals in their own respective experiences by means of a personal relationship. Note what eradicated the doubt of Thomas and pushed a confession of faith across his lips – a personal experience with the risen Jesus.

Because Jesus provides our best insight into God, the new reality of the resurrection of Jesus gives us confidence regarding the certainty of the promise, "You need never be alone; God is with you." One gospel writer placed such assurance explicitly on the lips of Jesus: "Where two or three are gathered in my name," Jesus says, "I am there among them." The implications of this promise energize our participation in worship, to be sure, but those implications stretch far beyond corporate worship.

The resurrection narratives make up a relatively small percentage of the material in the gospels. However, that small amount of material provides us with a large amount of truth. The risen Christ appeared in the midst of a small group of fearful, discouraged disciples. Jesus appeared on the shore of a lake in which some of his followers were fishing. As reported in the text for today, Jesus appeared to a man who questioned almost everything and doubted reports of the resurrection of Jesus. In a familiar place, Jesus shared a meal with some of his followers. Not long after that, Jesus joined two travelers reeling from shattered dreams to walk with them, talk with them, encourage them, and then to break bread with them. Jesus appeared to individuals who knew him well enough to avoid the use of titles and call him "Jesus." But Jesus also showed up among people who had never enjoyed a one-to-one conversation with him. Jesus appeared among people who spoke boldly of their faith. Jesus also appeared among individuals struggling with the possibility of faith.

Do you sense a truth running through all of these observations and pulling them together like a golden thread? No one was, or is, left out! The risen Christ comes to all people – the confident, the disturbed, the discouraged, the self-assured, the doubting, the grieving, the rejoicing, the fearful, the hopeful. No time or no location – geographically or spiritually – falls outside the reach of the risen Christ. We can experience the divine presence when worshiping, working, playing, or struggling, whether we are in a sanctuary or an office, whether it is a festival day or a miserable day or in the middle of the night. The risen Christ comes to us, and stays with us.

When we speak or write of our personal encounters with Christ, the story of the resurrection grows and continues. Each installment that we bring to the story is as peculiar and particular as those in the gospels. Now, as in the gospel narratives, diversity marks our varied encounters with Jesus. However, that diversity gives way to unity when, even in different voices, we speak of the rock-bottom reality at stake here – Christ comes to us!

The truths that spring from the affirmation of the gospel writers and our personal experience are overwhelming. We are never alone; God is with us. The closer we are with God, the closer we are drawn to each other. There is no challenge that we cannot meet and negotiate together.

We serve a risen savior! God is alive and among us. You ask me how I know. You inquire as to the reasons for my faith in the risen Christ. My answer, not unlike the answer you might have heard from Thomas, draws from many sources, but this one is primary – I know Christ lives because he lives within this fellowship and he lives within my heart! Amen.

– C. Welton Gaddy

April 30, 2006

3rd Sunday of Easter

Lessons

RCL	Acts 3:12–19	1 Jn 3:1–7	Lk 24:36b–48
Roman Catholic	Acts 3:13–15, 17–19	1 Jn 2:1–5	Lk 24:35–48
Episcopal	Acts 4:5–12	1 Jn 1:1–2:2	Lk 24:36b–48
	or Mic 4:1–5	or Acts 4:5–12	

Introductions to the Lessons

Lesson 1

(1) Acts 3:12–19 (RCL); Acts 3:13–15, 17–19 (RC)

In a public sermon delivered before a large crowd at Solomon's Portico, a part of the temple area in Jerusalem, Peter reviewed the key components of salvation history. He ended the sermon with a call to repentance.

(2) Acts 4:5–12 (Epis)

When political and religious leaders in Jerusalem asked Peter and John by what authority they spoke, Peter, inspired by God's Spirit, explained that their good work was being done in the name of Jesus Christ and called the leaders to recognize Christ.

Lesson 2

(1) 1 John 3:1–7 (RCL)

The love of God is known most clearly through Christians' identity as "children of God." The reality of that identity is not dependent upon recognition by the world, but is a consequence of the revelation of God.

(2) 1 John 2:1–5 (RC); 1 John 1:1—2:2 (Epis)

The author of 1 John writes out of personal experience in order that the children of God may know the joy, forgiveness for sins, and fellowship available in Christ. Children of God obey the commandments of God and walk as Jesus walked.

Gospel
Luke 24:36b–48 (RCL/Epis); Luke 24:35–48 (RC)

While the two people who met Jesus on the road to Emmaus were telling others about the risen Christ, Jesus appeared among them. After his greeting of "Peace be with you," Jesus explained that all that had happened was a fulfillment of God's intention.

Theme

Making peace is an important form of celebrating the resurrection of Christ.

Thought for the Day

Christ greeted us with the word *peace* and promised us the reality of peace. Hearing the greeting of Christ should send us running to take up the work of making peace a reality.

Call to Worship

One: Come children of God, let us worship God.
All: We will worship God and keep God's commandments.
One: Come, blessed recipients of Christ's peace, let us worship God.
All: We will worship God and live as peacemakers in Christ's name.

Pastoral Prayer

O God, the courage of the early disciples challenges us. With fidelity to your divine authority, they spoke prophetically and acted compassionately at great risk to themselves personally. The gospel was proclaimed, hurting people were helped, and the Christian community was strengthened. Our loyalties, on the other hand, tend to vacillate between competing authorities. Rationalized timidity takes a heavy toll on public expressions of our faith. Justifications for inaction deny people in need the bold compassion consistent with the character of Jesus. God, grant us clarity about to whom our ultimate loyalty belongs. God, grant us generosity in our sharing with people in need. God, grant us fidelity to living out our identity as your children. God, grant us courage in speech and action, so that we may provide credible evidence of the power of the risen Christ and bring new life to individuals and to communities. Amen.

Prayer of Confession

Holy God, we want to be known as your children, "children of God"
living as emissaries of the love of God. But, we know ourselves and readily
confess our sins. We seek fellowship with you even as we shun fellowship
with others. We deceive ourselves, thinking that we are good enough
to judge others while failing to look realistically at our own weaknesses,
faults, and sins. We affirm commandments that we refuse to obey. Words
of love come from hearts in which prejudice resides. Even as we confess
our wrongs, however, we rejoice in your promise of forgiveness. If we
confess our sins, you, who are faithful and just, will forgive us our sins
and cleanse us from all unrighteousness. Grateful for that assurance, we
confess and repent, requesting the grace and strength that will enable us to
walk as Christ walked. Amen.

Prayer of Dedication of Gifts and Self

O God, the easiest gifts to offer in your name are the gifts of things. With
little effort and not much thought, we can give away a bit of money, a
loaf of bread, a bag of clothes, or a pair of shoes that hurt our feet. We
find it far more difficult to give when the gift most needed is that of words
of reconciliation, or strategies for nonviolent solutions to conflict, or the
gift of ourselves as bridges that bring people together. In this moment
we dedicate to you both the things that we give with ease and the most
difficult gifts we ever offer, ourselves. Amen.

Sermon Summary

Hearing the greeting of Christ who just came from the grave should send
us running to the most important places in our lives to take up the work
of making peace a reality.

Hymn of the Day
"Thine Is the Glory"

In Luke's accounts of the risen Jesus and his disciples, it's as if Jesus is
intentionally teaching them that he is always with them, even when he is
not with them bodily. Here again, Jesus' eating with and inviting them to
see and touch his wounds affirm the reality of his resurrection.

Edmond Budry's "Thine Is the Glory" is a fine choice for today. The second verse, in particular, is perfect: "Lo, Jesus meets thee, Risen from the tomb! Lovingly he greets thee, Scatters fear and gloom." Handel's tune, JUDAS MACCABAEUS, composed in 1746 for his oratorio of the same name, fits the text splendidly.

Children's Time

Shout the Good News!

Preparation: Bring an inflatable globe or beach ball.

(Whisper "Jesus is alive" to two or three children.) How do you feel when someone keeps a secret from you? (Left out, sad, mad.) How do you feel when you are keeping a secret? (Important.) I'm going to whisper something important to all of you. Jesus is alive! Let's whisper it softly all together. Now let's say it in a soft voice. (Repeat "Jesus is alive!") Now a little bit louder.

Did Jesus want his followers to keep his new life a secret? (No.) Jesus told them to tell everyone about his new life. This good news isn't a secret. It isn't only for a special group of people. Jesus' good news is for all of the people in the world. Is this happy news or sad news? (Happy news.) Let's share our Easter happiness.

(Throw the earth ball to a child while saying "Jesus is alive!" The child who catches the ball throws it to another, repeating the message.)

Prayer: Dear Jesus, your happy Easter news is not a secret. Your Easter news is for all people. Help me to tell someone about you every day. Amen.

The Sermon

Peace! What Happened?

Hymns

Beginning of Worship: "Joy Dawned Again on Easter Day"
Sermon Hymn: "O God of Love, O God of Peace"
Closing Hymn: "Now Is the Time Approaching"

Scripture

Luke 24:36b–48 (For additional sermon materials on this passage, see the January 2006 issue of *The Clergy Journal* and the 2005 May/June planning issue of *The Clergy Journal*.)

What on earth happened about peace, I mean – about peace on earth? Everything looked so promising. Hopes were high. Speaking against the backdrop of the hope annunciated by the Hebrew prophets – Isaiah identifying the Messiah as the "Prince of Peace" and Micah envisioning the Messiah restoring creation to its original shalom – the risen Christ repeatedly greeted his followers saying, "Peace be with you." Earlier he had told them, "Peace I leave with you; my peace I give to you" (Jn 14:27). Jesus spoke of the legacy of his ministry in terms of peace – "Peace be with you."

What on earth happened? What sidetracked the advance of the peace of Christ? What usurped the reign of peace? And what, if anything, with the help of God and the power of the risen Christ, can we do to recover peace or to realize peace for the first time?

I do not know the whole story, but I know a part of it. We can discover something of what happened to peace by focusing on what has happened to the three foundations of the Christian life according to the apostle Paul in 1 Corinthians 13. Of course, I speak of faith, hope, and love; of which, the man from Tarsus identified the greatest as love. It stands to reason that if the risen Christ is empowering us in the world and if all is well with faith, hope, and love, we should know peace. That very observation again prompts the question, "What happened?"

Here is a part of what happened.

First, people politicized faith. The whole thing started out innocently enough. A proper emphasis on the importance of belief led to an affirmation of the significance of convictions – beliefs that a person holds inviolable; bottom-line tenets regarding what is important in religion and life.

People who prized convictions placed a premium on certainty, on an ability to say, "Without a doubt, we are right and all who disagree with us are wrong." At this point, a movement that initially emphasized inclusion became exclusive. Within the mindset of a rigidly prescribed orthodoxy, to view another person as different is to label that person as "spiritually inadequate," "morally wrong," "lost," or "in darkness."

Within Christianity, a healthy evangelism deteriorated into a sick militarism. Claiming the cross as their imprimatur, crusaders resolved to take the world for Christ – by physical force if necessary. Governments got involved, legally mandating that citizens align themselves with the correct faith and its rituals. The terminology that developed around faith stood in sharp contrast to the spirit of the Christ who made faith possible. Congregations sang "Onward Christian Soldiers marching as to war," encouraged their members to become "prayer warriors," and sent missionaries to subdue cultures as much as to serve people.

Individuals, communities, and eventually nations began to draw lines of distinction between who was right and who was wrong. Predictably, controversy developed and eventually physical violence erupted as people – people with convictions held with certainty – fought over differences in beliefs inspired by the Prince of Peace.

When faith was politicized, peace was compromised.

People pushed hope into a distant future related to another world. Ignoring the biblical truth that the roots of hope reside in the past and reach into the present, people could identify themselves as advocates for peace while involving themselves in movements that made peace impossible. Affirming the teachings of Jesus on peace as good counsel for sometime in the future, many people made no effort to understand peacemaking as a contemporary enterprise, related not only to internal peace, but also to peace in the world. I cannot count how many times I have heard someone justify an escalation of conflict by citing a single gospel text on war while ignoring the large blocks of material on peace in the teachings of Jesus. In pious tones, these people appeal to the scriptural assertion that there will be "wars and rumors of wars" as if it were their responsibility to assure its fulfillment.

What is real here?

Once people relegate hope to the future, they can ignore the urgency of obedience to the Messiah's call to peace and assure one another that we must live "realistically" in the present. Jesus' words, "Peace be with you," are interpreted either as a comment on internal peace rather than as a promise for external peace in the global community or as a comment about peace in the world to come. Thus, comforted by the internalization of peace or by the assumption that the ethic of Jesus was intended for a time far off, people dismiss Christ's imperative to work for peace and come to expect conflict as the norm in our present life together.

Faith, hope, and love; and the greatest of these is love.

People placed conditions on love. Though Jesus practiced and commended unconditional love, followers of Jesus decided that unconditional love was impractical. Thus, even people who claimed to follow Jesus decided that they were responsible for loving only people of whom they approved. They challenged all who did not meet with their approval to become acceptable enough to be loved. Indeed, as so often happens, they cloaked their excluding prejudices in the language of piety. "You know if we love those people like they are," the rationale developed, "they may never change for the better."

Jesus was as driven by compassion as by conviction. When, in Jesus' name, people condemn and even demonize those who don't share their faith, peace receives a fatal blow. Jesus included everybody within the embrace of his love. When, in Jesus' name, people restrict their love and welcome fellowship only with people who think, believe, and behave like themselves, peace suffers immeasurably.

Look again at the risen Christ. Hear him as he says, "Peace be with you." Jesus touched the present with hope saying, "Peace I leave with you." Surely the risen Christ weeps over the absence of peace in our world as Jesus wept over the city of Jerusalem because the people there did not know the things that make for peace.

We know what has happened to peace in the past. The story of peace in the stretch of time immediately before us is yet to be written; and we will write that story.

"Peace be with you," Jesus said. What happens next with peace depends to a great extent on the words and actions of people like us. So, hearing the greeting of Christ who came from the grave, should send us running to the most important places in our lives to take up the work of peacemaking. Amen.

– C. Welton Gaddy

May 7, 2006

4th Sunday of Easter

Lessons

RCL	Acts 4:5–12	1 Jn 3:16–24	Jn 10:11–18
Roman Catholic	Acts 4:8–12	1 Jn 3:1–2	Jn 10:11–18
Episcopal	Acts 4:(21–31) 32–37	1 Jn 3:1–8	Jn 10:11–16
	or Ezek 34:1–10	or Acts 4:(23–31) 32–37	

Introduction to the Lessons

Lesson 1
(1) Acts 4:5–12 (RCL); Acts 4:8–12 (RC)

When political and religious leaders in Jerusalem asked Peter and John by what authority they spoke and acted, Peter explained that their good work was being done in the name of Jesus Christ and called the leaders to recognize the unique identity of Jesus.

(2) Acts 4:(21–31) 32–37 (Epis)

After the apostles were released from jail and told to quit preaching the gospel, they met with their friends and began preaching the gospel again. Members of this early Christian community pooled their possessions so that no one within the community was in need.

Lesson 2
(1) 1 John 3:16–24 (RCL)

Real love finds expression in action. We know that we abide in Christ when we obey his commandments to believe in him and to show love toward one another.

(2) 1 John 3:1–2 (RC); 1 John 3:1–8 (Epis)

The love of God is known most clearly through Christians' identity as "children of God." The reality of that identity is not dependent upon recognition by the world, but is a consequence of the revelation of God.

Gospel
John 10:11–18 (RCL/RC); John 10:11–16 (Epis)
Jesus identifies himself as the good shepherd, who lays down his life
on behalf of his sheep. Jesus knows his people like a shepherd knows
his sheep and desires oneness among them. Followers of Jesus know
the voice of Jesus the shepherd and obey. God is pleased with Jesus
the good shepherd.

Theme
To know the reality of the Good Shepherd is to experience peace and
to work for community.

Thought for the Day
The Good Shepherd sees to it that each member of the flock is in the
fold – protected and secure, fed and made comfortable, peaceful. This
is an open invitation, a source of great comfort, an enduring promise,
and an awesome challenge for every one of Jesus' followers.

Call to Worship
> **One:** Affirming the diversity within this congregation, I call
> each of you to participate in the unity of worship.
> **All:** We unite our voices and gifts into one communal offer-
> ing of praise to God. To the living God – our abiding
> shepherd – we give praise, glory, honor, and the devotion
> of our lives. Amen.

Pastoral Prayer
In these moments together, O God, enable us to hear the voice of the
Good Shepherd once more. Empower us to embrace the divine vision
of peace. Guide us into a realization of the resurrection. Fill us with
the inspiration, power, persistence, and courage to pursue the building
of a world in which personal dignity, emotional comfort, spiritual
encouragement, and international peace are as common as breathing.
O Good Shepherd, please save your sheep! Amen.

Prayer of Confession

O Good Shepherd, not all is well within the fold of grace or, for that matter, within the courts of justice or along the paths of the rest of the world. Wants protrude like the bloated bellies of hungry youngsters and fulfillment seems as impossible in any one realm as in another. The green pastures now lay red and rocky, made ugly by the spiritual strip-mining of selfishness. The still waters, the very sight and sounds of which restore calm, now induce fear as they roar, foam, and roll – threatening to overflow their banks destructively. Recognizing right paths is made difficult by moral ambiguity and religious insensitivity. We do fear evil. We see more military weapons than we do shepherds' staffs. We sleep with restlessness rather than with comfort. We run from the presence of our enemies, seeking distance from them rather than a table before them. Those who follow us bear no resemblance to goodness and mercy. Why, sometimes we feel a spiritual homelessness that is every bit as real as the lack of a home is in the life of the man who sleeps under a bridge every night. O Good Shepherd, not all is well within the fold of grace or, for that matter, within the courts of justice or along the paths of the rest of the world. Forgive us, God, for our contributions to the problems. Lead us to become part of the solutions. Amen.

Prayer of Dedication of Gifts and Self

As a good shepherd dedicates all of his or her talents, skills, and life to the care of a flock, so we dedicate all of our talents and skills to you, O God. For you are the shepherd who, in turn, directs us to care for all of your flocks, to work for the betterment of all of your people. Amen.

Sermon Summary

To know the reality of the resurrection of the Good Shepherd is to experience peace and to work for community.

Hymn for the Day
"The King of Love My Shepherd Is"

Among the loveliest of biblical passages is Psalm 23, a reading often paired with today's gospel lesson. Both describe a shepherd: the psalmist, one who leads the sheep safely home; John, one who cares so much for the flock that he lays down his life for them.

Henry Williams Baker's paraphrase of Psalm 23, "The King of Love My Shepherd Is," is a fine choice for today. The language is such that the hymn doesn't seem a repetition of the psalm; indeed, Baker's rendering is, to my ear, as exquisite as the psalm itself. The gentle Irish melody, ST. COLUMBA, is first choice for melody.

Children's Time

The Good Shepherd

Preparation: Before worship, set out nametags and markers. Encourage everyone to wear nametags today so you all can call each other by name.

Good morning! My name is Pastor (your name). What are your names? (Let children say their names at the same time.) When I call out each one of your names, I want you to stand up and sit down quickly. (Call out each child's name.) Why do we have names? (Accept responses.) Who gave us our names? (People who love us.) Who calls you by your name? (Parents, friends, family members, teachers.)

During Jesus' time there were lots of shepherds. Shepherds took care of sheep. They often named each one of their sheep. The sheep recognized their own shepherd's voice. In the evening, the shepherd would call the sheep by name, gathering them into a large pen to keep them safe from wolves and thieves.

Jesus says that he is our Good Shepherd. Jesus knows each one of us by name. Jesus cares for us like a good shepherd cares for his sheep. Jesus is watching over us in the daytime and the nighttime. We all belong to Jesus' flock. Jesus sends people to call us by name, to share his love and care.

Prayer: Dear Jesus, thank you for watching over us like a good shepherd cares for his sheep. We love you. Amen.

The Sermon

The Good Shepherd, Anger, Peace, and Resurrection

Hymns

Beginning of Worship: "My Shepherd Is the Living God"
Sermon Hymn: "Peace I Leave with You, My Friends"
Closing Hymn: "Savior, like a Shepherd Lead Us"

Scripture

John 10:11–18 (For additional sermon materials on this passage, see the February 2006 issue of *The Clergy Journal*; for sermon materials on Acts 4:5–12, see the 2005 May/June issue of *The Clergy Journal*.)

Frederick Buechner stunned me with his recollection of a show at Sea World. Five or six killer whales were released into a large tank, racing around in circles, jumping, splashing, and spewing – playing! Suddenly Buechner found himself weeping. He had the sensation of watching a jubilant dance of creation. Later he learned that other members of his family also had tears in their eyes during the show.

Several years later, while speaking at the College of Preachers at the National Cathedral in Washington, D.C., Buechner recounted what happened to him at Sea World in Orlando, Florida. After his presentation, the Dean of Salisbury Cathedral in England asked Buechner if he would take a look at a part of a sermon that he, the dean, had preached a few weeks earlier. The passage that Buechner read from the dean's sermon described the priest's recent visit to a place near Orlando, Florida, where, amid an extraordinary spectacle in the water, he suddenly discovered that his eyes were filled with tears.

What was going on here? Buechner explained that tears came to him, the dean, and others while watching killer whales at play because they had caught a glimpse of the Peaceable Kingdom. They had seen what creation could be, but is not.

I understand Buechner's tears. I recall with a smile the Hebrew writers describing the playfulness of the sea monster named Leviathan. I am moved to the core of my being by the ancient vision of the prophets –

people beating swords into plowshares and refusing to study war any more, while animals that usually attack each other lie down together in peace. I can reflect for hours on American artist Edward Hicks' painting, *Peaceable Kingdom*. The joy nearly breaks my heart.

I know and love the biblical anticipation of a realm of peace and the holy presence that inspires it. I ache for a realization of that anticipation, fearing that we may have given up on both the ancient vision of that realm and the divine presence who makes it possible. Then I see Jesus. Through the eyes of the gospel writer named John, I see Jesus as "The Good Shepherd" – a metaphorical alias for "the Prince of Peace," which was, of course, another metaphor and another alias for the Messiah, the Christ, the revelation of God. Thinking of God as a loving shepherd sets before our hearts other soothing images – quiet waters, green pastures, goodness and mercy on the move, and even a valley of death in which travelers find light.

A good shepherd sees to it that each member of the flock is in the fold – protected and secure, fed and made comfortable, peaceful. Our hearts leap when we read that promise from the Risen one – the Good Shepherd, alias the Prince of Peace.

Our gospel text is not the only story in the news today or the only vision vying for our attention. While moving hurriedly through a busy airport recently, I caught a glimpse of CNN's caption, "Breaking News." I stopped and watched. Sounds of sirens, chaos, and weeping assaulted my ears. A girl in her early teens had just blown herself to bits in Jerusalem – a suicide that was an act of homicide. I watched emergency workers sprinting from one injured person to another and ambulances loaded with stretchers screaming their way toward hospitals. I studied the faces that flashed across the screen – pain etched like knife cuts into the bearded face of an elderly man who was severely wounded, fear that had frozen like icicles on the face of a youngster, grief that in torrents of tears ran down the face of a young woman. Suddenly, like the unexpected spasm of an upset stomach, I felt anger boiling within me.

Questions quickly followed. Had a deranged political operative promised this little girl that she could gain wealth for her family by giving her life? Or, had some crazed cleric, prostituting the very name of religion, manipulated texts in the Q'uran so as to convince the child that blowing up her body to kill some of her enemies would gain her a fine heavenly reward? What was going on here? Is there no answer to this craziness?

Where was the Good Shepherd? Why didn't religion make a difference there that day? Would the ancient visions of peace have authority only when all other authorities had been attended to and satisfied?

What good is faith? I yelled at God in my silence. Why did you send prophets to raise our hopes for peace and titillate our expectations by Jesus' promise of peace? If people cannot pursue peace in the Holy One in the Holy Land, then where?

What difference does faith make in us? How little has to be at stake before religious faith trumps our tendencies toward bickering, fighting, and deadly violence? Why have we turned peace into one of those values that we feel good about lauding but never serious about realizing?

Is the Good Shepherd weeping, or is he also angry? "Peace to you," the risen Christ said, "My peace I leave with you." This was the Good Shepherd speaking. So why on this far side of Easter are we still fighting – whether with bombs or words? Why is peace now relegated more to the realms of Mother Goose rhymes and political campaign rhetoric than to a global possibility? Did God fill us with an appetite that cannot be satisfied?

What are the consequences of the resurrection of Christ among us? I harbor a strong hunch that the vision and tears of Frederick Buechner at Sea World, the shock waves of terror that emanate from the deadly work of a suicide bomber by a bus stop in Jerusalem, the surge of anger in my soul as I set before televised coverage of the Middle Eastern violence, the frustrated possibilities for peace within us individually and as a church, and the words of the good shepherd named Jesus all have something to do with the resurrection of Christ. To know the reality of the resurrection is to experience peace and to work for community. To be without that power is to be in trouble.

How goes it with us? O God, may we allow the Good Shepherd, the Prince of Peace, the living Christ to move among us in such a manner that we are empowered to live the divine vision of people at peace. So let it be, shepherd God, so let it be. Amen.

– C. Welton Gaddy

May 14, 2006

5th Sunday of Easter

Lessons

RCL	Acts 8:26–40	1 Jn 4:7–21	Jn 15:1–8
Roman Catholic	Acts 9:26–31	1 Jn 3:18–24	Jn 15:1–8
Episcopal	Acts 8:26–40	1 Jn 3:(14–17)	Jn 14:15–21
	or Deut 4:32–40	18–24	
		or Acts 8:26–40	

Introduction to the Lessons
Lesson 1
(1) Acts 8:26–40 (RCL/Epis)

Guided by the Spirit of God, Philip met an Ethiopian on the road from Jerusalem to Gaza. Philip joined the stranger in his chariot, discussed scriptures written by Isaiah, and introduced him to Jesus. When the man from Ethiopia requested to be baptized, Philip baptized him.

(2) Acts 9:26–31 (RC)

Barnabas helped the Christians in Jerusalem set aside their fear of Paul by telling them of Paul's vision on the Damascus road and Paul's advocacy for Jesus in Damascus. Immediately the Christians in Jerusalem accepted Paul into their fellowship.

Lesson 2
(1) 1 John 4:7–21 (RCL)

Love is the *sine qua non* of Christian experience. Love is from God. If we are born of God and know God, we love like God loves. If we love God, we love each other.

(2) 1 John 3:18–24 (RC); 1 John 3:(14–17) 18–24 (Epis)

Real love finds expression in action. Jesus expressed love in laying down his life for others, for us. We know that we abide in Christ when we obey his command to believe in him and to show love toward one another.

Gospel

(1) John 15:1–8 (RCL/RC)

Jesus identifies himself as the true vine of God. Believers in Jesus are the branches of that vine. The best evidence of people's union with the vine is their good works, by which is God honored and with which God is pleased.

(2) John 14:15–21 (Epis)

People who love God obey God's commandments, but no one has to do this alone. God fills us with the Spirit of God – the Spirit of Truth – who remains even when Jesus is not physically present.

Theme

Christian baptism is an important act of declaration, promise, and identification with which to begin the Christian pilgrimage.

Thought for the Day

The road that unfolds before us after Baptism is the pathway to spiritual maturity as a brother or sister of Christ and a child of God forever.

Call to Worship

One: Let us worship God, the Lover.
All: God is love.
One: Let us obey God, the Lover.
All: We will worship God in loving praise and obey God in loving service.

Pastoral Prayer

O God, we thank you for the example of people like Philip. We are inspired by his sensitivity to your voice, the immediacy of his desire to move at your direction, the ease with which he engaged a stranger on the road, the breadth of his knowledge of the Holy Scriptures, the expertise with which he answered the stranger's spiritual questions, and the enthusiastic spontaneity with which he baptized a new Christian. O God, we are inspired, but also challenged. Help us to live so that we may respond to your voice, engage strangers, interpret your word, and celebrate the faith that you will for us and for all of humankind. Amen.

Prayer of Confession

Love is such a slippery word for us, O God. We speak of love in exalted tones while engaged in actions that call attention to the lack of love in our lives. We love people generally, but maintain a long list of people whom we hate. We love a sense of community, but not at the expense of relinquishing selfishness disguised as individuality. We love democracy, but turn away from the hard work of civic participation that makes democracy possible. We love education, but refuse to pay the taxes that make quality education for everybody a reality. We love peace, but not so much as to seek reconciliation with our enemies. We love you, O God, but excuse our lack of obedience to your commandments by labeling them "too idealistic for expression amid the realities of our world." O God, forgive the inconsistencies of our lives – so self-evident in our talk of love – and mute our words of love until our speech is resonant with our actions. Amen.

Prayer of Dedication of Gifts and Self

As we give ourselves to water, O God, so do we give to you all that we have and all that we are. Make us as generous in our giving in your name as we are wet after having been baptized in Jesus' name. Amen.

Sermon Summary

Christian baptism is an important act of declaration, promise, and identification with which to begin the Christian pilgrimage.

Hymn of the Day
"Lord of All Hopefulness"

What stands out to me most in this text is Jesus' use of the word *abide*: "Abide in me as I abide in you." Stay connected to, remain rooted in, hold fast to the vine. Jan Struther's "Lord of All Hopefulness" imagines this abiding in the ordinary moments of our days. "Be there at our waking...Be there at our labors...Be there at our homing...Be there at our sleeping." Her text is a prayer that God fill our days with bliss, strength, love, and peace. SLANE, an Irish folk melody, fits the text impeccably.

Children's Time

Different, but One in Christ

Preparation: Bring face paints or face paint markers and a mirror. Invite several artistic youth to help you.
(Paint a simple cross on each child's cheek. Invite the children to check the results in the mirror.) Did you know that there are people in northeast Africa that paint their faces with fancy designs? Each day they paint a new design. Many people around the world are different from us. Their food, clothing, homes, and jobs are different than ours. They speak in different languages.

In today's Bible story we meet Philip, one of Jesus' followers. God sent Philip to talk to an Ethiopian, an African who lived in the same country as the face-painting artists do today. Philip noticed right away that the man was different than he was. The Ethiopian had never heard of Jesus. But Philip taught him all about Jesus. The Ethiopian listened to Philip's words, believed in Jesus, and Philip baptized him. The Ethiopian became a Christian. And Philip learned that Jesus' love was for everyone!

Prayer: Dear Jesus, help us to share your love with all kinds of people. Amen.

The Sermon

Rethinking Christian Baptism

Hymns

Beginning of Worship: "Immortal Love, Forever Full"
Sermon Hymn: "Take Me to the Water"
Closing Hymn: "God, Our Author and Creator"

Scripture

Acts 8:26–40 (For additional sermon materials on this passage, see the February 2006 issue of *The Clergy Journal* and the 2005 May/June planning issue of *The Clergy Journal*.)

What in the world does getting wet have to do with being spiritual? Why the urgency of the Ethiopian to wade into a body of water to experience baptism back then? And, today, what makes us believe that a person is more acceptable to God and a better member of a church as a result of having been baptized? Why do Christians persist with the practice of baptism?

Well, you would expect a life-long Baptist, which I am, to know the answers to those questions. After all, we get our denominational name as a result of insistence not only on the importance of baptism, but also on the method of baptism, the commitment of a candidate for baptism, and the appropriateness of the person administering baptism. What about you? How do you understand the significance of baptism? What does getting wet have to do with being spiritual?

The strongest answers to that question may be the more negative ones. For example, baptism is not about winning God's favor in order to receive God's acceptance. Nothing happens in baptism that makes a person more acceptable to God than was the case prior to baptism. God's acceptance of us, like God's love for us, is strictly a matter of grace.

Is Christian baptism important? Yes; the answer is an emphatic one. At the same time, however, baptism is neither uniquely Christian – the religious rite of baptism predated Christianity – nor a sure-fire guarantee of mature spirituality. It is an important act with which to begin the Christian pilgrimage. Baptism is an act of declaration, promise, and identification, but what comes after baptism is as important as the act itself in the determination of mature discipleship.

Early followers of Jesus consented to be baptized as a means of declaring that their lives were devoted to following God's way by means of the leadership of Jesus. Baptism was an open declaration of faith that marked a turning point in the way a person lived.

A few times in my pastoral ministry, I have participated in a baptism in which the person's baptism was laced with such a sense of importance – even urgency. I remember baptizing a young man from Japan who told me that his immersion in the water in Jesus' name would mark the end of his inclusion as a son in his family of birth. A woman whom I baptized in Rio de Janeiro shared a similar story about rejection from her family.

I recall several times baptizing Vietnamese and Cambodian adults who walked into the water with a look of severity induced by the negative ramifications of this act within their worlds of family and employment, but who came up out of the water with a spontaneous expression of "hallelujah."

Most of us have been to the water again and again. It's just another baptism, we tend to think as we learn of a baptism within the church. It's the expected thing to do. Can anything spiritually significant happen by getting wet in Jesus' name?

Let me summarize what the baptism of a believer means from the perspective of Christianity and what baptism can mean experientially. Christian baptism is a declaration of Christian commitment – an external act reflective of an internal decision. The candidate enters the water or receives the water to declare once and for all, "I have given my life to Christ."

Christian baptism is a means of identification with Christ. "As Jesus lived by the principle of suffering love, so I will live," the believer declares in baptism. Inevitably that will involve dying and rising again; not just one time but many times as forgiveness is extended, as grace struggles for supremacy, as persistence in love faces the challenge of deadly resistance.

Christian baptism is an act of obedience to Christ. Before I baptize an individual I usually say that I am baptizing the person "in obedience to the command of our Lord and Savior Jesus Christ." Baptism is an act of obedience early in the life of a new Christian that signals an intention to obey faithfully all of the commandments of Christ throughout one's life as a Christian.

Christian baptism is an affirmation of fellowship and unity. In baptism, a person opens his or her arms to a family of faith. Remember that it was in the context of writing about baptism that the apostle Paul pointed out that we are all one in Christ – Jews and Gentiles, slaves and free people, men and women, African Americans and Asians, rich and poor, employed and unemployed. To be baptized is to be united with all others who are one in Christ.

When we are baptized, we identify with all of those in the history of our faith who have been baptized in Jesus' name. Reciprocally, we become recipients of their affirmation and the beneficiaries of their loving support.

Now, does everybody know all of this about baptism when they are baptized? No. At least, I didn't. In traditions that practice infant baptism, the baptism is a ringing declaration of God's grace that will be understood as the infant grows into adulthood. Regardless of our respective religious traditions, most likely, few, if any, of us brought a comprehensive awareness of the meaning of the act to the moment of our baptism.

Baptism marks a start, the beginning of a journey, not the end of one. It is an early act appropriate, even important, for our embarkation upon a pilgrimage with Christ. Undoubtedly that was the intent that fueled the urgency of the Ethiopian's desire to be baptized. We walk away from our baptism to study, to learn, to love, to serve, to grow – like an infant coming from the womb to mature as an adult. That is why it is important to read the biblical stories on baptism, stories like the one before us today. It's important to remember our baptism from time to time and to recall the promise and potential of a life filled with obedience to Christ, commitment to Christ, identification with Christ, and support for the unity of all who are baptized in the name of Christ.

When we get wet in baptism, it is best that we never completely dry off. We do well to touch the water of baptism again and again – in our minds if not with our bodies. The road that unfolds before us as we emerge from baptism is the pathway to spiritual maturity as a brother or sister of Christ and a child of God forever.

What does getting wet have to do with spirituality? Maybe nothing. But, then again, when you really think about it, maybe everything.

– C. Welton Gaddy

May 21, 2006

6th Sunday of Easter

Lessons

Introduction to the Lessons

Lesson 1
(1) Acts 10:44–48 (RCL); Acts 10:25–26, 34–35, 44–48 (RC)

Peter is summoned to the home of Cornelius, a Roman centurion; preaches the gospel for the first time to Gentiles; witnesses the descent of the Holy Spirit upon all who are present; and offers baptism to the first non-Jewish converts to Christianity.

(2) Acts 11:19–30 (Epis)

Through the preaching of men from Cyprus and Cyrene, the gospel is brought to Gentiles in Antioch, where Barnabas and Saul then minister among those converts, who are identified as "Christians" for the first time.

Lesson 2
(1) 1 John 5:1–6 (RCL)

The author sings of the love of God in obedience to God's commandments as the faith that conquers the world.

(2) 1 John 4:7–10 (RC); 1 John 4:7–21 (Epis)

The author draws readers a portrait of God, whose essence as love is revealed in the act of God sending God's Son into the world.

Gospel
John 15:9–17 (RCL/RC/Epis)
As he prepares for his crucifixion, Jesus offers the assembled disciples the key to their life together. Once he is gone: they are to love one another.

Theme
God's Spirit is given anew.

Thought for the Day
[T]he maxim of the kingdom is that of all love and all revolution: *ecce, omnia novo facio* – behold, I make all things new.
> – Charles Williams, *He Came Down from Heaven*

Call to Worship
One: Let us make a joyful noise to the Lord, all the earth.
All: Let us break into joyous song and sing praises.
One: Let us sing praises to the Lord with lyre and trumpets and melody.
All: Let us worship the Lord, to whom the seas, the floods, and the hills sing with joy.
> – Adapted from Psalm 98:4–8

Pastoral Prayer
From its very beginning, O God, your church has been built upon a foundation of love: a love that surrounds us, supports us, and sustains us. Your love sent your Son Jesus among sinful human beings to live out new ways of relating to one another and to you. Your Son loved us even to his own death, drawing us back to you from the long estrangement of sin. His resurrection sings of your great and gracious love, calling us in turn to love one another. For that love, supreme and sublime, yet particular and present, which draws us together as your church, we thank you, O God. May we seek in this life to grow ever closer to your loving perfection. We pray in the name of him who is Love, even Jesus Christ our Lord. Amen.

Prayer of Confession

All we need is love – isn't that right, O God? All we need is love, to help us live in peace and harmony. Yet we are anything but loving people. We place our trust in grasping for wealth, in searching for personal power and physical pleasure, in exploiting the natural world, in settling old scores, and in confiding in weapons of destruction, because these promise quick results. Love takes too much time. Justice costs too much effort. But time and cost didn't stop your loving us. As we realize the price of your love, we hang our heads before the cross and ask for your forgiveness. Love us back into relationship with you, that we may love one another and draw ever closer to your Son, who is Love, even Jesus Christ our Lord. Amen.

Prayer of Dedication of Gifts and Self

What is love, O God, but giving? What is love, but your giving your Son, whose death and resurrection bring undeserved forgiveness in abundance? What is love, but offering back to you what we have already received from your overflowing grace and care? Bless our gifts, we pray, that they may be used in love for the least of your children. Bless our lives, we pray, with peace and justice and mercy, so that we may work for the coming of your reign upon earth. Through the risen Christ we pray. Amen.

Sermon Summary

For those who seek in every age to follow faithfully as disciples of Jesus Christ, the recognition and welcoming of the Holy Spirit and the Spirit's gifts becomes a new Pentecost, a radiant empowerment for mission and ministry.

Hymn of the Day
"No Greater Love"

Today's gospel lesson conflates a number of Johannine themes: abiding in Jesus' love, completeness of joy, loving one another as Jesus loved us, no longer servants but friends, Jesus choosing us, our appointment to bear fruit. Each of these leads to different musical choices.

However, for those "wanting it all," there is Michael Joncas' "No Greater Love," a work whose text is this very pericope. The refrain is meant for all to sing; the chant-like verses, however, are intended for a cantor or choir. A fine traditional choice is Somerset Lowry's "Son of God, Eternal Savior," set to IN BABILONE.

Children's Time

Entering Into God's Family

Preparation: Bring a spray bottle filled with warm water.

How many of you have a sister? A brother? How does someone become a member of a family? (They are born, adopted, and get married are possible responses.) Are all families the same? (Accept responses.) Some families have a grandma and two grandsons. Others have a mom, dad, and three daughters. How are families the same? (The people in families love and care for each other.)

One of Jesus' followers was named Peter. God sent Peter to talk to a group of Roman soldiers. They did not worship God. They didn't know about Jesus. But when Peter told them the happy Easter story, they listened and they believed. They asked Peter how they could join God's family. All Peter needed was water. Peter baptized the soldiers with water and they became Christians, members of God's family.

(Lightly spray a mist over the children.) You are members of God's family too, like those Roman soldiers. Every time you drink water, take a bath, or water a plant you can remember that you belong to God's family.

Prayer: Dear God, thank you for making us part of your family. Amen.

The Sermon

A New Spirit-Giving; A New Pentecost

Hymns
Beginning of Worship: "O For a Thousand Tongues to Sing"
Sermon Hymn: "And Can It Be, That I Should Gain"
Closing Hymn: "Come, Holy Ghost, Our Hearts Inspire"

Scripture

Acts 10:44–48 (For additional sermon material on this passage, see the 2005 May/June planning issue of *The Clergy Journal*; for sermon materials on John 15:9–17, see the February 2006 issue of *The Clergy Journal*.)

May 24, 1738, is a milestone date for United Methodists and others who trace their theological heritage from the Rev. John Wesley. On that day, Wesley – recently returned to England from a disastrous missionary trip to Georgia – was at a prayer meeting, listening to a reading from Martin Luther's *Preface to the Epistle to the Romans*. At about 8:45 p.m., the person reading was describing "the change which God works in the heart through faith in Christ." At that moment, later recounted by Wesley in his Journal: "I felt my heart strangely warmed. I felt I did trust in Christ, Christ alone, for my salvation; and an assurance was given to me that He had taken away my sins, even mine, and saved me from the law of sin and death."

Wesley's heart-warming experience of conversion, ever thereafter associated with the meeting on Aldersgate Street in London, where it occurred, proved the turning point in a life that up to that moment had been drifting. Some 268 years later, it is appropriate to remember that John Wesley contributed significantly to the faith of the church catholic, because of the witness of Aldersgate and the changes it brought to his life.

John Wesley, the fourteenth of twenty children born to the Rev. Samuel and Susanna Annesley Wesley (1703), grew up in the rectory of the Anglican Church in Epworth, England, where his father was priest of the parish church. Samuel's income was never sufficient to support his family; Susanna became adept at "making do." Perhaps her greatest contribution to the ten children who survived to adulthood was the individual home schooling she provided. The children grew in learning, in social graces, in faith, and in profound respect for their mother's intelligence and integrity. Her three sons (Samuel Jr., John, and Charles) and seven daughters (Emilia, Susanna, Mary, Mehetebel, Anne, Martha, and Kezia) were raised with love, discipline, and creativity. From an early age, John appreciated that his mother was different from most other women – far ahead of her time, in significant ways.

Susanna Wesley continued to be John's teacher and counselor as the people called Methodists began to evolve from small groups that came together for prayer and spiritual discernment to a powerful renewal movement within the Church of England. Once the smallest Methodist groups, or "classes," had become too numerous for all of them to be under his direct personal attention, John learned, to his distress, that women were taking up leadership roles. He turned to his mother for advice. Susanna listened, then asked a single question: "Have they fruits?" Stunned, John had to admit that they did. Then, his mother observed, what was the problem? From that point onward, at least in England within John Wesley's own lifetime (ending in 1791), women figured prominently in Methodist leadership. Those whose gifts had been for so long neglected by the established church were welcomed within Methodism. Ministry became the province of both men and women.

For the early Wesleyan movement, the recognition and welcoming of the ministry of women became a recognition and welcoming of a new Spirit-giving, a new Pentecost.

Trying to deal with a new perception of how the Spirit works is also a problem for the apostle Peter. In Acts 9, we find Peter in the port city of Joppa, where he has healed the widow Dorcas (or Tabitha), much beloved of the disciples there. In Acts 10, Peter's path crosses with that of a Roman officer named Cornelius, a pious and devout Gentile who gives alms and prays to God, but who has not converted to Judaism. After Cornelius sees an angel of God, who tells him to send to Joppa for Peter, Cornelius becomes anxious to hear what Peter has to say to him.

Peter, in the meantime, has also had a vision. As he is up on the roof of the house of Simon the Tanner, praying, he sees three times "something like a large sheet coming down, being lowered to the ground by its four corners. In it were all kinds of four-footed creatures and reptiles and birds of the air" (Acts 10:11–12). Then, Peter hears a voice, telling him to kill and eat these creatures, declared unclean in Jewish law, because God has now deemed them clean. Talk about confusion! What is Peter to do with this puzzling image?

At this point, the messengers that Cornelius has sent from Caesarea arrive in Joppa, looking for Peter. Perplexed, but also intrigued, Peter listens to Cornelius' emissaries, and the next day, he returns to Caesarea with them to meet Cornelius. As instructed by God, Peter then summarizes the gospel, bearing witness to Jesus Christ as Lord of all. Peter continues the story through Jesus' death and resurrection, reporting how God allowed the risen Christ to appear to God's own chosen witnesses.

As Peter speaks, the Holy Spirit falls upon all who hear him – even though his audience is not Jewish. That it is truly a Spirit-giving is shown by the group, who speak in tongues and extol God, traits the readers of Acts would readily associate with the Spirit's activity on Pentecost. Peter orders the baptism of all who are present, and Cornelius becomes the first Gentile convert to Christian faith.

For the infant Christian church, the recognition and welcoming of Cornelius and his companions in Caesarea as converts becomes an occasion of a new Spirit–giving, a new Pentecost.

As the church moves through the season of Easter toward Christ's departure on Ascension Day and the giving of the Holy Spirit on Pentecost, it is important for us to remember that the discernment of how faith in Christ moves in human lives is not the same in every time and place. What makes Cornelius exceptional, in the mid-first century, is that he is a devout and pious man, but not a Jew – and his gifts are recognized as Spirit-given. What makes Peter so extraordinary is that he is called to a different understanding of who can become disciples through the gifts of the Spirit. What makes John Wesley unique, in eighteenth-century England, is his willingness to be taught, by his mother and by his own conversion experience and its aftermath, that males are not the only ones who receive gifts and offer fruits for ministry. Never static, never stagnant, never complete, our lives as disciples of Jesus Christ are ripe for new Spirit-giving as well, and for the opportunities to use such gifts for the furthering of faith in Christ in our own time.

For those who seek in every age to follow faithfully as disciples of Jesus Christ, the recognition and welcoming of the Holy Spirit and the Spirit's gifts becomes a new Pentecost, a radiant empowerment for mission and ministry. This is our faith, under the Mercy.

– Nancy E. Topolewski

May 25, 2006

Ascension Day

Lessons

RCL	Acts 1:1–11	Eph 1:15–23	Lk 24:44–53
Roman Catholic	Acts 1:1–11	Eph 1:17–23	Mk 16:15–20
Episcopal	Acts 1:1–11	Eph 1:15–23	Lk 24:49–53
	or Ezek 1:3–5a,	or Acts 1:1–11	or Mk 16:9–15,
	15–22, 26–28		19–20

Introduction to the Lessons

Lesson 1
Acts 1:1–11 (RCL/RC/Epis)
After reminding readers of the actions, teachings, death, and resurrection of Jesus, Luke reports Jesus' promise of the Holy Spirit to the disciples and his ascension into heaven.

Lessons 2
Ephesians 1:15–23 (RCL/Epis); Ephesians 1:17–23 (RC)
Paul offers a prayer for believers at Ephesus, calling upon God to grant them knowledge of God's power, working in Christ's resurrection and ascension.

Gospel
(1) Luke 24:44–53 (RCL); Luke 24:49–53 (Epis)
Appearing to the disciples just before his ascension, Jesus instructs them to remain in Jerusalem until they have received the promised gift of power from God to bear witness to the good news of repentance and forgiveness of sins.

(2) Mark 16:15–20 (RC)
In the longer ending of the gospel, Mark (as recorded by some early manuscripts) reports Jesus' post-resurrection appearance to the disciples, his commission to preach the good news, and his ascension into heaven.

Theme

The Ascension marks Christ's distant presence.

Thought for the Day

[A]scension Day is properly the most solemn feast of our Lord Jesus: for this day…he began to sit on the Father's right hand in bliss and took full rest of all his pilgrimage before.

— *Mirror of the Blessed Life of Jesus Christ* (translated by Nicholas Love)

Call to Worship

One: Let us clap our hands; let us shout to God with loud songs of joy.

All: For God has gone up with a shout; the Lord with the sound of a trumpet.

One: Let us sing praises to God; let us sing praises to our Sovereign.

All: For God is Sovereign over all the earth. We sound God's praise in song.

— Adapted from Psalm 47:1, 5–7

Pastoral Prayer

God of resurrection power, we remember on this Day of Ascension that our Lord Jesus Christ appeared one last time to his disciples, then left them to be with you. We cannot imagine such power, nor can we create it for ourselves. Yet in raising your Son from death, and in his triumph over the grave, your power has forever changed the sentence of death that has followed humankind from our earliest beginnings. In offering us the opportunity to turn our lives around, to turn away from sin, you offer resurrection power to the least of your human children. May we, who gaze in wonder at your Son's ascension, be empowered to proclaim his words and deeds to the ends of the earth; we pray in the name of him who is Love, even Jesus Christ our Lord. Amen.

Prayer of Confession

O God, we stand with open mouths, gazing into heaven as your Son ascends, astonished by the spectacle. Yet, we fail to understand what we are called now to say and to do. We know that his resurrection has broken the power of death; we know that he has proclaimed forgiveness of sins for those who repent; we know we have been called to tell that good news to the ends of the earth. Confident of our own salvation, we fail to change our own hearts and to amend our lives – much less preach the gospel to others. Forgive us our slothful complacence. Raise us from the stagnancy of false security, that we may join faithful disciples in all ages, living the gospel's resurrection power and sharing justice, peace, and forgiveness in our broken world. We pray through the name of him who is Love, Jesus Christ our Lord. Amen.

Prayer of Dedication of Gifts and Self

O Lord, we offer ourselves to your service. We have hands; use them to build and to heal. We have feet; use them to go where there is need. We have hearts; use them to love this broken world. May all that we offer be empowered to spread the good news through the work of your church in the world; through the ascended Christ we pray. Amen.

Sermon summary

In Christ's distant presence, we offer our lives and our witness to the good news of his resurrection and ascension, and his sovereignty until he comes again – until we are ultimately with him.

Hymn of the Day
"Hail the Day That Sees Him Rise"

Concluding the first part of the Luke–Acts narrative, the scene of Jesus' ascension is simple but visually powerful: Jesus lifts up his hands to bless his disciples one last time, and as he does so he is transported to heaven.

Charles Wesley's "Hail the Day That Sees Him Rise," from 1739, is a hymn written also for today. Originally a work 10 verses in length, none of them is used today in an unaltered form; even the "Alleluia" after each line was added in the middle of the nineteenth century. Robert William's LLANFAIR brings out both the majesty and might of Wesley's text.

Children's Time

Jesus' Ascension

Preparation: Bring in a shallow white bowl filled about halfway with water, a pepper mill set on a coarse grind, and liquid dishwashing soap. Do you ever lie on your back to watch the clouds? What shapes do you see? It's fun to imagine while we watch the clouds.

Forty days after Easter, Jesus' followers saw something wonderful in the clouds. But it wasn't something they imagined. It was real. It was time for Jesus to return to God, his Father, in heaven. Jesus gathered his followers and said, "I will send you the gift of the Holy Spirit. The Holy Spirit will go with you as you tell people about my life, death, and resurrection. Tell everyone this good news – to the ends of the earth." Then Jesus was lifted up, and a cloud took him out of their sight.

(Gather around the bowl. Have a child add pepper to the water.) Let's pretend that the pepper is all of Jesus' followers, including us. Jesus said that we should go to the ends of the earth. Watch what happens to the pepper when we add a drop of soap to the water. (Add one drop of soap in the center of the bowl.) Jesus wants us to spread out just like that pepper – to go everywhere to tell all people about his love.

Prayer: Dear Jesus, help us tell all people, near and far, about your love. Amen.

The Sermon

Ascension: Christ Distant, Yet Present

Hymns
Beginning of Worship: "Jesus Shall Reign"
Sermon Hymn: "Christ Is the World's Light"
Closing Hymn: "I Love to Tell the Story"

Scripture

Acts 1:1–11 (For additional sermon materials on this passage, see the 2005 May/June planning issue of *The Clergy Journal*; for sermon materials on Ephesians 1:15–23, see the February 2006 issue of *The Clergy Journal*.)

The mid-1970s, when I was a seminarian, was a heady time to be in theological school. Within the denomination of which I was then a part, women were discovering and heeding the call to ordained ministry in ever-increasing numbers. While I was a rarity at home, only the second woman from my presbytery to seek ordination, I was delighted to discover that I had several dozen female compatriots at Princeton Theological Seminary. The face of theology, as well as that of theological education, was changing at a rapid pace. There were women, persons of color, and persons from the Southern Hemisphere in my classes. There were feminist, black, and liberation theologies to learn about. For me, coming from the relatively insular, overwhelmingly Caucasian and Roman Catholic world of north-eastern Pennsylvania, this intellectual climate was both stimulating and more than a little bit intimidating.

Allied with these "new" theologies was the growing belief that in order to be "relevant" to a rapidly diversifying world, the church needed to move away from traditional God-talk and find fresh ways to speak of ancient truths. I found myself torn between the rather amorphous faith of my childhood and what I continued to learn in school. One of the biggest stumbling blocks for me during this period had to do with the Ascension.

All through my childhood and young adulthood, I had affirmed in the weekly recitation of the Apostles' Creed that Christ "ascended into heaven," and that he now "is seated at the right hand of God, the Father Almighty." The words were familiar, but what did they mean? How could persons living in an economically developed, scientifically literate environment continue to believe in something that appeared so patently counterintuitive? Would the church not do better to drop belief in the Ascension – along with other troublesome doctrines like virgin birth – and join the modern era?

Over the course of the years between my matriculation in 1975 and graduation in 1978, I struggled to "make sense of" the Ascension. I know now that Providence intervened in this long quest by helping me to arrive at the understanding that the Ascension, like so many other components of Jesus' life and interaction among human beings, was not susceptible to empirical analysis. Ascension is story-language that describes something otherwise indescribable – the departure of the risen Christ to reign with God. In a sense, the Ascension focuses our life in faith, because it is the beginning of the church's witness to the truth of the resurrection without the bodily presence of Christ to spur that witness on.

On Ascension Day, we acknowledge that the Jesus who walks in history is the Christ who reigns in faith. He is both beyond us and above us: beyond us, in that we cannot domesticate him or limit him; above us, as the One who will be our judge in God's time, discerning whether we have truly been faithful disciples.

Luke tells us that Jesus speaks these words to the assembled disciples, before he leaves them: "You will receive power when the Holy Spirit has come upon you; and you will be my witnesses in Jerusalem, in all Judea and Samaria, and to the ends of the earth" (Acts 1:8).

What does Jesus mean by, "You will be my witnesses"? I believe we can identify three related levels of meaning:

First, being Jesus' witnesses means testifying on his behalf to the truth. We believe we have known the truth, because Jesus has made it known to us. This truth is everything written about him in the law of Moses, the prophets, and the psalms, and it has been fulfilled.

Second, being Jesus' witnesses means sharing the content of his message. His Good News about repentance and forgiveness of sins transcends anything the world has to offer.

Third, being Jesus' witnesses means living out his teachings in the world. Like the ripple effect of throwing a pebble into a puddle of water, the apostolic testimony begins in Jerusalem and moves outward to all Judea, Samaria, then to the ends of the earth. Its ramifications cannot be limited.

We can measure the faithfulness of our witness by responding to questions like these: Do we search out opportunities to share our faith with those who have never heard of Christ? Do we govern the words we speak and the ways we relate to other people from an understanding that Kingdom values are not cultural values? Do we welcome one another as Christ welcomes us? Do we live in hope, knowing that life with Christ is not confined to the hereafter, but begins right here, right now? Do we love one another as God has loved us – loved us so much that God sent the Son to be among us as one of us, to die our human death, and to be raised up from that death by God's love and power?

As Christ ascends, he reminds us to be his witnesses everywhere, testifying to the powerful acts of God in Jesus that have broken down the dividing walls of sin and lifted us above even the limits of death. Classical Christian doctrine says that Christ reigns over us from the other side of death. He is the One who redeems and judges us. This in turn means that we who believe in him are accountable as his messengers. The risen and ascended Christ remains present with us, who know him only by faith.

The great cathedral in York, England, was built during the Middle Ages, when illiteracy was virtually universal. Those who planned and constructed this massive edifice thus took great pains to teach the faith through art. In one of the side chapels, the unknown craftsmen created a unique and ingenious testimony to the Ascension. There, on the ceiling, at the top of the archway, is a boss (central decoration), showing eleven faces gathered in a circle. They are the Twelve, minus Judas Iscariot, who are with Jesus as he departs. At the very center of the boss is a pair of feet – all that would be seen, in the mind of the artists, as Jesus ascends.

Christ is both distant from us and present with us. This visual image in York is consonant with the story-witness of Acts: In Christ's distant presence, we offer our lives and our witness to his lordship until he comes again, until we are fully with him at last.

This is our faith, under the Mercy.

– Nancy E. Topolewski

May 28, 2006

7th Sunday of Easter

Lessons

RCL	Acts 1:15–17, 21–26	1 Jn 5:9–13	Jn 17:6–19
Roman Catholic	Acts 1:15–17, 20–26	1 Jn 4:11–16	Jn 17:11–19
Episcopal	Acts 1:15–26	1 Jn 5:9–15	Jn 17:11b–19
	or Ex 28:1–4, 9–10, 29–30	or Acts 1:15–26	

Introduction to the Lessons

Lesson 1
Acts 1:15–17, 21–26 (RCL);
Acts 1:15–17, 20–26 (RC);
Acts 1:15–26 (Epis)

After Jesus' ascension, Peter explains to the believers in Jerusalem how the scriptures were fulfilled by the actions of Judas Iscariot and calls for the election of a replacement for Judas, in order to reconstitute the Twelve.

Lesson 2
(1) 1 John 5:9–13 (RCL); 1 John 5:9–15 (Epis)

According to the author, crowning his witness in this epistle of love, believers have in the Son the testimony to God's eternal life.

(2) 1 John 4:11–16 (RC)

The author sets forth his central message about the love of God in sending Jesus, and the need for believers to love one another in testimony that Jesus is the Son of God.

Gospel
> **John 17:6–19 (RCL);**
> **John 17:11–19 (RC);**
> **John 17:11b–19 (Epis)**

During his High Priestly Prayer, Jesus affirms to God the work he has done among the disciples, and asks God's protection for them once he has left them.

Theme

Preparing for mission means putting our house in order.

Thought for the Day

Order and simplification are the first steps toward the mastery of a subject – the actual enemy is the unknown.

> – Thomas Mann, *The Magic Mountain*

Call to Worship

One:	Rejoice, O earth; the Lord is Sovereign.
All:	Let us worship the Lord, who reigns with justice and righteousness.
One:	Rejoice, O earth; the Lord is righteous.
All:	Let us worship the Lord, who is exalted far above other gods.
One:	Rejoice in the Lord, all righteous ones;
All:	Let us give thanks to God's holy name.

> – Adapted from Psalm 97:1, 2, 9, 12

Pastoral Prayer

Gracious God, so many needs surround us: those who suffer from sickness of body or mind; those who labor in unsatisfying jobs; those without homes, without help, without hope; those who serve in the military far from home; those whose families are wracked by dissent; those without families or friends; those who struggle against poverty or the addiction to money and power; those who draw near to the end of life and the final mystery of death. Beyond our individual concerns are those of the world: for justice and freedom for all people; for leaders who serve their people without exploitation; for careful stewardship of the natural world. As we await your Spirit, help us to open our hearts to you and to others, shining forth the love with which you have blessed the world, even Jesus Christ our Lord, who is your mercy and our peace. Amen.

Prayer of Confession

As far back as we can remember, gracious God, we have been told that you are love, and that all who love are born of you and know you. We accept this truth in our minds, but our actions tell a very different story. We confess that we have rationed our love – confined it to those who place few demands upon us because they are so much like us. We have failed to act in love toward the poor, the homeless, the stranger; toward those we deem our enemies or our nation's foes; toward those who have nothing to give in return; toward those we believe we cannot help. Forgive our lack of love. Help us, through the change of heart and life that is true repentance, to grow in knowledge and love of you; through him who is Love Himself, Jesus Christ our Lord. Amen.

Prayer of Dedication of Gifts and Self

Out of faithfulness, in love, and from love, you have given us all that we have, O God. Help us in turn to give to others out of the bounty you provide us, out of faithfulness, in love, and from love, so that the work of your church may continue in the world. We offer this prayer in the name of the risen and ascended Christ. Amen.

Sermon Summary

The story of the election of Matthias reminds us that before we embark on the journey of making disciples for Jesus Christ, we must be prepared: we must put our house in order before we close the door behind us.

Hymn of the Day
"The Christ Who Died but Rose Again"

Today we hear a portion of what Raymond Brown calls Jesus' Final Discourse, an extraordinary portion of John's gospel where Jesus prays for his disciples. He prays for their protection, their unity, their sanctification – all so that their joy may be complete.

A wonderful hymn that complements this passage is Granton Douglas Hay's "The Christ Who Died but Rose Again," a paraphrase of Romans 8:34–39, asserting that nothing can separate us from God's love. A more commonly found traditional alternative is Luther's "A Mighty Fortress"; a well-known contemporary choice is Joncas' "On Eagle's Wings."

Children's Time

Pray Always

Preparation: Bring in paper and a red crayon, a toy car, a shower cap, and a spoon.

I'm going to act out some things we do just about every day. Try to guess each thing I act out. (Draw a picture with your red crayon. Move the toy car around the group. Put on the shower cap and pretend to take a shower. Use the spoon and pretend to eat soup.)

When can we pray? (Accept responses.) Can we pray when we're coloring with red? (Yes.) Can we pray when we're riding in a car? (Yes.) Can we pray in the bathtub? (Yes.) Can we pray before we eat? (Yes.) When do you pray? (Accept responses.)

In today's Bible story, the disciples had to make a very important decision. They prayed to ask God to help them make the right decision. Can we pray to ask God to help us make a good choice? (Yes.) We can pray to God at any time and in any place.

Prayer: Dear God, it's good to know that we can pray to you any time in any place. Thank you for always hearing our prayers. Amen.

The Sermon

Between Ascension and Pentecost: Putting Our House in Order

Hymns
Beginning of Worship:	"All Hail the Power of Jesus' Name"
Sermon Hymn:	"Hail, Thou Once-Despised Jesus"
Closing Hymn:	"Crown Him with Many Crowns"

Scripture

Acts 1:15–17, 20–26 (For additional sermon materials on this passage, see the 2005 May/June planning issue of *The Clergy Journal*; for sermon materials on John 17:6–19, see the February 2006 issue of *The Clergy Journal*.)

"I can't die yet – I haven't put my house in order!" The emaciated man lying on a hospital bed in his living room had been failing for months. Paradoxically, it was clear to everyone in the room that day that although he was dying, he retained much of his old authority. He beckoned his wife and children, who came and stood beside the bed. He motioned to his wife to sit next to him. Then he began to speak. His voice did not falter as he explained what he wanted them to do.

Charlie was a World War II veteran who had worked for a number of years as a private building contractor. He had been an officer in the local VFW post, who went with the honor guard for veterans' funerals, both to stand beside the caskets during calling hours, and then to go to the cemeteries for whatever final honors were requested by the families. When there were little American flags to be placed at cemeteries for Memorial Day or July Fourth, Charlie was there. When large American flags were taken from caskets and folded for presentation to families, Charlie knew just what to do. He had raised his daughter and son in the church and had lived to see them both married, with families of their own. For more than two years, he had waged a valiant battle against esophageal cancer. After being a "take charge" person all his life, Charlie had engaged an enemy against whom he could not prevail. But he had no intention of going "gentle into that good night." He would rage against his dying until his last breath.

After he spoke to his immediate family, Charlie called his brothers and their wives to his bedside and went through his instructions for them. I watched, fascinated, as every person in the crowded living room in turn listened to him. At last, he turned to me and said, "It's time for communion." I fought back tears as I followed the liturgy. I asked everyone to hold hands, and we prayed for Charlie. Then, knowing that the family needed time alone, I said my good-byes and slipped out into the chill January afternoon.

Two days later, Charlie's wife Sally called. "I just wanted to thank you for helping Charlie to put his house in order. He died a few moments ago. He was – and is – at peace." For my friend Charlie, putting his house in order meant he could end his life in peace.

Putting their house in order is what we find the eleven remaining disciples of Jesus doing in today's lesson from Acts 1. After a brief synopsis of the story of Judas Iscariot, who betrayed Jesus and effectively facilitated Jesus' death, Peter tells the whole group of perhaps 120 persons that it is time to find a replacement for Judas. There must be a full complement of twelve, in order to fulfill the mission Jesus has called the disciples to begin.

Why twelve? From the very outset of his ministry, Jesus surrounds himself with followers. We know the names of the twelve men who form his inner circle, those who work most closely with him, but very few others are identified by name. From the "special section" of Luke (between 9:51 and 18:14), we know that unnamed persons are attracted to Jesus, but for various reasons do not join him on the road to Jerusalem. Undoubtedly there are others, like Mary and Martha and their brother Lazarus, who are Jesus' close personal friends but who are not numbered among the core group. The Twelve have special responsibilities. The Twelve are to carry on now that Jesus is gone, ascended to God. The Twelve, in order to do this work, must again be twelve – just as God named twelve tribes to be his chosen nation of Israel.

Why wait until now, when Jesus is gone, to replace Judas? Couldn't Christ been done this before his ascension, so that the "right" person might be added to the company? After all, Judas' betrayal has fractured the sacred community. It will be important to find someone worthy. But Jesus leaves the replacement up to those he leaves behind. In the first act of the community on its own, Peter announces the taking of a vote. It is up to them to heal the fracture.

Two qualifications are set: First, the person chosen will have accompanied the Twelve the whole time Jesus was among them, beginning with his baptism by John and ending with his ascension. Second, the one elected will become a witness with the eleven to the resurrection. Neither candidate, Justus or Matthias, is ever mentioned again, but that is not important. What is vital to the story is that the disciples know a replacement must be found and that they are in concert with God, praying for guidance and casting lots to make the decision. When Matthias is selected, the house is once again in order.

This story stands in sharp contrast and pragmatic challenge to our Western cultural predilections of "spontaneity" and our "go-with-the-flow," stream-of-consciousness lifestyle that assumes no preparedness or order is necessary before we take action on anything. The eleven disciples know that they cannot simply depart Jerusalem whenever they feel like it. Their work is too important to trust to chance, but must be undergirded with personnel and prayer, so that they are ready to face whatever dangers, drama, and difficulties lie ahead.

As we look toward the Spirit-filling of Pentecost, can we do any less than put our house in order? Do we seek prayerfully for direction, asking God to guide us effectively in the church's primary task, making disciples for Jesus Christ? Our preparedness and our actions – or lack thereof – speak far more eloquently than the slogans we pitch. Until our house is in order, we are just not ready to be disciples.

The election of Matthias reminds us that we must put our house in order before we close the door behind us. We are to put our house in order before we embark on the journey from this life to the next, or from Jerusalem to the ends of the earth, or from where we are to wherever we are going. The early church preserved this story as counsel. We ignore it at our dire peril, as if the very ministry of the apostles, and our very lives, were at stake – because they were, and they are.

This is our faith, under the Mercy.

– Nancy E. Topolewski

June 4, 2006

Day of Pentecost

Lessons

RCL	Acts 2:1–21, or Ezek 37:1–14	Rom 8:22–27, or Acts 2:1–21	Jn 15:26–27, 16:4b–15
Roman Catholic	Acts 2:1–11	1 Cor 12:3–7, 12–13	Jn 20:19–23
Episcopal	Acts 2:1–11, or Isa 44:1–8	1 Cor 12:4–13, or Acts 2:1–11	Jn 20:19–23 or Jn 14:8–17

Introduction to the Lessons

Lesson 1
Acts 2:1–21 (RCL); Acts 2:1–11 (RC/Epis)
The apostles, gathered in Jerusalem, receive the gift of the Holy Spirit, which enables them to speak in other languages and empowers Peter to explain to skeptics how that gift was foretold through the prophet Joel.

Lesson 2
(1) Romans 8:22–27 (RCL)
Paul describes the Holy Spirit as that which intercedes with God on behalf of human beings, who wait in hope for redemption.

(2) 1 Corinthians 12:3–7, 12–13 (RC); 1 Corinthians 12:4–13 (Epis)
Paul addresses the nature of spiritual gifts – apparently an issue to the church in Corinth – as multifaceted, but all of equal value to the whole body of Christ.

Gospel
(1) John 15:26–27; 16:4b–15 (RCL)
Jesus tells the disciples, gathered in the upper room on the last night of his earthly life, about the coming of the Advocate, the Spirit of truth, who will guide them once he has gone from among them.

(2) John 20:19–23 (RC/Epis)

After Jesus appears to the disciples on the evening of the resurrection, Thomas, not present to see him, declares his disbelief, until he can see Jesus for himself.

Theme

The Holy Spirit empowers grace.

Thought for the Day

The grace of the Holy Ghost is not bound to any law.

— St. Gregory the Great

Call to Worship

One   Let us worship the Lord, who in wisdom has created the world.

All: Let us worship the Lord, who gives good things to the creation.

One: Let us worship the Lord, who sends forth the Spirit to the world.

All: Let us worship the Lord and sing praises to God as long as we live.

— Adapted from Psalm 104:24, 28, 30, 33

Pastoral Prayer

One: God of Easter, you freed your Son from the clutches of death.

All: Send us your Holy Spirit, we pray.

One: God of Ascension, you raised your Son to join you in glory.

All: Send us your Holy Spirit, we pray.

One: God of Pentecost, you poured your Spirit upon the apostles.

All: Send us your Holy Spirit, we pray.

One: God of the church, your Spirit's gifts empower disciples.

All: Send us your Holy Spirit, we pray.

One: God of compassion, you see the sufferings of the world.

All: Send us your Spirit to uphold us in need.

One: God of eternity, you guard all of time.

All: Send us your Spirit to guide us to everlasting life.

One: God of love, you loved us so much that you sent us your Son.

All: Send us your loving Spirit, we pray in the name of him who is Love Himself, Jesus Christ our Lord. Amen.

Prayer of Confession

One: O God, whose grace surrounds us, whose Spirit sustains us: we confess that we have failed to be your faithful disciples.

All: Forgive us, O Lord.

One: We confess that we have neglected the Spirit's gifts in us. You have given us wisdom and knowledge, faith and healing, but those gifts have languished unused.

All: Forgive us, O Lord.

One: We confess that we have been concerned with position and privilege, focused on the mistaken perception that we alone possess true faith.

All: Forgive us, O Lord.

One: Forgive us our neglect and presumption, our self-centered understanding of the gospel.

All: Help us, through your Spirit, to be the people you would have us be, loving you and our neighbors, and working together as the body of Christ; we pray in Christ's holy name. Amen.

Prayer of Dedication of Gifts and Self

One: For your Spirit's gifts to each of us,

All: We thank you, gracious God.

One: For the bounty of daily life; for strength and health, for food and shelter,

All: We thank you, gracious God.

One: For family and friends; for those who sustain us and support us,

All: We thank you, gracious God.

One: We offer our gifts, as an expression of our thanks and praise.

All: We pray that you will use them, as you use the Spirit's many gifts, to hasten the coming of your kingdom on earth; we pray, as the body of Christ, in his holy name. Amen.

Sermon Summary

The birth of the church at Pentecost is hopeful, exciting, even mysterious, as the gift of the Holy Spirit empowers the church to dream – to move forward into a future beyond our wildest imagining.

Hymn of the Day
"On Pentecost They Gathered"

Just as there are many preaching themes found in today's readings, so are there a number of hymns appropriate to the occasion. Tanzanian Wilson Niwagila's "Gracious Spirit, Heed Our Pleading" sounds great with drums. David Haas' "Send Us Your Spirit" is an excellent contemporary choice, as is Marty Haugen's driving "Send Down the Fire."

Jane Parker Huber's "On Pentecost They Gathered" is a traditional hymn that stands out because, unlike many others, it so clearly refers to the events of Pentecost. MUNICH, the German chorale harmonized by Felix Mendelssohn, adds a sense of jubilation to Huber's text.

Children's Time

A Birthday Surprise!

Preparation: Bring a box fan with an extension cord, a large pillar candle, and matches.

In today's Bible story, Jesus sends a surprise party for the disciples. Before Jesus ascended into heaven he said, "Wait in Jerusalem and you will receive the gift of the Holy Spirit." One day, while the disciples were waiting, a sound like a strong wind filled the house. (Turn on the fan.) Suddenly divided flames appeared in the air over each disciple's head. (Turn off the fan and light the candle.) The disciples watched in wonder and surprise as these beautiful flames flickered over their heads.

The sound of wind and the flames announced Jesus' gift of the Holy Spirit, a birthday gift for Jesus' church, the Christian church. The Holy Spirit helped all the disciples speak other languages. They rushed out into the streets of Jerusalem and told everyone about Jesus, each speaking in a different language, so that everyone could understand. Three thousand people believed and were baptized. With the gift of the Holy Spirit, the church began.

Let's sing "Happy Birthday" to the church. (Sing, then all blow out the candle together.)

Prayer: Dear Jesus, thank you the gift of the Holy Spirit. Help us, every day, to share your story. Amen.

The Sermon

Pentecost: The Hole in the Cellar

Hymns

Beginning of Worship:	"Spirit of Faith, Come Down"
Sermon Hymn:	"Come, Holy Ghost, Our Souls Inspire"
Closing Hymn:	"Come Down, O Love Divine"

Scripture

Acts 2:1–21 (For additional sermon materials on this passage, see the 2005 May/June planning issue and the February 2006 issue of *The Clergy Journal*.)

Leontine T. C. Kelly was one of the first women to be elected to the episcopacy in the United Methodist Church (her election was in 1984). I heard her speak in 1979. She told the following story, which has stayed in my memory for some twenty-seven years as one of the most compelling I have ever heard.

At the time this story took place, Bishop Kelly was about eight years old. One day her father (a Methodist minister) and mother were out shopping. Her brothers took advantage of their parents' absence by teasing her. "Come into the cellar, Teenie," they wheedled. "We've found something we want to show you." Curious about what she thought was a game, she went to the cellar.

What her brothers had found was a hole in the cellar floor. As brothers often do, they needed someone smaller than themselves to help with the necessary exploration. In spite of loud protests from Teenie, they lowered her into the hole, hoping to find out how deep it was.

Somewhere in the midst of Teenie's terrified screams, her parents returned home. Hoping to get her brothers into what she expected would be a whole lot of trouble, she reported what they had done to her. Much to her surprise, her Papa was remarkably mild in his response. "I think we've found something," her Papa said.

Without saying another word, Papa went next door to the church, taking a flashlight with him. A few minutes later, he returned, his face aglow. "I think we've found something," Papa said. "There's a hole just like this one, in the cellar of the church."

Papa gave the boys each a flashlight. Before taking his own flashlight and returning to the church, he told the boys to go down into the hole. Papa did the same at the church. When all of them met in the middle, in the space between the church and the parsonage, Papa's guess was confirmed.

In excited tones, Papa told his gathered family that the holes in the cellars meant that the church had been a stop on the Underground Railroad, which had helped many runaway slaves escape to freedom in the north in the years leading up to and during the Civil War.

"This is why God put us here, in this church," Papa explained. "The hole in the cellar means we have a purpose, a heritage, and a reason for being."

Leontine Kelly went on to remark that at the time, she hadn't understood what her father meant, that it was only years later that she came to realize what the discovery of the hole in the cellar signified. The congregation of which her Papa was pastor was African American, impoverished, hurting. Finding out where they came from – that their church had been a symbol of freedom for sorely oppressed people – gave the congregation the courage to move forward, to dream, to hope.

For the church, today is very much like the day when Leontine Kelly's family discovered the hole in the cellar. Today is Pentecost, that time 50 days after Easter when, as Luke tells us in Acts 2, the assembled disciples receive the Holy Spirit. They have been in Jerusalem since Jesus' ascension, obeying his instructions to wait there for the Holy Spirit. They are probably not at all sure what they await, but they stay, because Jesus has told them to wait.

Suddenly, on that day we call Pentecost, placid routine is exploded. The Holy Spirit is indeed bestowed on each one, in "tongues as of fire," and they receive the ability to communicate the good news of Jesus Christ to those who have not yet heard it, in their own languages. On the Day of Pentecost, the church is born. The people assembled in Jerusalem that day know where they have been. Now they receive the courage to face the unknown future – to dream, to hope, to go beyond their wildest imaginings.

Pentecost has been a day of finding a hole in the cellar for me, and for the churches I have served over the past thirty years, because Pentecost has been the day that confirmation classes have been received into the full membership of the church. Many cellars of despair – being small-membership congregations, being churches facing serious financial problems because of circumstances beyond their control, having so many good and active people leave the area to find jobs to sustain their families – have been illuminated by the preparation of young persons who will join the succession of generations seeking to become faithful disciples of Jesus Christ. Confirmation bears witness to a unique truth: In spite of debt, quarreling, and a history full of things that all of us would change if we could, the church has continued to witness in each place.

What is "the church"? It is each of us, caring for one another in the name of our Lord Jesus Christ. The confirmation of young persons is a sign of continuity with those gathered in Jerusalem to await the Holy Spirit: aware of the past, yet looking in eager anticipation toward the future.

The meeting of our Annual Conference always concludes with the service of ordination and commissioning, when those deemed worthy by the Conference enter symbolically into new relationships in the ministry of the church. Each time I witness this service, my thoughts are drawn back to another time and place, when I knelt among the elders of the presbytery to be ordained to the gospel ministry. Each time I remember, I begin to understand a bit more deeply what the outpouring of the Holy Spirit must have meant to the apostles, what finding the hole in the cellar must have meant for Leontine Kelly and her family. I remember the weight of hands upon my head, the inability to control the tears that seemed to spring from nowhere, the strong and loving arms that embraced me when at last I stood, a minister of the gospel.

Each time we celebrate Pentecost, the church affirms and lifts up all that is hopeful, exciting, and mysterious about our faith. Each time we celebrate Pentecost, we experience again the birth of the church and our roots in salvation history. We celebrate again the mountaintops and the holes in the cellar that compel us to move forward to follow the Lord Jesus Christ beyond where we have dared in our wildest dreams to aspire.

This is our faith, under the Mercy.

– Nancy E. Topolewski

June 11, 2006

Trinity Sunday

Lessons

RCL	Isa 6:1–8	Rom 8:12–17	Jn 3:1–17
Roman Catholic	Deut 4:32–34, 39–40	Rom 8:14–17	Mt 28:16–20
Episcopal	Ex 3:1–6	Rom 8:12–17	Jn 3:1–16

Introduction to the Lessons
Lesson 1
(1) Isaiah 6:1–8 (RCL)

This lesson recounts the call of the great prophet Isaiah. He has a fantastic vision of God's glory against which he interprets his own insignificance. God has another idea, however, and calls him to serve.

(2) Deuteronomy 4:32–34, 39–40 (RC)

Moses appeals for the people's obedience because of the previously-recounted saving acts of God. He exhorts his people to faithfulness because God is above all other gods, and concludes by pointing to the gifts of home and land, once yearned for when they were enslaved.

(3) Exodus 3:1–6 (Epis)

On the sacred mountain, Horeb, Moses comes face–to–face with God. From a burning bush that is not consumed, he hears God declare God's continuity of care in the course of his own history.

Lesson 2
Romans 8:12–17 (RCL/Epis); Romans 8:14–17 (RC)

Paul makes a case to the congregation in Rome that our relationship with God makes us God's adopted children, worthy of the trust and courage that this tie implies. He reminds us that the adoption is legal – there are two witnesses: our own sighs and the Spirit's.

Gospel

(1) John 3:1–17 (RCL); John 3:1–16 (Epis)

Nicodemus, a member of the religious elite, comes under cover of darkness to speak with Jesus as he could not in the company of his peers. Jesus engages him in a conversation about being born again of the Spirit.

(2) Matthew 28:16–20 (RC)

Following Jesus' direction, the eleven disciples went to the designated mountain. Jesus met them there and issued "The Great Commission" to go into all the world, baptizing and teaching. His charge is bolstered with the promise that he will be with us always.

Theme

We are made worthy of doing God's work by the one who calls us.

Thought for the Day

If in doubt about your call to serve, remember the one who calls you.

Call to Worship

One: We begin in the name of the one whose mystery is beyond us.
All: We stand before the ultimate mystery, seeking understanding.
One: Open yourself to us today, O God.
All: Teach us your ways, that we might serve you and the whole creation.

Pastoral Prayer

Holy God, you are a mystery to us, beyond the capacity of our imaginations. From your voice came the whole creation, and it rests in your hands. On this Sunday, give us the peace to rest in this mystery and the confidence that you call our names and welcome us into your family. Give us the spirit of those who belong, so that we might be your hands in the world with confidence and grace. In Jesus' name we pray. Amen.

Prayer of Confession

It is so easy for us to lapse into fear, forgiving God. When your way is different from the path so many walk, we can easily get lost. We fear that we will not fit in, that we will not have enough, that we will waste our effort on futile causes. Our fear keeps us from living passionately as you have created us, and we do not trust the vision of justice and mercy you offer. Remind us that we are your own, and that we need not be afraid. Rekindle your vision in us, that we might be renewed in our callings. Amen.

Prayer of Dedication of Gifts and Self

We offer to you, gracious God, those things around us and within us that you first gave to us. We offer to your service our material goods, that they may be tools to create a better world. We offer to your service our selves, created and gifted by you, to do and be all that you have imagined for us for the sake of your creation. Amen.

Sermon Summary

Our lives can be hopeful and confident, passionate and giving, because we know we are heirs of God's promises.

Hymn of the Day
"Give to Our God Immortal Praise!"

Nicodemus came to Jesus in the dead of the night seeking enlightenment. It's difficult to know how many of Jesus' ideas Nicodemus grasped, but his parting words could not have been clearer: "For God so loved the world that he gave his only Son, so that everyone who believes in him may not perish but may have eternal life."

Our own response to this good news could scarcely be put better than by Isaac Watts in "Give to Our God Immortal Praise." "He sent his Son with pow'r to save, from guilt and darkness and the grave." DUKE STREET, attributed to John Hatton, fits Watts' ebullient text marvelously.

Children's Time

Three-In-One

(Ask for three volunteers. Assign each a number: 1, 2, or 3. Have this group of three stand in a circle and hold hands.)

Child #1, raise both your hands. Now lower your hands. Child #2, raise your hands. Now lower your hands. Child #3, raise your hands. Now lower your hands. What happens when they raise their hands? (One hand of each of the other children in the group raised too.)

(Now name Child #1 as "Father," Child #2 as "Son," and Child #3 as "Holy Spirit." Repeat the activity, saying, "Father, Son, and Holy Spirit" instead of "one, two, three." Note again how all are connected.)

Today we remember the Holy Trinity. Trinity means three. God's love for us comes in three different ways: God the Father (touch head of Child #1) created the earth and planned for the cycle of the seasons and day and night. God the Son is Jesus (touch head of Child #2), who came to earth to teach us about God's love. God the Holy Spirit (touch head of Child #3) is with us, helping us to love God and love others. God is all three of these together. Where does a circle begin? Where does a circle end? Like a circle, God's love is never–ending.

Prayer: Dear God, thanks for loving us in three terrific ways – through creation, through Jesus, and through the Holy Spirit. Amen.

The Sermon

The Story Is Yours

Hymns

Beginning of Worship: "Holy, Holy, Holy"
Sermon Hymn: "Lead Me, Guide Me"
Closing Hymn: "My Life Flows on in Endless Song"

Scripture

Romans 8:12–17 (For additional sermon materials on this passage, see the 2005 May/June planning issue and the February 2006 issue of *The Clergy Journal.*)

It's a big, bad world out there and problems can be so intractable. Think for minute of the world's trouble spots. You have seen them on the news and you have read about them in the papers. What will it take to solve these conflicts? When will we learn that ethnicity is not a reason to hate another? That there are plenty of natural resources to go around? That we can protect our earth and still live abundantly? That there are ways to be sure all have enough?

And, of course, you don't necessarily have to look "out there" to see intractable problems. Even the best of marriages have minefields. Even the warmest parent-child relationships are strained in one way or another. Even healthy congregations have weak links that diffuse vitality and hope. Even our community has cracks through which people fall.

A person could get discouraged. There is so much to do and so few resources. What can one person do? We may confess that God has called us. We may seek to join the voices of the angels and sing God's praise and speak of God's glory. But on a day-to-day basis, do you believe you can make a difference?

Those of us who show up for worship know we have plenty of inadequacies when it comes to being instruments of God's peace. How can we save the world, when we have trouble deciding what kind of Sunday school curriculum to use, or what color the carpet should be in our worship space, or who is considered a "good" Christian?

Few of us would live as passionately as Paul did. Remember that Paul had been a persecutor of the church. As Saul, before his conversion, he had worked to eliminate this upstart faith, not enhance it. Then, one day, he has a vision and suddenly he changes parties. Not only does he change parties, but he becomes as vigorous a proponent of his new "home" as he was of his old ideologies. He did not, in embarrassment, withdraw to the edges and live out his life in anonymity.

That may be how we would see it, we who worry about how we will be seen, what people will think of us. There was a time, remember, when "flip-flopping" was a real negative (2004 U.S. presidential election). We admire people who are sure, who don't change their minds. We want people who think they can change the world. We will even relinquish our own power to someone with that kind of charisma.

But we do this because we are afraid, and that is exactly what Paul, as Saul, knew best as well. He was terrified of the way this new religion was threatening the world he knew and understood. Instead of wallowing in his fear, he set out to destroy the threat. From all we know, he was quite effective.

What Paul discovered on that road to Damascus – in the vision that both blinded him and opened his eyes – was that fear is not the response of faith. We do not have to protect ourselves or our standing. We do not have to fight for our place in the family of God. "You did not receive a spirit of slavery to fall back into fear, but you have received a spirit of adoption" (Rom 8:15).

Slaves, in Paul's day, had no place but the one given them by their masters. They did not have a family, a family name, or a family history. Similarly, they did not have a family future – no heirs, nothing to leave or pass on. Slaves' stories were the stories of their masters, not their own. So they feared being cut off from even this, as miserable and unjust as this was.

Saul was a slave to his masters' stories. He did not see himself in the story. He did not see the way he could or would influence the story. In fear, he strove to merely fortify it and protect it lest it be lost.

But Saul would influence the story. As Paul he came to see what it meant to be already a part of the family. He did not need to grasp the story, but let it fill him. In doing so, he found the freedom God had intended all along. In doing so, the story became his story, and he gained a family name, a history, and a future. In doing so, the story lived on. This story can not be lost.

Now, what about you, us, and our intractable times? Do we live in fear that the story will be lost? If we are honest with ourselves, then yes. We do. But need we? Honestly? No.

For the story is ours. We have been adopted. In our yearning to be God's own, our spirit joins God's yearning for us, and we have the witnesses necessary to make the adoption "legal." It is done. Already. We have a place, a name, a history, and a future.

So, we have a place in the story. We are not called to change the whole world – that is God's job. But we are called, as members of the family, to care deeply, and do what we can, based on the gifts we have been given. We are called to make a contribution, because the story lives on in each and every one of us. Each and every one of us will influence the story and give it just a little more spice.

What is at risk? Oh, sure. There might be those who will look at you a bit funny. Why be hopeful in an intractable world? Why be passionate about beauty and truth and justice in a world that seems so much more interested in profit and getting ahead and end-of-the-year bonuses? Why love when what is returned to you is hate or, worse, indifference?

Why? Because it will make a difference. Because the story is yours and it is mine – the story of God's redemption through Jesus; the story of such limitless love and acceptance; the story of life rising from death. This is a story worth telling no matter what distracts us. This is a story that confirms our worth and worthiness. This is a story that invites us into life. Brothers and sisters in Christ, welcome to the family. Amen.

– Catherine Malotky

June 18, 2006

Second Sunday after Pentecost (Proper 6)
RC/Pres: 11th Sunday in Ordinary Time

Lessons

RCL	1 Sam 15:34—16:13	2 Cor 5:6–10 (11–13), 14–17	Mk 4:26–34
Roman Catholic	Ezek 17:22–24	2 Cor 5:6–10	Mk 4:26–34
Episcopal	Ezek 31:1–6, 10–14	2 Cor 6:1–10	Mk 4:26–34
Lutheran	Ezek 17:22–24	2 Cor 5:6–10 (11–13) 14–17	Mk 4:26–34

Introduction to the Lessons
Lesson 1
(1) 1 Samuel 15:34–16:13 (RCL)

The Lord regretted Saul's kingship and sent Samuel in search of a replacement. After disguising his search with a believable story, Samuel goes to Bethlehem to find Jesse and his sons. There he anoints not the oldest or most prominent, but David, the youngest.

(2) Ezekiel 17:22–24 (RC/Luth)

Ezekiel prophecies about the coming Messiah by using the cedar tree as an image. Begun as a mere cutting, the mighty tree will welcome all to its branches, and all will know that God is the Lord.

(3) Ezekiel 31:1–6, 10–14 (Epis)

God commands Ezekiel to use the cedar as an image of strength and power in a prophecy to Pharaoh. God points out through this image that although the tree (Egypt) was strong and sure, it will fall because of its pride.

Lesson 2
2 Corinthians 5:6–10 (11–13), 14–17 (RCL/Luth);
2 Corinthians 5:6–10 (RC);
2 Corinthians 5:1–10 (Epis)

The writer of 2 Corinthians explains that as long as we live in time and space, we are, in some ways, separated from Christ. At the same time, we are never really apart from him. In Christ, our world is bigger than the one we see.

Gospel
Mark 4:26–34 (RCL/RC/Epis/Luth)

Jesus explains the nature of God's reign. As the mustard seed begins small, but grows to a sturdy bush, so God's reign might not look like much now, but in time, all will find a home there.

Theme
God's drive for life is powerful and sure.

Thought for the Day
I can trust God's desire for life for me and for the whole creation.

Call to Worship
One: O Lord, our God, Creator of the whole universe,
All: We are full of your life.
One: Gardens and fields, once at rest, bring forth life.
All: We turn to you, O source of life. We listen, to learn and to hope.

Pastoral Prayer
God of surprises, you offer us a vision of life in you. Our ancestors in faith saw you at work in their world, and we are the heirs of their testimony. Teach us to see you at work in our world, to rejoice in your insistence, and to trust your vision for our own well-being as well as the whole creation. We pray in Jesus' name. Amen.

Prayer of Confession

When all we can see is winter, God, we fail to see and trust in your promise of new life. We do not trust the power of the seeds of life you have planted in each of us, and we do not trust the power of your vision to transform the world through us. Encourage us. Turn our eyes again to the cross and empty tomb, that we might know your power to bring life to all. Amen.

Prayer of Dedication of Gifts and Self

Thank you, God, for the seeds of life you have given us. We dedicate ourselves to tending this precious gift, to nurturing ourselves and our world with all the resources you have provided. In Jesus' name we pray. Amen.

Sermon Summary

One of God's most fundamental gifts to us is the life force that rests in each of us. Like the power of the seed to grow into the plant it was created to be, we are drawn into our lives by God's power. Though it may at times seem insignificant, God's power is present and will grow.

Hymn of the Day
"God, Who Stretched the Spangled Heavens"

Jesus was one of the great parable tellers of all time, using them to help his listeners imagine God's kingdom. Musicians, hymn writers, and other artists share in this creative task when they forge words and ideas that help us ponder what being a Christian looks like today.

In "God, Who stretched the Spangled Heavens," Catherine Cameron prods us to think about just that. We share creative powers with God, she declares, and asks God to guide us in using these powers to "serve others" and "honor you." This outstanding text makes HOLY MANNA sound like it was composed yesterday.

Children's Time

Planting Seeds

Preparation: Bring in a planter filled with potting soil, zinnia or marigold seeds, a watering can with water, and wet wipes. Choose a location outside where the children can watch the seeds grow.

(Place a seed on your palm.) Look at this little seed. God has a plan for this seed. What will happen when we plant it? (It will grow into a flower and the flower will produce many more seeds. Those seeds will grow into flowers.)

Jesus wanted all of his followers to spread the good news of his love. He said that his followers are like seeds. We grow strong in God's love, then we tell others the good news of God's love. And so the message continues to spread and grow, like a garden planted with many, many flower seeds.

Let's all plant one seed. (Have each child use one finger to poke a hole in the soil and drop in one seed. After all have planted a seed, smooth over the soil. Wipe off dirty fingers. Water the seeds.) I'll put this planter (name the location you have chosen). You can watch your seeds grow into big strong plants. And you can grow big and strong in God's love by telling others about Jesus.

Prayer: Creator God, help us to grow big and strong, like beautiful flowers, so we can share the story of your Son, Jesus. Amen.

The Sermon

God's Garden

Hymns
Beginning of Worship: "Come, All You People"
Sermon Hymn: "Rise Up, O Saints of God"
Closing Hymn: "You Are the Seed"

Scripture
Mark 4:26–34 (For additional sermon materials on this passage, see the 2005 planning issue and the March 2006 issue of *The Clergy Journal*.)

In today's gospel text, Jesus offers two insights into who God is and how God works in our world. So, this will be a two–part sermon…

Part I

What is blooming in your garden these days? Gardener or not, aren't plants a miracle? Evidence of the power of seeds is all around us at this time of year. Those of us who itch to have our hands in the dirt know that we can do quite a bit to support a healthy growing environment, providing appropriate site and light, but we also know that we cannot make that seed grow. That is the miracle. That spark of life, that energy, is of God.

It's an apt metaphor, then, for God's reign in our world. We can do important work for the sake of God's reign. For ourselves, we can prepare and nourish our spiritual lives through prayer and study of God's word. We can worship, discern, and listen. For those close to us, we can support and welcome and be community for each other. For those we do not know, both human and nonhuman, we can share our gifts and give our resources and offer prayer. Yet, we cannot make faith grow. We cannot bring life from nothing or from death. We cannot manufacture that drive within us to be who we have been made to be. These things are of God and from God.

So how do we understand God's realm? How is God most at work in our world? Perhaps it is this life force that is the seed within each of us. Certainly, we see God's drive for life at work in the Easter story. Life out of death – this is God's most fundamental movement and a powerful promise to each of us. Though we can, and do, confound God's progress on a regular basis, God still draws us into the life we have been given.

Think of how you have grown through tragedy. Think of how your relationships deepen when the hard work of reconciliation is true and honest. Think of the astounding ability of the creation to heal itself in spite of our abuse. Think of how Jesus rose from the dead, how he was not silenced, as his detractors would have preferred. This impulse to live, grow, and become is of God.

This is God's desire for us – that we live fully, that the whole creation live fully. We participate, certainly. We fertilize the soil that is our own souls, our communities, our world. We have much to contribute. We water and feed the plants that spring from God's holy seeds in us. We can do much damage if we don't take seriously the power of our contributions, but we can also do much good when we heed God's call. Yet, nothing we do or don't do can steal from the seeds the impulse to grow. Resilient, and even sometimes stubborn, we can trust this impulse as God's gift.

Part II
Gardeners know that the mustard seed is not the smallest, in spite of Jesus' claim in this metaphor. However, mustard plants can grow quite tall, some as tall as 10 feet. Those of you who know things about invasive exotics, also known as weeds, know that garlic mustard can take over a garden like a bulldozer if given a couple of good seed-producing years. This mustard may not be tall, but it's vigorous.

That said, this metaphor was not spun by a botanist. Jesus used this image of the surprising mustard seed to help explain the reign of God. The take–away message? God's reign starts small, but just wait. In no time, we will be making our home in its branches.

Imagine Jesus' followers sitting at his feet, surrounding an itinerant preacher. The religious momentum of the day was not with them. As a matter of fact, neither was the political momentum. They were a people living under political occupation by the Romans. Military bullying was not unusual. They could be drafted into the service of a Roman soldier at any time.

They were also a people living under religious occupation. Lest the Romans feel threatened by Jewish solidarity, the Pharisees and other religious leaders who were in charge at the time were careful to keep their corporate noses clean. Though many Jewish laws were in opposition to Roman practice (for example, the Caesar, or emperor, was not god, according to Jewish beliefs), the Pharisees held together a tenuous peace. The Jews could continue to practice their faith, as long as they didn't get too uppity with the Romans. They continued to wait for the Messiah, but they didn't flaunt the liberation edge of that hope.

In this context, imagine the relatively few people who had gathered to hear Jesus. Even if there were hundreds, they were not Roman occupiers or local religious leaders. They were, most likely, folks on the edge, who dared to be seen listening to Jesus. If his message of love and justice captivated them, could they have been too hopeful with Roman soldiers around every corner? Could they have been optimistic about their chances when the religious authorities of their day kept things on such a short leash?

And now think about us, followers of Jesus. Imagine us, hearing of a God who desires all to have enough to eat, all to live in peace and safety, all to know God's love. And remember the most recent newscast you have seen or today's newspaper headlines. Is such a world just a pipedream? Not according to God's will and way. So you may offer a small contribution. You may challenge one racist or sexist joke. You may send $25 or even $100 to support international efforts to deal with AIDS – a drop in the bucket. You may offer safe harbor for one refugee, or dry one tear of someone who grieves.

But, it starts small, Jesus said. Remember that in no time, that smallest of seeds will grow into a surprisingly tall and vigorous shrub. Even we will find a home in the branches. There will be room and shelter enough for all.

This is a promise. This is one to trust. It may start small, but just you wait...

– Catherine Malotky

June 25, 2006

Third Sunday after Pentecost (Proper 7)
RC/Pres: 12th Sunday in Ordinary Time

Lessons

RCL	1 Sam 17:(1a, 4–11, 19–23) 32–49	2 Cor 6:1–13	Mk 4:35–41
Roman Catholic	Job 38:1, 8–11	2 Cor 5:14–17	Mk 4:35–41
Episcopal	Job 38:1–11, 16–18	2 Cor 5:14–21	Mk 4:35–41 (5:1–20)
Lutheran	Job 38:1–11	2 Cor 6:1–13	Mk 4:35–41

Introduction to the Lessons
Lesson 1
(1) 1 Samuel 17:(1a, 4–11, 19–23) 32–49 (RCL)

At Socoh, the Philistine army massed to fight Israel. Their bravado was incarnate in the giant, Goliath. David, yet a young man, offered to take him on, rejecting normal protection offered by his king. David slew Goliath with a sling and a stone in the name of the Lord of hosts.

(2) Job 38:1, 8–11 (RC);
Job 38:1–11, 16–18 (Epis);
Job 38:1–11 (Luth)

After experiencing grievous losses, Job challenges God to hear his lament. From a whirlwind God responds, clarifying that God's wisdom and will is far beyond what humans can comprehend.

Lesson 2
(1) 2 Corinthians 6:1–13 (RCL/Luth)

The writer of this text points out the distortions that have been attached to those who have been in ministry with the Corinthians. The writer appeals to the Corinthians to open their hearts to the word, so that they might know the day of salvation.

(2) 2 Corinthians 5:14–17 (RC); 2 Corinthians 5:14–21 (Epis)
Defending the ministry of reconciliation with the Corinthians, the writer appeals to them to see themselves as new in Christ and to no longer regard others from a human point of view.

Gospel
Mark 4:35–41 (RCL/RC/Luth); Mark 4:35–41 (5:1–20) (Epis)
Jesus and his disciples left the crowds and set out in a boat for the other side of the sea. However, a great windstorm arose and threatened to swamp the boat. When Jesus calmed the wind and waves, the disciples were left to wonder just who he was.

Theme
God's power is over all.

Thought for the Day
We can trust God's power to redeem whatever lies in our path.

Call to Worship
One: O Lord our God, ruler of the universe,
All: In your wisdom you have formed us.
One: Open us to your power,
All: That we might be at home in you.

Pastoral Prayer
O God, the vagaries of life swirl around us. The winds of change drive our lives in ways we could not expect. Be both our buoy and commander. Remind us that you are the creator and sustainer of life, for us and for the whole creation. In Jesus' name we pray. Amen.

Prayer of Confession
Forgive us, God, our panic when we lose sight of you. We are shortsighted and need your steadfast vision and compassion. When we cannot see or trust your life-giving ways, remind us that you are always there. Amen.

Prayer of Dedication of Gifts and Self

Though we may relinquish our gifts and our selves with reluctance, we offer them today. We choose, today, to trust that you will always provide what we need, and therefore give freely, without fear that we will come up short. In our giving, shore up our faith, that our giving might be even more generous next time. Amen.

Sermon Summary

When we face chaos, we easily forget that God is still god. It is harder to see and trust God's transcendent power, but it is there redeeming our losses and drawing us into life.

Hymn of the Day
"Jesus, Savior, Pilot Me"

The Earth's oceans, seas, and other large bodies of water hold a certain mystique for us. We are impressed by their size, respectful of their depths, aware of their wildness. It is no wonder that when a great windstorm arose on the sea, threatening to swamp their boat, the disciples were scared to death.

In "Jesus, Savior, Pilot Me," Edward Hopper likens our life journey to crossing a tempestuous sea, where "unknown waves" hide "rock and treacherous shoal." Jesus is the one who guides us; the one who says to the waves, "Be still"; the one who leads us safely to the other shore, saying "Fear not, I will pilot thee."

Children's Time

Jesus Is in the Middle of the Storm

What are you afraid of? (Accept responses. Add your own.) How many of you are afraid of storms? Today's Bible story is about a time when Jesus' disciples were afraid.

Please help me tell this story by making sound effects. Now, let's imagine that we are Jesus' disciples. We are sailing in a boat, gently rocking on the Sea of Galilee. (Rock back and forth.) Jesus is sleeping in the back of the boat. It begins to sprinkle. (Snap your fingers slowly.) It changes into a steady downpour. (Rub palms of hands together in a circular motion.) Then the storm hits. (Slap palms loudly on legs.) The wind howls. (Say, "Ooooo." Continue to slap palms on legs.) The boat is in the middle of a storm. Waves splash over the sides of the boat. The boat is filling with water. It's going to sink. "Wake up, Jesus, we're going to die!" the disciples cry out. Jesus wakes up. "Peace! Be still!" (Stop slapping palms.) And the storm stops. "Who is this?" the disciples wonder. "Even the wind and the waves obey him."

Who stilled the storm? (Jesus did!) Whenever we are in the middle of a storm or we're frightened, we can remember that Jesus is with us, watching over us.

Prayer: Thank you, Jesus, for watching over us in scary times. Amen.

The Sermon

Even for the Leviathan

Hymns

Beginning of Worship: "Word of God, Come Down on Earth"
Sermon Hymn: "Many and Great, O God, Are Your Works"
Closing Hymn: "On Our Way Rejoicing"

Scripture

Mark 4:35–41 (For additional sermon materials on this passage, see the 2005 May/June planning issue and the March 2006 issue of *The Clergy Journal*.)

It is common for us to hear Christians talking about having a personal relationship with God. There are many intimate details in the gospels that help us bond with God, to know Jesus as one of us. He wept at Lazarus' tomb. He changed water into wine for the sake of the wedding party. He was born, a baby in a stable. He rested and prayed. We can imagine that we know him.

Having a personal Savior is, indeed, desirable. If God were nothing but vast and other, to what would we cling when we are lost and alone? In baptism, you were welcomed into God's family, but not as some generic human being. God welcomed you, the unique you. We can imagine, when we so need comfort and cannot find it among our peers, that Jesus is there with a hug and listening ear. We need this intimacy. In fact, it was the point of God's incarnation – to be here in time and space with us.

There are other times when an intimate God is nice, but not first and foremost what we need. Sometimes we need a god of power – one who is definitely in control, because we are so not. Sometimes we need a big daddy who will rescue us from the bullies. Sometimes we need a great mother who will provide the order and safety we need when the world is spinning out of control.

Our ancient forebears in faith understood this, too. Remember the first story of creation, and God's power to transform the "without form and void" of pre-creation into order and grace. Recall the rhythm: "And God said…" "And there was.." "And God saw that it was good." "And it was evening and it was morning."

Even in the telling of the story, we are comforted by the repetition – we can learn to expect what is next. On the seventh day God rested, as you will recall. This order was God's great gift to us, who so yearn to know what is next.

But there remained then as there do now, places in our world that defy order. The ancients talked about the Leviathan that lived in the deep seas, chaos incarnate. They talked about Gehenna, the place where smoldering fires burned always, a place of fear and unknown.

And for us? Don't we yearn for order when ones we love die before their time or when circumstance or luck or fate or whatever you might call it burdens us with differences that challenge us, sometimes even our very survival? What about the power of the natural world, which can change us and our world in an instant? What about influences far beyond our control that pinch our lives – war, environmental degradation, poverty (our own or others), family dysfunction that reaches back generations and from which we are supposed to heal? When we know the capriciousness of life, when we are forced to or allow ourselves to see clearly the tenuous thread that connects us to the life we imagine, what then? Then we need a god who can stand up to the Leviathan – a big, powerful, all-everything god.

We, like the disciples, will come to Jesus, asleep in the stern as we are twisting in the wind. We will beg him, "Teacher, do you not care that we are perishing?"

How many of us have done just such a thing? The Psalms are full of these kinds of appeals. We will call in our relationship – demand that God hold up God's end of this covenant with us. "God, where are you? Show your face. Get me out of this!"

Because God is faithful, God will do so, one way or another. Rarely will it be instantaneous as it was on the boat that night. But, God's peace will come. New life will rise again, even if it happens slowly. This is God's promise, made manifest in Jesus, and we can give testimony that even the worst is redeemed in one way or another eventually. This is God's way with us…which makes Jesus' next question so difficult. "Why are you afraid? Have you still no faith?"

Well, yes. When we face the Leviathan, when chaos threatens to tear apart the world as we know it, when the rug is pulled out from under us…then, yes. We panic, even though we know from the witness of our own lives and the lives of our forebears that God is faithful.

Brothers and sisters, we can feel ashamed. Or, we can turn our eyes to the cross where we will see, once again, the God who is so like us, flesh and blood, and to the grave, where we will see, in its emptiness, the God obeyed by even the wind and sea.

We have both kinds of gods. Jesus was in the stern that night, asleep on the cushion, we are reminded. He was not a super–human. He didn't sleep standing up or anything else extraordinary. He slept on a cushion, no doubt, because it was more comfortable. He was tired after teaching the crowds all day. Like us, he was flesh and blood – one of us, with us. He ate. He slept. He wept. He loved. He got angry. And he died.

But three days later, when his friends and followers were just begin-ning to wake up to the devastating reality of what had happened to him and to them, his tomb was emptied. Jesus was alive again, risen. Now this was beyond reason. This was out of the ordinary. This simply didn't happen. A dead man was alive again. He is not just completely like us, he is also God, quite other, quite powerful, quite beyond our imagining. He is one who can stand face-to-face with the Leviathan, whatever shape that monster takes in our lives in these days. He is one who can stand face-to-face and demand, "Peace! Be still!" And it will be so.

We will be forgiven over and over again for our panic. We will come again to believe that this God, both intimate and so beyond, is our God, who loves us and promises us a future in God's love. Be filled with great awe, sisters and brothers, for the wind and the sea obey. We are safe. We are God's.

– Catherine Malotky

July 2, 2006

Fourth Sunday after Pentecost (Proper 8)
RC/Pres: 13th Sunday in Ordinary Time

Lessons

RCL	2 Sam 1:1, 17–27	2 Cor 8:7–15	Mk 5:21–43
Roman Catholic	Wis 1:13–15; 2:23–24	2 Cor 8:7, 9, 13–15	Mk 5:21–43 or 5:21–24, 35–43
Episcopal	Deut 15:7–11	2 Cor 8:1–9, 13–15	Mk 5:22–24, 35b–43
Lutheran	Lam 3:22–33 or Wis 1:13–15; 2:23–24	2 Cor 8:7–15	Mk 5:21–43

Introduction to the Lessons

Lesson 1

(1) 2 Samuel 1:1, 17–27 (RCL)

At Ziklag, a messenger comes to David to report the defeat of Israel's army and the death of the king, Saul, and his son, Jonathan on Mount Gilboa. This text is David's lament over Saul and Jonathan.

(2) Wisdom of Solomon 1:13–15; 2:23–24 (RC)

This text works out the theological difficulties behind the fact that we all die. Asserting that God did not create death, the author goes on to point to the envy of the devil as the cause of death.

(3) Deuteronomy 15:7–11 (Epis)

The sabbatical year (or the year of release), like the jubilee year, was a way God's people managed their socioeconomic life within the context of faith. Debts are forgiven in the sabbatical year, so it is for the sake of the poor who otherwise would have been burdened from generation to generation.

(4) Lamentations 3:22–33 (Luth)
With words of comfort and hope, the poet appeals for patience and a long view of God's work in our lives. God is faithful. God's love never ceases.

Lesson 2
    2 Corinthians 8:7–15 (RCL/Luth);
    2 Corinthians 8:7, 9, 13–15 (RC);
    2 Corinthians 8:1–9, 13–15 (Epis)
One of Paul's great mission projects was to gather a collection for the poor in the Jerusalem church from the Gentile congregations he mentored. This was a concrete way for him to demonstrate to the skeptical leaders of the Jerusalem church that they were all one in Christ.

Gospel
    Mark 5:21–43 (RCL/RC/Luth); Mark 5:22–24, 35b–43 (Epis)
Having just left the country of the Gerasenes because the people were afraid of him, Jesus lands before a great crowd by the sea. A religious leader's daughter and an outcast/unclean woman both are beneficiaries of Jesus' healing.

Theme
Our giving reflects our hearts.

Thought for the Day
God's welcome is for all.

Call to Worship
    One: God of the outcast and sinner,
    All: God of the religious elite and everyday saints,
    One: Be with us as we worship.
    All: Open our eyes to the wideness of your embrace.

Pastoral Prayer

We gather to worship you, God. Our voices rise to you with voices very like our own, and voices very different. Crack open our preconceived notions about your holiness. Reveal to us the limitlessness of your body. In Jesus' name we pray. Amen.

Prayer of Confession

O God. You call us to generosity, but we are too often blind to those in need and blind to our own need. Open our hearts to your vision of your body. Teach us to give and to receive. Help us to see with your eyes and live the magnitude of your grace. Amen.

Prayer of Dedication of Gifts and Self

We offer ourselves and our gifts to your service. Increase in us joy in giving, and bless us with generosity. Amen.

Sermon Summary

Paul's appeal to the Gentiles for the church in Jerusalem made active Paul's conviction that God welcomes all, regardless of the differences we perceive divide us.

Hymn of the Day
"O Christ the Healer, We Have Come"

Mark reports the predicaments of Jarius' daughter and the woman with a hemorrhage in generous detail. To the astonishment of all, Jesus heals both. Yet, Mark infers through both instances that one's faith in Jesus' power to heal is of paramount importance.

F. Pratt Green's "O Christ, the Healer, We Have Come" provides words to our yearning to be healed, both on a personal level and in the communal/societal dimensions of our lives. W. Walker's tune DISTRESS matches the depth of this remarkable text.

Children's Time

Fair Balance

Preparation: Make a balance by punching a hole through the top of both layers of sandwich–size plastic bags. Tie a 10-inch length of yarn through the top of each bag and tie to opposite ends of a coat hanger. Bring in a handful of coins. Place the coins in one bag and leave the other one empty. Bring two apples.

Stand up. Now stand on one foot. How long can you balance on one foot? Good job. Now you may sit down. What does balance mean? One meaning is that when you have two sides, one side equals the other side. Here's one example. (Place one apple in each of your hands.) Like one apple = one apple. Now let's look at this balance. (Place the top of the hanger over your finger.) Is this hanger balanced? (No.) How can we balance it? (Move some coins into the empty bag.) Transfer coins into the empty bag until the hanger is balanced. Do you think we have an equal amount of money in each bag? (Yes.) How do you know? (Because the hanger is balanced.)

In today's Bible story we hear from a teacher named Paul. Paul was one of Jesus' followers. He taught people about Jesus' love. Paul talks about a fair balance. Paul tells the people in the churches to share what they have with others. The people who have more than enough should share with people who don't have enough. Then the people can live in a fair balance, with enough food, clothing, and shelter for everyone.

Prayer: Dear Jesus, help us to make a fair balance in our lives by sharing what we have with others. Amen.

The Sermon

Welcome to the Body

Hymns

Beginning of Worship: "Here in This Place: Gather Us In"
Sermon Hymn: "Love Divine, All Loves Excelling"
Closing Hymn: "Breathe on Me, Breath of God"

Scripture

2 Corinthians 8:7–15 (For additional sermon materials on this passage, see the March 2006 issue of *The Clergy Journal*; for sermon materials on Mark 5:21–43, see the 2005 May/June planning issue of *The Clergy Journal*.)

This is not the typical stewardship time of year. Generally the temple talks and charts and graphs and budget line items show up in the fall. But the text from 2 Corinthians plops us right in the middle of the stewardship conversation.

Note how carefully Paul frames the conversation. "I do not say this as a command, but I am testing the genuineness of your love against the earnestness of others" (2 Cor 8:8). He's working with shame here, and competition. "Is your love genuine enough," he wonders, "and how will you measure up to the giving of others?" Most stewardship gurus would cringe, quite frankly. We should be giving out of the goodness of our hearts – because it is the right thing to do, because we need to give to others. We shouldn't base our stewardship campaigns on shame and competition.

Yet, that is precisely where Paul lands. Of course, this collection has a most interesting historical context. Paul was in conflict with the leaders of the Jerusalem church, specifically Peter and James. The theology of the new church was in transition, and Paul was out in front of the pack. The fundamental question was, "Does a Gentile have to become a Jew before he or she can claim to be a follower of Jesus?" Peter (at least initially) and James insisted that Gentiles did indeed need to observe Jewish law in order to count themselves among the body of Christ. Paul, who once was a persecutor on behalf of the Jews, did not. He felt called to reach out to the Gentiles, and believed passionately that they were as included in Jesus' welcome as the Jews.

So, we could interpret this collection as a peace offering, a political gesture on Paul's part to win over his detractors in Jerusalem. On the other hand, the collection was much bigger than merely a "proof text" for Paul's political gain. Theologically, his issue was that Jesus was for all people, regardless of their religious origins or cultural heritage. Whether or not people circumcised their sons or ate ham, the body of Christ was open to all.

Supporting each other, especially those who find themselves on the margins of life – even if they are very different – is a mark of faith. Could this text encourage you and me in any way, other than to give more to prove our genuineness of heart and to demonstrate that we are more generous than our neighboring faith communities?

When our forebears worshiped, it would seem that they did not deal with issues of diversity as we do today. Certainly those who sat next to them in the pews were ethnically similar, and even vocationally similar. Perhaps some of our brothers and sisters in faith in very small, isolated, rural communities may still have this kind of worship experience, but for most of us, this is not the case any more. We are a transient people, rarely more than a generation in one place anymore. We bring a wide variety of life experiences to church with us, and often many ethnic traditions. We are socioeconomically diverse, if not within congregations, then certainly within denominations, and most certainly within the whole body of believers.

Our forebears differed with each other, of course. And, to be sure, sometimes those differences divided the community. Our differences seem to light up the night sky: evangelical or mainline? pro–choice or pro–life? gay rights or love the sinner? praise worship or traditional? bingo or not? church discipline or lax standards?

And often, isn't it true, we choose to voice our allegiance with our wallets. Now, if Paul had followed our typical modern strategy, he would have broken away from the Jerusalem church and formed his own denomination, at first loosely knit and soon enough institutionalized. He would have thumbed his nose at Peter and James, set up pension plans, created constitutions, and incorporated. He certainly wouldn't have been fund–raising for the poor in Jerusalem.

But Paul believed something that would not let him break away, at least not ultimately. The body of Christ is much bigger than the limits we might imagine. God's welcome is for all people, and what we understand to be God's will, changes. Think of the healings we read about in the gospel lesson. From the vantage point of Jesus' followers, he should have ignored Jairus. After all, the religious leaders of his day gave him grief all the time. And the woman with the hemorrhage was considered unclean.

She had been excluded from the worshiping community from the first day she bled 12 years earlier. Yet, Jesus reached out to Jairus and his daughter. Jesus did not reject, and even affirmed, the bleeding woman who dared touch him for healing.

So who is in charge of the church? Whose gaze do we follow when we look for God's children? Our corporate structures? They can be wrong. Our own vision of who is "Christian enough" to be counted in? We can be terribly shortsighted.

God calls us to see with the eyes of Jesus' generosity. God calls us to discern without our own biases who has needs and to give all that we can. God also calls us to see how those we might perceive as needy might just have something to give in return.

We stand humbly before our God, whose generosity is so beyond our imagining. But we also stand welcomed into God's embrace, a beneficiary of that same generosity God offers to all. Thanks be to God.

– Catherine Malotky

July 9, 2006

5th Sunday after Pentecost (Proper 9)
RC/Pres: 14th Sunday in Ordinary Time

Lessons

RCL	2 Sam 5:1–5, 9–10	2 Cor 12:2–10	Mk 6:1–13
Roman Catholic	Ezek 2:2–5	2 Cor 12:7–10	Mk 6:1–6
Episcopal	Ezek 2:1–7	2 Cor 12:2–10	Mk 6:1–6
Lutheran	Ezek 2:1–5	2 Cor 12:2–10	Mk 6:1–13

Introduction to the Lessons
Lesson 1
(1) 2 Samuel 5:1–5, 9–10 (RCL)

David enters sovereign leadership through divine calling recognized by the tribal elders. Covenantal relationship is accompanied by the edict to remain pastoral: be a shepherd to the people.

(2) Ezekiel 2:1–7 (Epis)

Ezekiel's call sets him on his feet. He is forewarned: many will reject what he has to say, yet he is to declare, "Thus says the Lord."

Lesson 2
2 Corinthians 12:2–10 (RCL/RC/Epis/Luth)

The church wrestles with competing hallmarks of leadership: outwardly expressed ecstatic power and the acceptance of limited finitude. Paul chooses the less spectacular so that Christ may be known.

Gospel
Mark 6:1–13 (RCL/RC/Epis/Luth)

Jesus' hometown questions the validity of his leadership because it is more than was expected. In response, Jesus sends out the disciples with new leadership responsibilities.

Theme

Leadership has many challenges, some of which come from those whom we seek to serve.

Thought for the Day

One can acquire everything in solitude – except character.

– Marie Henri Beyle (1783–1842)

Call to Worship

One: Jesus came to his hometown. His teaching astounded everyone.
All: Where did he learn these things?
Right: He seems so wise.
Left: He claims to be more than we know him to be.
Men: We watched this boy grow up here.
Women: His family still lives here.
All: Why do we question leaders who are familiar to us?
One: Jesus sent the twelve out in pairs.
Right: Walk only with a staff.
Left: Rely only on today's bread.
Men: Don't pack extra clothes.
Women: Rely on God for today's needs.
All: God calls us to new ministries today.

Pastoral Prayer

O God, each one of us faces a mixture of certainty of what to do and doubt that we are the right ones to carry out your plans. Give us courage to live in your ways. Provide insight to those who prepare for leadership in your church. Give them courage to stand up to criticism, patience to endure the slow processes of change, and wisdom to discern when to challenge and when to affirm.

We thank you for the many people who have led us to be people of greater faith. Assure them that their weaknesses have not hindered your graciousness from being known, but rather have been opportunities for us to know your grace.

Speak to us through the leaders we know, so that we may hear the ways you call us to be faithful. Let us boast of one another's accomplishments that display your transforming grace. Amen.

Prayer of Confession

O God, too often we boast of our own abilities, so others will know our hard work. We talk about the magnificent things we have done, so others will know how strong our faith is. We emphasize how exceptional we are, so others will know how much you love us. Forgive our foolishness and remind us how your grace is known through our weakness. Help us to accept where we are weakest, so that your strength may be revealed.

We want to be sent out individually to be part of your justice-making. In our excitement we forget that ministry can be lonely; in our enthusiasm we forget that you sent out the disciples in pairs, so that they could minister together. Forgive us when we refuse to join together in ministry, for your grace is better known through our relationships. Forgive us when we promote ourselves more than we proclaim you. Amen.

Prayer of Dedication of Gifts and Self

God, the gracious gifts we receive are given because you accept who we are and have hope in what we are becoming. You give so that we may use your gifts in ways that make your grace known. In your grace, we come to know who we are in relationship to you, to ourselves, to one another, to the world. We dedicate these gifts to the church's work of teaching, preaching, healing, and accepting those whom others see as weak. As you call and send us in new ways, we dedicate these gifts to strengthening leaders in the church. Amen.

Sermon Summary

This sermon is written from the point of view of one who has known the one who is called in a new way, yet doubts the validity of the calling. The speaker continues to question this person whom they have known, surprised at the way the person expresses call. This questioning alternates with "common sense advice" for leaders.

Hymn of the Day
"The Church of Christ, in Every Age"

Jesus sent disciples out two by two, instructing them to travel light and giving them the power to heal. Lo and behold, their mission was a success! They "cast out many demons, and anointed with oil many who were sick and cured them."

"We have no mission but to serve," declares Fred Pratt Green in "The Church of Christ, in Every Age." Perhaps those first Christian missionaries we hear about today were driven by such an ideal. William Knapp's WAREHAM is a fine melody for this text, with a steady sense of flow to the phrases and a triple meter that captures well the stress of the words.

Children's Time

The Strongest Love of All

Preparation: Bring in a vase of flowers, a piece of fruit, and a pillow. What is this season called? (Summer.) Summer is part of God's plan. Summer is a time when plants grow strong.

God plans for us to grow strong, too. What are some things that God gives us to help our bodies grow strong? (Accept responses.) Eating healthy foods like this fruit (hold fruit) keep us strong. Everyone stand. Can you do jumping jacks with me? (Do a couple of jumping jacks.) Exercise helps to keep our bodies strong too. And when we're tired what do our bodies need? (Sleep. Rest your head on the pillow and snore.) All people and animals need to rest.

God wants us to be happy too. What makes you happy? (Accept responses.) Beautiful flowers of summer, blue skies, and green grass all make me happy. God made a beautiful world for us to enjoy and care for. It is the power of God's love that keeps us strong. What can we do to thank God? (Sing, pray, worship, tell others about God's love.)
Prayer: (Have the children echo you.) Dear God, / thank you for the many ways / your love keeps us strong. / Thank you for this warm, growing season / of summer. / Amen.

The Sermon

Who Do You Think You Are?

Hymns
Beginning of Worship: "God of Grace and God of Glory"
Sermon Hymn: "Called as Partners in Christ's Service"
Closing Hymn: "Sent Forth by God's Blessing"

Scripture

Mark 6:1–13 (For additional sermon materials on this passage, see the 2005 May/June planning issue of *The Clergy Journal*; for sermon materials on 2 Corinthians 12:2–10, see the March 2006 issue of *The Clergy Journal*.)

Watch your tone of voice! We taught you better than that. Just who do you think you are? You can't come in here and talk to us that way! Show some respect for your elders!

You have been away for a while. We know you have grown up some, and that you have learned a great deal. Yes, we heard how you won awards and were appointed as leader of those groups. Yes, that is quite an accomplishment; that is not in dispute. Yes, it is important that other leaders have recognized your abilities.

But we know you from way back. Look, we are your bone and flesh. We know what kind of kid you were. Some of us wiped your nose before you knew how to do that for yourself. We were the ones who helped you find your lost toys.

Remember when you fell and scraped your knees and elbows over by my home? I was the one who stopped to help. Do you remember the time when you gave yourself a black eye? I was the one who dried your tears. And just how many splinters did I remove from your fingers?

Some of your teachers are here, too. They taught you letters and numbers. They helped you memorize Bible verses and prayers. Almost everyone here remembers the time you got up and read the Scriptures for the first time, your voice barely above a whisper, so shaky that we could barely hear you. We all expected so much more from you.

Now you come in here saying these kinds of things. Just who do you think you are? I think you've developed a bit too high of an opinion of yourself. How dare you tell us what you think we are doing wrong! Aren't you at all thankful for the way we raised you?

You can't just come in here saying those kinds of things and expect us to listen politely. Change! You want us to change? Just who do you think you are? Repent? How dare you judge us that way! Who are you to tell us that we are living incorrectly? Who are you to tell us that God has a different plan? What authority do you think you have to tell us to change our ways?

Called by God, huh? Tell us more about that. Did you feel like your spirit left your body, like you were standing above your body? Did you have some special experience where you were given special visions from God? Did you receive a special revelation from God about how things are going to be? Did it come from long hours of study and contemplation? How did other people help you better understand how God might use you? We want to know just how you got this opinion of yourself.

Just what are you supposed to be anyhow? A prophet? A king? A shepherd of people? Do you expect to be selecting national leaders single-handedly? Are you called to teach and preach? What kind of messenger are you? Are you also called to administration? How well do you handle church budgets? And how do you expect to bring in new members to our congregation?

If God has chosen you, then why do you walk with a limp? Why is your eyesight a little dimmer than it used to be? I saw you walking this morning, a little stiff, complaining of a poor night's sleep. If you are called by God, then why does your body still ache? Just who do you think you are?

I hope you hear that we really love you and want what is best for you. We want you to have a long and successful ministry. We want people to love you and listen to what you have to say. Just take our advice and do it in a nice way. You do not always have to make others angry with you in order to be heard. You do not have to be so outrageous at every event. Tone down some of the dramatics. We like the way you bring God into everything, but soften the message a bit. After all, do you really think that God is going to show up in some new way? Do you really believe God's grace is really changing everything in the universe?

How dare you accuse us of not listening to God! How dare you accuse us of not understanding God's work! We've put our whole lives into building up this church. And now you accuse us of being too proud of what we have done? Just who do you think you are? You come here with your raggedy friends – none of you has an extra shirt, none of you seems to have planned for tomorrow's meals. You call yourselves leaders for the church. Just what kind of example are you? None of you seems to be saving up money for long-range development of your ministry. Just how do you expect to sustain this lifestyle you are living?

Do you not hear what people are saying about you? People are insulting you behind your back. They are planning to hurt you. They are planning to imprison you. If you treat them the way you have treated us, I can see why. Why aren't you concerned for your safety? Show a bit of prudence and think about what you are saying.

I don't know who you think you are, but I think you need to straighten out your faith. If you expect us to recommend you as a leader to other congregations, you are going to have to change a bit yourself and begin to live like normal people do. Otherwise no one will ever take you seriously. You will not get anywhere if you keep insulting people, telling them that God feels they have rebelled against God's ways. You will not be welcomed unless you have some kind words once in awhile. And think about wearing a nicer shirt and shoes. You need to dress in a respectable manner if you want people to pay attention to you. People will call you a fool and dismiss your faith because you are not living wisely. You will always have a home here, but shape up before the whole world rejects you. After all, you want to be remembered as a sensible leader, don't you?

– Thom Bower

July 16, 2006

6th Sunday after Pentecost (Proper 10)
RC/Pres: 15th Sunday in Ordinary Time

Lessons

RCL	2 Sam 6:1–5, 12b–19	Eph 1:3–14	Mk 6:14–29
Roman Catholic	Amos 7:12–15	Eph 1:3–14	Mk 6:7–13
		or 1:3–10	
Episcopal	Amos 7:7–15	Eph 1:1–14	Mk 6:7–13
Lutheran	Amos 7:7–15	Eph 1:3–14	Mk 6:14–29

Introduction to the Lessons
Lesson 1
(1) 2 Samuel 6:1–5, 12b–19 (RCL)
With celebratory parades, music and dance, offerings and festive foods, David and the people of Israel move the Ark of the Covenant.

(2) Amos 7:7–15 (Epis/Luth)
After two oracles, Amos is counseled to move to another town. Amos responds that he is not an appointed court official, but called by God.

Lesson 2
Ephesians 1:1–14 (RCL/RC/Epis/Luth)
Having been chosen by Christ, we are set apart as adopted children, given forgiveness, wise understanding, and a destined inheritance. We are marked with the seal of the Holy Spirit.

Gospel
Mark 6:7–29 (RCL/RC/Epis/Luth)
The disciples are sent out in pairs but without provisions. Meanwhile, the court of Herod fears that Jesus is John resurrected, for Herod had previously ordered John executed.

Theme

Commitment to accepting God's invitation to transformation asks us to reexamine our understanding.

Thought for the Day

Commitment is healthiest when it is not without doubt, but in spite of doubt.

– Rollo May

Call to Worship

One: David and the people brought the ark.

All: They came with music, singing, and dancing!

One: Amos said God would measure the people like a plumb line measures a wall.

All: Even though unpopular, he followed God's command.

One: God has adopted us as children so that we may know grace.

All: Because of God's grace, we look forward to the time when God will gather all things together.

One: Jesus sent out the disciples in pairs.

All: We come together now to worship God with one another!

Pastoral Prayer

Holy One, whose presence is through all of history: before you created the universe, you adopted us as your children. You gather us together to sing and dance as we testify to your grace. You call us to look again at how we live, so that we may measure up to your standards. Grant us wisdom to discern how to be faithful in these days – times of competing values, times of competing needs, times when our best intentions are often rejected. Place in us the faith to stand up when it seems we are alone and the faith to journey with others to see you do new things. Teach us to be your trustworthy people as we seek to proclaim, to heal, and to live in your justice. We ask this in the name of Christ, our very foundation. Amen.

Prayer of Confession

God, you love us like a parent. Help us accept your discipline, so that we may live as your adopted children. We have looked at others and despised them for what we see as a lack of good taste. We have not examined our own ways to make sure they are aligned with your ways. Forgive us when we refuse to hear your word because it comes from an unfamiliar source. We are quick to assume that only certain people with certain credentials have the ability to speak to us, especially about the ways we have taken your redemption for granted. Help us to claim our heritage as your disciples, so that others may know your grace. Forgive us for the ways we have restricted your announcements of transformation, especially when we have sought to eliminate the messengers of your judgments of us. We ask this as your children. Amen.

Prayer of Dedication of Gifts and Self

O God, our parent and our benefactor, our spirits dance as we bring these symbols of the ways you have blessed us. Hearts of joy sing your praises, responding to the grace we have inherited. We return these gifts of thanks to you asking that they may be transformed. Use them, so that all may be gathered to you in the fullness of your redemption. Shape them, so that we may be disciplined followers of your paths. Through them reveal the good news of your salvation offered graciously. Use them to distribute food to all, to support those who proclaim repentance, and to send out ministers of healing. As we give these gifts, may we learn to rely on your everyday gifts every day. Amen.

Sermon Summary

Each of the scriptures presents unusual actions by the main characters. We are asked to reconsider how God is acting, to consider our faith commitments, and to discern new tasks of faithfulness as we accept the invitation to new ministries.

Hymn of the Day
"You Are the Way"

In addition to filling us in on the gruesome demise of John the Baptist, the big issue here is Jesus' identity. Herod, ever superstitious, thinks Jesus is John come back from the grave to haunt him, while his advisors guess Jesus is Elijah or some new prophet.

George W. Doane's "You Are the Way," inspired by Jesus' words to Thomas, is a direct, powerful affirmation of who Jesus is. DUNDEE, with its unvaried rhythm and straightforward harmony, is the tune that best expresses Doane's text.

Children's Time

The Holy Spirit

Preparation: Bring brightly colored feathers, one per child. You can get these at a craft store.

What does it mean to be adopted? (Accept responses.) Some families adopt children from far away. Some children adopt children from the same cities they live in. Did you know that all of us are adopted? God adopted us. When we are baptized, we became God's children. That means we belong to two families – our family at home and God's family. We are all brothers and sisters in Christ.

In today's Bible message, Paul, one of Jesus' followers, writes: "All of God's children are adopted through Jesus Christ and are marked with the seal of the Holy Spirit." We can't see God's Holy Spirit, but it lives all around us, filling our lives with love. If we could see the Holy Spirit what do you think it would look like? (Dove, flame, cross, and a heart are possible answers.) One symbol of the Holy Spirit is a dove. The dove is soft and gentle like a feather. (Give each child a feather.)

Brush the feather against your cheek. How does it feel? Now hold your feather in your hand. How much does it weigh? Now blow on it. What happens? The seal of the Holy Spirit is like an invisible feather, soft and light, gently surrounding us with God's love. When you return to your seats, share a feather kiss with your family members.

Prayer: Dear God, thank you for adopting us into your family and marking us with the soft, loving seal of your Spirit. Amen.

The Sermon

Looking Again

Hymns

Beginning of Worship: "Let Justice Flow Like Streams"
Sermon Hymn: "O God of All Your People Past"
Closing Hymn: "Send Me, Lord"

Scripture

Mark 6:7–29 (For sermon materials on Ephesians 1:3–14, see the 2005 May/June planning issue and the March 2006 issue of *The Clergy Journal*.)

We need to look at David again. He and selected leaders of Israel are bringing the Ark of the Covenant to Jerusalem. The ark is God's protective presence and promise of prosperity for people of faith. There is music, singing, and dancing.

We look back on David and perceive him to be free in spirit, free in his praise of God. But what David is doing was not normal. It was not appropriate for a leader of his stature to be publicly dancing – especially in a religious ceremony. His exuberance offends some people. David's wife is offended when she looks from her window and sees him dancing. It seems he is breaking away from tradition.

Sometimes our commitments to new ways of doing things appear inconsistent with the ways that things have been done before. As we seek to be people of faith responding to the new things God is doing, we are challenged to discern how to keep God's people together. The radical changes to which God invites us are intended to include others, not to push them away.

We need to look at Amos again. God gives Amos a word of challenge to deliver. God has been measuring Israel like a carpenter using a plumb line measures the straightness of a wall. Amos must announce that the places of worship shall be destroyed, the people carried away, and the king killed. Not a popular change to announce. And the king's advisor, who has already warned the king, instructs Amos to flee to go elsewhere with his prophecies.

Amos is not the normal religious leader. He does not work for the religious institution, nor did his father. Amos tells the king's advisor that his business is not religious. In fact, there is a sense of wistfulness as Amos shares his identity as a farmer. But the words he speaks are directly from God.

Sometimes God's transformation in the world is demonstrated through unexpected people. We get used to trusting the same leaders, but sometimes God goes against what we know to be common sense. We need to remain open to God's actions that seem to come from unusual sources. When we speak with conviction from our faith, we are challenged to discern how to accurately represent God.

The opening to the letter to the Ephesians lists blessings for which God is to be praised: God has already blessed us in Christ, we are chosen in Christ, and through Christ we are adopted children of God. These blessings result in redemption and forgiveness, wisdom and insight, and inheritance according to God's plan for the fullness of creation. Marked with the seal of the promised Holy Spirit, we are not passive recipients of God's grace, but instructed to praise God for these blessings so that the redemption God has given may be known by others.

Sometimes we are so confident in our faith that we take it for granted. We need reminders that the blessings in our lives are not from anything we have done, but are gifts given at God's pleasure. When we praise God for all that has been done on our behalf, we must discern how to share the good news in ways that invite others to accept God's grace. God's blessings bring transformation to all of creation, and we are a testimony to God's actions.

To be in Christ is to be in a new relationship with all of creation, for the resurrection of Jesus has transformed the very ways that God relates to the universe. Do we trust the inheritance God has promised more than our weekly paychecks, more than our savings accounts, more than our investment packages? Are we able to accept our identity as God's adopted ones as more important than titles that praise our leadership – director, president, chairperson, prophet, minister? Are we prepared to live dependent only on God's grace?

We need to look at the disciples again. Jesus sent them out with a new mission. He instructed them to rely on God for their daily needs: no bag for extras, bread only for today, and without money to provide a security net "just in case we run into trouble." They were to take with them only those things they needed for traveling to a new place: a walking stick and sandals. For support, they were sent out in pairs.

Sometimes our faith requires that we leave what is familiar. Even the familiarity of a change of clothes may need to be set aside as we go out to see, share, and announce the new things God is doing. We are challenged to discern the essentials for this new ministry. Who are the best companions for this journey of faith?

Jesus warns the disciples that some places will not receive them well. There is no promise of easy living as God's adopted children. There is no promise of prosperity or popularity. How willing are we to accept that this is our identity in Christ, that this is our status as those adopted by God because we have a relationship with Christ? The transformations God invites us to be part of will challenge us to new ways of relating to others. We need to look at Jesus again. The new ways he did ministry had a lot of people talking. Some people saw Jesus as the prophet Elijah, expected to announce the new reign of God. Some people saw Jesus as one of the ancient prophets, one who spoke out against social injustices while showing a new way.

Sometimes the new ministries we do will be compared to ministries of people who came before us. We get the same responses that their ministries brought – both positive and negative. We are called to be transformed as we live in the presence of God – but that does not mean everything will be brand new or unique to us. We must discern how to honor our ancestors of faith.

We need to look at ourselves again. Hearing God's call to transformation, being committed to living in a new way, seeking to be agents of change and growth – these are ways we demonstrate our faith, our relationship with God. How are we being invited to transformation? How is it similar to what God has done before? How might our excitement offend others? In what ways are we accepting others, and in what ways might we be excluding them? What are the essential tools we need for this new ministry? And how will we continue to discern God's way? These are questions of faith.

– Thom Bower

July 23, 2006

7th Sunday after Pentecost (Proper 11)
RC/Pres: 16th Sunday in Ordinary Time

Lessons

RCL	2 Sam 7:1–14a	Eph 2:11–22	Mk 6:30–34, 53–56
Roman Catholic	Jer 23:1–6	Eph 2:13–18	Mk 6:30–34
Episcopal	Isa 57:14b–21	Eph 2:11–22	Mk 6:30–44
Lutheran	Jer 23:1–6	Eph 2:11–22	Mk 6:30–34, 53–56

Introduction to the Lessons
Lesson 1
(1) 2 Samuel 7:1–14a (RCL)
As David plans to build a Temple, God declares that God will provide David with a household of descendants and that it is a descendant who will build the Temple.

(2) Jeremiah 23:1–6 (RC/Luth)
Israel's leaders are metaphorically compared to shepherds who have permitted the flock to be scattered. God promises a new shepherd who will bring safety.

(3) Isaiah 57:14b–21 (Epis)
Through the prophet, God confesses divine anger toward the wicked. The message is mixed: the wicked will both be healed and will be denied peace.

Lesson 2
Ephesians 2:11–22 (RCL/RC/Epis/Luth)
The writer of Ephesians proclaims that Christ proclaims peace to those far and near, to Jews and Gentiles. Strangers and aliens are now recognized as citizen saints of God's household.

Gospel
Mark 6:30–34, 53–56 (RCL/RC/Epis/Luth)
Jesus and the disciples attempt to go on a retreat, but the crowds keep following them. Jesus uses this as an opportunity for teaching.

Theme
The responsibility of leadership includes facing the unexpected.

Thought for the Day
Leadership should be more participative than directive, more enabling than performing.

– Mary D. Poole

Call to Worship
Voice 1: The disciples came to Jesus saying,
All: This is a lonely place, and it is late. Send the people away so that they may go and buy their food.
Voice 1: Jesus answered them:
Voice 2: You give them something to eat.
Voice 1: The disciples said:
All: Do you expect us to spend 200 days of pay on bread for them to eat?
Voice 1: Jesus responded:
Voice 2: Go and see how many loaves we have.
Voice 1: The disciples reported back:
All: We have five loaves and two fish.
Voice 1: Jesus said,
Voice 2: This is enough.

Pastoral Prayer
Divine Deliverer, you promise to be like a shepherd, gathering the scattered together. You invite us to join you as shepherd-leaders for your people. We want rest from our enemies, and you present us with yet more crowds of needy strangers. We pray this day, Gentle Shepherd, that you would heal us in body

and spirit, so that we may announce your peace. Revive our souls, so that we may welcome your people without obstruction. Shape us as leaders and worthy stewards as we learn more of what it means to accept your wisdom, justice, and righteousness, so that we may be your disciples. We pray in the name of our pastor, Jesus. Amen.

Prayer of Confession

Uniting God, You call us to be one united humanity of peace without violence. And yet we divide ourselves by things we think are important. You offer us reconciliation, and we focus on differences. You provide us with places of familiarity, and we focus on our past when we felt like outsiders. You lead others to our community so they can be accepted, and we see strangers who must be tested for trustworthiness. We meet saints, but see them as sinners. Forgive us our shortsightedness. Help us to see others as citizens of your household so that our human relationships may be a place where you dwell. We pray this in the peaceful name of Jesus. Amen.

Prayer of Dedication of Gifts and Self

Giver of gifts, we often pay so much attention to money that we overlook that you have given us many resources to use in serving others. With these gifts we ask for vision to look past our sanctuary, past our friends, and past our bank accounts to reassess what gifts we have to offer. Use these gifts, and use our lives to heal the wounds and feed the hunger of this world. We lift up those who are currently studying to be your ministers as they recognize the blessed gifts in their lives. We pray as your servants, Amen.

Sermon Summary

Jesus repeatedly surprises the disciples with the ways he teaches them to become spiritual leaders. By word and deed his message is, "This is who I am. How will you relate to me?"

Hymn of the Day
"Healer of Our Every Ill"

Reading through the Synoptic Gospels, one is struck by how central healing was in Jesus' ministry. Wherever he and his disciples went, people rushed to him with their sick friends and relatives in tow, believing he could heal them in mind, body, and spirit.

Marty Haugen's "Healer of Our Every Ill" is a sincere appeal for God's healing, peace, vision, and hope. "Give us peace beyond our fear," Haugen writes fervently, "and hope beyond our sorrow." The melody is especially attractive, with either guitar or piano providing pleasing accompaniment.

Children's Time

A Big Picnic in the Grass

Preparation: Bring little fish crackers and a couple of big blankets.
Let's pretend that we're on a picnic. Come and sit on these blankets with me. The sunshine feels so nice and warm. What will we eat on our picnic? (Accept responses and comment on how tasty they'll be.) Oh, no! There's an ant. (Walk your fingers across the blanket toward one of the children then toward another.) We'll have to cover the food to keep the ants out.

One day Jesus was on a picnic. Guess how many people were eating with him? (Accept responses.) Jesus' picnic was a very big one – over 5,000 people. But one thing was missing: the food. The disciples found five small loaves of bread and two small fish to Jesus. Jesus gave thanks for the fish and bread and fed the crowd. After everyone had eaten, Jesus said to his disciple, "Gather all of the leftovers." And the disciples filled twelve baskets with leftovers! With a simple meal of bread and fish, Jesus taught the crowd to trust in God's love and care.

Now let's eat some fish together. (Distribute fish crackers.) Whenever you eat a meal, you give thanks for the good food God has given you.
Prayer: Creator God, thank you for sending Jesus to fill us up with your love. Amen.

The Sermon

Unexpected Leadership

Hymns

Beginning of Worship: "Savior, Like a Shepherd Lead Us"
Sermon Hymn: "O Savior, Let Me Walk with You"
Closing Hymn: "Community of Christ"

Scripture

Mark 6:30–56 (For additional sermon materials on this passage, see the 2005 May/June planning issue of *The Clergy Journal*; for sermon materials on Ephesians 2:11–22, see the March 2006 issue of *The Clergy Journal*.) Jesus and the disciples have been busy. They've visited Jesus' hometown, where his teaching and preaching style were considered with suspicion. Jesus has sent the disciples out in pairs to do their own ministry. The authorities have taken notice of Jesus, and are disturbed by the similarities between Jesus and that troublemaker, John the Baptizer.

All this sets the stage for the events of today's gospel reading. Jesus and the disciples are reunited. The disciples are filled with excitement as they share the stories of their experiences. Jesus recommends that they go on a retreat to debrief the experiences, to mine them for insight, improve ministerial practices, and refine theological reflection. This is a seminary course.

The deserted place may be a place away from the luxuries of civilization, a place where the awareness of their dependence on God can be heightened, or it may just be a place where there are fewer distractions. We need time to ourselves, time away from the regular demands of our lives to be rejuvenated, to reflect on our experiences, to nurture our spirits. Sometimes this can be done alone and sometimes, like in this passage, it is done with others with whom we share our passions for and works of ministry.

People want to join what Jesus and the disciples are doing; they are paying attention to what they do, who they are with, and where they are going. When Jesus and the disciples get into a boat to go away by themselves, the crowd follows along the shoreline.

Imagine arriving at the retreat center, anticipating a time of rest and intentional reflection, only to be met by a large crowd. Jesus sees the crowd and is moved to compassion. Is it because this is a pathetic group of people that society has abandoned? Is it because he perceives their lives are so empty that they have become star-struck and have followed him? Or is it, instead, that Jesus senses their devotion to a new way of being, their yearning for transformation, their eagerness to learn, their willingness to be discipled?

Why do we follow Jesus? Are we looking for a status boost because we can be associated with Jesus, with the disciples, with a particular congregation in a particular denomination? Or are we followers of Jesus who come to the church to confess and explore our transformed life, to learn from other disciples how to live this new life, to take a risk in doing something we haven't done before because we trust God to be with us?

Those beloved followers of Jesus who just experienced ministry in pairs overlook the compassion Jesus has for these other followers. That is not to say they are without compassion. Their very comments demonstrate concern for all these people: "It's late, and we're in the middle of nowhere. Tell them it is time for them to go into the nearby towns so that they can get their dinners."

Jesus has a simple reply: "You feed them."

Let's imagine we are among the disciples: a huge crowd suddenly shows up at our worship service. After the service, someone suggests, "Let's have lunch with everybody who is here." You can almost here the church treasurer sputtering, "Do you know how much that would cost? We might be able to pay for it, but which budget line will cover this expense?" That's how the disciples respond. "Us? Feed them? Do you have any idea how much that would cost? Two hundred denarii." The denarii was a single coin, usually given to a day-laborer for a day's work. The disciples, as peasant workers, probably got this much for their own work. The disciples are not mean people. They are not even people of disbelief. They are people who want to be faithful, and in this case it translates to being good stewards.

Jesus is asking them to reconsider the resources they have to be faithful. It's not just about how we spend our money; it's not just about how we meet people's physical needs. Being faithful is helping people help each other. "How much bread do you have? You saw that the people were hungry; you recognized their need. Did you think about sharing your own food with others?" We know the answer: they didn't think of that. We know this because they had to go find out how much bread they had: five loaves and two fish, a modest meal for about a dozen people.

Jesus gives thanks and shares the meal with everyone who is there. There is more than enough for everyone, enough to have leftovers for a long time.

It is time to go back to their retreat. Jesus sends the disciples off in the boat to continue the retreat. Jesus stays behind with the crowd, knowing the crowds will want to say "Hello" and "Thank You" and "We hope to see you soon."

Then Jesus does this strange thing. In the evening, Jesus sees the boat of the disciples moving slow because they are heading into a strong wind. Jesus waits until the morning to join them. He walks out – walks on top of the water – expecting to pass them by. It is like the youth who declares in a traffic jam, "I can walk faster," gets out of the car, and walks to prove it.

This activity scares the disciples; they think this is some supernatural being. When Jesus speaks, they realize it is their familiar rabbi. Still they feel tricked, betrayed: "You point out that we're not thinking about all the possibilities we have to be faithful. You feed a huge crowd with a meal meant for us. Now you come out here strolling by – you're not even supposed to be able to walk here! We don't understand; what's going on!"

Jesus does not respond. He gets in the boat and travels with them to the next village, and other villages, and marketplaces, and farming communities, and cities. People await Jesus, bringing more people: the lame, the sick. We're not told how the disciples react to this; they seem to be stepping back to wonder, to contemplate, to get perspective. In word and deed, the message of Jesus is, "This is who I am. How will you relate to me?"

– Thom Bower

July 30, 2006

8th Sunday after Pentecost (Proper 12)
RC/Pres: 17th Sunday in Ordinary Time

Lessons

RCL	2 Sam 11:1–15	Eph 3:14–21	Jn 6:1–21
Roman Catholic	2 Kgs 4:42–44	Eph 4:1–6	Jn 6:1–15
Episcopal	2 Kgs 2:1–15	Eph 4:1–7, 11–16	Mk 6:45–52
Lutheran	2 Kgs 4:42–44	Eph 3:14–21	Jn 6:1–21

Introduction to the Lessons:

Lesson 1

(1) 2 Samuel 11:1–15 (RCL)

David tries to cover up his affair with Bathsheba by making it seem her husband conceived the child. When Uriah's piety prevents this, David commands that Uriah be placed in a unit at the battlefront.

(2) 2 Kings 4:42–44 (RC/Luth)

Elisha uses a little food to feed many people.

(3) 2 Kings 2:1–15 (Epis)

Elijah and Elisha travel together until Elijah is taken up in a chariot. Elisha receives a piece of Elijah's clothing as a symbol of Elijah's spirit.

Lesson 2

(1) Ephesians 3:14–21 (RCL/Luth)

A pastoral prayer of intercession offered on behalf of the church that may have originated in a blended Jewish-Gentile liturgy.

(2) Ephesians 4:1–7, 11–16 (Epis)

The writer of Ephesians exhorts the church and its members to live worthily of its call from Christ: in unity, honoring diverse gifts, seeking authentic maturation.

Gospel

(1) John 6:1–21 (RCL/RC/Epis/Luth)

Near the Passover holiday, Jesus feeds a large crowd with a boy's lunch. Jesus then withdraws to a mountain for solitary prayer, and rejoins the disciples by walking across the lake.

(2) Mark 6:45–52 (Epis)

This is the parallel in Mark to the reading from John (see above).

Theme

We are called by God to come together.

Thought for the Day

Individual commitment to a group effort – that is what makes a team work, a company work, a society work, a civilization work.

– Vince Lombardi

Call to Worship

One:	We seek to be worthy of God's calling.
Left:	With humility and kindness,
Right:	With patience,
Left:	Bearing with one another in love,
Right:	Seeking unity
All:	In the Spirit of peace.
One:	Speaking the truth in love,
All:	We desire to grow up with Christ as our head.
Right:	We are joined and knitted together by God!
Left:	We are equipped to do Christ's work.
All:	We seek to be worthy of God's calling.

Pastoral Prayer

Living God who speaks in breeze and wind, guide us to recognize the leaders you place among us. We give thanks for the many different kinds of leaders: pastors and caregivers, politicians and business leaders, teachers and prophets. When transitions call them and us to new places, we trust that you will provide us with new leaders worthy of your calling. It is harder for us to open ourselves to you and accept that you call us to be leaders also – evangelists and teachers, healers and servants, the ones who speak out against wrongdoing, and the ones who help feed the hungry. Be with us now as we accept this new mantle as your chosen leaders in the world today. Amen.

Prayer of Confession

You are our Father and Mother, and every human family carries your name, Holy One. We proclaim that you have transformed our lives, but reluctantly we permit ourselves to be strong in your Spirit. We claim to be your people, but we do not allow our hearts to set roots in your love for all that is created. We flaunt our knowledge of the church in order to cover up how little we understand of your loving presence. We are so certain that we are right in our thinking, our beliefs, and our ways of doing things that we declare ourselves saints and judge others as sinful. Open our imaginations, so that we may be filled with your fullness. Open our hearts, so that we may dwell in faith. Unite us as your church, so that your glory may be shared with all. Amen.

Prayer of Dedication of Gifts and Self

O God, we have seen the signs of what you do in the world. People have been healed. Leaders have been provided. Crowds gather without violence to learn your ways. A boy gave Jesus his lunch of bread and fish and Jesus used it to feed five thousand and more. We dedicate these gifts as a testimony of how we come together in your name. Receive these gifts from our everyday lives and transform them into something miraculous so that people may be united. Through these gifts may yet more signs of you in the world be seen – in the simple acts of sharing a meal, in learning together what God can do, in prayer-filled retreats, in experiencing the unexpected. With the saints of many eras we pray. Amen.

Sermon Summary

As we claim the challenge to continue to pursue maturity in Christ, we must ask, "What do we want to be when we grow up?" and "How will we be when we grow up?" These are questions for the church as a body of individual believers and a corporate, unified body.

Hymn of the Day
"You Satisfy the Hungry Heart"

In the symbol-rich world of John's gospel, it's impossible to miss the Eucharistic connotations in today's reading. There were only five barley loaves and two fish to feed five thousand people on that mountain, yet the meal lasted until everyone was "satisfied."

Omer Westendorf's "You Satisfy the Hungry Heart," set to Robert Kreutz's BICENTENNIAL, is a beautiful choice for this text. As John's gospel does, Westendorf and Kreutz's hymn makes clear that Jesus' meal is meant to alleviate much more than physical hunger. This is a deeply satisfying hymn deserving wider usage.

Children's Time

Neighbors Near and Far

Preparation: In large letters write "Jesus" on a 9-inch square of heavy paper. Draw four identical crosses on 9-inch squares of paper.
(Give the four crosses to four older children. Spread them out as far as possible in your worship space – to the north, south, east, and west. If you have young children, have an adult stand with them. In the very center of your worship space have a child stand, holding the "Jesus" sign.)

Do all the people in the world live in our country? (No.) Do people all around the world speak the same language as we do? (No.) Paul, one of Jesus' followers, writes that the good news of Jesus' love is for all people, all around the world. Jesus loves people in every place. (Invite the four children holding crosses to move slowly until they are all standing around the child holding the "Jesus" sign.) Is Jesus' love for people who live in the North? (Yes!) South? (Yes!) East? (Yes!) West? (Yes!) Jesus' love is for everyone!

Prayer: Dear Jesus, help us find ways to spread the story of your love to the north, south, east, and west. Amen.

The Sermon

When the Church Grows Up

Hymns

Beginning of Worship: "The Church's One Foundation"
Sermon Hymn: "In the Midst of New Dimensions"
Closing Hymn: "When Minds and Bodies Meet as One"

Scripture

Ephesians 4:1–7, 11–16 (For sermon materials on John 6:1–21, see the 2005 May/June planning issue and the March 2006 issue of *The Clergy Journal*.)

"What do you want to be when you grow up?" Depending on how grown up we are when asked, we give different answers. Small children answer according to what they think are exciting activities: firefighter, astronaut, doctor. Later in childhood, the answers cluster around activities the children enjoy doing most: computer game designer, painter, dancer, writer of books. In early adolescence, the answers typically involve some aspect of what will bring notoriety and fame: musician, movie star, athlete.

The nuance of the question changes when it is asked during later adolescence. At this stage in life "What do you want to be when you grow up?" really means "What do you plan as a career for yourself?" We allow "be" to become "do," and we define "doing" by income-providing labor.

Later, we jokingly ask the same question of adults when they are going through a major life change, as if the transition they are in indicates that they have not yet "grown up." Somehow, "grown up" translates into absolute stability – certainly not inviting changes that are disruptive or uncontrollable.

Is it fair to ask this question of the church? Imagine what the conversation might be like. "Hello, Church. I haven't seen you in a long time. I remember when you were just this big; look how you have grown. Tell me, what would you like to be when you grow up? What is exciting to you now? What do you enjoy doing most? How will you plan for dependable change?"

This is not just an exercise of religious imagination. We need to ask this question of the church today. We can listen in on the conversation when the writer of Ephesians asked this question of the first-century church. It is a letter meant to encourage the church – as a single entity and as a group of many individuals – as the church does its best to be faithful.

This section of Ephesians begins by both affirming and challenging the church to be worthy of the call it has received from Christ. The writer then lists a variety of ways saints are equipped to promote that unity. We are told that the pursuit of unity is a maturing process.

We may be tempted to read this passage as though it were asking each one of us, "What do you want to do when you grow up to be in the church? Would you like to work as an apostle? Apostles are the ones who are set apart to share their personal experiences with Jesus and how that becomes a way of life. Would you like to do the work of a prophet? Prophets speak to the present; they tell us when we are not living well to the way God would have us live. Perhaps you would prefer to do the work of an evangelist? They speak the good news, declaring that God is offering salvation and that this changes the way we are in the world. Perhaps you would rather work as a pastor or teacher, doing the one-on-one work, the work within the congregation as it strives to be faithful in the nitty-gritty decisions of everyday living."

We must be careful about reading this passage as though it were a Christian career-counseling center. This is not a list of job opportunities that we get to select from; these are called roles in the church. The writer is telling us that God gives many gifts for many different responsibilities. We are challenged to reevaluate our perceptions of these leaders, for they have received gifts of leadership by the grace of God.

At the same time, these leaders are being warned to not think that they are set apart from everyone else. Their gifts are given so that unity in Christ may be better known, better lived. These leaders have already been given advice on how they can live in these roles: like everyone else, they are to live in humility and gentleness, patience, approaching all with love. Perhaps we have the entire question wrong. Instead of "What do you want to be when you grow up?" the question might be "How do you want to be when you grow up?" Imagine how different the answers would be if we asked that question instead. "How would you like to be when you grow up?" Small children might answer with words like happy, playing all the time. Older children might answer with the feelings that engage them most: I want to be excited, I want to be adventuring, I want to be loving and loved. Adolescents might answer I want to be noticed, I want to be meaningful, I want to make a difference wherever I am.

How might the church answer when asked, "How will you be when you grow up?" The epistle writer offers some suggestions. Humility and gentleness, so that we are sincere in our self-evaluations in ways that do not put others down. Patient and loving, so that we can grow together. Seeking unity as much as possible. Why is this the way we should be? Because we are called as followers of Christ to live out Christ's way.

The writer of Ephesians anticipates what others will say when we state, "Our church is still growing up." To admit "We are learning new ways to understand how God is at work among us" is to invite ridicule. So, the writer of Ephesians tells us to act like grown-ups. Don't be easy to manipulate. Know who you are and stand your ground. Know what you believe and stand by it. People are going to try to trick you; be smart and avoid it even while you promote unity.

How will you be when you grow up? How will we be as we continue to grow as the church that God has called us to be? It is easy to say, "Let us find joy in our unity." Now we have the challenge from the church of the first century to accept this identity and work at it together.

– Thom Bower

Appendices
Resources for Preparing to Preach
by David H. Schmidt

Of the writing of commentaries, there is no end. The following bibliography offers one person's review of commentaries and overviews that a pastor might consult as she or he prepares the sermon. The first sections cover books that can be used all three years of the Revised Common Lectionary. These are followed by comments about books for the portions of the lectionary covered in this year's *Minister's Annual Manual.* They are grouped by gospels, then epistles, and, finally, Old Testament. An effort is made to include some of the newer works coming on the market as well as some standard volumes that time has shown to be helpful to pastors. A variety of theological perspectives are included. With the growing use of computers, a few of the burgeoning software resources have been included.

One-Volume Commentaries

One-volume commentaries that can be used throughout the three-year cycle include: James L. Mays, general editor, HarperCollins Bible Commentary, rev. ed. (HarperSanFrancisco, 2000). Published in cooperation with the Society of Biblical Literature, this one-volume commentary provides good, brief information that reflects the current state of scholarship. There are good overview articles as well as comments on each book (including the Deuterocanonical Books).

A second, current one-volume work is Raymond E. Brown et al., The New Jerome Biblical Commentary, re. ed. (Paulist Press, 1989). Both of these works are now available on a Logos Bible Software CD-ROM, along with Matthew Henry's Commentary and the Bible Knowledge Commentary.

Logos Research Systems also makes available the Harper's Bible Dictionary and Doubleday's Anchor Bible Dictionary. They also have the Interpretation Commentaries series, Intervarsity Press New Testament Commentary series and others, and are working on the International Critical Commentary series.

Abingdon Press has released the entire New Interpreter's Bible on CD-ROM. Word Biblical Commentary is on a disk with Greek and Hebrew texts and numerous Bible translations. Biblesoft has packages that include such older series as Matthew Henry's Commentaries, Wycliffe Commentaries, Keil & Delitzsch's OT Commentary, Adam Clarke's Commentaries, and Jamieson-Fausset-Brown commentaries. Several software companies provide the Holman Bible Dictionary and/or others with some of their packages. Zondervan has released The Expositor's Bible Commentary, edited by Frank Gaebelein on CD-Rom.

Books for Study of the Psalter for All Three Years

Overview and Theology: H. J. Kraus's Theology of the Psalms (Augsburg, 1986) is a good discussion by a scholar who has also published a major commentary (below). James L. Crenshaw's The Psalms: An Introduction (Eerdmans, 2001) offers a fair and thorough overview of recent discussion. For a work that invites looking at the Psalms in a new way, J. David Pleius' The Psalms: Songs of Tragedy, Hope, and Justice, The Bible & Liberation (Orbis, 1993). J Clinton McCann and James C. Howell, Preaching the Psalms (Abingdon, 2001) challenges the preacher to recover the Psalms for sermon material.

Commentaries: H. J. Kraus' Psalms 1-59 and Psalms 60-150 (Augsburg, 1987, 1989) are the standard works full of detail. J. Clinton McCann covers the Psalms in the New Interpreter's Bible, vol. 4 (Abingdon, 1996). Richard J. Clifford Psalms 1–72 and Psalms 73–150, Abingdon Old Testament Commentaries (Abingdon, 2002, 2004), provide an informed and relatively inexpensive set designed for the pastor. K. Schaefer's Psalms, *Berit Olam*: Studies in Hebrew Narrative and Poetry (The Liturgical Press, 2001) is a recent Roman Catholic study. James L. May's Psalms, Interpretation Commentaries (John Knox, 1994) is a fine expository work that can be used alongside any of the above commentaries.

Books for Study of Acts for All Three Years

Overview: Mark Allen Powell's What Are They Saying About Acts? (Paulist Press, 1991) will provide a good introduction to the state of research on Acts. Jacob Jervell's The Theology of the Acts of the Apostles (Cambridge University Press, 1996) offers an up to date review of the theological issues.

Commentaries: W. H. Willimon's Acts, Interpretation Commentaries (John Knox, 1988) gives a sound expository start for the pastor. Then use one or more of the following for exegetical support: E. Haenchen's The Acts of the Apostles: A Commentary (Westminster, 1971) is a significant reference. Robert W. Wall's "The Acts of the Apostles," New Interpreters' Bible, vol. 10 (Abingdon, 2002) offers a Wesleyan exposition and exegesis. Luke Timothy Johnson's The Acts of the Apostles, Sacra Pagina vol. 5 (The Liturgical Press, 1992) is a recent Roman Catholic study with a fresh translation, notes and interpretation that provides another viewpoint. Joseph A. Fitzmyer's The Acts of the Apostles, Anchor Bible vol. 31 (Doubleday, 1998) is a good replacement volume in that series. Howard Clark Kee, To Every Nation Under Heaven: The Acts of the Apostles (Trinty Press International, 1997) includes helpful notes from archaeology along with good commentary. C.K. Barrett's Acts of the Apostles, International Critical Commentary, 2 volumes (T & T Clark, 1993, 1998) is a significant recent study on the Greek text.

Books for Study of the Gospel Lessons
Matthew (Year A)

Overviews: Jack Kingsbury, Matthew, Proclamation Commentary, 3rd ed. (Evangel, 1998) or D. Senior, What Are They Saying about Matthew? Rev. & Exp. (Paulist Press, 1996) will give one a good summary of the current discussion on Matthew. Kingsbury also has a good review in his Matthew as Story, 2nd ed., rev. & enl. (Fortress, 1988). U. Luz, The Theology of the Gospel of Matthew (Cambridge, 1995) provides a theological overview from a scholar. Luz is the author of the multivolume commentary listed below.

Commentaries: A recent helpful source is M. Eugene Boring, "The Gospel According to Matthew," The New Interpreter's Bible, vol. 8 (Abingdon, 1995). This volume also includes Mark and introductory studies on the New Testament. Other expository support is found in Douglas R. A. Hare, Matthew, Interpretation Commentaries (John Knox Press, 1993). Ulrich Luz, Matthew 1–7: A Commentary and Matthew 8–20: A Commentary (Augsburg, 1989, 2001) is completing a major study. David E. Garland, Reading Matthew: A Literary and Theological Commentary on the First Gospel (Crossroad, 1993) comes at the text from another approach. Daniel J. Harrington, The Gospel of Matthew, Sacra Pagina, vol. 1 (The Liturgical Press, 1991) is a solid Roman Catholic work. D. A. Hagner, Matthew 1–13 and 14–28, Word Biblical Commentary (Word, 1993, 1995) is a strong recent evangelical study. Malina and Rohrbaugh's Social-Science Commentary on the Synoptic Gospels (Fortress, 1992) provides another approach.

One might be interested in the patristic use of Matthew well researched in Manilo Simonetti's Matthew 1–13, and 14–28, Ancient Christian Commentary on Scripture (IVP, 2001).

Mark

Overviews: Paul Achtemeier's Mark, Proclamation Commentaries, 2nd rev. ed. (Fortress, 1986) or Frank J. Matera's What Are They Saying about Mark? (Paulist Press, 1987) provide an opening overview. W. R. Telford's The Theology of the Gospel of Mark (Cambridge, 2000) will give a theological overview. An interesting book that introduces a variety of modern approaches to Mark is Janice C. Anderson and Stephen D. Moore's Mark and Method: New Approaches in Biblical Studies (Augsburg Fortress, 1992).

Commentaries: Expository studies include Lamar Williamson Jr's Mark, Interpretation Commentaries (John Knox, 1983) or Bonnie Bowman Thurston's Preaching Mark (Fortress, 2002). Pheme Perkins' "The Gospel of Mark," The New Interpreter's Bible, vol. 8 (Abingdon, 1995) has both solid expository and exegetical material. Other options for exegetical study might include John R. Donahue and Daniel J. Harrington's The Gospel of Mark, Sacra Pagina vol. 2 (Liturgical Press, 2002), James R. Edwards' The Gospel according to Mark, Pillar New Testament Commentary (Eerdmans, 2002), or Morna D. Hooker's The Gospel According to St. Mark, Black's New Testament Commentary (Hendrickson, 1992). Eduard Schweizer's The Good News According to Mark (John Knox, 1970) continues to provide solid help for preaching. Ched Myers' Binding the Strong Man and Who Will Roll Away the Stone (Orbis, 1988, 1994) challenge us to take a new look at a familiar gospel.

John (Years A & B)

Overviews: Gerald S. Sloyan's What Are They Saying about John? (Paulist, 1991) provides a fine overview of current scholarship. D. Moody Smith's John, Proclamation Commentary, 2nd ed. (Fortress, 1986) is an alternative. He also provides a theological overview in The Theology of the Gospel of John (Cambridge University Press, 1995). Wes Howard-Brook, John's Gospel and the Renewal of the Church (Orbis, 1997) can stimulate one's thinking. Robert Kysar's Preaching John (Fortress, 2002) will prime many pumps.

Commentaries: Raymond E. Brown's The Gospel According to John, Anchor Bible 29, 29A (Doubleday, 1966, 1970) has become a standard two-volume work for exegetical study. Couple this with the expository effort of Gerald Sloyan's John, Interpretation Commentaries (John Knox, 1988) for a solid set of resources. Gail R. O'Day's "The Gospel of John" in The New Interpreter's Bible, vol. 9 (Abingdon, 1995) is an interesting study in a volume that also includes Luke. Charles H. Talbert's Reading John: A Literary and Theological Commentary on the Fourth Gospel and the Johannine Epistles (Crossroad, 1994) is a fine study using the newer literary approach. Ben Witherington III, John's Wisdom: A Commentary on the Fourth Gospel (Westminster/John Knox, 1995) offers another perspective. Bruce J. Malina, Social Science Commentary on the Gospel of John (Fortress, 1998) is study that also can cause one to look at the text in a different way. Francis J. Moloney's The Gospel of John, Sacra Pagina (The Liturgical Press, 1998) is another recent study.

Books for the Study of the Epistle Lessons
Romans

Paul J. Achtemeier's Romans, Interpretation Commentaries (John Knox, 1985) provides excellent expository materials. C. K. Barrett's Romans, Black's New Textament Commentaries, 2nd ed. (Hendrickson, 1991) continues to be a strong exegetical support. Brendan Byrne's Romans, Sacra Pagina vol. 6 (The Liturgical Press, 1996) compliments the above drawing on rhetorical study. Joseph A. Fitzmyer's Romans, Anchor Bible, vol. 33 (Doubleday, 1993) is an option. Douglas J. Moo's The Epistle to the Romans, New International Commentary on the New Testament (Eerdmans, 1996) is a strong evangelical offering. A detailed study based on the Greek is found in C. E. B. Cranfield's A Critical and Exegetical Commentary on the Epistle to the Romans, 2 vol., International Critical Commentary (T & T Clark, 1975, 1979).

1 and 2 Corinthians

William A. Beardslee's First Corinthians: A Commentary for Today (Chalice Press, 1994) is a good book aimed at the pastor and teacher. Richard B. Hays' First Corinthians, Interpretation Commentaries (John Knox Press, 1997) and Ernest Best's Second Corinthians, Interpretation Commentaries (John Knox, 1987) provide good expository work. J. Paul Smalley offers exegetical and expository insight in "First Letter to the Corinthians," New Interpreter's Bible, vol. 10 (Abingdon, 2002) and "Second Letter to the Corinthians," New Interpreter's Bible, vol. 11 (Abingdon, 2000). Ben Witherington III, Conflict and Community in Corinth: A Socio-Rhetorical Commentary on First and Second Corinthians (Eerdmans, 1995) offers a study by an evangelical. Gordon D. Fee's The First Epistle to the Corinthians New International Commentary on the New Testament (Eerdmans, 1987) is a fine detailed evangelical study. Raymond F. Collins' First Corinthians, Sacra Pagina vol. 7 (The Liturgical Press, 1999) and Jan Lambrecht's Second Corinthians, Sacra Pagina vol. 8 (The Liturgical Press, 1999) are helpful additions in that series. Other helpful volumes include Richard A. Horsley's First Corinthians, Abingdon New Testament Commentaries (Abingdon, 1997), Victor Paul Furnish's Second Corinthians, Anchor Bible 32A (Doubleday, 1984), and C. K. Barrett's The Second Epistle to the Corinthians, Black's New Testament Commentary (Hendrickson, 1973).

Ephesians

Pheme Perkins' "Letter to the Ephesians," The New Interpreter's Bible, vol. 11 (Abingdon, 2000) is a good starting place. Markus Barth's Ephesians, Anchor Bible 34 and 34A (Doubleday, 1974) continues to provide a detailed study. Ralph P. Martin's Ephesians, Colossians, and Philemon, Interpretation Commentaries (John Knox, 1991) offers additional expository material. Ernest Best's A Critical and Exegetical Commentary on Ephesians, International Critical Commentary (T & T Clark, 1998) provides a good study of the Greek text. And Rudolf Schnackenburg's Ephesians: A Commentary (T & T Clark, 1991) is a good Roman Catholic study.

Philippians

Morna D. Hooker's "Letter to the Philippians," New Interpreter's Bible, vol. 11 (Abingdon, 2000) has both exegetical and expository material. Fred B. Craddock's Phillipians, Interpretation Commentaries (John Knox, 1985) offers a brief expository study. It could be supplemented by Markus Bockmuehl's The Epistle to the Phillipians, Black's New Testament Commentary (Hendrickson, 1998) or Gordon Fee's Paul's Letter to the Phillipians, New International Commnetary on the New Testament (Eerdmans, 1995). There is a study of the Greek text in Peter T. O'Brien's The Epistle to the Phillipians, New International Greek New Testament (Eerdmans, 1991).

1 Thessalonians

Abraham J. Malherbe, The Letters to the Thessalonians, Anchor Bible 32B (Doubleday, 2000) is a helpful study. Earl J. Richard, First and Second Thessalonians, Sacra Pagina (The Liturgical Press, 1997) offers a good philological study. Beverly Roberts Gaventa's, First and Second Thessalonians, Interpretation Commentaries (John Knox Press, 1998) gives a good expository study. Abraham Smith, "The Second Letter to the Thessalonians," The New Interpreter's Bible, vol. 11 (Abingdon, 2000) also offers exegetical insight along with his expository study. Ernest Best, A Commentary on the First and Second Epistles to the Thessalonians, Black's New Testament Commentaries (Hendrickson, 1972), continues to be significant. C. A. Wanamaker, The Epistles to the Thessalonians, New International Greek Testament Commentary (Eerdmans, 1990) gives a somewhat unconventional study from the Greek text.

1 John

C. Clifton Black's "First, Second, and Third John," The New Interpreter's Bible, vol. 12 (Abingdon, 1998) is a good recent study. D. Moody Smith's First, Second, and Third John, Interpretation Commentaries (John Knox, 1991) offers helpful expository insight. These could be supplemented with Raymond E. Brown's The Epistles of John, Anchor Bible 30 (Doubleday, 1982) or Stephen Smalley's First, Second, and Third John, Word Bible Commentary (Word, 1984). Rudolf Schnackenburg's rich theological study is available as The Johannine Epistles: Introduction and Commentary (Crossroad, 1997).

Books for the Study of Some of the Old Testament Texts
Genesis

Walter Brueggeman, Genesis, Interpretation Commentaries (John Knox, 1982) is an excellent expository work. Terence E. Fretheim, "The Book of Genesis," The New Interpreter's Bible, vol. 1 (Abingdon, 1994) is another helpful place to start. An inexpensive but helpful set would be Donald E. Gowan's Genesis 1–11: From Eden to Babel and J. Gerald Janzen's Genesis 12–50: Abraham and All the Families of the Earth, International Theological Commentary (Eerdmans, 1993). A fine evangelical set are Gordon J. Wenham's Genesis, 2 vols., Word Biblical Commentary (Word, 1987, 1994). David W. Cotter's Genesis, Berit Olam (The Liturgical Press, 2003) is a new, sometimes provocative, confessional study.

Exodus

Walter Brueggeman's "The Book of Exodus," The New Intrepreter's Bible, vol. 1 (Abingdon, 1994) may be a good place to start. Terence E. Fretheim's Exodus, Interpretation Commentaries (John Knox, 1991) is also a good expository study. William H. C. Propp's Exodus 1–18, Anchor Bible 2 (Doubleday, 1999) begins a fine study. Waldemar Janzen's Exodus, Believers Church Bible Commentary (Herald Press, 2000) sees salvation not liberation as the key to Exodus. N. M. Sarna's JPS Torah Commentary on Exodus (JPS, 1991) provides interesting insights from a Jewish scholar.

1 and 2 Samuel

Walter Brueggeman's First and Second Samuel, Intrepretation Commentaries (John Knox, 1990) offers an excellent expository start. P. Kyle McCarter's First Samuel and Second Samuel, Anchor Bible 8 and 9 (Doubleday, 1980) provide solid exegetical support. Bruce C. Burch's "First and Second Samuel," The New Interpreter's Bible, vol. 2 (Abingdon, 1998) is an alternative to the above books. Gnana Robinson's Let Us Be Like the Nations: A Commentary on the Books of First and Second Samuel, International Theological Commentary (Eerdmans, 1993) offers reflection for an international reflection. Finally, Walter Brueggeman's David's Truth (Fortress, 1985) is a stimulating supplement.

Isaiah

Joseph Blenkinsopp's Isaiah, Anchor Bible 19, 19B, 19C (Doubleday, 2000, 2002, 2003) is a replacement set in that series where one scholar studies the whole book. Brevard S. Child's Isaiah, Old Testament Library (Westminster, 2001) is another stimulating of the whole book. Walter Brueggemann, Isaiah 1–39, 40–66, Westminster Bible Companion (Westminster John Knox, 1998) is a third such study. Expository help for Isaiah of Jerusalem comes from Christopher R. Seitz's Isaiah 1–39, Interpretation Commentaries (John Knox, 1993). Seitz also edited, Reading and Preaching the Book of Isaiah (Fortress, 1988) which can assist the pastor in thinking about the use of Isaiah during the year. He also is the author of "Isaiah 40–66" in The New Interpreter's Bible, Vol. 6 (Abingdon, 2001). Gene M. Tucker provides "Isaiah 1–39" in that same volume. Paul D. Hanson's Isaiah 40–66, Interpretation Commentaries (John Knox, 1995) provides expository work on later Isaiah. R. Clements's Isaiah 1–39, New Century Bible Commentary (Eerdmans, 1980) and R. N. Whybray's Isaiah 40–66, New Century Bible Commentary (Eerdmans, 1975) provide good inexpensive commentaries. A more detailed set would be O. Kaiser's Isaiah 1–12, Old Testament Library, 2nd ed. (Westminster, 1983) and Isaiah 13–39, Old Testament Library (Westminster, 1974) plus Claus Westermann's Isaiah 40–66, Old Testament Library (Westminster, 1969).

2005–2006 Writers

Sermons and Prayers

Andrea La Sonde Anastos
(UCC) Greenfield, MA
Apr. 9, 13, 14, 16, 2006

Thom Bower
(UCC) Westchester, IL
July 9, 16, 23, 30, 2006

Rod Broding
(ELCA) Battle Lake, MN
Nov. 13, 20, 24, 27, 2005

John R. Bucka
(ELCA) Blaine, MN
Mar. 12, 19, 26, Apr. 2, 2006

C. Welton Gaddy
(Bap) Monroe, LA
Apr. 23, 30, May 7, 14, 2006

Robert L. Kinast
(RC) Indian Rocks Beach, FL
Sept. 4, 11, 18, 25, 2005

Catherine Malotky
(ELCA) Minnetonka, MN
June 11, 18, 25, July 2, 2006

David Wesley Reid
(Bap) Reading, MA
Jan. 22, 29, Feb. 5, 12, 2006

Rosemary A. Rocha
(UCC) Edina, MN
Oct. 2, 9, 16, 23, 2005

William M. Schwein
(UMC) Carmel, IN
Aug. 7, 14, 21, 28, 2005

Melissa Bane Sevier
(PCU) Versailles, KY
Feb. 19, 26, Mar. 1, 5, 2006

John R. Throop
(Ep) Peoria, Illinois
Dec. 4, 11, 18, 24, 25, 2005

Nancy E. Topolewski
(UMC) Vestal, NY
May 21, 25, 28, June 4, 2006

J. Barry Vaughn
(Ep) Philadelphia, PA
Oct. 30, 31 Nov. 1, 6, 2005

Norman W. Wahl
(ELCA) Rochester MN
Jan. 1, 6, 8, 15, 2006

Children's Time

Sandra Anderson
(ELCA) Moorhead, MN

Preaching Resources

David H. Schmidt
West Lafayette, IN

Hymn of the Day Selections

Douglas Thompson
(Ep) Apple Valley, MN

Four-Year Church Year Calendar

	Year A **2004**	Year B **2005**	Year C **2006**	Year A **2007**
Advent begins	Nov. 28	Nov. 27	Dec. 3	Dec. 2
Christmas	Dec. 25	Dec. 25	Dec. 25	Dec. 25
	2005	**2006**	**2007**	**2008**
Epiphany	Jan. 6	Jan. 6	Jan. 6	Jan. 6
Ash Wednesday	Feb. 9	Mar. 1	Feb. 21	Feb. 6
Palm Sunday	Mar. 20	Apr. 9	Apr. 1	Mar. 16
Maundy Thursday	Mar. 24	Apr. 13	Apr. 5	Mar. 20
Good Friday	Mar. 25	Apr. 14	Apr. 6	Mar. 21
Easter Day	Mar. 27	Apr. 16	Apr. 8	Mar. 23
Ascension Day	May 5	May 25	May 17	May 1
Pentecost	May 15	June 4	May 27	May 11
Trinity Sunday	May 22	June 11	June 3	May 18
Reformation	Oct. 31	Oct. 31	Oct. 31	Oct. 31
All Saints' Day	Nov. 1	Nov. 1	Nov. 1	Nov. 1

Calendars for 2005 and 2006

JANUARY 2005	FEBRUARY 2005	MARCH 2005	APRIL 2005
S M T W T F S	S M T W T F S	S M T W T F S	S M T W T F S
30 31 1	1 2 3 4 5	1 2 3 4 5	30 1
2 3 4 5 6 7 8	6 7 8 9 10 11 12	6 7 8 9 10 11 12	2 3 4 5 6 7 8
9 10 11 12 13 14 15	13 14 15 16 17 18 19	13 14 15 16 17 18 19	9 10 11 12 13 14 15
16 17 18 19 20 21 22	20 21 22 23 24 25 26	20 21 22 23 24 25 26	16 17 18 19 20 21 22
23 24 25 26 27 28 29	27 28	27 28 29 30 31	23 24 25 26 27 28 29

MAY 2005	JUNE 2005	JULY 2005	AUGUST 2005
S M T W T F S	S M T W T F S	S M T W T F S	S M T W T F S
29 30 31	1 2 3 4	31 1 2	1 2 3 4 5 6
1 2 3 4 5 6 7	5 6 7 8 9 10 11	3 4 5 6 7 8 9	7 8 9 10 11 12 13
8 9 10 11 12 13 14	12 13 14 15 16 17 18	10 11 12 13 14 15 16	14 15 16 17 18 19 20
15 16 17 18 19 20 21	19 20 21 22 23 24 25	17 18 19 20 21 22 23	21 22 23 24 25 26 27
22 23 24 25 26 27 28	26 27 28 29 30	24 25 26 27 28 29 30	28 29 30 31

SEPTEMBER 2005	OCTOBER 2005	NOVEMBER 2005	DECEMBER 2005
S M T W T F S	S M T W T F S	S M T W T F S	S M T W T F S
1 2 3	30 31 1	1 2 3 4 5	1 2 3
4 5 6 7 8 9 10	2 3 4 5 6 7 8	6 7 8 9 10 11 12	4 5 6 7 8 9 10
11 12 13 14 15 16 17	9 10 11 12 13 14 15	13 14 15 16 17 18 19	11 12 13 14 15 16 17
18 19 20 21 22 23 24	16 17 18 19 20 21 22	20 21 22 23 24 25 26	18 19 20 21 22 23 24
25 26 27 28 29 30	23 24 25 26 27 28 29	27 28 29 30	25 26 27 28 29 30 31

JANUARY 2006	FEBRUARY 2006	MARCH 2006	APRIL 2006
S M T W T F S	S M T W T F S	S M T W T F S	S M T W T F S
29 30 31	1 2 3 4	1 2 3 4	30 1
1 2 3 4 5 6 7	5 6 7 8 9 10 11	5 6 7 8 9 10 11	2 3 4 5 6 7 8
8 9 10 11 12 13 14	12 13 14 15 16 17 18	12 13 14 15 16 17 18	9 10 11 12 13 14 15
15 16 17 18 19 20 21	19 20 21 22 23 24 25	19 20 21 22 23 24 25	16 17 18 19 20 21 22
22 23 24 25 26 27 28	26 27 28	26 27 28 29 30 31	23 24 25 26 27 28 29

MAY 2006	JUNE 2006	JULY 2006	AUGUST 2006
S M T W T F S	S M T W T F S	S M T W T F S	S M T W T F S
1 2 3 4 5 6	1 2 3	30 31 1	1 2 3 4 5
7 8 9 10 11 12 13	4 5 6 7 8 9 10	2 3 4 5 6 7 8	6 7 8 9 10 11 12
14 15 16 17 18 19 20	11 12 13 14 15 16 17	9 10 11 12 13 14 15	13 14 15 16 17 18 19
21 22 23 24 25 26 27	18 19 20 21 22 23 24	16 17 18 19 20 21 22	20 21 22 23 24 25 26
28 29 30 31	25 26 27 28 29 30	23 24 25 26 27 28 29	27 28 29 30 31

SEPTEMBER 2006	OCTOBER 2006	NOVEMBER 2006	DECEMBER 2006
S M T W T F S	S M T W T F S	S M T W T F S	S M T W T F S
1 2	29 30 31	1 2 3 4	31 1 2
3 4 5 6 7 8 9	1 2 3 4 5 6 7	5 6 7 8 9 10 11	3 4 5 6 7 8 9
10 11 12 13 14 15 16	8 9 10 11 12 13 14	12 13 14 15 16 17 18	10 11 12 13 14 15 16
17 18 19 20 21 22 23	15 16 17 18 19 20 21	19 20 21 22 23 24 25	17 18 19 20 21 22 23
24 25 26 27 28 29 30	22 23 24 25 26 27 28	26 27 28 29 30	24 25 26 27 28 29 30

Index of Sermon Texts